Relational Economics and Organization Governance

This interdisciplinary book series examines recent developments concerning the "relational view" in economics. While the relational research perspective primarily has roots in philosophy, sociology and economic geography, this series offers contributions to the relational view from such diverse fields as institutional and organisational economics, management, organisational theory, and mathematics. Focusing on a relational approach to contracts and governance, leadership, rents, global cooperation, intersectoral cooperation and civil society, the series welcomes theoretical and empirical research on relational structures in market theory, institutional and organisational economics, the resource-based view of the firm, organisational studies, behavioural economics and economic sociology. Within this range of fields, researchers are invited to contribute to the further development of a relational view in economics.

More information about this series at https://link.springer.com/bookseries/16570

Lucio Biggiero · Derick de Jongh · Birger Priddat · Josef Wieland · Adrian Zicari · Dominik Fischer
Editors

The Relational View of Economics

A New Research Agenda for the Study of Relational Transactions

Springer

Editors
Lucio Biggiero
University of L'Aquila
L'Aquila, Italy

Birger Priddat
Witten/Herdecke University
Witten, Nordrhein-Westfalen, Germany

Adrian Zicari
École Supérieure des Sciences Économi
Cergy-Pontoise, France

Derick de Jongh
Department of Business Management
University of Pretoria
Hatfield, South Africa

Josef Wieland
LEIZ
Zeppelin University
Friedrichshafen, Baden-Württemberg
Germany

Dominik Fischer
Zeppelin University
Friedrichshafen, Germany

ISSN 2662-9852 ISSN 2662-9860 (electronic)
Relational Economics and Organization Governance
ISBN 978-3-030-86525-2 ISBN 978-3-030-86526-9 (eBook)
https://doi.org/10.1007/978-3-030-86526-9

This Springer imprint is published by the registered company Springer Nature Switzerland AG
The registered company address is: Gewerbestrasse 11, 6330 Cham, Switzerland

Contents

Part I Introduction

Preface 3
Josef Wieland

Manifesto for a Relational Economics 9
Lucio Biggiero, Derick de Jongh, Birger P. Priddat, Josef Wieland, and Adrian Zicari

Part II Economic Theory and Relational Method

Relational Economics: Theoretical Framework and Managerial Implications—A Short Introduction 17
Josef Wieland

Why We Could Need a Relational Economics and Why Standard Economics and Its (Orthodox) Derivations Do not Help 43
Lucio Biggiero

Modeling Relational Transactions 75
Josef Wieland, Albrecht von Müller, Andrej Nikonov, Leonhard Teichert, Sebastian Lehrack, and Lukas Törner

Part III Shared Value Creation and Social Responsibility

Bringing Inspiration from the Past: A Renaissance Manual for Merchants 97
Adrian Zicari

Shared Value Statement: New Perspectives on Measuring Business Value Creation 111
Marco Möhrer

Managing Global Production Networks: Towards Social Responsibility via Inter-organizational Reliability? 133
Jörg Sydow, Elke Schüßler, and Markus Helfen

Incentives, Autonomous Motivation, and Bank Managers' Socially Responsible Behavior 159
Vincent Bouchet, Stefan Linder, and Nicolas Mottis

Part IV Global Value Networks and Relational Contracts

Transcultural Cooperation in Global Networks. A Contribution to the Research Program of Relational Economics 193
Julika Baumann Montecinos

Leadership in Multi-stakeholder Partnerships (MSPs) that Address the SDGs: Relational Leadership and Ubuntu in Dialogue 213
Yolande Steenkamp, Dominik Fischer, and Derick de Jongh

Relational Contracting in Practice: A Route to Relational Economics? 229
Tim Cummins and Sally Guyer

Part V Epistemology and Relational Economics

Relational Processes in Whitehead's Metaphysics and Commons' Economics. The Relevance of Cosmology for Economic Theory 249
Michael Schramm

Relational Money—Working to Define the Conditions of Non-payment 277
Christian Fiedler

Reasons Theoretical Underpinnings, and Core Features of a Novel Paradigm of Acting in Economics 299
Albrecht von Müller

Contracts as Cooperation: About an Implicit Ethics of Transactions ... 311
Jean Müßgens and Birger P. Priddat

Editors and Contributors

About the Editors

Lucio Biggiero is a professor at University of L'Aquila (IT). His background is in industrial economics, and his scientific research rounds on inter-firm networks and coordination, economic theory, and organizational design. His works employ mostly social network analysis and agent-based simulation modeling. Empirical studies concern various types of economic networks, like knowledge and R&D collaboration, ownership, and international trade.

Derick de Jongh is a professor and director of the Albert Luthuli Leadership Institute, University of Pretoria, South Africa, specializing in corporate citizenship and responsible leadership. He is passionate about creating learning opportunities through research and education that build individual and institutional capacity. He contributes to the emerging responsible leadership approach through relevant research aimed at informing strategy and policy, and by influencing and shaping undergraduate and postgraduate curricula to be more responsive to and relevant in broader society. He has been collaborating with the Leadership Excellence Institute Zeppelin (LEIZ) at Zeppelin University in their Transcultural Leadership and their Relational Economics projects since 2018. He is a co-author of the Manifesto for Relational Economics initiated by Josef Wieland.

Birger Priddat is a senior professor of economics and philosophy at the University of Witten/Herdecke and Zeppelin University in Friedrichshafen. Previously, he held the chair of economics and philosophy at Witten/Herdecke (since 1991) and Zeppelin University. His primary research interests are philosophy of economics, institutional economics, history of economic thought, and digital modernization.

Josef Wieland is a professor of Institutional Economics, Organizational Governance, Integrity Management, and Transcultural Leadership at Zeppelin University in Friedrichshafen and director of the Leadership Excellence Institute Zeppelin

(LEIZ). He is the initiator and president of the German Forum Compliance and Integrity (FCI). He served as the former chairman of the German Network of Business Ethics (DNWE) and is currently as the chairman of DNWE's advisory board. He is a member of the National CSR Forum of the BMAS (German Federal Ministry of Labour and Social Affairs) and serves on the jury board for the "CSR Prize" of the German government. He received the Max Weber Prize for Business Ethics of the IW (German Economic Institute) in 1999. In 2004, he received the highly estimated State Research Prize for Applied Research from the State of Baden-Württemberg, Germany. From 2017 until 2021, he was the Vice-President (Research) of Zeppelin University, Friedrichshafen, Germany.

Adrián Zicari is a professor in the Accounting and Management Control Department at ESSEC Business School. He is Academic Director of the Council on Business & Society. Born in Argentina, he holds a doctorate from Universidad Nacional de Rosario, Argentina, and an MBA from Universidad Adolfo Ibáñez, Chile. Before entering academia, he was a controller in healthcare organizations in Argentina. He is also the honorary representative of Buenos Aires City in Paris. His research interests include measurement systems and management practice in sustainability. His work appears in several academic journals: Journal of Business Ethics, Journal of Cleaner Production, Comptabilité-Contrôle-Audit, Corporate Social Responsibility, and Environmental Management, Social and Environmental Accountability Journal, BMC Health Services Research, and Harvard Business Review—Latin American Edition. He is one of the series editors for the Relational Economics and Organizational Governance book series, Springer.

Dominik Fischer is a post-doctoral researcher at the Chair of Institutional Economics at Zeppelin University. His research focuses on strategy and governance in global value chains with an emphasis on emerging markets based on relational economics. He also focuses on innovation and cooperation in stakeholder networks.

Contributors

Julika Baumann Montecinos Zeppelin University, Friedrichshafen, Germany

Lucio Biggiero University of L'Aquila, L'Aquila, Italy

Vincent Bouchet Ecole Polytechnique, Palaiseau, France

Tim Cummins Leeds University Business School, Leeds, UK

Derick de Jongh Department of Business Management, University of Pretoria, Hatfield, Pretoria, South Africa

Christian Fiedler Zeppelin University, Friedrichshafen, Germany

Dominik Fischer Zeppelin University, Friedrichshafen, Germany

Sally Guyer Durham University Business School, Durham, UK

Markus Helfen Freie Universität Berlin, Berlin, Germany

Sebastian Lehrack Cognostics AG, Pullach i. Isartal, Germany

Stefan Linder ESSEC Business School, Cergy, France

Nicolas Mottis Ecole Polytechnique, Palaiseau, France

Marco Möhrer Zeppelin University, Friedrichshafen, Germany

Jean Müßgens Zeppelin University, Friedrichshafen, Germany

Andrej Nikonov Cognostics AG, Pullach i. Isartal, Germany

Birger P. Priddat University Witten/Herdecke, Zeppelin University, Friedrichshafen, Germany

Michael Schramm University of Hohenheim, Stuttgart, Germany

Elke Schüßler Johannes Kepler Universität Linz, Linz, Austria

Yolande Steenkamp Department of Business Management, University of Pretoria, Hatfield, South Africa

Jörg Sydow Freie Universität Berlin, Berlin, Germany

Leonhard Teichert Cognostics AG, Pullach i. Isartal, Germany

Lukas Törner Zeppelin University, Friedrichshafen, Germany

Albrecht von Müller Parmenides Foundation, Ludwig-Maximilians-Universität München, München, Germany

Adrian Zicari ESSEC Business School, Cergy, France

Part I
Introduction

Preface

Josef Wieland

For several years now, in the field of economics a research perspective has gradually emerged that can be characterized as the "relational view." Thinking in terms of relations has a venerable tradition in, for example, network theory, economic geography, complexity research and relational sociology. In economics, various research programs have contributed to this trend. Examples there of are institutional and organizational economics, as well as several variations of the resource-based view of the firm, that are increasingly focusing on relational elements such as relational contracts, relational governance and relational rents. These relational elements serve as fundamental aspects of grasping economic transactions and value creation in global and regional networks. The central aspect of relational goods, as covered in the perspective of happiness research also belongs to this context. In terms of organizational and management theories, the stakeholder theory of the firm and relational leadership approaches are fundamentally based on a relational view. This trend, only briefly outlined here, corresponds to an advanced epistemological and methodological reflection on how the previously mentioned research approaches can be mathematically formalized in economics and the management sciences.

An implicit paradigmatic reorientation is a shared component of these research developments. Essentially, they no longer observe economic and social behavior as a series of dyadic, discrete exchanges on the market but instead as relational, multi-sectoral transactions involving multiple actors. Accordingly, relational transactions are powerful attractors for various behavioral and decision logics, while the optimally friction-free interaction influences said transactions' economic and social performance. In this context, the successful continuation of the relation, its pattern and structure formation, and the adaptability of the governance mechanisms required for the cooperation of actors and events are essential to private and societal value creation. This also poses challenges for the basic assumptions of methodological

J. Wieland (✉)
Zeppelin University, Friedrichshafen, Germany
e-mail: Josef.wieland@zu.de

L. Biggiero et al. (eds.), *The Relational View of Economics*, Relational Economics and Organization Governance, https://doi.org/10.1007/978-3-030-86526-9_1

individualism and the various approaches based on rational choice. The same is true for the relation between discipline-specific and interdisciplinary research, which is evolving in keeping with societal challenges and explorations of research.

The contributions gathered in this book are the outcomes of a research conference organized in 2019 by the Leadership Excellence Institute at Zeppelin University, Friedrichshafen. The conference's goal was, on the basis of an interdisciplinary discourse, to explore and discuss the topic of Relational Economics from various perspectives.

The first major outcome of the conference was the formulation of a *Manifesto for a Relational Economics* jointly written by *Lucio Biggiero, Derick de Jongh, Birger P. Priddat, Josef Wieland and Adrián Zicari*, which, as Chapter II of this book, discusses the shared intentions of the editors of the book series "Relational Economics and Organization Governance."

In turn, Part II *Economic Theory & Relational Method* brings together articles that concern themselves with theory building and methodological questions. Josef Wieland, in his article *Relational Economics: Theoretical Framework and Managerial Implications—A Short Introduction*, proposes a categorical taxonomy for Relational Economics, chiefly focusing on questions concerning the dynamic development of pattern and structure formation in transactions and their governance structures. In the article *Why We Could Need a Relational Economics and Why Standard Economics and Its (Orthodox) Derivations Do not Help,* Lucio Biggiero explores potential elements of a new field of research, Relational Economics. As, methodologically and epistemologically speaking, they are based on the complexity sciences, he especially favors behavioral and evolutionary economics, analytical and relational sociology, and organization science as building blocks for a new research approach. In their article *Modeling Relational Transactions*, the authors Josef Wieland, Albrecht von Müller, Andrej Nikonov, Leonhard Teichert, Sebastian Lehrack and Lukas Törner put forward a proposal for using actor-based network theory to model these transactions. Here, the dependence of cooperative value creation on the availability and qualities of polyvalent cooperation corridors is at the heart of the discussion.

In Part III *Shared Value Creation & Social Responsibility*, precisely this concept of shared value creation and social responsibility is explored in more detail from the standpoint of strategic management. Adrian Zicari reflects on Benedetto Cotrugli's (1458) book on the art of trade in his article *Bringing Inspiration from the Past: A Renaissance Manual for Merchants*. Relational interpersonal relationships, the dimension of time in contrast to the standard annual period, and business ethics serve to embed economic operations in the logics of private and public affairs; in turn, this embeddedness can be used to fathom the scope of relational economic analysis. Marco Möhrer then takes a deeper and more technical approach to the discussion of stakeholder value creation. In his article *Shared Value Statement: New Perspectives on Measuring Business Value Creation*, the goal is to identify and measure a firm's tangible and intangible value creation by means of a Shared Value Statement (SVS). This culminates in a proposal for sustainability-based or relational accounting for firms. The relation between economic and social value creation in inter-firm and global production networks is also the main focus for Jörg Sydow, Elke Schüßler and Markus Helfen. Their article *Managing Global Production Networks: Towards Social Responsibility via Inter-organizational Reliability?* addresses from a network perspective the question of whether, and if so, under which conditions, global production networks can yield, in addition to the desired economic effects, social upgrading. Their conclusion: inter-organizational reliability and social responsibility can be promoted through the suitable management of network production, the mechanisms of which require further research. Vincent Bouchet, Stefan Linder and Nicolas Mottis subsequently discuss the efficacy of managers' bonuses in precisely the same context. Their article *Incentives, Autonomous Motivation, and Bank Managers' Socially Responsible Behavior* presents empirical evidence to support the thesis that financial rewards are a poor incentive for Socially Responsible Behavior (SRB) among managers.

Part IV *Global Value Networks & Relational Contracting* also investigates the requisite conditions for successful value creation in networks, though it does so in various other directions. Julika Baumann Montecinos concentrates on the challenges posed by the fact that global value creation always involves transcultural cooperation. Her article, *Transcultural Cooperation in Global Networks. A Contribution to the Research Program of Relational Economics*, analyzes the relevance of cultural factors in the process of economic value creation. These factors can, for example, serve as a form of transcultural commons that view diversity as a potential opportunity to achieve a shared learning process. Yolande Steenkamp, Dominik Fischer and Derick de Jongh address the same question from the other side, namely, with regard to leadership in transcultural collaborations. From a theoretical standpoint, *Leadership in Multi-stakeholder Partnerships (MSPs) that Address the SDGs: Relational Leadership and Ubuntu in Dialogue* focuses on the similarities and differences between Western theories of relational leadership and the African ontology ubuntu. From a practical standpoint, the frame of reference is provided by the global, cooperative implementation of the UN's Sustainable Development Goals as a process of resource sharing. The effectiveness of SDG-related activities ultimately depends on successful setting the two relational leadership concepts in relation. Tim Cummins and Sally Guyer show in their article *Relational Contracting in Practice: A Route to Relational Economics?* that the evolution of the relational economy as a networked world of cooperation between multiple actors is hindered by an institutional, procedural and regulatory deficit. In this regard, relational contracting could serve as a catalyst and bridge-builder, provided it is understood as a process of contracting and not just a specific type of contract. In turn, the theoretical and practical implications of adopting this stance are discussed.

The epistemological aspects of Relational Economics are addressed in Part V *Epistemology & Relational Economics.* Michael Schramm examines precisely these aspects in his article *Relational Processes in Whitehead's Metaphysics and Commons' Economics. The Relevance of Cosmology for Economic Theory.* One of the main focus areas involves the question, which applies to all theoretical work, of how the "messiness" of reality and the resultant response, namely the reduction of complexity, can produce sound theoretical and practical insights. In this regard, the poly-dimensionality of transactions and their networks is an important factor.

Christian Fiedler's article *Relational Money—Working to Define the Conditions of Non-payment* employs a dogma-historical reconstruction of the theory of money put forward by John R. Commons to provide points of departure for a relational theory of money. He shows that, for Commons, above all the temporal distance involved in cooperative projects is what provides the basis for his monetary and financial market theory. Separating the definition of the economic process from the generation of the desired profit leads to a view of money as an institution, the key functions of which are the creation of, negotiation of and release from debt. Accordingly, money takes on a processed form that can accommodate the asymmetry of process and event, one in which the relation between firms, banks and financial markets develops its dynamics.

In his article *Reasons, Theoretical Underpinnings, and Core Features of a Novel Paradigm of Acting in Economics*, Albrecht von Müller explores the potential ramifications for a social theory of behavior resulting from fundamental epistemological discussions in the modern natural sciences. When said theory's paradigmatic core is based on an assumption of self-unfolding processes, it has consequences for the conceptualization of human and cooperative behavior. For the standard economy, this behavior is based on rational choice. Jean Müßgens and Birger P. Priddat point out in their article *Contracts as Cooperation: About an Implicit Ethics of Transactions* that relational transactions have always required a "minimal sociology" that obeys various decision logics, not necessarily maximizing personal gain. In addition, a discussion on the ethical prerequisites for a gift economy yields new insights into the digital economy.

Relational Economics is a work in progress. All of the articles gathered here represent valuable contributions to various facets of a relational view on economics and their further investigation. I would like to thank all conference participants and the authors for their valuable input. By publishing this work, the editors' hope is that it will foster the emergence of a distinct research agenda, as a contribution to economic theorization in times characterized by rapid and disruptive societal and economic transformation. In terms of preparing this book, I would like to especially thank my co-editor Dominik Fischer, and also Jean Müßgens, Pauline Fiedler and Mara Sagert, who did a wonderful job. Anyone who has coordinated an edited work from concept to author management, to technical implementation knows what I mean. Matthew Fentem at gonative language solutions supplied high-quality translations for selected texts.

Friedrichshafen, Germany
Fall 2021

Josef Wieland

Josef Wieland is professor of Institutional Economics, Organizational Governance, Integrity Management, and Transcultural Leadership at Zeppelin University in Friedrichshafen and director of the Leadership Excellence Institute Zeppelin (LEIZ). He is the initiator and president of the German Forum Compliance and Integrity (FCI). He served as the former chairman of the German Network of Business Ethics (DNWE) and currently as the chairman of DNWE's advisory board. He is a member of the National CSR Forum of the BMAS (German Federal Ministry of Labour and Social Affairs) and serves on the jury board for the "CSR Prize" of the German government. He received the Max Weber Prize for Business Ethics of the IW (German Economic Institute) in 1999. In 2004, he received the highly estimated State Research Prize for Applied Research from the State of Baden-Württemberg, Germany. From 2017 until 2021, he was Vice-President (Research) of Zeppelin University, Friedrichshafen, Germany.

Manifesto for a Relational Economics

Lucio Biggiero, Derick de Jongh, Birger P. Priddat, Josef Wieland, and Adrian Zicari

There is no such thing as a dyadic and discrete exchange transaction in a modern network economy. Economic, private and social value creation results from the investment and relationing of multiple resources by individual and collective actors from the economy, civil society and politics. The willingness and ability to build and continue such complex relationships through social cooperation are fundamental and constitute the core of Relational Economics.

1 Societal Change and Economic Theory

The forms, mechanisms and processes of economic value creation have been subject to rapid and dynamic changes over several decades.

The development of business models based on worldwide cooperative networks has substantial consequences for regional and national economies. These business models challenge the political applicability of conventional general equilibrium models and theories on international trade. At an industry and organisational level,

L. Biggiero
University of L'Aquila, L'Aquila, Italy

D. de Jongh
University of Pretoria, Pretoria, South Africa

B. P. Priddat
Witten/Herdecke University, Witten, Germany

J. Wieland (✉)
Zeppelin University, Friedrichshafen, Germany
e-mail: Josef.wieland@zu.de

A. Zicari
ESSEC Business School, Cergy-Pontoise, Cergy, France

L. Biggiero et al. (eds.), *The Relational View of Economics*, Relational Economics and Organization Governance, https://doi.org/10.1007/978-3-030-86526-9_2

the empirical developments of intra-sectoral and trans-sectoral networks of cooperation can no longer be characterised solely by microeconomic market assumptions and transaction cost governance.

Nowadays, disruptive innovations mainly facilitate and speed up the development and utilisation of digital and exponential technologies, including platforms that severely impact cooperative business models. These changes require new forms of organisation and a new conception to further integrate the diversity of governance mechanisms in economic theory.

The predominance of the financial markets in the economic system, the emergence of a narrow group of markets and society-dominating companies, particularly in the field of future technologies, have reached levels that pose unmet challenges to the relationship between civil society, state and the market. The relation between the visible and invisible hand to create effective competition and the associated questions of private and public value creation, distributive justice, and public welfare are not adequately addressed.

The worldwide challenges of sustainable business development and growth as well as public welfare affect stakeholder management, accounting, reporting, business strategy and monitoring of economic success and require the creation of shared value for all business and societal stakeholders. The core of these developments is that modern value creation is achieved by interlinking the resources of stakeholders originating from multiple economic as well as social systems and organisations.

All these points are facets of the aforementioned fundamental developmental dynamics of contemporary society's economies, increasingly pushing the underlying epistemological and methodological assumptions and concepts of economic theory building to the limits of their explanatory power.

2 The Case for Relational Economics

Conventional economic theory is characterised by methodological individualism, homo economicus, rational choice theory, discrete and dyadic exchange transactions, general equilibrium, individual as well as independent utility maximisation, the neoclassical theory of the firm, and the theorisation of moral and social values as external effects to name a few. They have massively reduced the descriptive, explanatory and prognostic capacity of mainstream economics. Thus, the economic and social applicability and recognition of mainstream economics have been shrinking in recent years and decades. This is not at all a new issue. They have been disputed from the beginning, and this has been the subject of long-running methodological debates. The problem is less the unrealistic underlying assumptions of conventional economics than the lack of analytical fruitfulness and the explanatory power of real economic developments.

The emergence of alternative, economic research programmes, such as the economics of governance, resource and capability theory of the firm, industrial economics, institutional economics, organisational economics, behavioural economics, managerial economics or stakeholder value creation, are reflections of this development. Even though these selective approaches are still an enriching exercise to deepen and broaden our understanding of economic life, they have not yet succeeded in creating a new integrative research paradigm and framework.

The authors of this Manifesto suggest taking a different path. It is the economy of complex, recursive and non-linear transactions as well as cooperative polyvalent resource networks in which the continuity of relations is a source of economic and societal value creation on its own, which asks for Relational Economics. To achieve this target, both conceptual and empirical research is plainly needed. We also aim to develop the required taxonomy of categories of economic theory formation as a fundamental objective in the development of a Theory of Relational Economics.

The development of Relational Economics as a comprehensive theory of the governance of regional, national and transnational economic transactions is of paramount importance. In doing so, we are convinced that it may contribute to creating a categorical framework and research agenda for the explanation and design of interconnected economic organisations and socially productive networks.

3 Defining the Research Agenda

Relational Economics, as a political economy, is concerned with the production and distribution of private and public value creation in the various sectors and organisations of society and their relationships with one another. The basic unit of their analysis is a relational transaction involving multiple actors.

Relationships bundle different types of economic and social value and are based on interests and norms. Relational transactions are economic exchange relationships that are designed for continuity and, in their course, become attractors of different perceptual frames and polyvalent decision logics. Economics, law, ethics, politics, technology, religion and other disciplines are those frames and logics that dock onto economic transactions and enter into relations that determine economic performance and its sustainable growth. This can only be understood and explained from the interaction of these relations and the adaptability of the required governance structures.

Therefore, the following fields are just a few possible illustrations of the relational research agenda:

- regional and global production clusters
- creation and distribution of relational rents
- corporate governance and relational contracting
- governance and innovation of exponential technologies
- happiness research and relational goods
- stakeholder management
- social responsibility
- sustainable development goals

- shared value creation and business ethics
- social accounting and integrated reporting
- leadership and transcultural management and
- relational society and complex adaptive systems.

Relational Economics is also concerned with the interaction and interference of regional, national, transnational and global economic as well as social transactions. It does not attempt to limit economic theory to personal relationships; instead, its epistemological and methodological perspective assumes that all being is relational.

The relationships between 'people and people', 'people and things', 'systems and organisations', 'structures and processes', 'past, present and future', 'different decision logics, and their semantics' are not bilateral relations but each of these events itself and their interaction with each other are relational. Through this lens, complexity is a multiplex of economic, social, political, artificial and natural interactions and they form the core of the nurturing field of relational research. Economic interactions are not limited to the relationships between agents mediated by prices.

Thus, the point of reference for Relational Economics is not the pure market relation but the relationing of multiple decision logics in and by different types of organisations and societal institutions. It is the unfolding process and the continuity of relational adaptive forms of governance for mutually determining economic and multivalent social decision logics in the cooperative process of economic transactions. Therefore, Relational Economics is interested in the interaction of economic, legal, technical, political, cultural and moral events and language games, which constitute the process and success of economic transactions.

Consequently, epistemologically and methodologically, Relational Economics focuses not upon the analysis of isolated and homogeneous individual or collective events but upon the process of relationing within and between these events. A relation is the form of the relationship between events. Relationality is the self-unfolding process of proportioning, networking and considering trade-offs of multivalent events or decision logics regarding the execution of a specific economic transaction and its contribution to economic value creation for all stakeholders. Forms and processes, the governance of relationality, and its continuation are fundamental elements of cooperative economic value creation for mutual benefit and thus the paradigmatic starting point of the relational view on economic transactions and the required governance for social cooperation.

Relational Economics is a constitutively process-oriented and interdisciplinary political economy. It is not only open to contributions from all areas of the social sciences and humanities, the natural sciences, philosophy of science, mathematics, and network theory but also encourages transdisciplinary cooperation. We invite interdisciplinary epistemological and methodological, fundamental and applied research as well as conceptual and empirical contributions to the discussion of these research topics.

Lucio Biggiero is professor at University of L'Aquila (IT). His background is in industrial economics, and his scientific research rounds on inter-firm networks and coordination, economic theory, and organizational design. His works employ mostly social network analysis and agent-based simulation modeling. Empirical studies concern various types of economic networks, like knowledge and R&D collaboration, ownership, and international trade.

Derick de Jongh is professor and director of the Albert Luthuli Leadership Institute, University of Pretoria, South Africa, specializing in corporate citizenship and responsible leadership. He is passionate about creating learning opportunities through research and education that build individual and institutional capacity. He contributes to the emerging responsible leadership approach through relevant research aimed at informing strategy and policy, and by influencing and shaping undergraduate and postgraduate curricula to be more responsive to and relevant in broader society. He has been collaborating with the Leadership Excellence Institute Zeppelin (LEIZ) at Zeppelin University in their Transcultural Leadership and their Relational Economics projects since 2018. He is a co-author of the Manifesto for Relational Economics initiated by Josef Wieland.

Birger P. Priddat is senior professor of economics and philosophy at the University of Witten/Herdecke and Zeppelin University in Friedrichshafen. Previously he held the chair of economics and philosophy at Witten/Herdecke (since 1991) and Zeppelin University. His primary research interests are philosophy of economics, institutional economics, history of economic thought, and digital modernization.

Josef Wieland is professor of Institutional Economics, Organizational Governance, Integrity Management, and Transcultural Leadership at Zeppelin University in Friedrichshafen and director of the Leadership Excellence Institute Zeppelin (LEIZ). He is the initiator and president of the German Forum Compliance and Integrity (FCI). He served as the former chairman of the German Network of Business Ethics (DNWE) and currently as the chairman of DNWE's advisory board. He is a member of the National CSR Forum of the BMAS (German Federal Ministry of Labour and Social Affairs) and serves on the jury board for the "CSR Prize" of the German government. He received the Max Weber Prize for Business Ethics of the IW (German Economic Institute) in 1999. In 2004, he received the highly estimated State Research Prize for Applied Research from the State of Baden-Württemberg, Germany. From 2017 until 2021, he was Vice-President (Research) of Zeppelin University, Friedrichshafen, Germany.

Adrián Zicari is professor in the Accounting and Management Control Department at ESSEC Business School. He is Academic Director of the Council on Business & Society. Born in Argentina, he holds a doctorate from Universidad Nacional de Rosario, Argentina, and an MBA from Universidad Adolfo Ibáñez, Chile. Before entering academia, he was a controller in healthcare organizations in Argentina. He is also honorary representative of Buenos Aires City in Paris. His research interests include measurement systems and management practice in sustainability. His work appears in several academic journals: Journal of Business Ethics, Journal of Cleaner Production, Comptabilité-Contrôle-Audit, Corporate Social Responsibility, and Environmental Management, Social and Environmental Accountability Journal, BMC Health Services Research, and Harvard Business Review—Latin American Edition. He is one of the series editors for the Relational Economics and Organizational Governance book series, Springer.

Part II
Economic Theory and Relational Method

Relational Economics: Theoretical Framework and Managerial Implications—A Short Introduction

Josef Wieland

Keywords Relational economics · Relational transaction · Governance · Network analysis · Shared value creation

This article introduces readers to the research program of Relational Economics. The fundamental categories for analyzing a relational view of economics—the transaction, governance, and cooperation rent—are developed in terms of their process logic for private and societal value creation. The management of stakeholder networks on one hand, and pattern and structure formation on the other hand, two important drivers of shared value creation in the relational economy are also included in the discussion.

1 The Relational Economy as a Self-unfolding Process

1.1 Phenomena and Theories

In this chapter, I will attempt to provide a brief introduction to the fundamental taxonomy of Relational Economics, a topic I have developed in more detail elsewhere (Wieland, 2018, 2020).[1]

Relational Economics is a political economy that focuses on the driving forces of and processes involved in private and public value creation. It is the governance of

[1] Although doing so involves a certain degree of redundancy, I have consistently sought to develop the relational view as a process, and to connect it with new or partly modified theoretical considerations.

J. Wieland (✉)
Zeppelin University, Friedrichshafen, Germany
e-mail: Josef.wieland@zu.de

L. Biggiero et al. (eds.), *The Relational View of Economics*, Relational Economics and Organization Governance, https://doi.org/10.1007/978-3-030-86526-9_3

relational transactions in modern societies, which constitutes the core of the theoretical and practical interest of Relational Economics. Relational Governance as a research program is interested in the process of ongoing, frictionless, and cost-effective value creation in multivalent collaborative networks of economic and societal, individual, and collective actors. Economic value creation through cooperation takes place not just in regional and global intra-firm and inter-firm networks; rather, from a systemic perspective, these networks also include financial, academic, political, and civil-societal actors (see Fernandez-Stark & Gereffi, 2019; Sydow et al. in this volume). These extra-firm connections, which I will refer to as stakeholder networks, are characteristics of modern economies. Universities and think tanks cooperate with firms in the area of exponential technologies and innovations for digital transformation (see Chang, 2017; de Moraes Silva et al., 2018; Geisler, 1995; Mascarenhas et al., 2018). The "networked information economy" (Benkler, 2006) is based on "peer production" (Benkler, 2017) and has led to a "substantial non-market sector" (Benkler, 2006, p. 131), which, compared to classical market solutions, has resulted in more effective access to knowledge and information as input factors of value creation. The UN Principles of Responsible Investors (PRI) and the Sustainable Development Goals (SDGs) encourage economic, political, and civil-societal actors to cooperate in the development of sustainability strategies for products and processes. Social standards and corporate strategies for respecting human rights in global supply chains are just as much part of this picture (Ruggie & Sherman, 2017) as the enforcement of legally binding regulations via Ethics and Compliance Management on the part of firms and their global networks (see Wieland et al., 2020).

These examples of relational transactions should suffice to illustrate the relevance of the issue at hand. Their theoretical quintessence, from the standpoint of Relational Economics, is as follows: modern economies are cooperative economies (see Wieland, 1998) and are based on the productive networking of local clusters and global value networks (see De Marchi et al., 2018) of economic, political and societal resources. Value creation derives from the involvement of multiple stakeholders who are the owners of these resources and yields a shared value for all invested resources (see Wieland, 2014, 2017a; Freeman et al. 2020).

The successful continuation of cooperation processes in value creation networks is one of the most fundamental prerequisites for and sources of value creation in modern economies. From the perspective of Transaction Cost Economics, the continuity and adaptivity of the requisite governance structures are the critical factors. In addition to contracts and organizational mechanisms, relational governance includes leadership and management processes that have to be integrated with the analysis as value-creating factors. Accordingly, Williamson's (1985, 2005) pioneering work on the economics of governance is a theoretical reference guide that provides the starting point for Relational Economics.

The relational governance research program also ties into the work of Elionor Ostrom (2005, 2010) on "polycentric governance". Viewed through this lens, the complexity of economic transactions, according to Ostrom (while referring to V. Ostrom, Thiebout, & Warren, 1961, p. 831) arises from the interaction of poly-contextural decision making agencies, which through this interactions become an "interdependent system of relations" (ibid.). Thus, the object of study changes from the linear interaction of independent actors to the study of the processes of a system of relations. The research interst of polycentric governance is the process of creation and processing the complexity of relational economies. "We need to ask how diverse polycentric institutions help or hinder innovativeness, learning, adapting, trustworthiness, levels of cooperation of participants" (Ostrom, 2010, p. 665).

The view of polyvalent transactions as relational transactions, and the institutional and organizational arrangements that make them possible, as relational governance is rooted in the work of Commons (1934/1990). It represents the theoretical core of his well-known assumption that an economic transaction is a relation involving multiple participants and various decision logics (ibid., p. 58), and that, through the execution of such transactions, the firm as a going concern comes into being and is continuously changed and reproduced (ibid., p. 53).

1.2 Processes and Experience

A relational economic theory in the tradition of Commons, Williamson and Ostrom (see Wieland, 2020; Schramm in this volume) is a departure from the static and equilibrium-based paradigm of conventional textbook economics. Commons' institutional economics reflects the process philosophy of Alfred N. Whitehead in which a process is understood as "the becoming of experience" (Whitehead, 1941, p. 166) and as the "relatedness of 'actual entities'" (ibid., Chap. xiii) and proceeds on the premise that the "'relatedness' is dominant over 'quality'" (ibid., Chap. xiii). Such a philosophy must, according to Whitehead, be not only coherent and logical but also practically applicable and adequate, that is, be observable through human experience (ibid., p. 3 f.). In this view, processes are "the becoming of experience" and "apart from experiences of subjects there is nothing, nothing, nothing, bare nothingness" (ibid., p. 167).

Accordingly, first of all, the reflection of practically relevant societal experience is what matters for the development of Relational Economics as a process theory.

Second, however, a process can only be understood immanently, as pattern and structure formation through the continual interaction and relationing of the events taking place within it. With regard to relational transactions and their governance, the phases of pattern formation and structure formation can be distinguished. In the pattern formation phase, economic transactions attract events from their societal environment. These events begin to interact with each other and change the nature of the transaction. In the course of this interaction, the ways in which the different events relate to each other, and in which the results of these relations are fed back into the process, form a temporalized pattern. We speak of structure formation when the temporary stabilization of the interaction of events from the first phase leads to the development and implementation of permanent governance structures. Their adaptivity shapes the interaction of events in such a way as to give rise to the continuity of the process of relationing and economic value creation. Continuity in the context of Relational Economics is non-linear continuity, i.e. the process of interaction of events enables the continuity of cooperation by changing its texture.

Third, the introduction of time—past, present, and future—is constitutive of economic value creation. Relational processes are self-unfolding in precisely this sense. Schumpeter (1950) explains this with regard to the analysis of macroeconomic structures and their evolution: "we are dealing with a process [...] as it unfolds through decades or centuries" and one "that incessantly revolutionizes the economic structure from within" [emphasis added] (p. 83). For the microeconomic analysis of the firm as a collective actor, Penrose (1959/1995) observed that its growth, both quantitative and qualitative, is the "result of a continuous on-going or 'unfolding' process" (p. 1) of interaction in a polyvalent "collection of productive resources" (ibid., p. 24) that are used to evoke and deliver "a bundle of potential services" (ibid., p. 25) for economic performance.

Adopting a relational view on the processes of economic value creation as defined in this manner has epistemological and methodological consequences for economics. Some of the most important consequences for its categorical taxonomy will be discussed in this paper. These involve the terms "transaction," "governance," and "cooperation rent." These terms are logically related, and the epistemic focus of Relational Economics as a political economy is on investigating this relation and its managerial ramifications.

2 The Relatedness of Relational Transactions

2.1 Exchanges and Transactions

Conventional microeconomic price theory views economic transactions as dyadic and discrete exchanges. Two individual actors are involved, who, in a finite time-frame t1, exchange goods for money or vice versa in a one-time act. The exchange relation created in the process is strictly limited to the actors' purely economic interests; personal relations and the actors' identities are wholly irrelevant. Coase (1937) suggested calling this type of transaction "exchange transactions co-ordinated through the price mechanism" (p. 393).

The Transaction Cost Theory developed by Williamson (1979, 1985, 1991), starting from market transactions, shifted the focus of economic analysis from discrete transactions to "discrete structural alternatives" (Williamson, 1991, p. 1). As a result, the way was paved for the analysis of the theoretical and practical characteristics of relational transactions as "ongoing contractual relations" (Williamson, 2005, p. 2) within economic theory. This supplementation (not supplanting) of the market perspective allowed him to distinguish between, on the one hand, economic interactions as the result of one-time or of ongoing contractual relations of market exchange and, on the other, organizational cooperation, the feasibility and corresponding transaction costs of which are in turn determined by discrete governance structures (market, firms, hybrids) (Williamson, 1985). As a result, he integrated the economic logic (economizing on transactions costs) and explicitly the logic of the law and that of private, contractual relational arrangements, in which the actors' identities are highly relevant, into economics. Building on this theoretical advance, Relational Economics proceeds under the assumption that effective and cost-efficient relational governance structures require the economic transaction itself to possess economically relevant relational qualities. Accordingly, its research interest, unlike that of Williamson, is not only in the comparative cost structure for the governance of a transaction but also in how governance can be shaped with a view to enabling cooperative value creation.

The observation and description of relational transactions were also the point of departure for the contractual theory contributions of Macaulay (1963) and Macneil (1974, 1978). Though Williamson refers to the latter, the concept of the relational transaction as the antonym of the exchange transaction does not serve as the starting point in his own work. Instead, when he defines the transaction so broadly and technically that it includes a microeconomic perspective on market transactions, he does so in an attempt to find a common basis for exchange and relational transactions:

> A transaction occurs when a good or service is transferred across a technologically separable interface (Williamson, 1996, p. 379).

This was likely one of the reasons why Macneil (1985) classified the Transaction Cost Theory, despite a few qualifying remarks, as belonging to neoclassical microeconomics (see p. 495f.). A few years earlier (Macneil, 1981), he had claimed that Transaction Cost Economics was significant for neoclassical standard economics' continuing development but not "sufficient for useful economic analysis of all contractual relations" (ibid., p. 1025, emphasis in original).

Williamson himself employs other distinctions:

> The transaction is a semimicroanalytic unit of analysis—more microanalytic than economics has characteristically been concerned with, but a larger unit than the decision premise (Williamson, 1996, p. 45).

When economic cost calculations regarding the ability of private contractual arrangements to adapt to future contingencies and the ethical opportunism of not wholly rational actors become important factors in the analysis, then the rational choice-based world of standard economics is no longer critically relevant. Yet unlike Commons (1950, p. 45), as previously mentioned, Williamson does not distinguish between exchanges and transactions; rather, he focuses on the dimensions of economic transactions. The attributed dimensions by which transactions can be distinguished and compared are their asset specificity, uncertainty and frequency; in this regard, the first dimension is also the most important (Williamson, 1985).

2.2 Exchange Transactions and Relational Transactions

In contrast to Williamson's Transaction Cost Theory, Relational Economics starts with the distinction between exchange transactions and relational transactions as having their own distinct dimensions and reference systems (see Wieland, 2020, Chap. 2). As previously mentioned, exchange transactions are dyadic and discrete, that is, there are only two actors involved in this type of transaction, who, in the market system, make their decisions using an economic code (price). Discrete transactions take place in the present (t1) and have neither a historical nor a future dimension. Here, the actors' identities have no relevance, and collective actors (organizations) are, as the result of methodological individualism, modeled as a "uni brain" (Machlup, 1963, p. 133), that is, as if they were individual actors. The mode of interaction is competition; the reference system is the market. Exchange transactions are a relation but are not relational. They are executed in a world of thing–thing relations.

Relational transactions are not discrete; rather, they are distinct. Distinct means that each one constitutes a limited, specific relation of events with characteristically defined qualities. Each transaction involves more than just two individual or collective actors who belong to different systems within society (such as the economy, law, civil society, politics, science, culture) and/or employ different decision logics (such as economic, legal, ethical, political, aesthetic). I (for a discussion of the relevant literature, see Wieland, 2020) have dubbed the first aspect the polycontextuality (belonging to multiple systems) and the second, the polycontexturality (using multiple decision logics) of relational transactions. It follows then that their execution is situated in a polylingual communicative environment with various language games (such as, for the economy: payment/non-payment; law: legal/illegal; science: true/false) that determine how transactions are assessed, and the mutual comprehension and integration of which are essential to a given transaction's chances of success and potential for creating value. The level and quality of a given societal actor's polylingual competence define how they perceive and grasp events in the context of their transactions, which can potentially dock with them. A given business model's standards for sustainability and integrity, for example, are the result of societal discourses. As such, they have a significant influence on the recognizability and manageability of new risks, on the general direction of product-based and process-based innovations; and thus on the firm's ability to capitalize on market opportunities. The capacity to understand and recognize the meaning of communications between diverse societal stakeholders critically influences a firm's ability and opportunities to cooperate across societal sectors. Accordingly, polycontextuality, polycontexturality, and polylingualism are not only what drive the relatedness of relational transactions but they are also the operationalization of the latter's function as the execution and reproduction of society.

The specific mode of interaction in relational transactions is cooperation; its reference system is the organization. Relational transactions seek to achieve continuity, making the past and the future relevant time dimensions for value creation. The identities of both individual and collective actors (such as their motivations, abilities and resources) are essential to executing transactions, since they influence their feasibility and the resulting economic benefits for the actors. Relational transactions are structurally coupled with the market system of the exchange transaction because their execution generates costs and earnings and/or attendant payments from/to actors on the market. While the relational transaction is the basic analytical unit of Relational Economics, its relation to the market-mediated exchange transaction is an important aspect of the research approach that I will explain in more detail in the following section (see Wieland, 2020, Chap. 4).

To sum up this discussion: relational transactions are dynamic attractors (see Wieland, 2020; Priddat, 2016; Müßgens & Priddat in this volume) for multiple societal actors, multiple decision logics, language games and their relationalization, that is, the continuity of the relation and the mutual influencing through interaction that this relation permits. Attractors are forms of interaction and generate complexity. Relational transactions are an ongoing process of polyvalent interactions, which leads to new pattern formations and the need to give form to them through appropriate governance structures. The distinction made here between discrete and relational transactions is of a purely analytical and definitional nature. Macneil (1974, pp. 696–718) pointed out that, from the standpoint of contract theory, the two terms essentially constitute two ideals or limiting cases, and that in economic practice, there is a continuum of mixed forms lying between them. In his eyes, criteria for a transaction to be classified as discrete include: (i) the degree to which the agreed-upon services can be specified, (ii) the unambiguousness with which they are communicated and (iii) the measurable reciprocity of the services. Criteria for a transaction to be considered relational include: (i) the desire to cooperate, (ii) the acceptance of, response to and handling of one's dependence on one's partner, and finally (iii) the mutual desire to continue cooperating.

Figure 1 applies this logic but replaces the criteria with the characteristics of discrete and relational transactions, as developed in this paper.

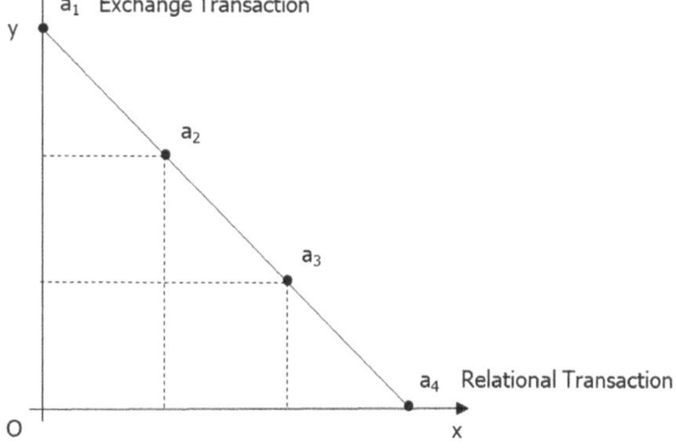

Fig. 1 Continuity of exchange–relation–exchange (from Wieland, 2020, p. 31)

An ideal discrete transaction is defined on the y-axis by the characteristics (i) dyadic, (ii) purely economic decision logic, (iii) no personal identity, and (iv) timeframe t_1. A distinct relational transaction is defined on the x-axis by the characteristics (i) multi-personal, (ii) polyvalent decision logics, (iii) personal identity, and (iv) timeframe t_0–t_1–t_n. The points a_1 (e.g. commodities) and a_4 (e.g. relational goods (see Bruni, 2013; Gui, 2005; Uhlaner, 1989)) demarcate the two types of transaction in their pure forms; the points a_2 and a_3 represent mixed forms, for example, long-term contracting or changing relations with a supplier over time (a_2), or the relation of permanent employment (a_3). Accordingly, the majority of economic transactions can be characterized as relational and classified as mixed forms, whose systematic governance structure is not the market, but rather the various forms of contract and organization. As Richardson (1972) already noted:

> …to refer to co-operation and market transactions as distinct and alternative modes of co-ordinating economic activity, we must not imagine that reality exhibits a sharp line of distinction; what confronts us is a continuum passing from transactions, such as those on organized commodity markets, where the co-operative element is minimal, through intermediate areas in which there are linkages of traditional connection and goodwill, and finally to those complex and interlocking clusters, groups and alliances which represent co-operation fully and formally developed (p. 887).

3 The Governance of Self-unfolding Processes

3.1 Governance and Process

If we view relational economic transactions as dynamic attractors for societal events—which, in turn, denote multiple actors and decision logics—we need to remember that these transactions are not only part of a process but are themselves simultaneously fluctuating processes, not static and isolated substances or qualities. The societal events that a transaction attracts and relationalizes are significant in their own right and for all other events (see Whitehead, 1968, p. 146). If a transaction is relational, it means that every attracted event is also an event that interacts (<->) with other events. Taken together, these events determine the configuration and dynamics of the transaction by the specific form of their relationalization. In formal terms, one might say that a relational transaction's distinctiveness results from interactions between different decision logics. If (for simplicity's sake) we assume only three dimensions are involved—an economic (e), a legal (l) and a moral (m) dimension—then the result is:

$$RTe, l, m <-> (e <-> l <-> m)$$

As such, in relational transactions related to exchange transactions, all forms of knowledge (e, l and m) are potential business knowledge, making them relevant for value creation. Viewed in this light, a relational transaction requires an adaptive governance structure, one that both permits and limits the constant interaction of its events, and by doing so, gives form to it. Macneil (1978) referred to this form, very much in keeping with Whitehead, as a "minisociety" (p. 901) of fluctuating events. In the theoretical context that will be developed here, I will refer to this form as Relational Governance, the purpose of which is, through its adaptive effectiveness, to stabilize and ensure the continuation of cooperative projects between actors.

I have discussed the parameters of Relational Governance and the relevant literature on the subject elsewhere (see Wieland, 2014, 2020, p. 50 ff.), so here I will limit myself to a brief summary. For the governance of a distinct relational transaction (RT), the perceptions and motivations of individual persons or agents (I) and their resultant actions and behavior are predominantly important. We expect homo oeconomicus to respond to the uncertainties and contingencies inherent to a cooperation project in a systematically different way than, for example, a Kantian virtue ethicist would. As such, the adaptivity of coordination and cooperation mechanisms, of the organizational form (O) of such a project, is relevant, because it can foster or hinder the interaction of events, as well as the actors' (I) rule compliance. Purely legally driven compliance systems have a different and less pronounced effect on the integrity of a firm's business model, in comparison with an Ethics and Compliance Management System (ECMS). Thus, the informal institutions of a given society (SII) are essential. These include the ethical values, traditions, and norms of a region but in our context also the communicative codes of the polycontextual and polycontextural events in a transaction, for example, the various imperatives of decision logics. Finally, we must consider the requirements of formal institutions (SFI), such as the law and contracts, which dock with relational transactions and influence their processes. The following formal representation

$$\mathrm{RTe, l, m} = \mathrm{f(I <-> O <-> SII <-> SFI)}$$

indicates that the effective and efficient execution of a relational transaction with the decision logics of the economy, law and morality depends on the adaptivity of the parameters I, O, SII, and SFI; on the effectiveness of each parameter; and on the amount of friction in relations between the parameters. A relational governance structure is itself a process that makes possible the processes in relational transactions as attractors for multiple events. Relational Governance is a permanent process of structure formation intended to ensure the continuity and adaptivity of relational transactions. In other words, it is a relation of parameters that, in turn, represent a network of relations. This is the nature of Relational Governance.

3.2 Interaction and Functional Equivalence

The structure $\mathrm{RT = f(I <-> O <-> SII <-> SFI)}$ is both complete and necessary. "Complete" means there are no further parameters for the governance of relational transactions; "necessary" means the parameters are only temporary functional equivalents of one another. "Temporary functional equivalents" means they are capable of assuming one another's functions in the specific context of a distinct transaction. In the process, however, the parameters I, O, SII, and SFI do not replace one another in terms of their existence or potential as effective events in the process of governance.

I have modeled elsewhere (see Wieland, 2014, Chap. 2) the interaction process between the parameters of relational governance as a relational mechanism involving various functional equivalences (see Cao & Lumineau, 2015; Ellickson, 1991; as well as the article in Journal of Institutional and Theoretical Economics 1994, Vol. 150 (1)). For the parameters of a governance structure as a distinct alternative mode of control for distinct relational transactions, the following applies:

(i) I, O, SII, and SFI can be substitutive for one another, that is, they can replace one another. One example: maxims of virtue ethics (I) being replaced by legal regulations (SFI).
(ii) I, O, SII, and SFI can be complementary, that is, they can increase or decrease one another's effectiveness. One example: the fit or misfit between the corporate culture (SII) and its policies and procedures (O).
(iii) I, O, SII, and SFI can be compensatory, that is, they can be used to compensate for individual parameters' lack of effectiveness. One example: compensating for a critical culture of corruption in a given region (SII) with the strong integrity culture practiced by a firm and its leadership (O, I).
(iv) I, O, SII, and SFI can be combined in order to increase the effectiveness of the structure as a whole. One example: the combination of formal compliance (O) and individual leadership.

Substitution, complementarity, compensation, and combination are the interactive, functional equivalences that determine a relational governance structure's adaptivity. Figure 2 portrays this discussion on functionally equivalent governance in the form of a matrix.

In order to illustrate relational governance as a self-unfolding process, the following section will revisit an example touched upon earlier. For one thing, our

Fig. 2 Functional equivalences of governance (see Wieland, 2020, p. 45)

	I	O	SII	SFI
Substitutive	x			x
Complementary		x	x	
Compensatory	x	x	x	
Combinational	x	x		

goal is to clarify the relationalization of distinct decision logics as events and attractors for a distinct transaction. For another, I wish to shed light on the process of the docking and mutual interaction of events as a minisociety, and on its consequences for the adaptive restructuring of the parameters of a relational governance structure on the part of the management. Finally, we will see that the processes of interaction between various societal governance structures have consequences for the events in other relational transactions. What emerges here is a process of societal change.

3.3 Case Study: Pattern and Structure Formation

Relational transactions as attractors for interacting events are subject to a continuous process of pattern and structure formation in their surrounding minisociety of events. The dynamics of spontaneous and temporary pattern formation require a governance structure to stabilize them, which must have the necessary adaptivity to continue the interaction of events as cost-effectively as possible. In the following, we will examine this in more detail with the help of a case study.

In 1977, the USA ratified the Foreign Corrupt Practices Act, and in 1987, the Sentencing Commission released the US Sentencing Guidelines (USSG), which among others were intended to enhance the effectiveness of the US legal system in an increasingly globalized business world. Legal events (FCPA, USSG) dock with economic transactions (e.g. global sales or purchasing) and fundamentally change their character. In terms of enforcing the law through sanctions, the US Sentencing Guidelines employ a combination of economic, legal and moral decision logics. First, they distinguish between individual actors (agents) and collective actors (organizations) and hold every organization responsible for ensuring its agents' legally compliant conduct. This organizational liability is specified by the organization's obligation to practice due diligence regarding the behavior of its agents. An agent is anyone who acts on behalf of the organization, including formally independent agents and partners in its global business network, as covered by the Foreign Corrupt Practices Act (FCPA). Such due diligence may be achieved and credibly expressed through effective ethics and compliance management for a given firm's business network. Its effectiveness/ineffectiveness can, for the transaction in question, result in a substantial reduction of/increase in the financial penalty in the event of wrongdoing (see USSG, 2018, § 8B2.1: Effective Compliance and Ethics Program, p. 517 ff.).

So, what we've learned so far is:

(i) that for a distinct economic transaction with an increased compliance risk, specific precautions are expected to preventively reduce this risk;
(ii) for the purposes of enforcing US law extraterritorially (l), ethical standards of conduct (m), and economic incentives (e) must be relationalized with one another. This must be done in such a way that the efficiency and effectiveness

of private governance structures increase the efficiency and effectiveness of state governance structures;
(iii) public and private ordering are combined to economize on transaction costs.

This new pattern of event interactions also has consequences at the level of other governance structures, in this case, at the macro level of the firm as an organization (see Fig. 6). The legal, financial, and reputation-related risks to the organization in the regional and global execution of its transactions are changed both qualitatively (new and prohibitive compliance risks) and quantitatively (increased compliance risks). At the organizational meso level, this leads to the introduction of an Ethics and Compliance Management System, which appears as a new organizational structure beside the existing Legal Department. This can, in turn, lead to conflicts concerning jurisdiction and to challenges for the corporate and leadership culture. These conflicts may have a positive or negative influence on the organization's fulfillment of its diligence-related responsibilities, and therefore take on a legal and financial relevance that they never had before. This change in the firm's governance structure leads to corresponding changes, say, to the creation of Compliance Offices at its partners (for example, suppliers and dealer networks). The implementation and monitoring of compliance by accounting firms and legal firms produce considerable costs and, at least initially, no earnings. However, these efforts might have a preventive effect with regard to future costs of criminal prosecution.

Finally, this reform of the US legal system has consequences at the organizational microlevel of the individual actor. Personal liability-related risks increase, there are new bureaucratic policies and procedures to adhere to at the firm, and lucrative markets and the revenues they represent are affected. Accordingly, the demands placed on a new leadership and business ethics lead to new standards of conduct and a new business purpose that must be routinized by individual and organizational learning processes. Before the implementation of the USSG, these demands were rarely explicitly voiced at firms, and in the curricula of business schools, they were rarely considered to be part of future managers' education. Subsequently, civil society organizations (NGOs like Transparency International) and business schools responded to the new demands by developing management standards and new business ethics programs in connection with their educational and research activities, working hand in hand with the corporate sector. As a result, NGOs and business schools can now support firms' efforts to implement Ethics and Compliance Management Systems and offer training material or continuing education courses on effective compliance management for the firms' managers.

Time is a constitutive factor in all processes. Developing and implementing generally accepted and practically effective standards of integrity and due diligence compliance took several years. They emerged from a combination of practical business experience and the expertise of standard setters and monitors in the legal, business, academic, and civil society systems. Today, they define a generally accepted set of legal and societal expectations that are continuously evolving. The specific implementation and enforcement of new legal regulations are not only due to state power but also to the interaction of polycontextual societal actors and a process of private and public value creation. While state power triggers the process, implementation is achieved through an interweaving of the logics of law, economics, civil society, morality, and management. Thus, economizing on transaction and relational costs transforms into effective third-party enforcement.

Though the process could be explored in much more detail, I will leave it at that. Reduced to a basic and fairly theoretical denominator: relational governance is the interlacing of polycontextual and polycontextural events in a governance structure (I, O, SII, SFI), the adaptivity of which is determined by the capacity of each parameter to replace, complement, compensate for, or to be combined with all other parameters. Polyvalent events are considered to represent the numerically incalculable complexity of trade-offs in price theory-based neoclassical economics and are, therefore, not part of its epistemic focus (see Jensen, 2002, 237 ff; Machlup, 1967, p. 21 ff.). According to Robert Axelrod (1997, p. 4) "[t]he main alternative to the assumption of relational choice is some form of adaptive behavior" when dealing with complex interactions. In Relational Economics, polyvalent events are theoretically and practically endogenized via a distinct governance structure, which allows us to analyze their role and the characteristics of how they function in private and public value creation: as shared value creation on the part of organizations. What in standard economics are considered to be market failures and trade-offs that could not be internalized by price theory can thus become value creation goals for strategic and operational management. Adaptivity through individual and organizational learning processes is central to the governance of economic complexity. In this way, economic complexities are transformed into economic opportunities, and externalities are transformed into relational business transactions.

4 The Cooperation Corridor and Relational Rent

4.1 Cooperation-Economic Opportunities and Organization

Cooperation-economic opportunities represent potential additional revenues for a given organization or network of organizations, simply because the resources of all its stakeholders are used collaboratively. When utilized through strategic and operational stakeholder management, they can deliver a competitive edge and, in the process, a relational rent (see Wieland, 2020; Möhrer in this volume).

Relational Economics views the firm as an organized relation of stakeholders' material and non-material resources and interests. The relevant stakeholders invest their distinct resources and—depending on the nature of the transaction and the requirements for continuing the cooperative relation—expect in return to receive both a factor income and a share of the jointly generated cooperation rent. Both types of income can be material and/or non-material in nature (see Wieland, 2014, 2020). Figure 3 illustrates this theoretical assumption of the firm as a nexus of stakeholders:

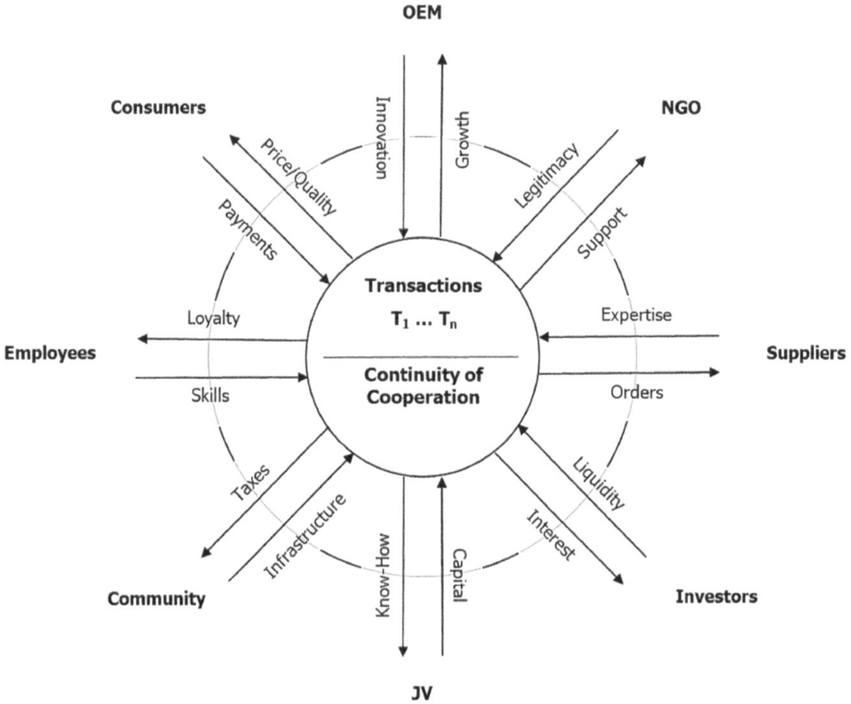

Fig. 3 The firm as a nexus of stakeholder relations (from Wieland, 2020, p. 71)

By applying this model to the previously discussed example of implementing the legal requirements for an Ethics and Compliance Management System (ECMS) as a distinct transaction intended to ensure the continuation of the cooperative project, we arrive at the following.

On the one hand, the figure shows stakeholders' interests or invested resources with regard to the transaction and the organization, as well as their (representative) expected returns. In this regard, we should note the unique status of the government (state) as a stakeholder. Unlike the others, its contribution is not based on a voluntary, formal or informal agreement, but on its societally legitimated power to create and enforce the law (see Van Oosterhaut et al., 2006, p. 532). Governments and state administrations are stakeholders of the firm, but not specifically investing stakeholders in the team, when they act as societal institutions for the creation and enforcement of universally valid regulations. These regulations are events that dock with a given organization's transactions. As such, they are entities in the polyvalent minisociety of these transactions as a distinct context. They do so as political and legal organizational systems, and therefore as stakeholders of society. In this role, they have a priority influence on the execution of distinct transactions and the continuation of organizations. They are their societal stakeholders, a function based on the social contract (see Donaldson & Dunfee, 1995), which determines the contractual relevance (see Wieland, 2014, p. 117) and therefore the priority of these stakeholders. With regard to legal regulations and their enforcement, all societal actors agree to accept and adhere to them. Commons (1934/1990) viewed this aspect as the "control of individual action by collective action" (p. 70), by which he was referring to all of a society's formal and informal institutions. To put it in an economic language: After joining the constitutional contract, firms are only free to choose within rules at the post-constitutional level (Buchanan, 1975, Chap. 2). Here, we can also see that the execution of relational transactions is simultaneously the execution of society and societal regulation.

On the other hand, from a process perspective, the horizontal relations (dashed circle in Fig. 4) between the stakeholders are relevant, since the desired new opportunities for cooperation can only be produced by the polycontextuality of their resources and the level of dynamism achieved in their interactions. These new opportunities manifest as events at various levels of an organization and its stakeholders, namely, at the level of the organization's processes (policies and procedures, communications topics), its structure (ECMS, Integrity and Compliance Department, settlement institutions) and its products (regulation, monitoring standards, earnings, trainings). Figures 5 and 6 illustrate these relations.

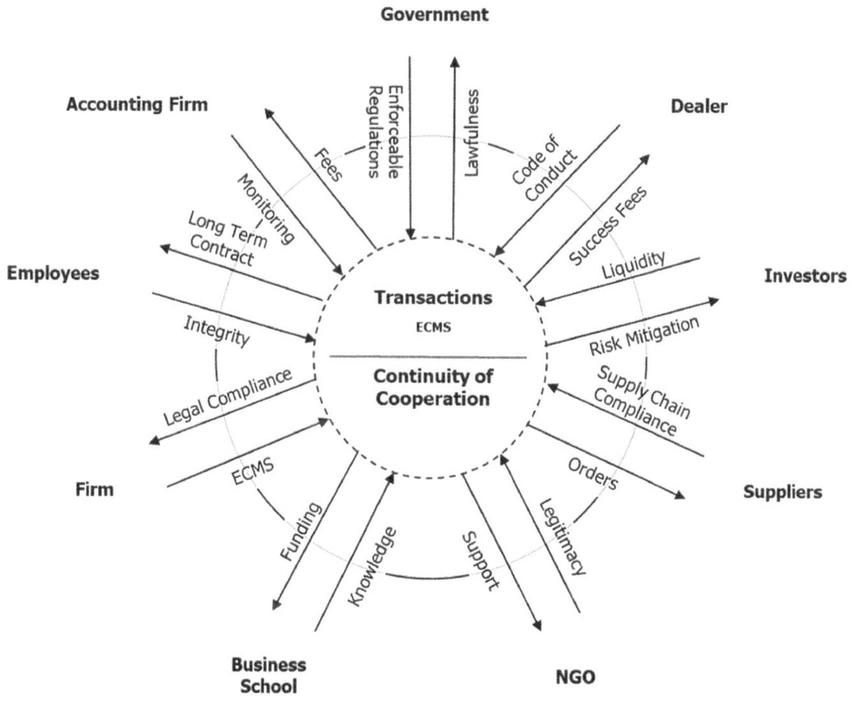

Fig. 4 Analysis of ECMS stakeholders

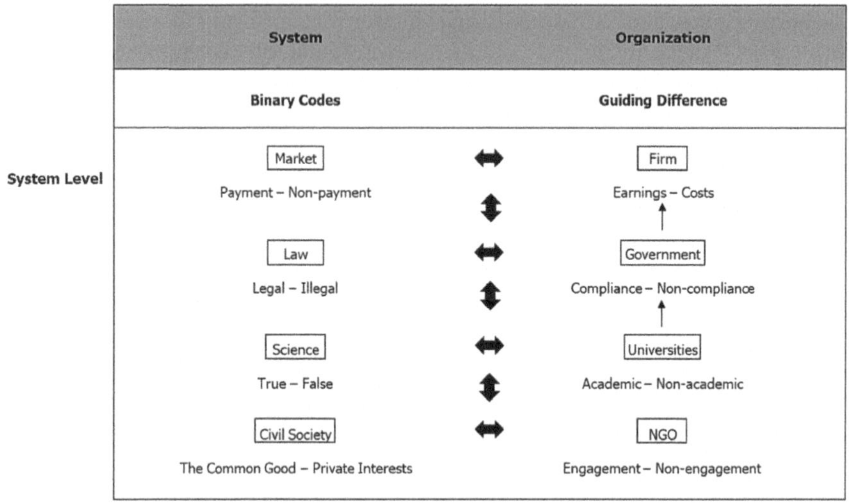

Fig. 5 System communications and organizational decisions

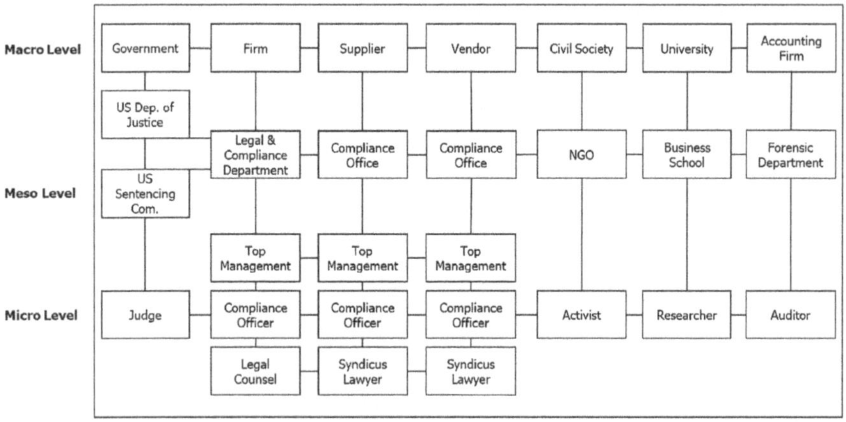

Fig. 6 Multi-level impacts of an ECMS

Figure 5 employs a system theory perspective (see Luhmann, 1989, 1995, 2012) to classify the actors mentioned in the case study in terms of their various contexts (market, law, science) and their organizational decision logics (firm: earnings/costs; government: compliance/non-compliance; universities: academic/non-academic). The interlacing of these language games into a chain of decisions takes place as follows: the US Sentencing Guidelines are part of the legal system and define standards of legality and their enforcement via third-party and self-enforcement or public and private governance. This reflects and expresses legal expectations (compliance).

What is more important, though: through the economic organization's guiding difference (earnings/costs), the penal system (criminal liability, financial bonus/penalty) can be directly conceived and cannot be rejected. Simultaneously, standards of integrity are formulated, the specifics of which can be developed in universities' Business Ethics programs in keeping with established academic and professional standards. This, in turn, promotes interactions between universities and firms from different industries, since the task of validating the credence and not merely functional existence of these efforts is generally considered to reside in the purview of academia or certified accounting firms rather than the general business world. The development of these programs entails costs for universities and accounting firms, which are (or should be) balanced by the corresponding earnings from providing management standards, continuing education, consulting and certified monitoring services. Here, the code "academic/non-academic" is structurally coupled with the economic codes "payment/non-payment" and "earnings/costs" while simultaneously maintaining the systemic and organizational differentiation. The functional logic and effectiveness of the USSG are based precisely on the premise that, while all organizations have to do business, not every organization is part of the economic system (see Weber, 1921/1976, Chap. II, § 1.4, 1.5).

Figure 6 examines these relations at the organization's macro, meso, and microlevels, as intra-firm, inter-firm, and extra-firm motivational, structural and functional consequences. Due to the docking of new decision-making contexts and their respective language games, the increasing complexity of the relational transaction is accommodated by implementing new and adapted governance structures (I, O, SII, SIF), which serve to enhance the effectiveness and efficiency of its adaptivity. This produces pecuniary and non-pecuniary costs and earnings at all levels but can also mean losing or gaining new opportunities for cooperation and value creation.

The figure is intended to show why purely legally driven compliance might only be efficient or effective to a limited extent, even if the event was set in motion by the legal system. First, it disregards the legal regulation's integrative ethical and economic logic and, therefore, does not ensure adherence, which might lead to liability, fines, and settlement costs. Second, it disregards the interaction between the logics of these three language games. A dominant legal logic has a crowding-out effect on ethical and economic logic and necessarily leads to other events at the level of organizations and their stakeholders. Uncertainty among and between actors, complying out of fear of punishment, a "tick-the-box" approach when it comes to implementing management systems, rigid legal communications and so on lead to a reformatting of the cooperative pattern (with regard to the willingness to cooperate, ability to cooperate and chances for cooperation) with negative economic and ethical consequences. To put it in more general terms: the effective and efficient adjustment of the decision logics and language games involved, which are what determine the breadth of and opportunities for access to a cooperation corridor for all stakeholders, defines the size of the relational rent and shared value creation that can be achieved (see the paper by Wieland et al. in this volume).

4.2 Triggers and Other Effects

In Figure 6, we saw how the introduction of the relational transaction "ECMS" gives rise to organizational differentiation. In Figure 7, we will now take a closer look into horizontal interactions between stakeholders (see dashed circle in Fig. 4) as events in the minisociety that has formed on and docked with this transaction. For this purpose, we will distinguish between the "trigger event" and its consequences as either "primary effects" or "secondary effects" in a network of events that influence the quality and quantity of its value creation.

In our case study, it is a societal stakeholder that launched the trigger event: the new regulations issued by the US Sentencing Commission in connection with the FCPA. This event necessitates changes in organizational governance and a redefinition of the role-based expectations for actors to live up to their responsibilities in connection with transaction-related "due diligence." Generally speaking, the trigger event affects the structure and motivation of a given organization, but potentially its products, too, as can readily be seen with regard to sustainability management. The trigger event diffuses into the network of stakeholders involved and changes the patterns and structures of their interactions. In a primary effect, within the firm's organizational setup, differentiation may occur with regard to, for example, its stakeholder perspective. In this case, the Top Management has to redefine the role-based expectations it is meant to represent, and the newly created Ethics & Compliance Department must prepare

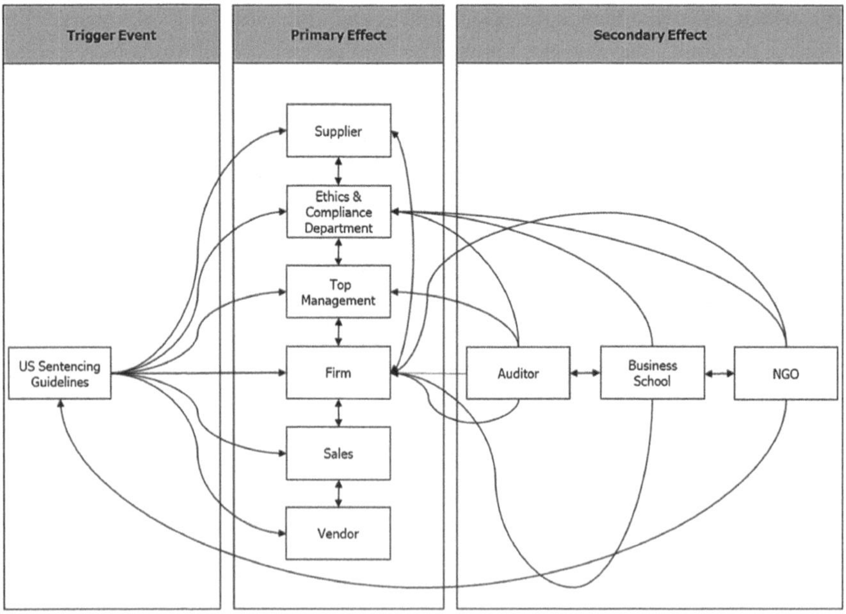

Fig. 7 Network of events

a host of new policies and procedures to process the effects of the trigger event within the organization. However, this can only work if all the previously mentioned actors (Top Management, suppliers, investors, etc.) become explicit stakeholders in the transaction and the organization and develop their own interests. This is achieved by legal detention strategies employed by the stakeholders on the one hand, and by the development of new and autonomous standards of professionalism regarding due diligence on the other hand. Whereas a Legal Department tends to focus on the options for creating legal leeway, and on finding latitude in interpreting legal regulations, the focus of the Compliance Office is on ensuring that public and in-house regulations are adhered to using a "zero tolerance" approach. With regard to aggressive shareholder value-oriented sales strategies, CEOs can no longer practice "willful blindness." This in turn has consequences for the effects of the systemic coding and the guiding difference within the organization. A compliance organization cannot make its adherence to the law dependent on the earnings and costs resulting from executing or not executing a given transaction; rather, it must be geared towards "zero tolerance" conformity with the law and enforce it. Expressed in theoretical terms: both the coding of the market system (payment/non-payment) and the guiding difference for the organization (earnings/costs) continue to apply to the assessment of transactions. Yet, within the organization or in connection with decision-making for a specific event or transaction, they can be temporarily suspended and replaced by a legal codification. At this point, the coding of the legal system becomes dominant from an inter-systemic standpoint. This is why, at the level of the organization, multiple language games can still be applied and understood. Its capacity for polylingualism is not constrained. However, the assessment and hierarchization of these language games with regard to the specific transaction "ECMS" are made by additionally using the societal guiding difference "conformity/non-conformity." Here, we see again that firms are organizations embedded in both the economy and society. In other words, the completion of their transactions always also represents the reproduction of the organization and society. Yet this reproduction of society can only be integrated in the organization's processes and events with the previously discussed emergence and addition of new governance structures (here, compliance). This has consequences not only for suppliers but also the sales organization and customers, who, with regard to the specific transaction, now have to adopt this organizationally modified decision-making effect in their minisociety. Their signal can only be one of their own conformity with the organization's conformity. The network interactions touched upon above produce economic, business-model and academic "secondary effects" at NGOs, auditing companies and business schools. They are triggered by observations. Secondary effects only have selective and contingent effects on the transaction, in the sense that new chances for cooperation can emerge. In terms of the overall effect, we can see that the combination of stakeholders' vertical and horizontal interactions constitutes the network of value creation. While polycontextuality and polylingualism remain unaffected by this combination, polycontexturality adopts a new mix of the relevance and effectiveness of the decision logics involved.

4.3 Relational Costs and Shared Value Creation

The process of interacting events just described presupposes and produces a recursive chain of causality at the level of individual and collective actors—willingness to cooperate <-> ability to cooperate <-> chances for cooperation <-> cooperation rent—, which I will also explain using the previously discussed example.

Willingness to cooperate: this is the fundamental prerequisite for the US Sentencing Guidelines and requires a shift from conflict to cooperation. First, from a legal standpoint, it means voluntarily relinquishing the privilege of not having to incriminate oneself through testimony or disclosures, and instead, offering full cooperation in determining the facts of the matter. This is rewarded with bonus points in terms of determining penalties, which can have financially positive effects. Furthermore, the willingness to cooperate is seen as an expression of the collective actor's ethical integrity, an aspect that is also viewed positively. On the part of the individual actors, this requires the development of an organizational culture that demands integrity and the willingness to cooperate in all of the organization's activities. As such, a culture of legal integrity that is designed to promote transparency and the willingness to cooperate is only one of many events within the set of events (others include standards of ethical conduct, and relational leadership (see Wieland, 2017b)) that can be used to promote integrity throughout the cooperative project.

Ability to cooperate: the US Sentencing Guidelines expect organizations and their stakeholders to be able to proactively practice compliance with the law and ethical integrity. This requires the previously mentioned policies, procedures, and structures within the respective organization, which are used to implement and monitor the processes, ensuring legal compliance and ethical integrity. In addition, training measures focus on enabling staff to actively practice the required willingness to cooperate. In global supply chains and value creation networks, acquiring transcultural competency (see Wieland & Baumann Montecinos, 2019) is another essential factor and enables individual and collective actors to accept and successfully address the risks of corruption arising from cultural diversity. This ability also applies, to use a different example, to investors as stakeholders, whose expectations regarding the return on investment (RoI) depend on their ability to develop sustainable investment concepts.

This willingness and ability to cooperate lead to an achievable corridor of chances for cooperation. Acquiring and honing these traits entail specific costs, which I refer to as relational costs (Wieland, 2020, Chap. 11). Relational costs differ from transaction costs, adaptation costs and cooperation costs in that they are exclusively connected to specific relational transactions. In systemic terms, they are produced by the costs of the requisite stakeholder management, by the negative consequences of suboptimal leadership qualities, and by the learning processes involved in ensuring that the transcultural nature of this type of transaction (see Wieland, 2020) is addressed with as little friction as possible. More general: Relational costs are the costs to create and maintain the willingness and ability to cooperate and continue cooperation. Figure 8 illustrates these relations.

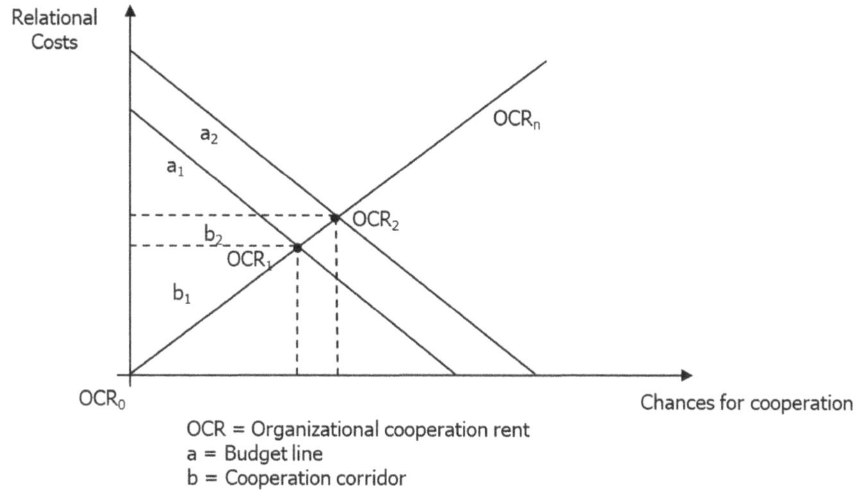

Fig. 8 Organizational cooperation rents and corridors (from Wieland, 2020, p. 149)

The budget line a1 marks the chances for cooperation that are available to a network of stakeholders at a given level of costs. The tangent OCR represents the organization's learning and development process, which produces an optimal cooperation rent at point OCR_1. The potential expansion of business by opening new global markets (for example, China's Belt and Road initiative) can only yield new revenues when, in addition to numerous other events, the adaptivity and the efficiency and effectiveness of the compliance or CSR management systems already in place, as well as the transcultural integrity, are adjusted. Assuming its willingness and ability to cooperate, the organization in question can achieve a larger potential cooperation corridor ($b_2 > b_1$), which is accompanied by budget line a_2 and the higher cooperation rent OCR_2.

That being said, the acceptance of the increased chances of cooperation depends on the willingness to take risks, as well as the ability to manage risks within the cooperative project, and assessing these parameters could lead to the non-expansion or even a reduction of the corridor. The cooperation corridor's strategic and operational management also involves choosing not to pursue chances for cooperation when there is insufficient willingness or ability to cooperate in connection with a given transaction.

This discussion can be summarized in a schema of relational value creation, based on the well-known "simple contractual schema" put forward by Williamson (2005, p. 12). This should serve to underscore the fact that value creation through cooperation, not the comparison of transaction costs, is what constitutes the epistemic interest of Relational Economics (Fig. 9).

Exchange transactions (ET) and their discrete exchanges generate a monopoly rent (MR) at best, but no cooperation rent (CR). In the intra-firm constellation RT_1,

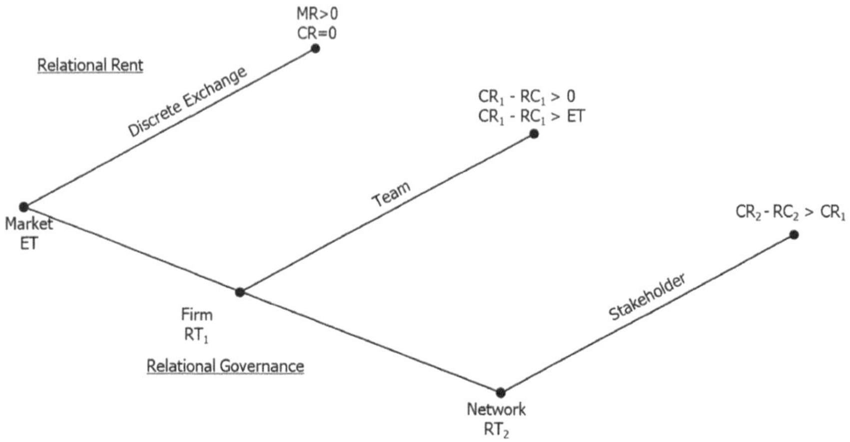

Fig. 9 Schema of relational value creation (from Wieland, 2020, p. 152)

on the other hand, the rent from cooperation is not merely the result of an inseparable production function (Alchian & Demsetz, 1972) and/or of the specificity of the resources invested, but also of the organizational capabilities (Teece et al., 2000), or in our context, the adaptivity of the governance structure selected (see Amit & Schoemaker, 1993; Wieland, 2014, 135 ff.). The residual claimant appropriates this rent after deducting the relational costs, particularly the costs of creating and maintaining the team. An inter-firm network (RT_2) and the firm as a nexus of polyvalent stakeholders are formed when the cooperation rent (CR_2) resulting from asset specificity, co-specialization and governance adaptivity, after deducting the relational costs of governance, is larger than the cooperation rent CR_1 for intra-firm cooperation.

5 Closing Remarks

From the perspective of Relational Economics, the realization of economic transactions and the value creation that can be achieved with them in a self-unfolding process take place in a well-defined cooperation corridor of interacting and multivalent events. In this regard, the relational transaction as an attractor for polyvalent contexts and decision logics is the basic unit of analysis. Relational governance, which consists of individual and organizational self-governance regimes and formal and informal institutions, must allow these multiple events to be structured in such a way that the relational costs can be minimized and factor incomes and cooperation rents can be generated. To that end, it can combine these parameters of governance so that the capacity of each one to temporarily serve as a substitute for, complement, compensate for, or be combined with all other parameters is enhanced. The relational governance structure's resulting degree of adaptivity determines not only the relational costs but also the size of the cooperation corridor and its appropriable rent. With regard to the three factors willingness to cooperate, ability to cooperate and chances for cooperation, both their scope and direction of action are determined by relational governance. Consequently, if cooperation is the analytical point of reference for Relational Economics, the organization of cooperation is its focus. The firm itself then becomes a nexus of the resources and interests of economic, political and other societal actors for private and societal value creation. Relational Economics is a Political Economy that seeks to understand the economy and society as a network of events whose relationalization leads to innovation in the form of changed or wholly new chances for cooperation in all systems of society.

References

Alchian, A. A., & Demsetz, H. (1972). Production, information costs, and economic organization. *American Economic Review, 62*(5), 777–795.

Amit, R., & Schoemaker, P. J. H. (1993). Strategic assets and organizational rent. *Strategic Management Journal, 14*(1), 33–46.

Axelrod, R. (1997). *The complexity of cooperation: Agent-based models of competition and collaboration.* Princeton University Press.

Benkler, Y. (2006). *The wealth of networks. How social production transforms markets and freedom.* YaleUniversity Press.

Benkler, Y. (2017). Peer production, the commons, and the future of the firm. *Strategic Organization, 15*(2), 264–274.

Buchanan, J. M. (1975). *The limits of liberty: Between anarchy and Leviathan.* University of Chicago Press.

Bruni, L. (2013). Relational goods: A new tool for an old issue. *ECOS Estudos Contemporâneos Da Subjetividade, 3*(2), 173–178.

Cao, Z., & Lumineau, F. (2015). Revisiting the interplay between contractual and relational governance: A qualitative and meta-analytic investigation. *Journal of Operations Management, 33–34*, 15–42.

Chang, S.-H. (2017). The technology networks and development trends of university-industry collaborative patents. *Technological Forecasting and Social Change, 118*, 107–113.

Coase, R. (1937). The nature of the firm. *Economica, 4*(4), 386–405.

Commons, J. R. (1934). *Institutional economics: Its place in political economy (Reprint 1990).* Transaction Publishers.

Commons, J. R. (1950). *The economics of collective action.* MacMillan.

De Marchi, V., Di Maria, E., & Gereffi, G. (Eds.). (2018). *Local clusters in global value chains. Linking actors and territories through manufacturing and innovation.* Routledge.

de Moraes Silva, D. R., Furtado, A. T., & Vonortas, N. S. (2018). University-industry R&D cooperation in Brazil: A sectoral approach. *The Journal of Technology Transfer, 43*(2), 285–315.

Donaldson, T., & Dunfee, T. W. (1995). Integrative social contracts theory: A communitarian conception of economic ethics. *Economics & Philosophy, 11*(1), 85–112.

Ellickson, R. C. (1991). *Order without Law. How neighbors settle disputes.* Harvard University Press.

Fernandez-Stark, K., & Gereffi, G. (2019). Global value chain analysis: A primer (2nd ed.). In S. Ponte, G. Gereffi, & G. Raj-Reichert (Eds.), *Handbook on global value chains* (pp. 54–76). Edward Elgar.

Freeman, R. E., Phillips, R., & Sisodia, R. (2020). Tensions in stakeholder theory. *Business & Society, 59*(2), 213–231.
Financial Stability Financial Services and Capital Markets Union. (2020). *Platform on sustainable finance—List of members.* Banking and Financial Services. https://ec.europa.eu/info/publications/eu-platform-on-sustainable-finance-members_de
Geisler, E. (1995). Industry–university technology cooperation: A theory of inter-organizational relationships. *Technology Analysis & Strategic Management, 7*(2), 217–229.
Gui, B. (2005). From transactions to encounters: The joint generation of relational goods and conventional values. In B. Gui & R. Sudgen (Eds.), *Economics and social interaction: Accounting for interpersonal relations* (pp. 23–51). Cambridge University Press.
Jensen, M. C. (2002). Value maximization, stakeholder theory, and the corporate objective function. *Business Ethics Quarterly, 12*(2), 235–256.
Luhmann, N. (1989). *Ecological communication.* Polity Press.
Luhmann, N. (1995). *Social systems.* Stanford University Press.
Luhmann, N. (2012). *Introduction to system theory.* Polity Press.
Macaulay, S. (1963). Non-contractual relations in business: A preliminary study. *American Sociological Review, 28*(1), 55–67.
Machlup, F. (1963). *Essays in economic semantics.* Prentice-Hall.
Machlup, F. (1967). Theories of the firm: Marginalist, behavioral, managerial. *The American Economic Review, 57*(1), 1–33.
Macneil, I. R. (1974). The many futures of contracts. *Southern California Law Review, 47*, 691–816.
Macneil, I. R. (1978). Contracts adjustment of long-term economic relations under classical, neoclassical, and relational contract law. *Northwestern University Law Review, 72*, 854–905.
Macneil, I. R. (1981). Economic analysis of contractual relations: Its shortfalls and the need for a "rich classificatory apparatus." *Northwestern University Law Review, 75*(6), 1018–1063.
Macneil, I. R. (1985). Relational contract: What we do and do not know. *Wisconsin Law Review, 4*, 483–526.
Mascarenhas, C., Ferreira, J. J., & Marques, C. (2018). University–industry cooperation: A systematic literature review and research agenda. *Science and Public Policy, 45*(5), 708–718.
Ostrom, E. (2005). *Understanding institutional diversity.* Princeton University Press.
Ostrom, E. (2010). Beyond markets and states: polycentric governance of complex economic systems. *American Economic Review, 100*(3), 641–672.
Ostrom, V., Tiebout, C. M., & Warren, R. (1961). The organization of government in metropolitan areas: atheoretical inquiry. *American Political Science Review, 55*(4), 831–842.
Penrose, E. (1959). *The growth of the firm (Nachdruck 1995).* Oxford University Press.
Priddat, B. P. (2016). Die Transaktion als Juxtaposition und als Kooperation. Differente Interpretation des Marktes. In H.-C. Schmidt am Busch (ed.), Die Philosophie des Marktes (pp. 207–226). Felix Meiner Verlag.
Richardson, G. B. (1972). The Organisation of industry. *The Economic Journal, 82*(327), 883–896.
Ruggie, J. G., & Sherman, J. F. (2017). The concept of 'due diligence' in the UN guiding principles on business and human rights: A reply to Jonathan Bonnitcha and Robert McCorquodale. *European Journal of International Law, 28*(3), 921–928.
Schumpeter, J. A. (1950). *Capitalism, socialism and democracy* (3rd ed.). Harper Torchbooks.
Teece, D. J., Pisano, G., & Shuen, A. (2000). Dynamic capabilities and strategic management. In G. Dosi, R. R. Nelson, & S. G. Winter (Eds.), *The nature and dynamics of organizational capabilities* (pp. 334–362). Oxford University Press.
Uhlaner, C. J. (1989). "Relational goods" and participation: Incorporating sociability into a theory of rational action. *Public Choice, 62*(3), 253–285.
United States Sentencing Commission. (2018). *Guidelines manual.* Retrieved from https://www.ussc.gov/sites/default/files/pdf/guidelines-manual/2018/GLMFull.pdf.
Van Oosterhaut, J. H., Heugens, P., & Kaptein, M. (2006). The internal morality of contracting: Advancing in the contractualist endeavor in business ethics. *Academy of Mangement Review, 31*(3), 521–539.

Weber, M. (1921). *Wirtschaft und Gesellschaft* (5th ed.). Mohr (1976).
Whitehead, A. N. (1941). *Process and reality*. The Free Press.
Whitehead, A. N. (1968). *Modes of thought*. The Free Press.
Wieland, J. (1998). Kooperationsökonomie: Die Ökonomie der Diversifität, Abhängigkeit und Atmosphäre. In G. Wegner & J. Wieland (Eds.), *Formelle und informelle Institutionen: Genese, Interaktion und Wandel* (pp. 9–33). Metropolis Verlag.
Wieland, J. (2014). *Governance ethics: Global value creation, economic organization and normativity*. Springer International Publishing.
Wieland, J. (Ed.). (2017a). *Creating shared value—Concepts, experience, criticism* (Vol. 52). Springer International Publishing.
Wieland, J. (2017b). Relationale Führung und intersektorale Governance. In M. Lehmann & M. Tyrell (Eds.), *Komplexe Freiheit: Wie ist Demokratie möglich?* (pp. 237–257). Springer Fachmedien Wiesbaden.
Wieland, J. (2018). *Relational economics: Ökonomische Theorie der Governance wirtschaftlicher Transaktionen*. Metropolis Verlag.
Wieland, J. (2020). *Relational economics. A political economy*. Springer.
Wieland, J., & Baumann Montecinos, J. (Eds.). (2019). *Transcultural leadership and transcultural competence*. Metropolis Verlag.
Wieland, J., Steinmeyer, R., & Grüninger, S. (Eds.). (2020). *Handbuch compliance management* (3rd ed.). ESV.
Williamson, O. E. (1979). Assessing Vertical market restrictions: Antitrust ramifications of the transaction cost approach. *University of Pennsylvania Law Review, 127*(4), 953–993.
Williamson, O. E. (1985). *The economic institutions of capitalism*. Free Press.
Williamson, O. E. (1991). Comparative economic organization: The analysis of discrete structural alternatives. *Administrative Science Quarterly, 36*(2), 269–296.
Williamson, O. E. (1996). *The mechanisms of governance*. Oxford University Press.
Williamson, O. E. (2005). The economics of governance. *American Economic Review, 95*(2), 1–18.

Josef Wieland is professor of Institutional Economics, Organizational Governance, Integrity Management, and Transcultural Leadership at Zeppelin University in Friedrichshafen and director of the Leadership Excellence Institute Zeppelin (LEIZ). He is the initiator and president of the German Forum Compliance and Integrity (FCI). He served as the former chairman of the German Network of Business Ethics (DNWE) and currently as the chairman of DNWE's advisory board. He is a member of the National CSR Forum of the BMAS (German Federal Ministry of Labour and Social Affairs) and serves on the jury board for the "CSR Prize" of the German government. He received the Max Weber Prize for Business Ethics of the IW (German Economic Institute) in 1999. In 2004, he received the highly estimated State Research Prize for Applied Research from the State of Baden-Württemberg, Germany. From 2017 until 2021, he was Vice-President (Research) of Zeppelin University, Friedrichshafen, Germany.

Why We Could Need a Relational Economics and Why Standard Economics and Its (Orthodox) Derivations Do not Help

Lucio Biggiero

Abstract The theoretical landscape of economic, management, and social sciences is already rather crowded to advance with light heart a further proposal. Therefore, this chapter aims only to offer elements to reason about the opportunity to create the new research field of Relational Economics. I suggest three main lines of reasoning that can help for this purpose. Firstly, I attempt to show that Standard Economics and its (orthodox) derivations do not provide the right theoretical background. Secondly, I argue that complexity science should be the methodological and epistemological framework on which developing Relational Economics. Finally, I outline five research streams—behavioral and evolutionary economics, analytical and relational sociology, and organization science—that could be the building blocks of the new approach. They are largely consistent and partially overlapped with each other, and thus, beyond the relatively different languages, it is not difficult to imagine its convergence to a unitary proposal.

Keywords Analytical sociology · Austrian economic theory · Behavioral economics · Complexity science · Economic interactions and networks · Emergence · Evolutionary economics · Organization science · Relational economics · Relational sociology · Self-organization · Standard economics · Transaction cost economics

1 Introduction

In front of the evidence that, according to Standard Economics (SE), economic agents interact through prices and quantities (Bridel, 2012; Zamagni, 1993), why should we need Relational Economics (RE)? A standard economist, in fact, would say that we do not need any further branch of economics, because the very concept of competitive equilibrium—be it partial or general—is already based on (economic) relations. The same could be argued for most of its derivations, like organizational and industrial

L. Biggiero (✉)
University of L'Aquila, L'Aquila, Italy
e-mail: lucio.biggiero@univaq.it

L. Biggiero et al. (eds.), *The Relational View of Economics*, Relational Economics and Organization Governance, https://doi.org/10.1007/978-3-030-86526-9_4

economics (Grandori, 2013; Schmalensee & Willig, 1989), which are based just on explicit or implicit contracts, and thus, supposedly, on agents' relations. Hence, if SE and its derivations were already relational, we would not need any other kind of dedicated field.

In this work, my attempt is to contend that view, to provide elements to consider the opportunity of identifying a specific theoretical space for RE, and then to outline the theoretical pillars on which it could be built. My first argument runs by claiming that "spot" economic interactions, as those supposed by SE, do not refer to relations, at least not in a strong and full sense of the word, which refers to *relatively stable connections*, often rather complex and irreducible to purely economic aspects. When considered this way, relations require and produce (as well relatively stable) socio-economic structures, be them groups, organizations, communities, or even largely aggregated entities, like industrial clusters, industries, regions, etc. Put differently, the interactions assumed by SE are not the full kind of interactions that good microeconomics should take into account (Elsner, 2012).

The real world is made of such structures (networks), in which agents cover given positions, and in turn, such positions influence to some extent their behaviors. Then, agents have (usually) enough degree of freedom to produce new behaviors (or choose some out of many possible behaviors) to induce changes in the structures. This view substantially coincides with the *structural individualism* proposed by analytical sociology (Hedström, 2005; Manzo, 2014), which hopefully had to be engaged as one of the pillars of RE. Conversely, economic agents of SE interact occasionally in a structure-less world, because their behaviors and socio-economic facts are taken as sharp oversimplifications of real-world phenomena. In the alternative between a wider, more consistent, and more formalized approach with its side effect of lacking explaining power, and a narrower, weaker, and less formalized approach providing effective but fragmented and episodic explanations, SE and its derivations sides on the first one, while RE should do the opposite. SE starts from a few supposedly evident and ideologically neutral assumptions about the real world, to which it adds a number of totally implausible further hypotheses required to make the theoretical model formalized and able to find optimal prices in general economic equilibrium (GEE).

Now, the criticism of lack of realism is all but new (Komlos, 2019; Landreth & Colander, 2001; Roncaglia, 2006; Screpanti & Zamagni, 2005), dating back to the very beginning of SE, and then renewed in at least two particularly significant waves: right after WW2 and, more recently, with the approach of critical realism (Pratten, 2013). What distinguishes this new "attack" is its base on the sound and effective findings of complexity science (Casti, 1989, 1994; Mainzer, 1994; Serra, 2010). Actually, a poorly investigated implication of complexity science is that the epistemology of classical science, which was based on a progressive approximation to real-world phenomena from a very abstract but highly consistent and wide theory, does not hold anymore. This logic was the necessary companion to legitimate and make sense of reductionism. Now, while on reductionism there is an extant literature, on the failure of approximation there is a knowledge gap. In this work, I cannot develop this point, because it is beyond its scope and would take too much space.

Among the various forms in which complexity affects socio-economic phenomena, I have focused on the two that seem more general, easier to be introduced here, more debated in economic literature, and more contrasting SE (and its derivations) with innovating research streams and the possible birth of RE. These two forms of complexity are the structural (network) dimension of socio-economic phenomena and its evolutionary characteristic, which in turn produces emergent outcomes, that is, new and unpredictable phenomena.

This work is structured in two parts. In the first one, six conceptual building blocks of RE are sketched: complexity science, which provides a cross-disciplinary conceptual (and also, implicitly, epistemological) framework; behavioral and evolutionary economics on the side of unorthodox research streams in economics; analytical and relational sociology on the side of unorthodox research streams in sociology; and finally, organization science. This way, RE would not spring out from scratch. On the contrary, those unorthodox research streams, each one from its own angles, already address almost all the fundamental ingredients to create the new approach.

The second part shows how different, distant, and even incompatible SE and some of its derivatives are from what RE could be. The main references will be two economic theories, one of which can be considered as the ever most influential in economic thought—the neo-Walrasian GEE (General Economic Equilibrium)—and the other one an approach whose influence was growing during last decades—the Austrian school of economic theory. The former is the theoretical framework on which it is based, through some of its variants, any standard course of microeconomics and macroeconomics, while the latter is recalling a special interest due to a supposed consistency with self-organization processes, which is considered one of the main traits of complexity science. Among the plethora of derivations from SE, the main concern will be given here to transaction cost economics (TCE), and to some less general theories.

It would have been logical to dedicate part of this contribution to the epistemological and methodological aspects involved by RE because actually it differs substantially from SE and its derivations under these two respects. While there is no space to discuss them here, some of those aspects have been dealt with in the recent volume by Biggiero et al. (2016) and more specifically in Biggiero (2016a). The main relational methods—social network analysis, NK-FL Boolean networks, artificial neural networks, and agent-based simulation networks—have been introduced and discussed there under both theoretical and empirical sides. Further, in line with Wieland's book (2018), which can be considered the first explicit and full attempt to outline RE, and with the Manifesto launching this book series, the reference level of this paper is micro. However, as evolutionary economics (EE) and analytical sociology (AS) already did, nothing prevents them to extend their scope to the macro level. This is why I preferred to keep the acronym as RE, without adding a restriction to organizational governance.

The last warning: due, on the one hand, to the small space that a chapter allows and, on the other hand, to the many theories and concepts involved, each theory is presented very schematically. I am aware that this can be annoying and even repulsive, but the main rationale of this contribution is not in the discussion of some single point or whether some specific element has been precisely assigned to a given theoretical framework or research stream. Rather, its interest should primarily lie in the underlining theoretical architecture and in the main arguments, which hopefully could help to discuss the opportunity to favor the birth of RE and, in case, its general outline.

2 Part I: Building Blocks

In what follows, by addressing its possible conceptual and epistemological building blocks, I attempt to outline what RE could be. The logic of this schema is placing the development of RE around some reference points, which had to be "merged" into one single approach, albeit taken in a broad sense. In fact, because of the current proliferation of research streams in economics and sociology, the suggestion to add a new one had to be already "forgiven" for itself, so it is not the case to follow a sectarian fashion. This call for a non-sectarian view becomes a true claim for pluralism and anti-foundationalism, in line with a pragmatist philosophy of science (Laudan, 1996; Putnam, 1995; Rorty, 1982).

Complexity science (COMP-S) plays the role of cross-disciplinary building block, while the other five—namely, Behavioral and Evolutionary Economics (BE-EE), Analytical and Relational Sociology (AS-RS), and Organization Science (ORG-S)—carry more discipline-specific and operational concepts. Hence, four theoretical roots of RE would come from non-orthodox and recent branches of economic theory and sociology. With some precursors in the 1950s (and even before), BE-EE includes two research streams that started approximately during the same time, at the beginning of the 1950s, but then received a strong impulse about 20 years after. The same can be said of AS-RS, which is even more recent than BE-EE. In terms of vintage, ORG-S is much older, because its very beginning dates back to the beginning of the nineteenth century, but nevertheless, this seniority did not produce a more solid and unitary framework.

It is worth reminding that, far more in this era of "economic thought fragmentation" (Roncaglia, 2006, 2019),[1] each of these research areas is variegated and often is poorly structured into handbooks or academic courses. The authors who rubric themselves into each of them usually share only some of the distinctive points. Evoking what Zygmut Bauman refers to the entire modern society, even in these knowledge fields everything is rather "liquid". As for ORG-S, we could say that it has been "liquid" since long, at least since the classical schools of thought have been criticized and overcome by many different approaches (Van de Ven & Joyce, 1981). Into this field, theoretical proliferation is very high and its various branches breed

[1] Indeed, excepted Colander's (2000), Roncaglia's and other books on economic thought history (Landreth & Colander, 2001; Roncaglia, 2006; Screpanti & Zamagni, 2005) overlook these research streams, which means that the landscape of economic theory would be already fragmented even without them. More or less the same happens with the books on the sociological thought history.

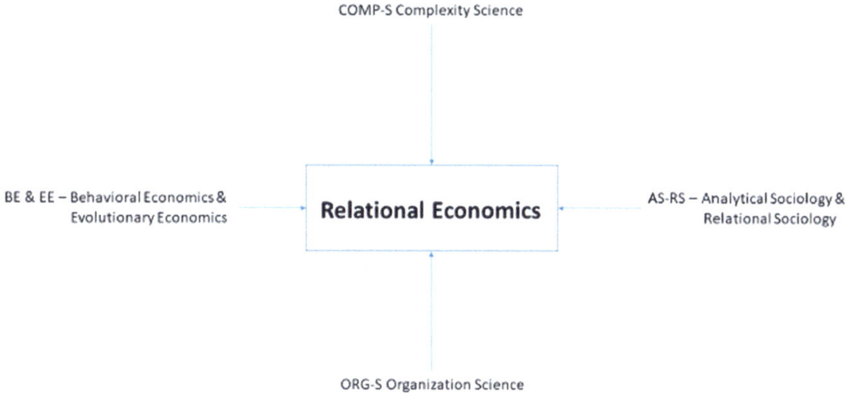

Fig. 1 Conceptual building blocks

with BE-EE, sociology and social psychology, as well as management engineering (Fig. 1).

2.1 The Complexity Turn in Social Sciences

Undoubtedly, since the 1980s we are witnessing at a "complexity turn" in social (and natural) sciences (Biggiero, 1998, 2001a, b; Casti, 1989, 1994; Chaitin, 1987a, b; Ekelund, 1991; Gell-Mann, 1994; Gleick, 1987; Goertzel, 1994; Hall, 1991; Holland, 1998; Jörg, 2011; Kauffman, 1996; Mainzer, 1994; Miller & Page, 2007; Prigogine & Stengers, 1984; Ruelle, 1991; Waldrop, 1992; Wolfram, 1994), and economics was not immune of it (Arrow et al., 1988; Arthur, 2010, 2015; Arthur et al., 1997; Barnett et al., 2004; Blume & Durlauf, 2006; Faggini & Vinci, 2010; Helbing & Kirman, 2013; Holt et al., 2010; Kirman, 2011; Lane et al., 2009; Rosser, 1991, 1999). The complexity turn is bringing a revolution in concepts, epistemology, and methodology, whose traits are still far to be acknowledged and discussed in their whole relevance and depth. The well-known literature on the history and philosophy of science (Kuhn, 1962; Lakatos, 1978; Lakatos & Musgrave, 1970; Laudan, 1990) suggests that a dominant paradigm does not crash soon under the criticisms of the new ideas, because science making is not a hyper-rational exercise where the best wins so clearly, and thus, the supporters of the current (wrong) one leave the scene. Things are much more complicated, especially in the domain of social sciences, where the possibility (and even the habit) of running experiments and providing rigorous proofs are much lower and recent than in natural sciences. Instead of a single ready-to-use new paradigm, there are many concurrent or rival theories and methods, whose languages and definitions are not so widely shared and acknowledged or even legitimated. The depth and breadth of criticisms are not well known neither enough supported by empirical evidence. This mess is evident even in reference to the main traits characterizing the complexity turn and even just concerning the meaning of complexity, which still lacks a common understanding. The variety of perspectives and definitions depends on the disciplinary background of who is theorizing complexity, be him/her a natural or social scientist or a philosopher.

Structural (relational) dimension. It is not possible here to discuss all the main traits characterizing the complexity turn, but, due to its relevance for RE, I deal with a couple of them. The first one addresses the fact that most socio-economic phenomena—as well as many natural or artificial phenomena—occur in a structural (relational) dimension: social and economic agents are not independent of one another, but rather they are connected through relatively stable relations, then giving rise to networks (systems, structures). The acknowledgment of the systemic nature of socio-economic and natural life dates back to the very birth of systems science about one century ago, and then it was developed with the rise of cybernetics right after WW2 (Glushkov, 1966; Klir, 1991). A system approach to social sciences received a strong impulse from the 1950s and 1960s (Forrester, 1961, 1968), especially in sociology (Buckley, 1967; Checkland, 1981, 1999), anthropology, and organization science (Beer, 1959, 1966, 1972; Churchman, 1979; Churchman & Verhulst, 1960; Sterman, 2000), while SE fiercely resisted to it. Most of the time, even when it was done, the reference to economic systems was deprived of peculiar properties, and it was just used to delimit a set of objects or facts.[2] The typical system property that a system's behavior is more (or different) than the simple sum or combination of its parts was usually neglected in SE (and in large part of sociology until the 1950s). Economic agents and the parts of an economy were considered in isolation, interacting only through the price mechanisms.

Most approaches of SE overlook the systemic property and the related fact that agents are non-independent in either price or non-price types of interaction. With the exception of network economics (Jackson, 2010a, 2014a), agents' behavior is studied only through standard statistics, which in fact is the method to take into account attributes distributed among independent cases-events-agents. No doubt, this view captures a fundamental dimension of reality: exactly the one looking at attributes distribution and groupings. However, there is also another ontological dimension, which is just that of the connections among cases-events-agents. The network (structural) dimension is relatively independent of the attributive dimension because agents or events can be connected through a variety of different ways, and at the same time, they can have more or less similar attributes. The two dimensions are not fully independent, because it is likely that, under specific circumstances, attributes influence the structure and vice versa. SE and most of its derivations resist acknowledging the network nature of socio-economic phenomena (Schweitzer et al., 2009),[3]

---

[2] Indeed, there are few but important exceptions, among which Boulding (1958, 1970, 1981) and Lange (1965, 1970) are particularly remarkable, which actually should be listed within what is currently labelled as "heterodox economics" instead of SE.

[3] Very highlighting is, in this sense, the explicit claim of the irrelevance of the network dimension for economic analysis made by an economist of the level of Kenneth Arrow (2009), Nobel Prize in 1972.

either because of the well-known inertia of scientific paradigms or because such an acknowledgment would affect heavily its ideological and theoretical framework (Biggiero, 2016a).

Emergence, evolution, dynamics. Economic, social, and technological innovations cannot be treated with equilibrium models, especially when innovations are endogenous. Indeed, being an evolutionary system means that all its elements, i.e., social actors, physical and environmental aspects, etc., may change over time because of exogenous and endogenous factors. By treating entrepreneurship and leadership as emergent outcomes of evolutionary processes, two recent papers (respectively, Foster & Metcalf, 2012; Yezdani et al., 2015) have relaunched the phenomenon of emergence into the economic analysis and underlined its incompatibility with SE.[4] Foster & Metcalf reviewed the development of evolution and dynamics as a research tradition in economics, which led over time to the constitution of what then became EE and linked it to the concept of emergence. With few pioneers' exceptions, emergence is a concept started during the 1960s with the development of computational modeling, firstly through cellular automata (Holland, 1998; Miller & Page, 2007; Waldrop, 1992; Wolfram, 1994, 2002) and then through agent-based modeling (Arthur, 2006, 2010; Cioffi-Revilla, 2014; Edmonds & Meyer, 2013; Gallegati & Richiardi, 2009; Gilbert, 2008).[5] The basic idea is that, with few simple rules of behavior, it is possible that recursively interacting agents create outcomes that were unpredictable according to the characteristics of single agents and definitely beyond their intentions. Further, despite they often could come from random initial states, such outcomes also show the property of being relatively stable and ordered structures (Feltz et al., 2006; Helbing, 2012; Smith & Stevens, 1996). Because single quasi-independent agents' random behavior might generate ordered macro-structures, the problem of emergence[6] has been strictly related to the micro/macro problem in sociology and economics (Squazzoni, 2012). Further, some economists have taken it as the best scientific legitimation of markets as ordered structures produced by a

[4] The opposite position was taken by Donzelli (1986), who contends the idea that emergent properties in GEE is wrong even from a pure epistemological and methodological point of view. Interestingly, this position was based just on the GEE model, which in fact does not allow any emergence. Put differently, if GEE were the right representation of the economy, then actually no emergence would be possible. Donzelli's mistake was precisely that he took GEE as a correct representation of real-world economy.

[5] See the story of the Santa Fè Institute told by Bertuglia and Vaio (2005), Casti (1994), Waldrop (1992). Indeed, the Nobel Prize for Economic Sciences Thomas Schelling was among the early scientists to design and apply, with the help of John Casti, a computational model on segregation dynamics.

[6] A precise definition of emergent phenomena and emergent properties—which do not coincide—is still a matter of debate and has been taken seriously only relatively recently by the philosophers of science (Corning, 2012; Taylor, 2015), who usually call it "supervenience". An attempt to define it in general and with a specific reference to economics has been done by Harper & Endres (2012).

self-organizing process of independent agents: the magic of the "visible hand" reformulated as spontaneous order from chaos.[7] Indeed, analogous emergent phenomena concern situations where agents are non-independent (but rather, embedded into networks), and the rules are more complicated and multiple, as it seems that happens in the real world.

2.2 Five Research Streams in Economics, Sociology, and Organization Science

Behavioral Economics. BE (Camerer et al., 2004a, b; Diacon et al., 2013; Kahneman, 2011; Thaler, 2015, 2016) leaves the traditional normative orientation of mainstream economics, according to which agents' cognition conforms to rational choice theory and they are supposed to be perfect—or quasi-perfect—optimizers. In the SE view, agents have no or mild computational limits, neither other kinds of flaws, like cognitive biases. They are perfect statisticians without emotions disturbing their calculative capabilities; they are selfish and competitive. Moreover, they do not look for cooperative solutions, which are left unexplored by most economists (Landreth & Colander, 2001; Roncaglia, 2006; Screpanti & Zamagni, 2005). BE challenges these postulates and attempts to search for empirical confirmations of them. Herbert Simon was the pioneer, who started criticizing the idealized model of *homo economicus* (1955, 1957, 1983, 1987). His main argument was focused on the computational limits of human cognition, which prevents the possibility to optimize choices and hinder the construction of utility or production functions, the two pillars of SE. To that framework, Simon opposed the idea that agents make satisfying instead of optimizing choices, which means that they stop searching for the right choice when they feel a solution is good enough. Such satisfaction comes from the—more or less aware—existence of levels of aspiration that each agent formulates in his mind (Simon, 1976, 1978, 1979). Consistent and supportive of this view is the emphasis on the economic and timing resources required by the activities employed to collect the pertinent information. That is, before the cognitive and timing resources needed to evaluate and compare the alternatives, operations and costs that are traditionally overlooked by SE[8] must be designed and (often) paid.

[7] I am obviously referring to the Austrian approach to economic theory (Gloria-Palermo, 1999), which magnifies the virtues of free markets and neo-liberalism. I will go back on this point in Part II.

[8] I wish to remark once more that this paper only sketches theories and authors. In the case of great and eclectic scientists like Simon, it results in a dramatic impoverishment and undervaluation of what he did (Augier & March, 2004). For instance, he anticipated many themes that have been later developed in BE, and attacked rational choice under many other respects: the supposed clear demarcation between facts and values, the role of intuition and heuristics, etc. Further, he was also firmly convinced that economics must be strongly rooted in real world, as any empirical science must do (Simon, 1997, 2001). This orientation is totally consistent with RE and all the other building blocks here introduced.

Simon's fellows and collaborators Michael D. Cohen, Richard M. Cyert, and James G. March (1994) brought forth that research stream by progressively extending the range of individual cognitive limits and dealing more closely with its implications for organizational decision-making. Some of the aspects triggered but less developed by Simon were investigated more deeply: for instance, not only the computational limits, meant as mere calculative capacity, but also limits of attention. Further, the supposed obvious sequence of problem identification, collection of alternatives, evaluation, and comparison was indeed rejected, at least according to agents' real-world behaviors, which resulted in not to follow this rational choice model.[9] Moreover, it was evidenced that many choices require circular decision processes because the set of alternatives should be changed according to the early stages of evaluations. Further, agents—be them isolated individuals or members of group decision making—make choices not only (and perhaps not mostly) after having collected and compared all alternatives but to a large extent by following rules or influential people or by imitation of who they consider the best (or just, better than them) (March, 1994).

The research on BE was further developed by other authors, some of whom specialized precisely in cognitive psychology or social psychology. Daniel Kahneman and Amos Tversky have been two fundamental reference points (Kahneman & Tversky, 2000; Kahneman et al., 1982; Thaler, 1991), and they gave a special impulse to the development of behavioral finance (Ackert & Deaves, 2009; Thaler, 1993). Their studies and criticisms of SE led to advance also a theory of decisions under uncertainty alternative to the standard expected utility theory: the prospect theory (Tversky & Kahneman, 1992). Further works (Kahneman, 2011; Taleb, 2007; Thaler, 2015; Thaler & Sunstein, 2009) have contributed substantially to BE research in various fields: finance, assurance, risk management, etc. because their studies were based not only on empirical observation through statistics but also on laboratory case studies. Actually, these latter have been largely used and finally well-acknowledged also through the 2002 Nobel Prize in Economic Sciences shared by Daniel Kahneman and Vernon Smith, this latter being one of the main experts in that method. Particularly corrosive of the rational choice theory are the criticisms of BE in the form of argumentation run by Gigerenzer (2008a, b).

Considering that, like all the building blocks here discussed, BE is a relatively young research program, and thus in full evolution, among its main discoveries, it is worth summarizing the following ones:

* Agents' behavior is far more complicated from what is assumed by the rational choice theory.

---

[9] The Garbage Can Model (Cohen et al., 1972; Lomi & Harrison, 2012), which was elaborated moving from empirical case studies of loosely coupled organizations, like schools and other public administrations, has shown that, in the practical decision-making of organizations, the sequence of the rational choice model can be completely reversed: solutions do not follow the problems for which they have been supposedly chosen, but rather, solutions, once adopted because of an easier or routine application, then search for problems that can bring them legitimation. In other words, agents do choose or do something, and then try to make sense of what they have chosen and done. This became then one of the themes later developed by Karl Weick in his emphasis on organizational sensemaking (1995).

* Cognitive limits are related not only to computational capacity but also to the limits of focused attention, and to the "distortive" role of values and emotions in decision-making processes.
* Intentional or unintentional heuristics, like rule-following and imitation, are pervasive in agents' behavior to compensate for their lack of cognitive capacity.
* Cognitive biases are also common features affecting all agents' behavior in each topic, even the most well cognitively equipped ones, like experts or researchers in that same field.
* Agents' risk aversion changes if it concerns losses or gains.
* Agents' risk behavior depends not only on incremental gains or losses but also on their actual endowment.

Evolutionary Economics. With Joseph Schumpeter as the acknowledged—but unaware at the time—"father" of what later will be defined as EE, this research stream has received a strong impulse by the publication of the Richard Nelson and Sidney Winter's book of 1982 (Nelson & Winter, 1982). There, it was established a strong conceptual link with Darwin's evolutionary theory and a focus on the role played by technological innovations as the drivers of economic change. The emphasis of economic theory was shifted from equilibrium prices to economic (and non-economic) characteristics of economic evolution. The biological analogy was all but new in the history of economic thought because biology and Alfred Marshall inspired already classical economists even more.[10] Schumpeter and Penrose further enhanced the analogies, but a systematic theorization that employs the typical concepts of evolutionary biology started only with Nelson & Winter. Over time, researchers in EE were taking more and more into account the main discoveries of complexity science (Arrow et al., 1988; Arthur et al., 1997; Hodgson, 1993, 2000; Loasby, 1991, 1999, 2001). In this sense, three collective volumes signed a turning point in EE evolution: Saviotti (2003), Dopfer (2005), et al. (2009). There, all the themes of EE are reformulated and combined with some of the main aspects of complexity science: basically, the above two discussed the network nature of economic phenomena and economic emergence. In brief, EE is centered on the following points:

i. A reduced focus on (if not even a tout-court rejection of) equilibrium, in particular of GEE.
ii. A strong emphasis on the evolutionary nature of the economic process and of technological innovations as its engine, considered as an endogenous force, which should be part of the economic analysis.
iii. A rejection of the typical assumptions of SE in regard to agents' behavior and their possibility to find optimal solutions, with a strong emphasis on the discoveries of cognitive sciences as concerning the possibility to make optimal decisions.

[10] In turn, biology took many analogies from economic theory too. Indeed, it was Darwin himself to write—in the Introduction to the Origins of species—to have borrowed the concept of competition for survival from economics.

iv. A consequent substantial rejection of rational choice theory, and thus, a wide sharing of many traits of BE.
v. A close view to real-world phenomena, with a crucial role given to firms and institutions, and their relationships.
vi. A strong and growing attention to the suggestions coming from complexity science.
vii. A pluralist methodological orientation, with a growing preference for relational methods and laboratory experiments.

Relational Sociology. RS was born officially with the Emirbayer's Manifesto in 1997. Since then, a number of books and handbooks have been published on the subject, even though the empirical works that would better show the distinguishing traits of this research stream do not abound. So far, it seems more a conceptual than an empirical project. Emirbayer stigmatizes the sociological research landscape as dominated by a substantialist approach, which he characterizes as static and focused on facts-events-objects, like systems and structure, and overlooking the dynamic and relational dimensions. He argues that even the interactions between systems or their parts are expressed in terms of variables, meant as universals that can explain the occurrence of a given phenomenon or the generation of a given structure. To these two facets of substantialism, Emirbayer opposes that "relational theorists reject the notion that one can posit discrete, pre-given units such as the individual or society as ultimate starting points of sociological analysis …" (1997: 288). He proposes to put relations—that he identifies with transactions—at the core of the analysis, and he makes explicit references to Nicholas Luhmann and Harrison White. The former (1995) was very much engaged in the exploration of some of the social forms of complexity, and the latter is (1981, 1993) an important scholar of Social Network Analysis (SNA). This way, an explicit bridge with complexity theory and one of the most important relational methods was cast. The connection with SNA (Knoke & Yang, 2008; Scott, 1992; Scott & Carrington, 2011; Wasserman & Faust, 1994)[11] is reinforced by referring to power not as a specific attribute intrinsic to some social actor, but rather, in line with SNA, as the result of the position covered by that social actor into a network of relations. The "election" of network analysis as the most consistent analytical method for RS becomes evident in a further reader (Dépelteau & Powell, 2013b), to which contribute directly to experts of SNA, like Harrison White. In other contributions (Dépelteau & Powell, 2013a; Donati, 2011), it is speculated that relations convey many different aspects with which two or more actors do interact or influence one another. This richness can be precisely translated into the SNA jargon with the concept of multiplexity (Wasserman & Faust, 1994), that is, a network whose actors are connected through many types of links.

Analytical Sociology. Like RS, AS also (Hedström, 2005; Hedström & Bearman, 2009; Hedström & Manzo, 2015; Manzo, 2014) has the merit to overcome old sterile sociological disputes on realism vs nominalism, subjective vs objective approaches, structure vs agency, and others. The main points of AS are the following:

---

[11] Actually, either Knoke and Scott and SNA are explicitly recalled by Emirbayer.

i. Solving the structure vs agency juxtaposition by proposing the concept of structural individualism, which gives the agents the main role, but takes into account that agents are embedded into a network of relationships, which constraints and contributes to agents beliefs and choices and, in turn, is shaped and changed by agents.
ii. Grounding explanations into the mechanisms through which agents interact among them and with their environments. This mechanism-based explanation is supposed to overcome the problems of ascertain causality, which instead are weakening traditional statistic-based explanations.
iii. Focusing on micro/macro problems, let say, the problems characterized by emergent properties at the macro level arising from repeated interactions at the micro level. Despite this emphasis, AS does not disregard dealing with other kinds of problems, occurring at the same level of aggregation (micro/micro or macro/macro), as it commonly happens.
iv. Adopting a true pragmatist epistemological orientation, which acknowledges the idea that, instead of obsessively pursuing general theories of society,[12] knowledge grow proceeds—at least during these times of knowledge fragmentation—by developing the so-called middle-range theories: that is, theories that focus some specific well-defined phenomenon, which is then rigorously modeled in a nomologic structure of explanation—a well-defined explanandum and its explanans.
v. Adopting agent-based simulation modeling as the paradigmatic method: indeed, it matches perfectly the structural individualism approach, because agents are the key players that generate structures, which in turn constraint or orient agents' behavior. Because of the algorithmic structure of the models, its outcomes are nothing else than the implications (deductions) from the assumptions and the rules (mechanisms) according to which agents are supposed to behave. In this perspective, the nomologic structure of explanation is called "generative explanation" (Epstein, 1999, 2007): the idea is that if you can generate a given phenomenon, then the corresponding model that generates it is also (one of) its possible explanations.

Organization Science. Despite ORG-S is the less structured of the five building blocks, it is possible to find in it at least three main fields (Van de Ven & Joyce, 1981), namely (i) organization design and coordination theory (Burton et al., 2006; Donaldson, 2001; Lomi & Larsen, 2001; Mintzberg, 1979), (ii) organization behavior and human resource management (Pfeffer, 1981, 1997), and (iii) managerial cognition and knowledge management systems (Gallupe, 2001; Zeleny, 2005). These three fields are largely overlapped to other disciplinary fields and research streams: for example, the former is shared with organizational economics and EE, the second

[12] Interestingly enough, economic theory and sociology aimed at the same goal: building general, all-encompassing, complete, and consistent theories. What the various versions of GEE did (and still do) in economic theory has been done by Weber's or Parson's theories in sociology. Indeed, this is not surprising, because in the nineteenth and twentieth centuries all disciplines had the same purpose. This illusion was allowed by the not-yet-acquired findings of complexity science.

one with the sociology of organization and social psychology, the latter with behavioral economics and organizational psychology. Interestingly, though ORG-S started by focusing on single organizations, then it extended its scope to the higher level of relations between organizations. The parallelism with EE goes so close that in ORG-S it has developed in the 1970s a field that recalls exactly evolutionary biology as well: the population ecology of organizations (Hannan & Freeman, 1977, 1989).

Being so fragmented and overlapped with other disciplinary fields, ORG-S is very pluralist in a methodological, conceptual and epistemological sense. ORG-S has embraced—at least in some of its research areas—complexity theory from its very beginning (Arrow et al., 2000; Biggiero, 2001b; Guastello, 2002; Mitleton-Kelly, 2003; Parker & Stacey, 1994; Priesmeyer, 1992; Richardson, 2005; Stacey, 1993, 1996; Stacey et al., 2000; Yolles, 2006). Destructuration and fragmentation is its strength because it can absorb all conceptual and methodological innovations, but also its weakness, because it was difficult to create enough cohesion to consolidate a core set on which grounding and developing the discipline. A clear sign of this lack of a comprehensive unifying theory is that, in each of the three main fields, we can find a lot of handbooks or textbooks, which usually introduce many rival theories per each of the topics touched into the book, without any sound and consistent connection across the topics. However, for our specific interest here, what really matters is that ORG-S can be a reservoir of "fragmented theories" that can feed the birth and development of RE.

3 Part II: What RE Should Not Be

It is not possible to extensively discuss here the characteristics of what could be collected under the label of SE, and even less the plethora of approaches that can be grouped under the umbrella of its "derivatives".[13] They are too many. However, it is possible to show that the neo-Walrasian GEE and the Austrian economic theory do not match many of the traits of the five conceptual building blocks above sketched. Further, I repeat the exercise done above for RE with some of SE derivatives—TCE and some variants including the network perspective. TCE, in fact, became the

[13] Let me repeat once more that the aim of this chapter is not providing a detailed and extensive account of SE and its current derivatives. It would be not sufficient even a dedicated volume, because there are many other versions or derivations not recalled here, like the game theory approach (Gintis, 2000) and the many attempts to make GEE compatible with dynamics (Gintis, 2007) and stability (Arrow & Hurwicz, 1958; Arrow et al., 1959), with its uncountable debates. Neither such a titanic effort would be so useful, because what matters is still the main argument: they all ignore complexity. Once complexity and a minimum requirement of realism and empirical test were claimed, then all those debates would look like the complicated reasoning made by Ptolemaic astronomers to account for inexplicable orbits. For a Copernican astronomer, it was not more the case to become expert in the calculations required by the old paradigm, because it would have been not helpful to find the truth. It was necessary to simply change the paradigm. Analogously, SE is a wrong and death paradigm, still (institutionally) dominant and powerful because of the inertia with which institutions change.

most important theory in the field of organizational and inter-organizational structures, seriously challenged only by the resource-based theory and by organizational-network theory.[14] Actually, TCE is a theory that, with respect to its rival theories, offers likely the highest number of publications and empirical tests. Nevertheless, I will attempt to show that it seems still too strictly enchained into its derivation from SE, thus suffering from most of its inadequacy to be put among the building blocks of RE. A last set of comments are left for many recent contributions that indeed match some of the features that I have outlined for RE, but are still not enough close to it.

3.1 The Inadequateness of Standard Economics

Since its very beginning, the reference model of GEE was that of an auction, where a neutral auctioneer calls for different prices/quantities of all goods produced and demanded in the economy (Bridel, 2012; Ingrao & Israel, 1990; Landreth & Colander, 2001; Roncaglia, 2006; Screpanti & Zamagni, 2005). The idea is that the economy is motionless before that equilibrium prices—defined as the prices for which no supplier or consumer would offer or demand more, following a rational choice mechanism—will be found for all the goods.[15] In fact, due to the interdependence of production costs and revenues, the vector of equilibrium prices must be defined simultaneously for all the goods, otherwise not all the variables would be taken into account and the solution would be incomplete and wrong (Arrow & Hahn, 1971; Bridel, 2012; Hahn & Petri, 2002; Ingrao & Israel, 1990; Kirman, 1976; Loasby, 1991; Zamagni, 1993). Of course, during the auction, consumers' preferences, production costs, and technology—this latter meant in the broadest sense as the knowledge about production plans and the present and future state of nature—must be invariant. Participants are supposed to know all the future demand and supply for any good and to be able to compare and compute all the goods and their prices so as to find the most convenient combinations. In the original versions, it was supposed that there is no uncertainty in the economy and that natural events are known as well. Alternatively, uncertainty was later introduced and treated in terms of expected utility theory. Further, participants cannot make coalitions, because these would modify the assumption of perfect competition, and finally, still to guarantee that assumption, the following conditions should hold:

i. A high number of exchangers (suppliers and consumers) per each good.
ii. Perfect mobility of production factors—work, capital, and natural resources—between all economic sectors.

[14] To place TCE within the neoclassical theory of firm, see Dietrich & Kraft (2012) and Schmalensee & Willig (1989), while for a less neoclassical—but still not truly alternative to that—view, see Grandori (2013).

[15] As well-known, there are different auction mechanisms, which indeed can give different results under specific situations, but indeed they are not so relevant for my essential reasoning.

iii. Constant returns to scale, because otherwise any discontinuity in the production functions would produce mobility barriers.
iv. Specialized producers, because the existence of joint production costs would create a serious hurdle to the existence and calculation of the equilibrium price vector.
v. No distinction between producers and consumers, else than their preferences, because possible different endowments of capital would produce monopolistic power.
vi. Finally, all agents (all the participants to the auction) are supposed to be selfish and to possess perfect rationality, that is, having no cognitive limits or biases.

Actually, in this model there is no need to have firms because the elementary unit of decision is the single individual and scale economies or externalities or technological discontinuities are supposed not to exist. As well, no common goods or natural monopolies are supposed to be. In compensation of this long list of necessary conditions, it can be demonstrated that all goods have a corresponding competitive market, that there is a vector of equilibrium prices, and that such prices guarantee market efficiency, and thus, the perfect allocation of resources across them.[16]

Now, there is no doubt that auctions are useful tools to combine supply and demand of some good and to find efficient prices,[17] and actually it is easier for everybody to access and have direct experience of it through the internet. However, from this acknowledgment to represent an entire economy as a huge auction, there is no logical or empirical consequence. It would be a misleading fiction, like others that are often employed by SE to induce the reader to transfer to real-world contexts what seems reasonable or likelihood for oversimplified cases. A typical example is that of marginal utility and the laws of decreasing returns: textbooks offer many examples that make sense in specific oversimplified cases, where an agent is facing a situation of a simple and local choice with only one criterion. This way the student is induced to believe that global and multi-criteria choices can be easily represented in the same way and can conform to the simple case.

It is not difficult to see that an entire economy—or even a single manufacturing or financial sector—cannot be represented as the "perfect auction" above described. Into the real world, and especially into the sectors of industrial goods, almost none of the above conditions do hold. Agents build coalitions and are far from being perfectly rational; information is costly and sometimes inaccessible; for many types of goods its performances are far from being evident: rather, they have to be experienced and carefully discussed in several meetings, thus summing up to a lot of sunk costs.

[16] Notice that one same good in different states of nature would configure a different good with its own specific market: the same umbrella in a rainy day configures a different and specific market than that umbrella in a sunny day. Agents are supposed to know all the corresponding demands and supply. Of course, all the available stock, demand and supply of oil and all fossil resources until the depletion of the last unit of resource are supposed to be known, because clearly its state in a future moment influences also the current demand and supply, and thus, it influences also current equilibrium prices of those goods as well of all the goods with which they are interconnected.

[17] Actually, Nobel Prize in Economic Sciences 2020 was awarded jointly to Paul R. Milgrom and Robert B. Wilson just "for improvements to auction theory and inventions of new auction formats".

Further, agents are heterogeneous with very different endowments in terms of capital and knowledge. Moreover, the future states of nature and markets are characterized by uncertainty in a strong sense, as actually complexity theory shows, and thus, expected utility theory cannot hold.[18] Finally, the very pre-condition of an auction (at least, as a GEE model), which is that exchanges take place only after its end, evidently does not hold.

There is an "original sin" undermining GEE from its very birth: it was thought to emulate classical physics. Leon Walras explicitly said that his aim was to apply the same model of Newtonian mechanics (Mirowski, 1989), and his disciple Vilfredo Pareto, who was an engineer as background, shared the same view. Hence, no surprise that SE, especially in the GEE versions, inherited also the epistemology of classical physics. It is easy to check that, starting from the true core of the model, which is built just on equilibrium instead of evolution and innovation (Loasby, 1991), it ignores the features of complexity theory (Arthur, 2006, 2010).

The Austrian approach to economic theory, especially in the Hayekian version, is remarkably different from the neo-Walrasian GEE model (Gloria-Palermo, 1999). Actually, there has been a bitter dispute between the two approaches, and even more with Keynesian economics (Wapshott, 2012) and with neo-Marxian approaches (Harvey, 2005, 2017). In fact, despite its many substantial differences, the latter two share the idea of a strong role of state and public administration, while Hayek was a hard opponent of this position and a convinced supporter of the self-organizing virtues of the free market. Therefore, since the post-Second World War, he and his theories were taken as paladins of neo-liberalism and fierce opponents of socialism, because of political-ethical reasons, and because of a supposed scientific legitimation claimed by his economic theory.

Indeed, Hayek shared with SE the same roots in neoclassical economics, namely that agents are selfish and that there is nothing strange that some people possess only capital and some others only labor force.[19] Hayek's main argument was just that an entire economy is too complex to allow a central (planned) governance (Hayek, 1945, 1967, 2002). Free markets would find the right and best solutions to efficiently allocate scarce resources and satisfy all the needs. The decentralized market mechanism would also avoid the distortions due to the power concentration of the centralized governance. Further, Hayek was borrowing from GEE the idea that, under conditions of perfectly efficient markets, prices contain all the information agents require

[18] Before the complexity turn in economic and social science, the standard reference of uncertainty in strong sense was the definition and discussion provided by Knight and Keynes. Now, complexity theory provides a plenty of examples and proofs of unpredicatability tout court or weak predictability, which prevent the reduction of uncertainty on terms of a set of probability functions.

[19] In line with the whole Austrian (main) research tradition of economic theory, Hayek shares with neoclassical economics also the fundaments of its theory of value, according to which the source of value lies into relative scarcity respect to the demand. Further, interests, profits, wages, and rents are the "natural" returns for the productivity of the corresponding factors of production—capital, entrepreneurship, labor, and land, respectively. In this sense, both the two mainstreams of SE that I am discussing here are totally juxtaposed to the neo-Marxian perspective (Brennan et al., 2017; Harvey, 2017).

to optimize their choices. Finally, as a common trait of all Austrian economic tradition, equilibrium was not considered so important, because a strong emphasis was given on the evolutionary nature of the economic process.

So, Hayek claimed to succeed where GEE was failing, that is to show not only that markets are the right and efficient governance mechanisms of economic transactions but also that such mechanisms can include evolution and the role of entrepreneurs. The small "detail" was, however, that while GEE was built on solid and formalized models, he could never provide them, and moreover, his "loans" from GEE were flawed: for example, prices contain all required information only if markets are efficient, agents' cognition is perfect, etc. Indeed, recent developments of the Austrian economic theory attempt to strengthen it also on this side by absorbing many traits of BE (Frantz & Leeson, 2013).[20]

Because of these weaknesses and, on the opposite side, the great consideration received by neo-Keynesian economic policy, Hayek and neo-liberalism was not so influential until the 1980s, when the pernicious combination of Thatcher and Reagan as, respectively, prime minister and president in the Anglo-American world, brought back neo-liberalism into vogue (Picketty, 2013). Noticeably—and more pertinent to our issue—its resurgence and continuing fascination depends also on a superficial understanding of the complexity theory as the scientific fundament of neo-liberalism, the grounding that Hayek was missing. In fact, computational models show that, under some circumstances, simple rules can lead independent (and possibly also selfish) self-organizing agents to generate ordered (and distributed) structures, without any central "super-agent" (institution) (Anzola et al., 2016; Biggiero, 1998; Boschetti, 2011; Cioffi-Revilla, 2014; Helbing, 2012). This possibility seemed to some authors the mathematical (namely, algorithmic) demonstration of what Hayek was looking for but did not reach himself (Hagedorn, 2015; Rosser, 2012). However, this can actually happen in some circumstances, while in others it can happen that the outcome of the self-organizing process leads to creating a structure that with free and efficient markets have nothing to do (Gallegati & Richiardi, 2009; Mautinovic, 2006; Moss, 2009). A self-organizing process can lead to the formation of oligopolies or even monopolies, to lack of freedom, and even to the extinction of entire communities: that is, the full repertoire shown by human history. Further, a large part of that literature, just starting from models on segregation and cooperation, show that the most efficient—or best survival in the long run—communities are those not characterized by all selfish agents, but rather by a significant share of mild or pure cooperative agents.[21] Therefore, though Austrian economic theory and neo-liberalism contain some elements in common with complexity theory, namely the emphasis on self-organizing processes leading to markets seen as spontaneous order beyond agents' will, nothing guarantees that such markets will be efficient. Further, Austrian economic theory should deny the

[20] This strategy of "neutralization by cooptation" is now followed also by SE (Ogaki & Tanaka, 2018), which employed it already with Keynesian macroeconomics through the "neoclassical synthesis" (Screpanti & Zamagni, 2005).

[21] For a survey of that debate through agent-based modeling, see Squazzoni (2012).

other form of complexity discussed above, the network nature of economic and social phenomena. In fact, this acknowledgment would imply: (i) the introduction of frictions into the free mechanisms of market adaptations; (ii) the further acknowledgment of unbalanced power relationships and capital endowments among agents, with the consequent economic, social, and political implications, depicting an all but free and liberal society.

3.2 Transaction Cost Economics

Among the many derivations of SE, TCE is one of the most interesting and, due to its emphasis on organizational and inter-organizational transactions as the constituting matter of economic relations, it can induce to believe that that theory (and transactions themselves) is the best reference of RE. There is a vast literature on the subject (see Williamson, 1975, 1981, 1985 among the many), which is also well known, because it represents perhaps the most important theoretical reference into the field of inter-organizational relationships and the theory of the firm.[22]

Three issues should be distinguished: (i) the first one concerns whether TCE could be taken as another building block of RE; (ii) the second one regards whether transactions as an important unit of analysis; (iii) and the third one concerns whether transaction perhaps are the right and distinctive elementary units for RE. Now I attempt to discuss these three points separately.

TCE evolved during the 45 years from its beginning. One of the general traits of its evolution has been the relaxation of the typical features of SE in the GEE version. However, as it is proposed even in the last versions (Williamson, 1996, 1998), TCE does not seem so fruitful for RE, because it is still too much enchained into SE. Williamson was a neo-classical economist, sharing all the main basic concepts, like isolated and optimizing agents driven by their utility functions, and firms described entirely by their production functions. The theoretical framework was that of partial equilibrium, where agents do not make coalitions and do not learn and make optimum choices in a static context: TCE treats alternative governance structures and mechanisms in a perspective of comparative statics. Even the key concept of transaction cost and its pivotal role to explain the otherwise "inexplicable existence of firms" was borrowed from Coase (1937), another distinguished neoclassical economist. Actually, in traditional GEE models there is no "space", no rationale for firms: single independent agents, who are rewarded by the price for their service, make decisions, and there is no information asymmetry, no opportunism, and no limits to cognitive capacity, etc. (see the discussion above, and Tsang, 2006). In fact, the TCE explanation of the raison d'être of firms that lies *only* in the existence of transaction costs

[22] Its founders—Ronald H. Coase and Oliver E. Williamson—have been rewarded the Nobel Prize for Economic Sciences, as well as the founders of the agency cost theory—the other main neo-contractualist theory of the firm.

cannot be accepted, because there are at least the following other and independent causes:

- Exploitation exerted by few privileged (or somehow powerful) over poor (or somehow powerless) people. If such exploitation is due to capital or knowledge or casts or pure brutal force or other social rules, it is a secondary aspect
- Technological discontinuities, which require to engage labor force not in single units and to employ capital in large minimum quantities (entry barriers)
- Complexity of coordination, which generates "organizational discontinuities" and power concentration within and between organizations
- Information asymmetries, which, in presence of imperfect (bounded) rationality and agents' opportunism, prevent the possibility to design optimal solutions.

Williamson (1991a, 1994, 1996) acknowledges the latter point and, to some extent, the third point, but not the former two. Therefore, we should acknowledge that even without transaction costs, organizations would exist. Further, and rather surprisingly, TCE (and all neo-contractualist theories) face with the problem of explaining the nature of firms as if they were the anomalies, that is, as if the normal—and thus, expected—form of governance of economic activities were markets, and as such, they did not require any particular explanation. This subversion of historical fact is rather surprising, because economic history and anthropology show exactly the opposite: organizations were at the beginning of human development, while markets came after. Moreover, such markets were very different from any neoclassical idea of equilibrium markets: neither efficient nor open.

Indeed, Williamson left from the pure orthodoxy in some sense, and in fact, especially after so much time spent dialoguing with sociologists and organization theorists (Williamson, 1981, 1991b, 1994), he was considered "heretic" by mainstream economics.[23] Actually, under the influence of Herbert Simon, who taught in the same university, Williamson claimed to adopt the idea of bounded rationality

---

[23] For instance, during the 1980s, he engaged a debate with sociologists and organization scientists on the role of power and strategies, which, according to these latter, were limiting current or expected transaction and production costs only to be a component among others to choose the best governance mechanism. Williamson's answer to these criticisms came at the beginning of the 1990s through a couple of papers that should be considered masterpieces for its capacity to express the point of view of standard economists with extreme clarity. In the first one he argues that "the only strategizing is economizing" (1991b), while in the second one he answers to another series of objections concerning the role of trust and other extra-economic variables by arguing that trust is nothing else than the masked way to express the risk assigned by agents to alters' behaviors, namely calculativeness-based trust (1993). It means that, at the very end, once he had to side definitely on these debates, his position was always that of SE. In fact, in both papers what lies at the ground is that the true core of SE is not even GEE, but something deeper: a theory of optimal decisions (Resnik, 1987) tout court, not only about strictly economic variables. And in fact, this is exactly the logic that is shared also by Austrian economic theory: everything that has some kind of utility for somebody can be dealt with rational choice theory, including common goods, natural "capital", health, trust, etc. Whether these assumptions allow to make efficient (competitive) markets and whether this outcome can be demonstrated formally are two very hard and different issues. The history of economic thought shows that these two things can be argued only into the totally unrealistic world of neo-Walrasian GEE, where anyway the stability and unicity of equilibrium cannot be demonstrated.

on one side, but on the other side, TCE was built on the idea that agents minimize the sum of production and transaction costs. This criterion can make hierarchical governance more convenient than market governance. However, as discussed above and in his several works, Simon spent all his life contesting the idea that agents can be optimizers of anything, and this is one of BE's key concepts. Therefore, because of its ambiguous anchoring to SE, TCE should not be considered among the building blocks of RE.

The second issue related to TCE concerns viewing transactions as an important unit of analysis. This idea is rather disputable. On one side, the transaction concept is fruitful because it is more micro-analytic than that of entire products, and thus, particularly useful when the choices concern complex products, like aircraft, or services, like higher education. However, on the other side, it seems much more related to the old material-based society and economy, instead of the present and future knowledge-based economy, where data, information, and knowledge seem to be the most important elementary units. Actually, the evolution of TCE into EE and ORG-S is already realizing a double transformation: (1) including transaction costs into an evolutionary perspective and (2) combining transaction with knowledge (through the related concepts of capabilities, learning, absorptive capacity, etc.).

Such doubts sound even more important when wondering whether to consider transactions as RE elementary analytical units. Actually, transactions are the outcomes of agents' behavior and interactions, not the causes themselves.[24] Of course, agents should consider them for their choices, but the true sources of actions and decisions can be only human agents or their collective entities (collective minds). In relational methods, transactions can be modeled as kinds of objects, which can occur in different states, and so transactions are also inputs for decision-making and, more broadly, influential factors of agents' individual and collective behavior. However, transactions lack autonomy, at least in the sense of intentions, decisions, or any other kind of cognitive expression.[25]

Other important reasons to keep (individual and collective) agents and not transactions, as RE elementary analytical units are the following:

- Relations come before transactions and entail them.
- Many (most?) types of relations do not imply or trigger transactions, but yet influence/create behaviors and beliefs.
- Many (most?) transactions require relatively stable relations.

---

[24] Just to remind: "A transaction occurs when a good or service is transferred through a separable connection under a technological respect. A stage of activity ceases when another starts" (Williamson, 1985).

[25] Things become much more complicated if non-human cognitive machines are involved into the analysis, and especially when concerning cognition-embodied robots, and even more in the case of "communities" of robots, now allowed by platforms of advanced distributed intelligent robots. I believe that they should be included into the category of non-human autonomous agents, even though this will imply a remarkable change of our entire approach to economic and social science and to its analysis (Biggiero, 2019). On the other hand, such a change cannot be avoided and neither delayed, as the fast robotization of economic and social life is showing.

- Transactions as elementary units do not resolve any of the problem that occurs when agents are chosen: there are still micro/macro problems, due to nonlinear and recursive effects of combinations between transactions.[26]

However, nothing is farther from me than the idea that transaction costs are not important in forming: (i) the boundaries and strategies of organizations, (ii) the structure and dynamics of inter-organizational networks, (iii) the set of competitive advantages, etc. What I found definitely not convincing is the way in which transaction costs are theorized in TCE. Paradoxical as it may seem, the true relevance of transaction costs and other concepts central for TCE, like opportunism, specificity, frequency, imperfect rationality, comes when such concepts are used outside and regardless of TCE. Actually, this process of "sterilizing" those concepts—by keeping and using them separately from TCE—is slowly occurring in the debate and studies trying to merge TCE with other very different approaches, like the resource-based view, network theory, etc. (Argyres & Zenger, 2012; Gulbrandsen et al., 2017; Jacobides & Winter, 2005; Schilling & Steensma, 2002). Actually, many of the supposed empirical proofs in favor of TCE (Carter & Hodgson, 2006; David & Han, 2004; Geyskens et al., 2006; Ghoshal & Moran, 1996; Marinescu, 2012) are indeed cases of employment of those concepts in very free schemas and settings, where the concepts and traits of transactions are almost always redefined and disentangled from TCE wider theoretical framework.

3.3 *A View at Some Theoretical Fragments*

Some recent approaches analyze highly specific problems while keeping as many as possible ingredients of SE, with the aim to allow the future extension and combination of those problems and their corresponding results in a wider framework. They attempt to run a kind of "reverse engineering" of GEE: start from single pieces in the hope that they could be combined in a unique framework. This type of approaches is often

[26] This is an aspect always overlooked by micro-analytical applications of TCE. On the other hand, it would be simply impossible because even the pure list of the combinations between all the transactions would be computationally intractable even for some simple group of activities. Not even imaginable for all the complex activities of a large organization. We would face with combinatorial outcomes of the magnitude of those made by Kauffman for the amino acids (1996). The type of reasoning that Kauffman develops in his Investigations (2000) could be applied to transactions, and actually it well shows the complexity and the enormous degree of freedom available for economic evolution. This is another way to support the idea of the impossibility to build a GEE. Indeed, at the Santa Fè Institute, Kauffman discussed a lot of times with some of the best mainstream economists of the world, among whom was the Nobel Prize Kenneth Arrow, and it is very nice to read his recent reflections on that period about the obsession of economists for equilibrium. Looking at the rather disputable and often inappropriate use of Kauffman's theories and models by standard economists (Biggiero, 2016c), it does not seem that they understood so much and well each other. In his later works (2016, 2019), Kauffman further excitingly expanded this line of reasoning to show the creative role of human beings in the future evolution.

based on a group of single agents, who possess many of the following common traits:

- They are de-contextualized, a-historical, selfish, and driven only (or mostly) by their utility function.
- They are more or less opportunistic, cognitively strong (often optimizers), almost always memory-less.
- They interact in a very specific setting to reach some well-defined goals.

A substantial difference of these approaches with SE and its derivations is that they usually do not provide their agents with perfect (or quasi-perfect) cognition and information, do not overlook information asymmetries, sometimes (not always) do not overlook transaction costs, employ simple memory mechanisms, and they can consider also coalition or group formation. Further, they embed agents into a network of relationships. Indeed, a substantial part of this literature is giving an important contribution to understanding just network formation processes, especially by taking into account the costs of relations. However—and this is a crucial point—also the ones who consider important some of the just mentioned aspects do not put them working altogether. They would likely give some of the two following answers: the problem could become mathematically intractable or at least the solution not optimal. On the other hand, for such authors the accusation of oversimplification would not be seen as a problem, because they share the pre-complexity -turn epistemology, according to which good science proceeds by aggregating results obtained from elementary cases. The edifice of economics would then be built by accumulating the knowledge produced by analyzing the bricks of such elementary cases.

Examples of these approaches are the contributions by Goyal (2007), Gintis (2000), Jackson (2010a, b, 2014a, b), Nagurney (1999, 2009; Nagurney & Dong, 2002), Easley and Kleinberg (2010), most of which are excellent combinations between economic theory and network analysis. In all of them, with some overlapping on the same problems, there is no attempt to build (or renew) any GEE, but rather the problems faced are usually defined on a very local and simplified base. Sometimes, as in Gintis, Goyal, Jackson, and Nagurney, there is the attempt to build some more general framework, which however does not go beyond the level of partial economic equilibrium. In other cases, the purpose to find equilibrium conditions, which is the standard economists' obsession since the marginalist revolution (Arthur, 2006, 2010; Landreth & Colander, 2001; Roncaglia, 2006; Screpanti & Zamagni, 2005) is even absent. Further, in some cases, there is also an explicit evolutionary—or at least, dynamic—approach, even though evolution is usually treated in a very simple way (Johnson et al., 2017). For example, out of the many different aspects that in a given problem could change, and out of the many ways in which that change could be designed, it is usually chosen just one changing event, and the simplest way of change. Despite these limitations, in many senses these scholars (and their vast works and authors of reference) leave SE and contribute to building the recent field of network economics.

However, they are still very far from what RE had to be because they lack two of RE's fundamental building blocks: behavioral economics and complexity theory.

Let us look first at the former failure. With few and partial exceptions, the agents considered into the models/studies of those authors are selfish optimizers, who do not form coalitions, have all—or most relevant—information, have strong rationality, and do not learn (or do it in a very simple way). As trivial but meaningful proof, we can see that cognitive limits and biases are not taken into account.[27] Even when some of the main traits of BE is considered—that is, for example, if there is information asymmetry and cost or some kind of cognitive bias—the trick used to run the study is always the same: considering only one of such traits at once and keeping the analysis at its simplest case. For example, in some study agents' rationality is limited to local facts—for example, they can observe only what happens to their neighbors there are no coalitions or alternatively they do not suffer of cognitive biases, do not employ heuristic reasoning, etc. In other words, they keep most features of agents in a SE perspective, including the use of (expected) utility functions. In the much rarer studies regarding firms or production behavior, the same over-simplifications do occur and, instead of utility functions, production functions and expected profit rates are employed. With few exceptions, deviations from rational choice theory are not admitted. The other lacking building block of RE concerns complexity science and its underlying implication that most (or at least some) over-simplifications cannot be considered (and compensated) as approximations, but rather as theoretical choices full of unpredictable consequences. For example, even the seemingly most innocent idea of "scale neutrality" has been demonstrated as false in many (most?) agent-based models (Biggiero & Sevi, 2009; Biggiero 2010, 2011, 2016b): what holds with 20 agents could not hold with 200. Put more broadly and strongly: a rather inexplored consequence of complexity is that—if not always and for all forms of complexity, al least in many (most?) cases—simple models cannot approximate what happens with less simple models. Therefore, we cannot follow a linearly incremental approach to knowledge growth.

4 Conclusions

For SE and its derivations is made by a galaxy of theories and its corresponding research streams, it would be simply impossible in a single paper to "measure the distance" between them what RE could be. Being aware that this is a disputable choice, I examined only the neo-Walrasian model of GEE, Hayek's version of the Austrian perspective on economics, transaction cost economics, and some other theoretical fragment in current developments of network economics. I argued that these economic theories and research streams are wrong or misleading, because its assumptions about agents' behavior, economic and social structure evolution, knowledge growth and learning do not (even approximately) correspond to what happens in the real world.

[27] Even at a quick sight, it is easy to see that authors like Gigerenzer, Kahneman, Thaler, Tversky are absent from the references of those works.

Further, I underlined that social and natural sciences are living a dramatic transformation due to the discoveries of complexity science, which make the criticism of oversimplification much more solid and deep than before. Complexity science itself is under evolution and clarification of its implications, and this not yet consolidated process allows old paradigms to resist the change. Among the many forms in which complexity occurs in economics and organization science, I have highlighted that most socio-economic phenomena have a stable structural (relational) dimension, which cannot be overlooked or treated only through standard statistics, and that when analyzed in a dynamic view, most problems are characterized by emergent outcomes, due to recursive interactions.

Then, I sketched five research streams that, in various degrees, are rather free from the "neoclassical chains" dominating SE and most of its derivations. Each research stream currently contains and brings forth important pieces of social and economic sciences, thus complementing (and often overlapping) each other to create a new approach. Perhaps, RE could be the outcome of that theoretical merger. In this perspective, I have stressed that transaction cost economics (and its derivations), though introducing important elements of novelty and improvements with respect to SE, is backward with respect to the main traits characterizing the five building blocks discussed above. In this perspective, it is worth reminding that it seems more appropriate that, instead of transactions, it is people and their embodied knowledge that had to play the role of RE elementary units.

The outcome of such a theoretical merger giving eventually birth to RE could be outlined as a real-world economic and management theory, in which:

- Theoretical abstractions should be "reasonable" or anyway as most as possible anchored to real behaviors and contexts.
- The degree of disaggregation and simplification should be accurately chosen and discussed from the perspective of complexity science.
- Structures and agents (structural individualism) are considered together in an evolutionary perspective.
- Agents, not transactions, are at the core of the analysis.
- Relational methods play a central role, especially in terms of mechanisms of interaction (Biggiero, 2016b).

The endeavor of building RE would require merging them in a unified framework. I am aware that this operation will be difficult and long, because, despite the several common ideas and methods, languages can sometimes differ considerably. Moreover, researchers are always very much attached to their conceptual references, and their identification in social, institutional and epistemic communities becomes usually even stronger with a newer research stream rather than with the mainstream. Indeed, the merger will be not done "in cold blood": a lot of time and contributions would be required. It should result as an emergent outcome, as it typically occurs in complex processes.

References

Ackert, L. F., & Deaves, D. (2009). Behavioral finance: Psychology, decision-making, and markets. South-Western Pub.

Anzola, D., Barbrook-Johnson, P., & Cano, J. I. (2016). Self-organization and social science. *Computational & Mathematical Organization Theory*.

Argyres, N. S., & Zenger, T. R. (2012). Capabilities, transaction costs, and firm boundaries. *Organization Science, 23*(6), 1643–1657.

Arrow, K. J. (2009). Some developments in economic theory since 1940: An eyewitness account. *Annual Review of Economics, 1*, 1–16.

Arrow, K. J., & Hahn, F. H. (1971). *General competitive analysis*. Oliver & Boyd.

Arrow, K. J., & Hurwicz, L. (1958). On the stability of competitive equilibrium I. *Econometrica, 26*, 522–552.

Arrow, K. J., Block, H. D., & Hurwicz, L. (1959). On the stability of competitive equilibrium I. *Econometrica, 27*, 82–109.

Arrow, K., Anderson, P. W., & Pines, D. (Eds.). (1988). *The Economy as an evolving complex system*. Addison-Wesley.

Arrow, H., McGrath, J. E., & Berdhal, J. L. (2000). *Small groups as complex systems: Formation, coordination, development, and adaptation*. Sage.

Arthur, W. B. (2006). Out-of-equilibrium economics and agent-based modelling. In L. Tesfatsion & K. L. Judd (Eds.), *Handbook of computational economics* (pp. 1551–1564). North-Holland.

Arthur, W. B. (2010). Complexity, the Santa Fè Approach, and nonequilibrium economics. *History of Economic Ideas, 18*(2), 149–166.

Arthur, W. B. (2015). *Complexity and the economy*. Oxford UP.

Arthur, W. B., Durlauf, S., & Lane, D. (Eds.). (1997). *The economy as an evolving complex system II*. Addison-Wesley.

Ashby, R. W. (1956). *An introduction to cybernetics*. Wiley.

Augier, M., & March, J. G. (Eds.). (2004). *Models of a man*. MIT Press.

Barnett, W., Deissenberg, C., & Feichtinger, G. (Eds.). (2004). *Economic complexity: Non-liner dynamics, multi-agent economies, and learning*. Elsevier.

Beer, S. (1959). *Cybernetics and management*. The English UP.

Beer, S. (1966). *Decision and control*. Wiley.

Beer, S. (1972). *Brain of the firm*. Penguin.

Bertuglia, C. S., & Vaio, F. (2005). Nonlinearity, chaos and complexity. The dynamics of natural and social systems. Oxford UP.

Biggiero, L. (1998). Complexity and self-organization: Consequences for capitalistic industrial organization. In G. Minati (Ed.), *First Italian Conference on Systemics* (pp. 185–198). Apogeo.

Biggiero, L. (2001). Sources of complexity in human systems. *Nonlinear Dynamics and Chaos in Life Sciences, 5*, 3–19.

Biggiero, L. (2001a). Managerial action and observation: A view of relational complexity. *Systemica, 12*, 23–37; reprinted in LUISS International Journal, 2000.

Biggiero, L. (2010). Exploration modes and its impact on industry profitability. The differentiated effects of internal and external ways to access market knowledge. In M. Faggini, & P. Vinci (Eds.), *Decision theory and choice: a complexity approach* (pp. 83–116). Berlin: Springer.

Biggiero, L. (2011). Knowledge redundancy, environmental shocks, and agents' opportunism. In J. Józefczyk, & D. Orski (Eds.), *Knowledge-based intelligent system advancements: systemic and cybernetic approaches. Advances in Artificial Intelligence Technologies (AAIT)* (pp. 252–281). Hershey (Penn, USA): IGI Global Publishers. https://doi.org/10.4018/978-1-61692-811-7.ch013.

Biggiero, L. (2016a). Network analysis for economics and management studies. In L. Biggiero et al. (Eds.), *Relational methodologies and epistemology in economics and management sciences* (pp. 1–60). Hershey, PA (US): IGI Global. https://doi.org/10.4018/978-1-4666-9770-6.ch001

Biggiero, L. (2016b). Conclusions: Methodological pluralism and epistemology between and beyond relational methods. In L. Biggiero et al. (Eds.), *Relational methodologies and epistemology in economics and management sciences* (pp. 397–411). Hershey, PA (US): IGI Global.
Biggiero, L. (2016c). NK simulation modeling. In L. Biggiero et al. (Eds.), *Relational methodologies and epistemology in economics and management sciences* (pp. 62–100). Hershey, PA (US): IGI Global. https://doi.org/10.4018/978-1-4666-9770-6.ch002.
Biggiero, L. (2019). A note on variety and hierarchy of economic and social systems. The system-network dualism and the consequences of routinization and robotization. In G. Minati, M. Abram & E. Pessa (Eds.), *Systemics of incompleteness and quasi-systems (207–220).* In *Proceedings of the Seventh National Conference of the Italian Systems Society*. Springer.
Biggiero, L., & Sevi, E. (2009). Opportunism by cheating and its effects on industry profitability. The CIOPS model. *Computational & Mathematical Organization Theory, 15*, 191–236. https://doi.org/10.1007/s10588-009-9057-3.
Biggiero, L., et al. (Eds.). (2016). Relational methodologies and epistemology in economics and management sciences. IGI Global.
Blume, L. E., & Durlauf, S. N. (2006). *The economy as an evolving complex system III*. Oxford UP.
Boschetti, F. (2011). Rationality, complexity and self-organization. *E:CO, 13*(1–2), 133–145.
Boulding, K. (1958). *Principles of economic policy*. Prentice-Hall.
Boulding, K. (1970). *Economics as a science*. McGraw-Hill.
Boulding, K. (1981). *Evolutionary economics*. Sage.
Brennan, D. M., Kristjanson-Gural, D., Mulder, C. P., & Olsen, E. K. (Eds.). (2017). *Routledge handbook on Marxian economics*. Routledge.
Bridel, P. (2012). *General equilibrium analysis: A century after Walras*. Routledge.
Buckley, W. (1967). *Sociology and modern systems theory*. Prentice-Hall.
Burton, R. M., Eriksen, B., Håkonsson, D. D., & Snow, C. C. (2006). *Organization design: The evolving state of the art*. Springer.
Camerer, C. F., Loewenstein, G., & Rabin, M. (Eds.). (2004). *Advances in behavioral economics*. Princeton.
Camerer, C.F., Loewenstein, G. & Rabin, M. 2004b. Behavioral economics: Past, present, and future. In C. F. Camerer, G. Loewenstein, & M. Rabin (Eds.), *2004 Advances in behavioral economics* (pp. 3–51). Princeton UP.
Carter, R., & Hodgson, G. M. (2006). The impact of empirical tests of transaction cost economics on the debate on the nature of the firm. *Strategic Management Journal, 27*(5), 461–476.
Casti, J. (1989). *Paradigms lost*. Avon Book.
Casti, J. (1994). *Complexification*. HarperCollins.
Chaitin, G. J. (1987). *Information, randomness and incompleteness*. World Scientific.
Chaitin, G. J. (1987). *Algorithmic information theory*. Cambridge UP.
Checkland, P. (1981). *Systems thinking, systems practice: Include a 30-year perspective*. Wiley.
Checkland, P. (1999). *Soft system methodology: A 30-Year retrospective*. Wiley.
Churchman, C. W., & Verhulst, M. (Eds.). (1960). *Management sciences: Models and techniques*. Pergamon.
Churchman, C. W. (1979). *The systems approach*. Dell.
Cioffi-Revilla, C. (2014). *Introduction to computational social science: Principles and applications*. Springer.
Coase, R. H. (1937). The nature of firm. *Economica*. 386–405.
Cohen, M. D., March, J. G., & Olsen, J. P. (1972). A garbage can model of organizational choice. *Administrative Science Quarterly, 17*, 1–25.
Colander, D. (Ed.). (2000). *Complexity and the history of economic thought*. Routledge.
Corning, P. A. (2012). The re-emergence of emergence, and the causal role of synergy in emergent evolution. *Synthese, 185*, 295–317.
David, R. J., & Han, S.-K. (2004). A systematic assessment of the empirical support for transaction cost economics. *Strategic Management Journal, 25*(1), 39–58.

Dépelteau, F., & Powell, C. (Eds.). (2013). *Applying relational sociology: Relations, networks, and society*. Palgrave MacMillan.
Dépelteau, F., & Powell, C. (Eds.). (2013). *Conceptualizing relational sociology: Ontological and theoretical issues*. Palgrave MacMillan.
Diacon, P. E., Donici, G.A. & Maha, L.G. 2013. Perspectives of economics—behavioural economics. *Theoretical and Applied Economics, XX*(7), 27–32.
Dietrich, M., & Kraft, J. (Eds.). (2012). *Handbook on the economics and theory of the firm*. Edward Elgar.
Donaldson, L. (2001). *The contingency theory of organizations*. Sage.
Donati, P. (2011). *Relational sociology: A new paradigm for the social sciences*. Routledge.
Donzelli, F. (1986). Il concetto di equilibrio nella teoria economica neoclassica (The concept of equilibrium in neoclassical economic theory). La Nuova Italia Scientifica.
Dopfer, K. (Ed.). (2005). *The evolutionary foundation of economics*. Cambridge UP.
Easley, D., & Kleinberg, J. (2010). *Networks, crowds, and markets: Reasoning about a highly connected world*. Cambridge UP.
Economics. (1968). *Economics, 5*(3), 9–23.
Edmonds, B., & Meyer, R. (Eds.). (2013). *Simulating social complexity. A handbook*. Springer.
Ekelund, I. (1991). *Au hazard*. Paris: Editions du Seuil.
Elsner, W. (2012). *Microeconomics of interactive economies: Evolutionary, institutional, and complexity perspectives*. Edward Elgar.
Emirbayer, M. (1997). Manifesto for a relational sociology. *American Journal of Sociology, 103*(2), 281–317.
Epstein, J. M. (1999). Agent-based computational models and generative social science. *Complexity, 4*(5), 41–60.
Epstein, J. M. (2007). Generative social science: Studies in agent-based computational modeling. Princeton UP.
Faggini, M., & Vinci, P. (Eds.). (2010). *Decision theory and choice: A complexity approach*. Springer.
Feltz, B., Crommelink, M., & Goujon, P. (Eds.). (2006). *Self-organization and emergence in the life sciences*. Springer.
Forrester, J. W. (1961). *Industrial dynamics*. MIT Press.
Forrester, J. W. (1968). *Principles of systems*. MIT Press.
Foster, J., & Metcalf, J. S. (Eds.). (2001). *Frontiers of evolutionary economics: Competition, self-organization and innovation policy*. Edward Elgar.
Foster, J., & Metcalfe, J. S. (2012). Economic emergence: An evolutionary economic perspective. *Journal of Economic Behavior & Organization, 82*, 420–432.
Frantz, R., & Leeson, R. (Eds.). (2013). *Hayek and behavioral economics*. Palgrave Macmillan.
Gallegati, M., & Richiardi, M. G. (2009). Agent based models in economics and complexity. In R. A. Meyers (Ed.), *Encyclopedia of complexity and systems science* (pp. 200–223). Springer.
Gallupe, B. (2001). Knowledge management systems: Surveying the landscape. *International Journal of Management Reviews, 3*(1), 61–77.
Gell-Mann, M. (1994). *The quark and the jaguar*. Freeman & Company.
Geyskens, I., Steenkamp, J.-B.E.M., & Kumar, N. (2006). Make, buy, or ally: A transaction cost theory meta-analysis. *Academy of Management Journal, 49*(3), 519–543.
Ghoshal, S., & Moran, P. (1996). Bad for practice: A critique of the transaction cost theory. *Academy of Management Review, 21*(1), 13–47.
Gigerenzer, G. (2008). *Rationality for mortals: How people cope with uncertainty*. Oxford UP.
Gigerenzer, G. (2008). *Gut feelings: Short cuts to better decision making*. Penguin.
Gilbert, N. (2008). *Agent-based models*. Sage.
Gintis, H. (2000). *Game theory evolving. A problem-centered introduction to modeling strategic interactions*. Princeton UP.
Gintis, H. (2007). The dynamics of general equilibrium. *The Economic Journal, 117*, 1280–1309.
Gleick, J. (1987). *Chaos: Making a new science*. Penguin.

Gloria-Palermo, S. (1999). *The evolution of Austrian economics: From Menger to Lachmann*. Routledge.
Glushkov, V. M. (1966). *Introduction to cybernetics*. Academic Press.
Goertzel, B. (1994). Chaotic logic. Language, thought, and reality from the perspective of complex systems science. Plenum Press.
Goyal, S. (2007). *Connections: An introduction of the economics of networks*. Princeton.
Grandori, A. (Ed.). (2013). *Handbook of economic organization: Integrating economic and organization theory*. Edward Elgar.
Guala, F. (2005). *The methodology of experimental economics*. Cambridge UP.
Guastello, S. (2002). *Managing emergent phenomena. Nonlinear dynamics in work organizations*. Lawrence Erlbaum.
Gulbrandsen, B., Lambe, C. J., & Sandvik, K. (2017). Firm boundaries and transaction costs: The complementary role of capabilities. *Journal of Business Research*.
Hagedorn, H. (2015). A model of Austrian economics. https://www.researchgate.net
Hahn, F. H., & Petri, F. (Eds.). (2002). *General equilibrium: Problems and prospects*. Routledge.
Hall, N. (1991). *The new scientist guide to chaos*. Penguin.
Hannan, M. T., & Freeman, J. (1977). The population ecology of organizations. *American Journal of Sociology, 82*.
Hannan, M. T., & Freeman, J. (1989). Organizational ecology. Harvard UP.
Harper, D. A., & Endres, A. M. (2012). The anatomy of emergence, with a focus upon capital formation. *Journal of Economic Behavior & Organization, 82*, 352–367.
Harvey, D. (2005). *A brief history of neoliberalism*. Oxford UP.
Harvey, D. (2017). Marx, capital and the madness of economic reason. Faber and Faber.
Hayek, F.A. v. (1945). The use of knowledge in society. *American Economic Review, 35*(4), 519–530.
Hayek, F.A. v. (1967). The theory of complex phenomena. In *Studies in Philosophy, Politics, and Economics* (pp. 22–42). University of Chicago Press.
Hayek, F.A. v. (2002). Competition as a discovery procedure. *Quarterly Journal of Austrian*.
Hedström, P., & Bearman, P. (Eds.). (2009). *The Oxford handbook of analytical sociology*. Oxford UP.
Hedström, P., & Manzo, G. (2015). Recent trends in agent-based computational research: A brief introduction. *Sociological Methods & Research, 44*(2), 179–185.
Hedström, P. (2005). Dissecting the social: on the principles of analytical sociology. Cambridge UP.
Helbing, D. (Ed.). (2012). *Social self-organization: Agent-based simulations and experiments to study emergent social behavior*. Springer.
Helbing, D., & Kirman, A. (2013). Rethinking economics using complexity theory. *Real-World Economics Review,* 64. http://rwer.wordpress.com/2013/07/02/rwer-issue-64/
Hodge, D. (2008). Economics, realism and reality: A comparison of Mäki and Lawson. *Cambridge Journal of Economics, 32*(2), 163–202.
Hodgson, G. M. (1993). *Economics and evolution: Bringing life back into economics*. University of Michigan Press.
Hodgson, G. M. (2000). *Evolution and institutions: On evolutionary economics and the evolution of economics*. Edward Elgar.
Holland, J. H. (1998). *Emergence: From chaos to order*. Oxford UP.
Holt, R. P. F., Rosser Jr., J. B., & Colander, D. (2010). The complexity era in economics. *Review of Political Economy*.
Ingrao, B., & Israel, G. (1990). *The invisible hand: Economic equilibrium in the history of science*. The MIT Press.
Jackson, M. O. (2010). An overview of social networks and economic applications. In J. Benhabib, A. Bisin, & M. O. Jackson (Eds.), *Handbook of social economics* (pp. 511–585). North-Holland.
Jackson, M. O. (2010). *Social and economic networks*. Princeton.
Jackson, M. O. (2014). *The past and future of network analysis in economics. In The Oxford Handbook on the economics of networks*. Oxford UP.

Jackson, M. O. (2014). Networks in the understanding of economic behaviors. *Journal of Economic Perspectives, 28*(4), 3–22.
Jacobides, M. G., & Winter, S. G. (2005). The co-evolution of capabilities and transaction costs: Explaining the institutional structure of production. *Strategic Management Journal, 26*(5), 395–413.
Johnson, J., Nowak, A., Ormerod, P., Rosewell, B., & Zhang, Y.-C. (2017). *Non-equilibrium social science and policy. Introduction and essays on new changing paradigms in socio-economic thinking*. Springer.
Jörg, T. (2011). New thinking in complexity for the social sciences and humanities. A generative, transdisciplinary approach. Springer.
Kahneman, D. (2011). *Thinking fast and slow*. Farrar, Straus and Giroux.
Kahneman, D., Slovic, P., & Tversky, A. (Eds.). (1982). *Judgment under uncertainty: Heuristics and biases*. Cambridge UP.
Kahneman, D., & Tversky, A. (2000). Choices, values, and frames. Russell Sage Foundation and Cambridge UP.
Kauffman, S. A. (1996). *At home in the universe: The search for the laws of self-organization and complexity*. Oxford UP.
Kauffman, S. A. (2000). *Investigations*. Oxford UP.
Kauffman, S. A. (2016). *Humanity in a creative universe*. Oxford UP.
Kauffman, S. A. (2019). *A world beyond physics. The emergence and evolution of life*. Oxford UP.
Kirman, A. P. (1976). *Introduction to equilibrium analysis*. North-Holland.
Kirman, A. P. (2011). *Complex economics: Individual and collective rationality*. Routledge.
Klir, G. J. (1991). *Facets of systems science*. Plenum Press.
Knoke, D. (2012). *Economic networks*. Polity Press.
Knoke, D., & Yang, S. (2008). *Social network analysis*. Sage.
Komlos, J. (2019). Foundations of real-world economics. What every economics student needs to know. Routledge, Taylor & Francis.
Kuhn, T. (1962). *The structure of scientific revolutions*. The University of Chicago Press.
Lakatos, I., & Musgrave, A. (Eds.). (1970). *Criticism and the growth of knowledge*. Cambridge UP.
Lakatos, I. (1978). *The methodology of scientific research programmes*. Cambridge UP.
Landreth, H., & Colander, D. C. (2001). *History of economic thought* (4th ed.). South-Western College Pub.
Lane, D., Pumain, D., van der Leeuw, S., & West, G. (Eds.). (2009). *Complexity perspectives in innovation and social change*. Springer.
Lange, O. (1970). *Introduction to economic cybernetics*. Pergamon Press.
Lange, O. (1965). Wholes and parts: A general theory of system behavior. Pergamon Press.
Laudan, L. (1990). *Science and relativism: Some key controversies in the philosophy of science*. University of Chicago Press.
Laudan, L. (1996). *Beyond positivism and relativism*. Westview Press.
Loasby, B. (1999). *Knowledge, institutions and evolution in economics*. Routledge.
Loasby, B. (2001). Time, knowledge and evolutionary dynamics: Why connections matter. *Journal of Evolutionary Economics, 11*, 393–412.
Loasby, B. (1991). Equilibrium and evolution. Manchester UP.
Lomi, A., & Harrison, J. R. (2012). *The garbage can model of organizational choice: Looking forward at forty* (Vol. 36). Emerald Group Publishing Limited.
Lomi, A., & Larsen, E. R. (Eds.). (2001). Dynamics of organizations: Computational modeling and organization theories. MIT Press.
Luhmann, N. (1995). Social systems. Stanford UP.
Mainzer, K. (1994). *Thinking in complexity. The computational dynamics of matter, mind, and mankind* (2007th ed.). Springer.
Manzo, G. (Ed.). (2014). *Analytical sociology: Actions and networks*. Wiley.
March, J. G. (1994). *A primer on decision making. How decisions happen*. The Free Press.

Marinescu, C. (2012). Transaction costs and institutions' efficiency: A critical approach. *The American Journal of Economics and Sociology, 71*(2), 254–276.
Mautinovic, I. (2006). Self-organization and design in capitalist economies. *Journal of Economic Issues, XL*(3), 575–601.
Metcalfe, J. S. (2010). Complexity and emergence in economics: The road from Smith to Hayek (Via Marshall and Schumpeter). *History of Economic Ideas, 18*(2), 45–75.
Miller, J. H., & Page, S. E. (2007). *Complex adaptive systems: An introduction to computational models of social life*. Princeton.
Mintzberg, H. (1979). *The structuring of organization*. Prentice-Hall Inc.
Mirowski, P. (1989). More heat than light: Economics as social physics, physics as nature's economics. Cambridge UP.
Mitleton-Kelly, E. (Ed.). (2003). *Complex systems and evolutionary perspectives on organizations. The application of complexity theory to organizations*. Elsevier Science.
Moss, S. (2009). Agent based modeling and neoclassical economics: A critical perspective. In R. A. Meyers (Ed.), *Encyclopedia of complexity and systems science* (pp. 176–184). Springer.
Nagurney, A. (1999). *Network economics: A variational inequality approach*. Kluwer.
Nagurney, A. (2009). Network economics. In D. Belsley & E. Kontoghiorghes (Eds.), *Handbook of computational econometrics* (pp. 429–486). Wiley.
Nagurney, A., & Dong, J. (2002). *Super-networks: Decision-making for the information age*. Edward Elgar.
Nelson, R. R., & Winter, S. G. (1982). *An evolutionary theory of economic change*. Belknap Press of Harvard University Press.
Ogaki, M., & Tanaka, S. C. (2018). *Behavioral economics: Toward a new economics by integration with traditional economics*. Springer.
Parker, D., & Stacey, R. (1994). *Chaos, management and economics: The implications of nonlinear thinking*. Institute of Economic Affairs.
Pfeffer, J. (1981). *Power in organizations*. Pitman.
Pfeffer, J. (1997). *New directions for organization theory: Problems and prospects*. Oxford UP.
Picketty, T. (2013). *Capital in the twenty-first century*. Belknap Press.
Pratten, S. (2013). Critical realism and the process account of emergence. *Journal for the Theory of Social Behaviour, 43*(3), 251–279.
Priesmeyer, H. R. (1992). *Organizations and chaos: Defining the methods of nonlinear management*. Quorum Books.
Prigogine, I., & Stengers, I. (1984). *Order out of chaos: Man's new dialogue with nature*. Bantam.
Putnam, H. (1995). *Pragmatism*. Blackwell.
Resnik, M. D. (1987). *Choices: An introduction to decision theory*. University of Minnesota Press.
Richardson, K. (2005). Managing organizational complexity. Philosophy, theory, application. Greenwich (CT), IAP.
Roncaglia, A. (2006). *The wealth of ideas. A history of economic thought*. Cambridge UP.
Roncaglia, A. (2019). *The age of fragmentation: A history of contemporary economic thought*. Cambridge UP.
Rorty, R. (1982). *Consequences of pragmatism*. University of Minnesota Press.
Rosser, J. B., Jr. (1991). *From catastrophe to chaos: A general theory of economic discontinuities*. Springer, US.
Rosser, J. B., Jr. (1999). On the complexities of complex economic dynamics. *Journal of Economic Perspectives, 13*, 169–192.
Rosser, J. B., Jr. (2012). Emergence and complexity in Austrian economics. *Journal of Economic Behavior & Organization, 81*, 122–128.
Ruelle, D. (1991). *Chance and chaos*. Princeton.
Saviotti, P. P. (Ed.). (2003). *Applied evolutionary economics: New empirical methods and simulation techniques*. Edward Elgar.
Schilling, M. A., & Steensma, H. K. (2002). Disentangling the theories of firm boundaries: A path model and empirical test. *Organization Science, 13*(4), 387–401.

Schmalensee, R., & Willig, R. (Eds.). (1989). *Handbook of industrial organization*. North-Holland.
Schweitzer, F., Fagiolo, G., Sornette, D., Vega-Redondo, F., & White, D. R. (2009). Economic networks: What do we know and what do we need to know? *Advances in Complex Systems, 12*, 407–422.
Scott, J., & Carrington, P. J. (Eds.). (2011). *The Sage handbook of social network analysis*. Sage.
Scott, J. (1992). Social network analysis: A handbook (2nd Edn., 2001). Sage.
Screpanti, E., & Zamagni, S. (2005). *An outline of the history of economic thought*. Oxford UP.
Serra, R. (2010). A complex view of complex systems science. *History of Economic Ideas, 18*(2), 19–44.
Simon, H. A. (1955). A behavioral model of rational choice. *Quarterly Journal of Economics, 69*, 99–118.
Simon, H. A. (1957). *Models of man*. Wiley.
Simon, H. A. (1978). Rationality as process and a product of thought. *American Economic Review, 68*, 1–14.
Simon, H. A. (1979). Rational decision making in business organization. *American Economic Review, 69*, 493–513.
Simon, H. A. (1983). *Reason in human affair*. Stanford UP.
Simon, H. A. (1987). Bounded rationality. In J. Eatwell, M. Milgate, & P. Newman (Eds.), *The new palgrave: A dictionary of economics* (Vol. I, pp. 266–268). Stockton Press.
Simon, H. A. (1976). From bounded to procedural rationality. In S. Latsis (Ed.), *Method and appraisal in economics*. Cambridge UP.
Simon, H. A. (1997). Models of bounded rationality. *Empirically grounded economic reason* (Vol. 3). MIT Press.
Simon, H. A. (2001). Complex systems: The interplay of organizations and markets in contemporary society. *Computational & Mathematical Organization Theory, 7*, 79–85.
Smith, T. S., & Stevens, G. T. (1996). Emergence, self-organization, and social interaction: Arousal-dependent structure in social systems. *Sociological Theory, 14*(2), 131–153.
Squazzoni, F. (2012). *Agent-based computational sociology*. Wiley.
Stacey, R. D. (1993). *Strategic management and organizational dynamics*. Prentice Hall.
Stacey, R. D. (1996). *Complexity and creativity in organizations*. Berrett-Koehler.
Stacey, R. D., Griffin, D., & Shaw, P. (2000). *Complexity and management. Fad or radical challenge to systems thinking?* Routledge.
Sterman, J. D. (2000). *Business dynamics: Systems thinking and modeling for a complex world (19)*. Irwin/McGraw-Hill.
Taleb, N. N. (2007). *The black swan*. Random House.
Taylor, E. (2015). An explication of emergence. *Philosophical Studies, 172*, 653–669.
Thaler, R. H. (1991). *Quasi rational economics*. Russell Sage Foundation.
Thaler, R. H. (2015). *Misbehaving: The making of behavioral economics*. Norton & Company.
Thaler, R. H. (2016). Behavioral economics: Past, present, and future. *American Economic Review, 106*(7), 1577–1600.
Thaler, R. H., & Sunstein, C. R. (2009). *Nudge: Improving decisions about health, wealth, and happiness*. Penguin.
Thaler, R. H. (Ed.). (1993). *Advances in behavioral finance*. Russell Sage Foundation.
Theurer, K. L. (2014). Complexity-based theories of emergence: Criticisms and constraints. *International Studies in the Philosophy of Science, 28*(3), 277–301.
Tsang, E. W. K. (2006). Behavioral assumptions and theory development: The case of transaction cost economics. *Strategic Management Journal, 27*(11), 999–1011.
Tversky, A., & Kahneman, D. (1992). Advances in prospect theory: Cumulative representation of uncertainty. *Journal of Risk and Uncertainty, 5*, 297–323.
Van de Ven, A. H., & Joyce, W. F. (1981). *Perspectives on organization design and behavior*. Wiley.
Waldrop, M. M. (1992). *Complexity: The emerging science at the edge of order and chaos*. Simon & Schuster.
Wapshott, N. (2012). *Keynes Hayek: The clash that defined modern economics*. Norton & Co.

Wasserman, S., & Faust, K. (1994). *Social network analysis: Methods and applications*. Cambridge University Press.
Weick, K. E. (1995). *Sensemaking in organizations*. Sage.
White, H. C. (1981). Where do markets come from? *American Journal of Sociology, 87*, 517–547.
White, H. C. (1993). Markets in production networks. In R. Swedberg (Ed.), *Explorations in economic sociology*. Sage.
Wieland, J. (2018). *Relational economics* (English edition, 2020, Springer). Metropolis Verlag.
Williamson, O. E. (1975). *Markets and hierarchies: Analysis and antitrust implications*. The Free Press.
Williamson, O. E. (1981). The economics of organization: The transaction costs approach. *American Journal of Sociology, 87*, 548–577.
Williamson, O. E. (1985). *The economic institutions of capitalism*. The Free Press.
Williamson, O. E. (1991). Strategizing, economizing, and economic organization. *Strategic Management Journal, 12*(75), 94.
Williamson, O. E. (1991). Comparative economic organizations: The analysis of discrete structural alternatives. *Administrative Science Quarterly, 36*, 269–296.
Williamson, O. E. (1993). Calculativeness, trust, and economic organization. *Journal of Law and Economics, 36*(1), 453–486.
Williamson, O. E. (1996). *The mechanisms of governance*. NY: Oxford UP.
Williamson, O. E. (1998). Transaction cost economics: How it works; where it is headed. *De Economist, 146*, 23–58.
Williamson, O. E. (1994). Transaction cost economics and organization theory. In N. J. Smelser & R. Swedberg (Eds.), *The handbook of economic sociology* (pp. 77–107). Princeton UP.
Wolfram, S. (1994). *Cellular automata and complexity: Collected papers*. Addison-Wesley.
Wolfram, S. (2002). A new kind of science. Wolfram Media Inc.
Yezdani, O., Sanzogni, L., & Poropat, A. (2015). Theory of emergence: Introducing a model-centred approach to applied social science research. *Prometheus, 33*(3), 305–322.
Yolles, M. (2006). *Organizations as complex systems. An introduction to knowledge cybernetics*. IAP.
Zamagni, S. (1993). Microeconomic theory: An introduction. Gregg Revivals.
Zeleny, M. (2005). *Human systems management. Integrating knowledge, management and systems*. World Scientific.

Lucio Biggiero is professor at University of L'Aquila (IT). His background is in industrial economics, and his scientific research rounds on inter-firm networks and coordination, economic theory, and organizational design. His works employ mostly social network analysis and agent-based simulation modeling. Empirical studies concern various types of economic networks, like knowledge and R&D collaboration, ownership, and international trade.

Modeling Relational Transactions

Josef Wieland, Albrecht von Müller, Andrej Nikonov, Leonhard Teichert, Sebastian Lehrack, and Lukas Törner

Abstract This paper proposes an actor-based approach to model relational transactions. The text entails a brief summary of the essential concepts of relational economics. The concepts of "resources of cooperation" and "cooperation corridor" are specified. Next, the study offers a guideline to model relational transactions in an n-dimensional vector space and describes the modeling of the emergence of transactions by focusing on multiple decision logics and an actor's context. The results of this investigation show relational economics can benefit from using actor-based approaches. Modeling a network of relational transactions is strong in showing cooperative value creation. Future research may apply this model to structure formation and the analysis of strategic choice. The second major finding is that this way with multi-dimensional accounting data polycontextural, global economic clusters and organizational, strategic learning processes can be researched.

Keywords Relational transactions · Network methods · Agent-based model · Cooperation · Strategy

1 Introduction

Recent approaches from the interface of physics and philosophy describe reality as a process of continuous self-unfolding. In the configuration of that, interactions lead to novel phenomena and thus the "process of reality" continues to unfold, also qualitatively, in neither fully deterministic nor fully random manner. Only because it is not fully deterministic there is the possibility of genuine novelty. Only because it is not purely random we can recognize and interpret certain patterns in what happens.

J. Wieland · L. Törner (✉)
Zeppelin University, Friedrichshafen, Germany
e-mail: Lukas.Toerner@zu.de

A. von Müller
Parmenides Foundation, Pullach i. Isartal, Germany

A. Nikonov · L. Teichert · S. Lehrack
Cognostics AG, Pullach i. Isartal, Germany

L. Biggiero et al. (eds.), *The Relational View of Economics*, Relational Economics and Organization Governance, https://doi.org/10.1007/978-3-030-86526-9_5

The important conceptual or "philosophical" contribution of relational economics is that it allows us to address and interpret the emergence of new relations, i.e., it enables us to process the phenomenon of ongoing constellatory self-unfolding in the domain of economics (cf. von Müller & Zafiris, 2018). Unlike traditional approaches in economic theory, it allows us to accommodate the openness of the future and the emergence of the genuinely novel. In the tradition of Oliver E. Williamson, the observational focus fundamentally transforms from discrete to relational transactions (cf. 1979; 1985). The mathematical approach presented in the following pages seeks to establish a formal framework in which these phenomena emerge, i.e., not ex-ante predictable but ex-post interpretable features of the overall system can be addressed and studied. Thus, an actor-based model develops relations among agents who are characterized by bounded rationality and have access to incomplete information.

Methodologically speaking, this requires the switch from algorithms that portray the behavior of the overall system to ones that portray the (multi-dimensional) behavioral optimization of individual agents (cf. Edwards, 2001; Hodge & Johnson, 1970). The emergent patterns in the interactions of those agents provide insights into the neither fully deterministic nor fully random evolution of the respective system. Accordingly, the emergent behavior of an agent-based model presumed here translates the central goal of relational economics into a formal representation that can be studied "empirically" on the basis of multi-dimensional accounting data (cf. Möhrer in this volume).

This has two key advantages: (a) a more suitable framework for examining evolving complex systems with an open future and (b) the ability to overcome the trap of "local optimization," i.e., the ability to appreciate that, in a self-unfolding context, what is good for the system as a whole may converge with what is best for the individual agent.

In the following, a mathematical model of a network of relational transactions is introduced. Here, the significance of transactions is presented as the foundation of relations between the individual and collective agents in terms of creating value in global economic networks. It lies in the nature of the problem that both conceptual and mathematical modeling are, from epistemological and practical standpoints alike, poorly suited to providing comprehensive descriptions of complex systems (cf. Whitehead, 1929). Instead, they yield insights into some specific aspects of the system in question. The focus of this paper is therefore on mathematical characteristics, parameters and effects of transactions in a polycontextual and polylingual environment. The question addressed is how actors in a space of divergent interests interact via relational transactions and how they are repositioned to one another. The scope of analysis includes the resources of cooperation and thus the heaviness of relations. To avoid conceptual confusion, it is important to point out that this focus does not guarantee insights into physical traded commodities and goods that are exchanged in the context of discrete transactions. Rather, we will seek to arrive at a profound understanding of the structural and systemic aspects of relational transactions themselves. The aim of this paper is to mathematically describe the function of relational transactions as attractors for the multiple decision logics applied by the agents involved.

In the first section, we will introduce the fundamental theoretical assumptions of relational economics that will be represented in the model. In turn, the second section clarifies the mathematical equivalents of these assumptions and begins building the model itself. Subsequently, we will discuss our results, the limitations of the model, the potential fields of application, i.e., modeling based on multi-dimensional accounting, and its theoretical implications for research, meaning the possibilities that arise from using the relational view to question orthodox models, analysis and paradigms in economics. Furthermore, we will discuss the practical implications of the model in the context of corporate strategy and complex decision-making processes.

2 Background and Essential Concepts

2.1 Relational Transactions

Generally speaking, two different strands of paradigmatic research orientation can be distinguished in the formation of economic theory. On the one hand, there is an interest in understanding the functional mechanisms of the market, and in investigating and predicting their quasi-lawful effects (cf. Herscovici, 2019; Schramm in this volume). In this paradigm, the market is a system of relative prices that mediates discrete "exchange transactions" between individual actors under competitive conditions and ideally brings them into equilibrium. In this context, "discrete" means that in an isolated and dyadic exchange, materializing in t_1, only its economic value is taken into consideration.

On the other hand, there is an interest in "relational transactions" (Wieland, 2018, 2020), which forms the focus of our research. Relational transactions are not executed via spot markets but via continuing relational contracts and organizations or, in more general terms, via cooperation. Not only the economic and technical resources for the effective and efficient execution of these transactions and cooperation projects are of importance. Rather, the actors' motivations and behavioral characteristics, moral preferences, experiences and future visions, the cultural imprints and convictions of organizations and societies, and the effectiveness of their legal and other institutional orders, also play a role, to name only a few parameters. These parameters represent different societal systems (e.g. economy, ethics, law, politics, civil society) that obey different decision-making logics, which are in turn crucial for the execution of relational transactions in the economy.

Modern societies are based on these functionally differentiated systems with distinct binary codings (cf. Luhmann, 1987, 1997) (e.g. economy: payment | non payment; politics: power | no power; civil society: common good | private interest) and consequently guiding differences in their organizational systems (firms: cost/earnings; political parties: government/opposition; NGOs: engagement/non engagement). Actors make decisions that are structured by the guiding difference and binary coding which are the context or encodings of the decision-making process. Relational economics views organizations as collective actors.

In a word, relational transactions, as cooperation projects, are attractors for polyvalent contexts, decision logics and sources of value creation. The theory of private and public value creation through cooperation, which refers to this relationship of transsectoral interactions, is the research field of relational economics (cf. Wieland, 2020, Ch. 7).

2.2 *Resources of Cooperation and Cooperation Corridors*

Creating value via collaborating actors means, firstly, that all actors involved expect to receive a factor income and rent from cooperation in return for the specific resources they invest. The higher the transaction specificity or organization specificity of their investment, the higher the added value produced by the cooperation. A cooperation rent is an additional income to stakeholders beyond explicit contracts (see Möhrer in this volume) that is generated by the higher productivity of collaborative value creation compared to a discrete individual investment on the part of the actor or the next-best cooperation project. A firm's cooperation rent is accrued as "supranormal profit," a type of profit that is above the market average and is appropriated by the organization (cf. Wieland, 2020; see also Möhrer in this volume).

It is, therefore, the individual and organizational willingness to cooperate (e.g. pro-social skills, preference for continuity) and ability to cooperate (e.g. specificity of resources, transcultural competency) that determine the cooperation corridor available to a given firm and thus the number of its chances for cooperation.

The costs involved in creating a cooperation corridor—transaction, adaptation, cooperation and relational costs—place a limit on the corridor's size (cf. Gibbons & Roberts, 2013; Tadelis & Williamson, 2013; Wernerfelt, 2016; White and Siu-Yun Lui, 2005). Social institutions—laws, ordinances, moral convictions, cultural traditions—are further constraining and enabling factors (cf. North, 1990, 2005). A firm's ability to cooperate therefore also includes its willingness and ability to pass up opportunities for cooperation that are organizationally or socially impermissible or undesirable. The model outlined in this paper describes actors' repositioning in terms of their willingness and ability to cooperate and is modeled in terms of whether the common cooperation corridor allows a transaction (cf. Wieland, 2020).

2.3 *Relations as the Central Problem*

The concept of the specificity of the invested resources, introduced in the last section, and its significance for the attainable level of the cooperation rent has certain implications, which will be emphasized here. First, the productivity of specifically invested resources depends primarily on the programs that a firm has at its disposal and with which it organizes its processes. Programs include risk management, value management, compliance systems, people management, and other management systems. These programs can either hinder or foster the competitive advantage arising from specificity. In the model, the programs help to gauge a given agent's performance regarding a particular societal sub-system and constitute his or her account balances.

Second, there is the problem of co-specialization, which is important when considering networks. Making specific investments as co-specialization is a characteristic of network resources and has been a subject of economic theory for quite some time (cf. Dyer & Sing, 1998; Gulati, 1999; Lavie, 2006). The specialization and investments provide information on an actor's accounts. These accounts represent an agent's performance regarding particular sub-systems of society. All actors in a network are the environment for each other and influence the competitiveness of all participating firms and the network as a whole. For each of the actors, the challenge consists in generating their own added value with resources that they do not fully own and control (cf. Dyer et al., 2018).

In the model presented below, the position of a given actor is the environment for all others. We assume that the four main independent variables for the dependent variable—relational transactions—are investment, preferences, knowledge and abilities. The specificity of resources is expressed by the position in a network and the reaction toward the context of the other actors' resources (cf. Seers & Chopin, 2012). In this way, the existing relational transactions help to explain the actors' positions. They also explain how other actors position themselves with regard to the transaction in terms of their own accounts.

This interdependence transforms a previously independent bilateral market transaction into a multilateral relational transaction. Oliver E. Williamson (cf. 1985, p. 61) has pointed out that this "fundamental transformation" has far-reaching contractual consequences, as it increases the complexity of the transactions and interactions. As a result, uncertainty regarding the behavioral expectations of the partners in a network takes on a new significance. Against this backdrop, the exploitation of shared knowledge and the use of co-specialized resources create a rent from cooperation in the network. Therefore, uncertainty leads to the need for adaptive governance structures that protect the relations in the network and enable the development of their specific performance (cf. Wieland in this volume).

Generally speaking, a transaction is a process to transfer property rights or things. "Transfer" can have various meanings: market exchange, for example, but also contracts or gifts (cf. Priddat & Müßgens in this volume). Network transactions are by definition not feasible as market transactions, and this is precisely where we can see their fundamental transformation from discrete to relational transactions. According to Willamson, the fundamental transformation lies in the transition from a discrete exchange transaction to a relational transaction and the necessary transition from market governance to relational governance. In brief, the relational transaction as an attractor for multiple decision logics is the result of this fundamental transformation.

"Fundamental transformation" refers to the fact that exchange transactions cannot be processed by relational governance and that relational transactions cannot be processed by market governance. The fundamental transformation does not start from

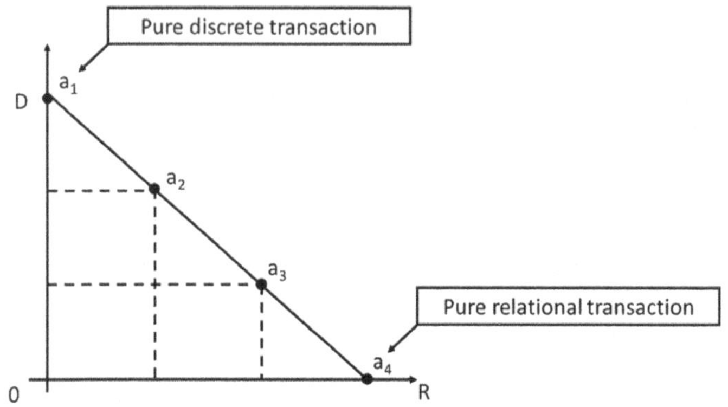

Fig. 1 Continuum exchange relation, a_1 and a_4 represent ideal types (from Wieland, 2020, p. 31)

a given threshold but is a process of continuous transition, which therefore requires a dynamic, relational form of governance (Fig. 1). This is associated with far-reaching demands on the adaptivity of relational governance structures (cf. Cao & Lumineau, 2015; Ellickson, 1991), which is precisely why we model relational transactions between actors and as a network, not in a market model notation.

3 Operationalizing Relational Transactions: Modeling

3.1 The Unit of Analysis: Classifying Transaction Attributes

More abstractly, and as a summary of the brief sketch of the core concepts of relational economics, we can say that the productive and at the same time adaptive governance of relations between multiple and multivalent events, which have a significant influence on the execution of transactions and thus on the cooperative economic value creation, factor incomes and relational rent, is the focus of relational economics. Actors in cooperative networks within and between firms, and between firms and other societal stakeholders, are at the center of the analysis as nodes within a network of relational transactions. Seen through this lens, firms, as collective actors, are constitutive resource networks of multiple stakeholders and at the same time temporary or permanent stakeholders in other local or global value creation networks. In the subsequent considerations on the development of a formal network model of relational transactions, we will therefore assume the following.

The essence of a network is the information and knowledge processed in and through relational transactions. They are the threads of the model which attract diverse and interacting events that make networks polyvalent. Relational governance structures, which we understand as the nodes of this network are necessary for the transactions' own effective and efficient execution.

The nodes of this network are economic and other social organizations. They are agents. From an inside-out perspective they represent resource networks in their own right; from an outside-in perspective they are collective actors in a transaction-specific network. They have peculiarities in the form of the resources they use for cooperation. The resources are balanced in accounts that capture a given agent's performance regarding a specific sub-system. To make accounts measurable, the balances of accounts can be evaluated using programs that are a mix of indicators. This is comparable to a multi-dimensional accounting approach. Taken together, these account balances determine the position of the nodes or actors within the network. In relational economics, a key assumption and major difference from neoclassical economics are that accounts are not solely guided by a financial context. Neither collective nor individual actors assess accounts on the basis of complete information; their assessments are influenced by their preferences, knowledge, abilities and specific prior investments determining their strategies.

The links between these nodes are threads. They represent and process the relations between the nodes in the network. Threads are, for example, formal contracts, and joint learning processes that create the relations between the various actors and events with a view to executing a mutually desired transaction. When a transaction takes place between two actors, a new thread is created and the interrelatedness of the network increases.

Nodes and threads, organizations and their network relations each have their own and a common contextual content, which lends both a certain heaviness (cf. Håkansson & Ford, 2002). These include financial and technical resources, private and shared knowledge, specific perceptions and classifications of events, and a common history with the desire to achieve continuity and cooperation. In the model, this aspect is expressed as resources of cooperation, which are invested by the agents involved in order to create a shared cooperation corridor.

"The heaviness is the result of complex interactions, adaptations and investments within and between the companies over time. Is not a world of individual and isolated transactions between companies. Instead, each business unit with its unique technical and human resources is bound together with many others in a variety of different ways through its relationships" (ibid., 133).

It is the quality of the links between the actors that defines the value-added capacity, the size of the cooperation rent for the entire network and each of its individual members. We represent the different qualities and the "heaviness" of the relations formally by the size of the cooperation corridor, which depends on the actors' accounts.

So far, we have discussed the need to model cooperation between firms and other societal stakeholders and introduced the main elements that are needed to model a network of transactions. In the following section, the mathematical characteristics of these theoretical elements of the model are listed and briefly introduced.

3.2 *The Elements of the Model*

In the following, an outline of the model's main elements is presented as a brief overview, before the mathematical details are provided in the next section.

i. *Contexts (C)*: Contexts are differentiated, autonomous systems of society in Luhmann's sense. In this paper, the exemplary sub-systems of interest are the market, law, civil society, ethics, religion and science. Each of these sub-systems (context: $c \in C$) makes use of its own semantic system and language and applies varying and distinct decision logics. The resulting polylingualism is captured in binary encodings for each functional systems' context (e.g. in the context of the market: payment/non payment).
ii. *Agents (X)*: For each agent, it holds that $x \in X$. Here, agents are organizations or individual entities that are involved in certain contexts and act according to their specific decision logics as a guiding difference. We assume that an agent is constituted by inherent accounts (account: $a \in A$). These accounts are mapped to and therefore represent the specific decision logics of the previously introduced functional systems. They have certain balances that capture the agent's performance within a system. This multi-dimensional accounting approach makes it possible to locate the agent in an n-dimensional (where n represents the number of all existing accounts/organizational systems) vector space, whereas every inscription of the vector that represents an agent is based on a particular set of account balances. To make accounts measurable, the balances of accounts $\sigma(t)$ can be evaluated by *programs* (P), which are sets of *indicators* (I) (indicator: $i \in I \in \{1, 0\}$). Indicators are classified as positive (G) or negative (N), which correspond to the binary encodings of a given context. This assessment is made using the function $P(I) \rightarrow \sigma$. Furthermore, agents voluntarily make choices and take actions in their contexts and can alter their focus on them. This allows us to represent agents with irrational or semi-rational preference orders. Hence, agents can shift their focus and adapt their assessment standards to other organizational systems/contexts. In the model, agents are represented as the nodes of a network.
iii. *Resources of Cooperation (RC_X):* Resources of cooperation are the most relevant element for successful economic cooperation and are the foundation of every transaction. In our model we understand them as *pro-social* abilities that an agent x contributes to a collaboration with an agent y: $RC_{x \rightarrow y}$. In contrast to the set of indicators of account balances as described in *ii*, the resources of cooperation depend on an evaluation of agent y's performance (account balances) carried out by agent x. This subjective evaluation is not based on perfect information, since x will most likely have only incomplete information, whether correct or incorrect, regarding y's account balances.

iv. *Cooperation Corridors (CC):* Cooperation corridors are polycontextual and polylingual relations between agents that go beyond individual market transactions. They depend on the involved agents' ability to cooperate and their willingness to cooperate. Cooperation corridors also depend on the resources of cooperation invested by the agents involved. It holds that $CC = RC_x \times RC_y$. From this follows that only if both parties involved contribute a marginal amount of resources can there be a cooperation corridor with a given probability. If one of the agents suspends the flow of $RC_{x,y}$, the corridor will collapse.

Transactions are represented as the threads between nodes (agents). The emergence and hence the existence of such threads depends on the elements RC_X and CC of the model. Interaction between agents respectively direct mutual exchange and impact is only given if resources of cooperation are invested to a marginal extent by all involved parties, a shared corridor of cooperation is thereby constituted and a transaction of a thread is eventually established on this basis. This means that a transaction takes place when a thread is created. Anyhow the transaction is not an element of the model for its own sake. Rather the resources in the cooperation corridor are the elements that create the thread called a transaction. Overall, a network of transactions emerges.

3.3 Modeling Relational Transactions

Having introduced the fundamental elements of the model, we will now turn to the relations between the individual elements and show how they interact and can evolve over time.

Even though the focus of analysis is on transactions as entities that establish relations between agents, first we must study the agents and their critical parameters. The key to modeling complex economic and social interdependencies and interactions between agents is their heterogeneity (cf. Gatti et al., 2018). The representation of agents as being ambivalent, preference-based, and imperfectly informed is a *conditio sine qua non* when mathematically describing relational transactions. Indeed, it is the scope of this model to deal with such agents. Therefore, our goal is to model the behavior of agents operating with imperfect information and bounded rationality. Accordingly, the need to employ an agent-based network approach becomes evident. The advantage of such approaches is the spatial specificity of agents. The approach captures the heterogeneity amongst agents and makes it possible to precisely define rules of interaction (cf. Namatame & Chen, 2016). Hence, it allows us to model the agents' behavior on the basis of their abilities, preferences, imperfect knowledge and specifically invested resources.

In this framework, an agent is represented by a fixed number of accounts and a certain number of contexts in which he or she operates (there are exactly as many accounts as there are potential contexts). The balances of accounts objectively describe the agent's position in the system. It should be noted that:

- The set of individual contexts for a given agent is a real sub-group of the set of all his/her accounts.
- There is a natural set of rules and impediments that limits the number of individual contexts for a given agent, making it impossible to maximize the balances of all his/her accounts simultaneously.

Accounts and Balances

Each agent has the exact same number and type of accounts (e.g. the market, law, civil society, ethics, religion and science). The balances of these accounts are defined on a finite range (defined by the number of indicators). Taken together, the balances of all accounts constitute a vector $\overrightarrow{\sigma_{is}}$ that describes the respective agent's position in a vector space:

$$\overrightarrow{\sigma_{is}} = \begin{pmatrix} \sigma_1 \\ \vdots \\ \sigma_n \end{pmatrix}$$

Therefore, the agent's position in an n-dimensional space will change depending on the balance of each account. In fact, this form of representation implies a multi-dimensional accounting approach that we will revisit later in the paper. Initially, at $t_0 t_0$ the balances of accounts are evaluated using the previously mentioned programs. A set of positive (G) and negative (B) indicators can be either fulfilled (1) or not fulfilled (0). An example of a negative indicator (B) could be the practice of child labor. If an agent does not practice child labor, the result is a tuple (B; 0), meaning the negative indicator "child labor" is not fulfilled. As the network is constantly evolving, the alteration of the account balances depends on interactions with other agents.

Contexts and Strategy Vectors

Regardless of the accounts, which can be seen as each agent's objective parameters, agents choose the contexts they predominantly operate in. These choices can be understood as the individual strategy of each agent. The choice of contexts is seen as a type of specialization. When a context is chosen, the corresponding semantic system and decision logic are adopted by the agent in question, and other agents' performance is assessed through the lens of the logic applied (see Fig. 2).

Agents define goal values for the contexts they operate in. These are composed of $\sigma_{is} + \delta_{ought}$ and describe what the respective agent is seeking to achieve with regard to a particular account (corresponding to an organizational system). Taken together, these values constitute a strategy vector $\overrightarrow{\sigma_{ought}}$. This strategy vector exhibits the following pattern and assigns each agent a tendency or direction in an n-dimensional vector space:

$$\overrightarrow{\sigma_{ought}} = \begin{pmatrix} \sigma_{is,1} + \delta_{ought,1} \\ \vdots \\ \sigma_{is,n} + \delta_{ought,n} \end{pmatrix}$$

The agent assumes that the context with the highest δ_{ought} is more important than the contexts with lower δ_{ought} values. This weighting is simultaneously a preference order for the corresponding accounts and eventually defines an agent's strategy. An example of a morally driven actor would be:

$$\delta_{ought,Ethics} > \delta_{ought,Market} \rightarrow s_{Ethics} \succ s_{Market} \succ s_{Rest}$$

These theoretical assumptions become relevant when introducing different kinds of strategies that agents can employ within the model in order to maximize their account balances. Even preference-based and information-lacking strategies can be used. The preference orders basically imply which contexts the agents primarily operate in. Furthermore, the subjective character of these preference orders makes it possible to capture each agent's choice of contexts, regardless of whether that choice can be explained rationally or is entirely irrational. Hence, the economically irrational strategies pursued by some agents in the network can easily be depicted in the modeled system of interactions.

Objective Repositioning of Agents via Transactions

In addition to the strategy vector, which indicates an agent's desired position in an n-dimensional vector space, the vector $\overrightarrow{\sigma_{is}}$ describes the factual position of an agent in space. Therefore, the actual repositioning of agents in a vector space solely depends on this vector. The alteration of an agent's account balances $\sigma(t)$ caused by a transaction with any other agent determines the agent's new location in an n-dimensional vector space. An objective evaluation of this delta can be mathematically expressed by the function $F(\overrightarrow{\sigma_x}, \overrightarrow{\sigma_y}) \rightarrow \Delta\overrightarrow{\sigma_x}$. The specification of this function

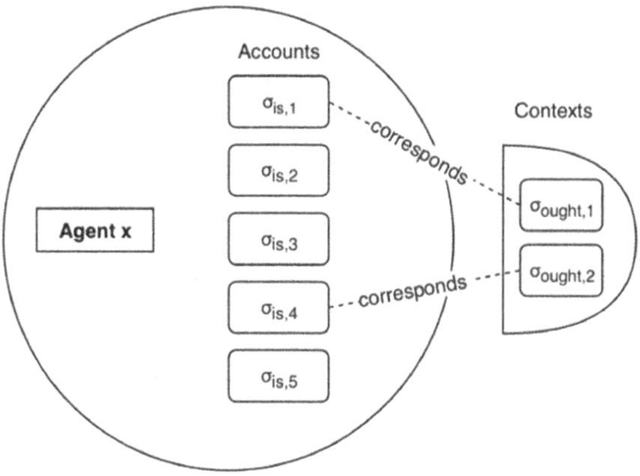

Fig. 2 Context of an agent mapping to certain accounts

differs from account to account. In the case of *ethics,* the following formula describes the delta of agent x's account balance σ_{Ethics}:$\Delta\sigma_{Ethics,x} = \left(\sigma_{Ethics,y} - \sigma_{Ethics,x}\right) * \epsilon$, where ϵ serves as a damping parameter to avoid unnatural jumpy evolution in just a few iterations.

3.4 Resources of Cooperation

Unlike the account balance vector $\overrightarrow{\sigma_{is}}$, an agent's strategy vector $\overrightarrow{\sigma_{ought}}$ is not an objective measure; rather, it is an individual lens or preference order used to assess other agents' account balances and their impacts on the agent's own balances (only those that correspond to contexts). When assessing a potential cooperation partner, $\delta_{ought,1}$, the agent's own contexts, the corresponding account balance $\sigma_{is,1}$ and the respective account balances of the other party are the only relevant parameters for an agent's decision on whether or not to invest resources of cooperation into a collaboration (the latter two values are combined in $\Delta\overrightarrow{\sigma_x}$). Since a given agent most likely has only flawed or at least non-perfect information regarding another agent's account balances $\overrightarrow{\sigma_y}$, the objective repositioning $\Delta\overrightarrow{\sigma_x}$ is distorted by a normally distributed probability mass function Ψ, such that:

$$F\left(\overrightarrow{\sigma_x}, \overrightarrow{\sigma_y}(\Psi)\right) \rightarrow \Delta\overrightarrow{\sigma_x}(\Psi)$$

By including Ψ in the assessment function, a network-inherent opacity is introduced, reflecting the assumption of imperfect knowledge amongst agents in a relational economic system. It is also the point of departure for individual and organizational learning processes to enhance actors' knowledge and abilities. In an evolutionary process, agents can adjust their strategies in each iteration, on the basis of the fruitfulness of existing transactions. This is essentially a learning process over time. If assumptions about other agents' performance were flawed, it will become apparent to the assessing agent at the end of the corresponding round. If other agents' actual performance was worse than their projected performance, the assessing agent can decrease the resources of cooperation invested; if their actual performance was better than their projected performance, the agent can increase the resources invested. For an example of such a learning process, see the contribution by Wieland in this volume. It follows that agents gain more knowledge about other agents' performance, the longer they cooperate with each other.

The following function describes the subjective assessment procedure used by x for the status quo of a cooperation partner y, the impact of a transaction with y on x's accounts, and the invested resources of cooperation for x: $F\left(\Delta\overrightarrow{\sigma_x}(\Psi), \overrightarrow{\sigma_{ought,x}}\right) \rightarrow RC_x$. More specifically, it holds that if the distance from an agent's potentially altered position (after the transaction) is smaller than the distance (d_{old}) from its initial position (before the transaction), the transaction in question is assessed positively and resources are invested.

$$\left|\overrightarrow{\sigma_{ought}} - \overrightarrow{\sigma_{is}}\right| = d_{old}$$

$$\left|\overrightarrow{\sigma_{ought}} - (\overrightarrow{\sigma_{is}} + \Delta\overrightarrow{\sigma}(\Psi))\right| = d_{new}$$

$$\Delta d = d_{old} - d_{new}$$

If the delta is positive or zero, the value of the binary coding of a given context will also be positive (e.g. in the case of the market: "payment"), while if it is negative, the opposite holds true (e.g. in the case of the market: "non payment"). This delta with regard to the agent's contexts is positively proportional to the resources of cooperation RC_x that the agent invests in cooperation. Moreover, resources of cooperation can be hypothetically approximated in order to predict other agents' cooperation strategies.

3.5 Cooperation Corridors

Taken together, the resources of cooperation define a corridor in which all preconditions for a transaction to emerge are fulfilled: $CC = RC_x \times RC_y$ (see Fig. 3). Hence, only if both parties involved invest a marginal amount of resources a cooperation corridor exists. If one of the agents stops the flow of $RC_{x,y}$, the corridor will collapse.

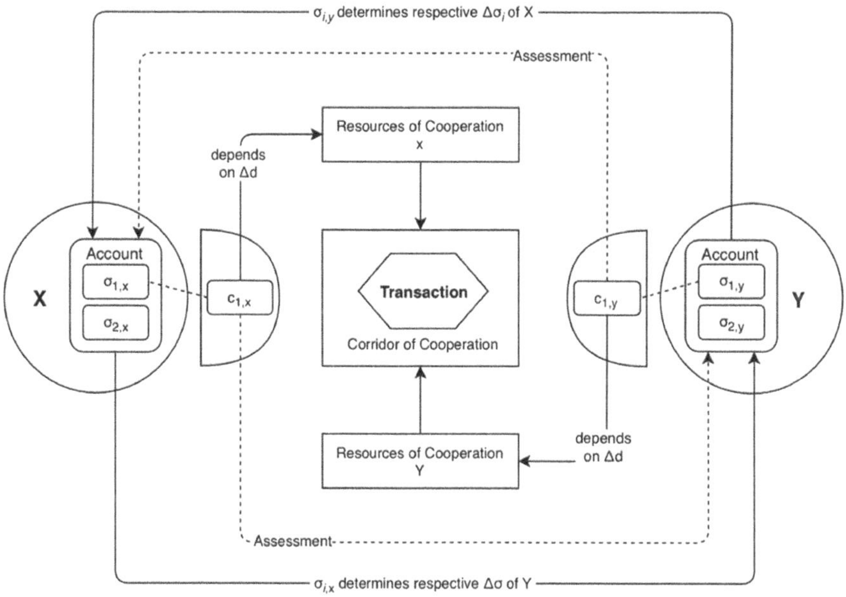

Fig. 3 Mechanisms of a relational transaction between two agents

The corridor itself does not cause any alteration of the agent's factual position; the position is only influenced when a transaction is executed.

Based on an approximated investment of cooperation resources, it is possible to define a hypothetical cooperation corridor CC_{hypo} of agents that are not yet directly interacting (no threads are established yet). This hypothetical corridor will be subsequently needed in order to calculate the probability of the emergence of new transactions. The following graphic (Fig. 3) takes into account the parameters defined above and represents the mechanisms of a relational transaction between two agents.

3.6 Transactions and Their Emergence

The probability of a transaction emerging depends on the hypothetical cooperation corridor between two agents: $p(T) = \alpha * CC_{hypo}$. If a corridor does not already exist, its hypothetical size is applied in order to determine the likelihood of emergence. This implies that an agent's chances to establish new collaborations increase with the increasing size of the hypothetical corridor. These probabilities are one pillar of the model's dynamic. But it is the actual existence of a relational transaction that allows agents to be altered, develop, progress or regress. Hence, the system can only be dynamic if relational transactions between agents are actually executed. When a relational transaction takes place, a thread is created between two nodes.

3.7 Dynamics Through Strategies

How to ensure the model is dynamic is a rather crucial question, given the fact that our goal is to explore the highly complex and dynamic relationships between interacting agents and how they mutually alter their positions in n-dimensional vector spaces. Therefore, in this section we introduce two possibilities to ensure the model is dynamic. Doing so means firstly ensuring the non-interruption (=continuation) of the relational transaction; secondly, different dynamics come from different accounts and are combined as the relation of a transaction.

1. Given that the number of contexts is smaller than the number of accounts (S > C), it is highly unlikely that an agent will focus on all accounts equally. Assume this scarcity constraint implies that the balances of accounts can only be maximized under restrictions. However, it also makes it possible to define different maximization strategies that agents could pursue by changing the δ_{ought} of their contexts or even choosing new or different contexts. As a result, analyzing agents' strategic choices, as well as their preferences, becomes plausible.
2. Another way to ensure the network is dynamic would be adapting the model in such a way that certain costs were assigned to δ_{ought}. Agents would then have

a new class of resources that would allow them to invest in higher δ_{ought} or a higher $\overrightarrow{\sigma_{ought}}$. Here, maximizing the balances of multiple accounts simultaneously would no longer be possible. The effect would be the same as for the first option. The complexities that could be added to the network of transactions between agents in order to ensure it is dynamic are virtually limitless.

4 Discussion

4.1 Limitations and Simplifications

In its current version, the actor-based model is to be understood as a minimal representation of the complex interactions and dependencies that evolve in networks of relational transactions. We made a number of simplifying assumptions regarding the nature and behavior of agents and the essence of transactions. These simplifications define some of the technical and theoretical limitations of the minimal configuration. In addition, the simplifications are attached to a logic of relational economics in which agents act on the basis of their preferences and uncertain information.

For the sake of simplicity, we chose not to model the details of how cooperation rents are achieved and influence the dynamic of the network. Although the concept of cooperation rent and factor income is certainly implicitly included in the model we propose, they are not yet explicitly observable or measurable. Though the current version of the model is presented here in its minimal configuration, it provides the basis for an even more detailed representation of relational transactions.

4.2 Output Analysis

4.2.1 Theoretical Implications

The relational transaction as an attractor for multiple decision logics is the result of this fundamental transformation. Therefore, an approach to modeling relational transactions is called for that can explain the strategic choices of actors with polyvalent decision logics. The approach here is to use a vector space, with each decision logic making up one dimension of the model. The positioning of the actors and their behavior toward one another is not only of practical interest but also offers an approach to analyzing strategy from a methodological point of view. Actor-based modeling allows us to situate relational transactions, as threads, at the core of the analysis.

The different strategies that agents could pursue by changing the δ_{ought} of their contexts or even choosing new or different contexts are of interest with regard to identifying patterns and studying events. The link to the investment of specific resources is evident. The respective positions of actors and constellations of actors for specific circumstances will be interesting for future research.

At the core of the analysis is the relational rent, as a key motivation to both partners in a transaction. In the approach presented here, the relational rent is an additional income to stakeholders beyond explicit contracts (see Möhrer in this volume) that is generated by the higher productivity of collaborative value creation compared to a discrete individual investment of the actor or the next-best cooperation project. Currently, this aspect cannot be incorporated directly; this step is subject to future advances in modeling research.

The strategy vectors employed by each agent are what we assume drive the model. The ways in which agents apply individual preference orders (contexts) in order to assess other agents and calculate the resources of cooperation that they are *willing* to invest are what define how transactions relocate the parties involved and redefine their abilities to cooperate. This aspect provides the model's long-term dynamic because it is possible to model agents with strategies that can change and adapt over time, depending on their current position.

By displaying the agent's *ability to cooperate* by means of vector $\overrightarrow{\sigma_{is}}$ and his/her *willingness to cooperate* by mapping the strategy vector $\overrightarrow{\sigma_{ought}}$, the model implicitly represents the foundations of the cooperation rent. In order to keep this initial version as simple as possible, we chose not to incorporate an explicit scale of rent measurement for the time being. But as an essential element of relational transactions, we sought to ensure that at least its constitutive elements (ability and willingness) were represented in the model. On the one hand, this makes it possible to draw inductive conclusions about the cooperation rent within the model; on the other hand, it paves the way for future versions that explicitly portray the cooperation rent.

Much of economic theory is based on modeling discrete transactions on markets, but in these times, when organizational networks need to be understood in more detail because they process more relational transactions, it is especially important to discuss proposals like ours that specifically focus on modeling relational transactions. This approach could then be seen as a first step in adapting the subject of analysis as we know it from discrete transactions to relational transactions. Among the many options are:

- Multiple event studies of relational transactions instead of discrete transactions
- Value chain analysis of ostensibly discrete transactions that are revealed to be relational transaction networks (cf. Gereffi, 2018)
- Make, buy or ally analysis and its contractual arrangements (cf. Child et al., 2005)
- Analysis of strategy trigger events and secondary effects (cf. Dyer and Singh, 1998).

The nature of the model presented here is purely agnostic: it does not seek to prove any particular assumptions, e.g. regarding agents' access to perfect information. Rather, it allows for different configurations representing different theoretical frameworks. As a result, the different predictions made on the basis of the assumptions of different economic theories can be reconciled.

Furthermore, one rather powerful implication is that the model allows us to study emerging clusters within a transaction network. As such, it will be possible to analyze whether groups of interacting agents exhibit similar preference structures and if they, according to their respective guiding differences, primarily interact with each other rather than with agents outside their cluster. The methodological option of analyzing patterns or clusters in networks is of help to examine relational transactions as attractors of polyvalent events. The structure formation is a limited dynamic process that can lead to recognizable clusters/patterns. This process from single transactions to cluster formation is a modeled process of constellatory self-unfolding (cf. Wieland in this volume).

Examples of such clusters could be the "green economy" and "dirty economy." Presumably, agents belonging to the latter cluster chiefly or exclusively focus on the organizational system "market," whereas those belonging to the former cluster have adapted the decision logics of the system "market" and are highly involved in the systems "ethics" and "civil society." Such effects would also enable predictions regarding the pull factor of such clusters. It would then be possible to determine whether a given cluster had reached critical mass within the network, allowing it to attract agents from other clusters (cf. Gereffi, 2018; Gereffi et al., 2005).

4.2.2 Practical Implications

The main idea behind this model is that each transaction is relevant for a diverse set of contexts, sub-systems, decision logics and semantic systems. Our goal was to examine the impact of such multi-dimensional relations on agents and the system they constitute. Within a quite narrow scope, the model makes these implicit results explicit. It is exactly this step that can be of added value not only for sciences but also for specific agents. In an increasingly complex world, it is becoming far more important to understand the logics and dynamics of the systems we are predominantly operating in. Agents can only make sound decisions based on a solid understanding of the nature of relations and the relevant parameters of fruitful transactions. Agents could create representations of themselves according to the logic of the model and could predict, based on its mechanisms and rules, how certain strategies and transactions would impact their position in an uncertain environment and how the overall system would respond.

There are multiple conceivable ways of gathering real-world data for this undertaking. One, in particular, seems to be promising—multi-dimensional accounting. By classifying agents' costs and revenues and mapping these inputs and outputs to the dimension of our social system, a clear definition of account balances becomes possible and the multi-dimensional evaluation of real-world transactions becomes practically feasible. As a result, the methods accounting for multi-dimensional data take on new strategic importance.

Account balances and their delta over time can be collected continuously and semi-automatically through interfaces with bookkeeping software and other digital systems that reflect a given firm's activities. These activities may concern financial investments into specific areas or non-financial measures (such as internal policies and regulations) that concern the accounts. In this way, benchmarking and ratings of market competitors can be employed to model decision-making strategies.

To analyze the net effect of investments into the different accounts, key performance indicators must be continuously obtained and monitored. By correlating their changes with the individual investments into the various accounts, the most effective measures for maximizing the individual account balances could be identified, a procedure that would enrich the analysis of strategic choice.

As a second step, the most relevant factors enabling collaboration could also be analyzed. These partially concern the individual account balances, but also the context and dynamics of the collaboration.

Lastly, the reverse effects of specific cooperation on individual account balances could be analyzed. Aggregated effect analysis could yield a quantified model that provides a strategic assessment of the selection and nature of cooperation, as well as firm-specific requirements. In this context, if each partner satisfies the account-specific requirements, a sufficient cooperation corridor can be established.

Methods used to simulate and visualize static snapshots and those used to analyze the dynamics of the proposed model could be beneficial for its broader analysis and interpretation. For this purpose, network-based representations are a natural choice, since they make it possible to show the transactions between all actors, and their relative heaviness. Particularly in the context of strategic planning processes in a world of rapidly increasing complexity, such visualizations provide an optimized overview. They can also be made interactive so that, by selecting specific relationships, more detailed information will appear that characterizes the history and status of the given relationship. Providing such tools to decision-makers in the current era means enhancing their ability to grasp and respond to highly complex situations.

References

Cao, Z., & Lumineau, F. (2015). Revisiting the Interplay between contractual and relational governance: A qualitative and meta-analytic investigation. *Journal of Operations Management, 33–34*, 15–42.

Child, J., Faulkner, D., & Tallman, S. (2005). *Cooperative strategy: Managing alliances, networks, and joint ventures*. Oxford University Press.

Dyer, J. H., & Singh, H. (1998). The relational view: Cooperative strategy and sources of interorganizational competitive advantage. *Academy of Management Review, 23*(4), 660–679.

Dyer, J. H., Singh, H., & Hesterly, W. H. (2018). The relational view revisited: A dynamic perspective on value creation and value capture. *Strategic Management Journal, 39*(12), 3140–3162.

Edwards, J. (2001). Multidimensional contracts in organizational behavior research: An integrative analytical framework. *Organizational Research Methods, 4*(21).

Ellickson, R. C. (1991). *Order without law. How neighbors settle disputes*. Harvard University Press.

Gatti, D. D., Fagiolo, G., Gallegati, M., Richiardi, M., & Russo, A. (Eds.). (2018). *Agent-based models in economics: A toolkit*. Cambridge University Press.

Gereffi, G. (2018). *Global value chains and development*. Cambridge University Press.

Gereffi, G., Humphrey, J., & Sturgeon, T. (2005). The governance of global value chains. *Review of International Political Economy, 12*(1), 78–104.
Gibbons, R., & Roberts, J. (Eds.). (2013). *The handbook of organizational economics.* Princeton University Press.
Gulati, R. (1999). Network location and learning: The influence of network resources and firm capabilities on alliance formation. *Strategic Management Journal, 20*(5), 397–420.
Håkansson, H., & Ford, D. (2002). How should companies interact in business networks? *Journal of Business Research, 55*(2), 133–139.
Herscovici, A. (2019). *Essays on the historicity of capital.* Palgrave Macmillan.
Hodge, B. J., & Johnson, H. J. (1970). *Management and organizational behaviour—A multidimensional approach.* Wiley.
Lavie, D. (2006). The competitive advantage of interconnected firms: An extension of the resource-based view. *Academy of Management Review, 31*(3), 638–658.
Luhmann, N. (1987). Soziale Systeme. Grundriß einer allgemeinen Theorie. In Frankfurt a. M.: Suhrkamp. (Luhmann, N. (1996). Social Systems. Stanford University Press.)
Luhmann, N. (1997). Die Gesellschaft der Gesellschaft (Band 1). In Frankfurt a. M.: Suhrkamp (Luhmann, N. (2012). Theory of society (vol. 1). Stanford University Press.)
Namatame, A., & Chen, S. H. (2016). *Agent-based modeling and network dynamics.* Oxford University Press.
North, D. C. (1990). *Institutions, institutional change and economic performance.* Cambridge University Press.
North, D. C. (2005). *Understanding the process of economic change.* Princeton University Press.
Seers, A., & Chopin, S. (2012). The social production of leadership. In M. Uhl-Bien & S. Ospina (Hrsg.), *Advancing relational leadership research: A dialogue among perspectives* (pp. 43–82). IAP.
Tadelis, S., & Williamson, O. E. (2013). Transaction cost economics. In R. Gibbons & J. Roberts (Eds.), *Handbook of organizational economics* (pp. 159–189). Princeton University Press.
von Müller, A., & Zafiris, E. (2018). *Concept and formalization of constellatory self-unfolding.* Springer.
Wernerfelt, B. (2016). *Adaptation, specialization, and the theory of the firm: Foundations of the resource-based view.* Cambridge University Press.
White, S., & Siu-Yun Lui, S. (2005). Distinguishing costs of cooperation and control in alliances. *Strategic Management Journal, 26*(10), 913–932.
Whitehead, A. N. (1929). *Process and reality: An essay in cosmology.* MacMillan.
Wieland, J. (2018). *Relational economics. Ökonomische theorie der governance wirtschaftlicher transaktionen.* Metropolis.
Wieland, J. (2020). *Relational economics. A political economy.* Springer.
Williamson, O. (1985). The economic institutions of capitalism. Firm, markets, relational contracting. Free Press.
Williamson, O. (1979). Transaction-cost economics: The governance of contractual relations. *The Journal of Law & Economics, 22*(2), 233–261.

Josef Wieland is professor of Institutional Economics, Organizational Governance, Integrity Management, and Transcultural Leadership at Zeppelin University in Friedrichshafen and director of the Leadership Excellence Institute Zeppelin (LEIZ). He is the initiator and president of the German Forum Compliance and Integrity (FCI). He served as the former chairman of the German Network of Business Ethics (DNWE) and currently as the chairman of DNWE's advisory board. He is a member of the National CSR Forum of the BMAS (German Federal Ministry of Labour and Social Affairs) and serves on the jury board for the "CSR Prize" of the German government. He received the Max Weber Prize for Business Ethics of the IW (German Economic Institute) in 1999. In 2004, he received the highly estimated State Research Prize for Applied Research from the State of Baden-Württemberg, Germany. From 2017 until 2021, he was Vice-President (Research) of Zeppelin University, Friedrichshafen, Germany.

Albrecht von Müller is professor at Ludwig-Maximilians-Universität, Munich. He is the founder and chairman of the Parmenides Foundation (www.parmenides-foundation.org). After his Ph.D., he worked at the Max Planck Institute for physics and became head of the "Stability-oriented Security Policy" research program. He was the founding director of the European Center for International Security and developed in 1983 the arms control paradigm of structural defense dominance, which later became a leitmotif of the CFE treaty. Müller developed the visual reasoning language Eidos. He publishes in the fields of philosophy, theoretical physics, complexity theory, cognitive science, and political studies.

Andrej Nikonov has a background in theoretical physics and after working in the Software industry for many years with an increasing focus on data science and artificial intelligence, he became a member of the Parmenides Foundation in 2011. He participated in research that strives for a sound understanding of how human reasoning tackles complexity and how, in turn, humans can be assisted in the endeavors of our modern society. In 2016, he also became the CEO of Cognostics AG (https://www.cognostics.de/). At Cognostics he has focussed on building personalized and AI-enhanced applications, in particular for the areas of eLearning and healthcare.

Leonhard Teichert has a background in philosophy and economics. He focused on exploring the interface between technology and society. Since 2016, he has been working at Cognostics AG, where he is involved in developing AI-based technologies that provide decision-makers with an improved basis for strategy development in an ever more complex world. In close collaboration with the Parmenides Foundation, he is researching system-oriented approaches to complexity management in politics and economics, intending to use new technologies to support rather than replace human cognition and capabilities.

Sebastian Lehrack studied physics and informatics in Munich with a constant focus on computational challenges. After his Master of Science in physics in 2014, he worked towards his Ph.D. in medical physics. In 2018, he defended his thesis on Ionoacoustics, an ultrasound-based in-vivo range detection method for particle cancer therapy, with 'magna cum laude'. After a PostDoc period at the department for medical physics of LMU Munich, he started working as a software developer for Cognostics in 2019. His work there concerns advanced decision support software for oncologists.

Lukas Törner is a doctoral student at the Chair of Institutional Economics at the Zeppelin University, Germany. He applies institutional theory to the management of non-financial data in the context of corporate sustainability. His dissertation project "The Importance of Sustainability Software" is funded by the German Federal Environmental Foundation. Previously, he studied environmental sciences, e-business, and management in Lüneburg, Vienna, and Friedrichshafen.

Part III
Shared Value Creation and Social Responsibility

Bringing Inspiration from the Past: A Renaissance Manual for Merchants

Adrian Zicari

Abstract This essay takes inspiration from one of the first books on business, the "Libro del'arte dela mercatura" (The Book of the Art of Trade), written by Benedetto Cotrugli in 1458, in the then Kingdom of Naples. That book is an occasion to reflect on the lines of relational economics, with the hope that the past can bring us inspiration for the future. First, there is a succinct presentation of the author, his historical context, the purpose and aims of that document. It is a comprehensive illustration of business practices in Italy during the times of the Renaissance, with an elaboration on the highest expectations for merchants. There is a brief comparison with another famous book, the "Summa Arithmetica", written by Fra Luca Pacioli some years later. Second, there is a short description of the book contents. During the four parts of the book, Cotrugli provides advice to the merchant on the principles and tools of trade, religious practice, civic and domestic life. Cotrugli sees the merchant as a learned person, somebody who can refer to different people in a fair, reliable way. He also highlights the value of a merchant's reputation, a point that relates with relational economics' interest in the continuity of relations. Finally, Cotrugli brings the idea of "enough". To Cotrugli's mind, profit need not be too much, but sufficient for living a good life. This latter point is relevant to the contemporary discussion on the planetary limits and much connected with the interest of relational economics for sustainable growth. Finally, there are some considerations about that book, in the light of our growing discipline of relational economics. Among others, a reflection about the scope of relational economics analysis, raising attention to the level of persons and families, a call for exploring time horizons other than the standard annual period and an invitation for a renovated look at business ethics. Relational economics as a nascent theoretical perspective can only profit from looking at different contexts and historical facts as an occasion for scholarly reflection. In this case, a manual for merchants, written more than 500 years ago, becomes an opportunity for some tentative comments around relational economics.

Keywords Relational economics · Benedetto Cotrugli · Accounting · Management · Merchants · Renaissance · Luca Pacioli

A. Zicari (✉)
ESSEC Business School, Cergy, France
e-mail: b00265409@essec.edu

L. Biggiero et al. (eds.), *The Relational View of Economics*, Relational Economics and Organization Governance, https://doi.org/10.1007/978-3-030-86526-9_6

1 Introduction

The relational economics project calls for a more comprehensive consideration of some frequently overlooked aspects of modern economic life. Among others, the importance of time in shaping long-term relationships among economic actors plays a key role (Wieland, 2014, p. 105) and the complex interactions among partners and competitors (Wieland, 2020, p. 43). Far from the conventional depiction of economic life as a collection of discrete, short-term, one-time transactions, which impact mainly in the local sphere, relational economics presents a more realistic, overarching view of how people deal with economic activities nowadays. Relational economics concerns, instead, with complex, network business agreements, kept and developed over time, and possibly at a larger scale, either international or global.

This unfolding intellectual project implies revisiting many realms of business studies, in the understanding that those associated disciplines can also benefit from the larger conceptual horizon of relational economics. Besides, the large scope of interest of relational economics, conversant for instance with politics, culture and religion, can further enrichen business disciplines, and provide new perspectives for both scholars and practitioners.

For this tentative inquiry, I take inspiration from one of the first books on business, the "Libro del'arte dela mercatura" (The Book of the Art of Trade), written by Benedetto Cotrugli in 1458, in the then Kingdom of Naples. This book is one of the earliest writings about business and it is arguably the first book that describes double-entry accounting (Hernández Esteve, 1992). While this book has been known for a long time, a recent discovery of an early edition of this book aroused the interest of accounting scholars (Sangster & Rossi, 2018). That edition, found in the National Library of Malta, has been translated to English in 2017 (Cotrugli, 1458). From now on, I refer to this translation done by John Francis Phillimore, edited by Carlo Ferraro and Giovanni Favero, and published in 2017.

This chapter does not pretend to be an academic study on Cotrugli's book, a task already done by other researchers, many of whom I cite in these pages. This chapter takes instead that book as an occasion to propose a reflection on the line of relational economics, with the hope that the past can bring us inspiration for the future.

While exploring the past may at first glance seem a mere "academic" pursue, there are in fact several reasons for this choice. First, the Renaissance was a moment of dramatic change, when many of the advances that characterize modern life began. For instance, Gutenberg's invention of the press, improvements in navigation technology and the gradual development of merchant companies (Adamo et al., 2020). As a moment of change, discovery and growth, the Renaissance remains a historical period that still speaks to our contemporary times. Second, the Renaissance witnessed the consolidation of a sophisticated system of money exchange and commercial credit all along Mediterranean ports (p. 67). This complex network of international trade, frequently regulated by the Lex Mercatoria (Leeson, 2006), was arguably a precedent of today's globalization. Third, and much related to the previous point, commercial and managerial practices at the time had gradually developed, mainly in an empirical way and with scarce systematization. Cotrugli was among the first who put in writing, in a systematic way, how these practices were happening at the time. Thus, this book gives us, through its fresh account of business practices in the Renaissance, an opportunity to reflect on our current time.

The remainder of this chapter is organized as follows. First, a succinct presentation of the historical context of Cotrugli's book. Then, a brief description of the book contents, with emphasis on the advice that Cotrugli provides to merchants. Finally, a discussion of Cotrugli's book in the light of our nascent discipline of relational economics.

2 Benedetto Cotrugli and His Book

Benedetto Cotrugli (ca. 1416–1469) was a merchant born in Ragusa (Dubrovnik), at that time an independent maritime republic, which is now part of Croatia. While he belonged to a family of merchants for at least three generations (Favero, 2017), it seems that Cotrugli had originally planned for an intellectual career. An unexpected situation, probably his father's death, forced him to abandon his academic studies in order to take over the family business (p. 24). Cotrugli began a career in business that led him to travel and live in several ports in the Mediterranean. He lived in Naples, where he was in charge of the Mints of the Kingdom (Perfetto, 2017), a prestigious role at that time. During a plague in Naples in 1458, Cotrugli settled some kilometers away from the city, in the castle of Serpico, now Sorbo Serpico, where he found the time to write down this book (p. 172). This was not the last book written by Cotrugli. Some years later, he also wrote a manual for sailors, "De navigatione", based on his extended experience and observation in the seas (Falchetta, 2013).

Cotrugli writes from his particular position as a scholar-turned merchant, having lived many years away from his natal Ragusa and being active in the civic life of the Kingdom of Naples. His stated purpose is to improve his profession (pp. 24–25). He thus makes a conscious effort to accurately describe commercial practices (or "best practices", as we would say today), with the aim of educating his fellow merchants and raising the reputation of trade as a professional calling. Among those commercial practices, he provides the first written description of double-entry accounting, in the now-famous Chapter XIII of the first part of his book (Hernández Esteve, 1992). While Cotrugli did not "create" double-entry accounting, he describes in detail, in a systematic way, the practices done at the time by professional merchants.

Beyond the historical importance of this Chapter XIII, the merit of the book lies in a comprehensive picture of the exemplary merchant, including advice on how a merchant should conduct his personal, civic and religious life. Besides, Cotrugli emphasizes the importance of trade for the prosperity of a city, thus making the case for the social role of merchants (p. 25). Possibly in order to signal the soundness of his arguments, Cotrugli makes frequent citations from classical authors, like Cicero and Seneca, along with copious references from Christian sources, like Thomas Aquinas, John Chrysostom and Saint Paul. Indeed, this kind of erudition would not be alien to a merchant, who according to Cotrugli should have a broad education, be able to speak well (p. 118) and be knowledgeable not only about the liberal arts but also about other disciplines like cosmography, philosophy, law and theology (p. 121).

While Cotrugli advises merchants to be proficient in Latin, the common language of the time (p. 118), he still chooses to write his book in the vernacular (i.e. ancient Italian), to make it more accessible to practicing merchants. While Cotrugli feels the need to justify this choice (p. 26), at that time many writers have already been using the vernacular, as it has been the case for Boccaccio, Petrarca and Dante. Besides, and according to the use at the time, he presents his book as a long letter sent to a colleague, a merchant named Francesco di Stefano, and he duly ends his writing by lauding the King of Naples (p. 172).

This book continues a tradition of manuals for merchants that trace back to the Middle Ages. Caunedo de Potro (2011) posits that more than a dozen manuals for merchants existed at that time. Many of these books were written by merchant-writers themselves (Suárez Pineda, 2012). These manuals were mostly used for training aspiring merchants in the "scuole d'abbaco" (abacus schools) that existed in Northern Italy since the thirteenth century (Carruthers & Espeland, 1991). However, the scope of those books was far beyond the mere description of accounting techniques. Caunedo de Potro (2011) highlights the role of these books as guidelines for professional behavior, thus presenting in writing the first notions of Business Ethics.

As Garstka (2018) poses, there was no distinction between ethical and technical aspects in those early works. This is the case of Cotrugli's book, where prescriptions for commercial practices are normally embedded in ethical considerations. For instance, he insists that a merchant has to be a good payer (p. 53) and has to promptly write down records of his transactions, in order to prevent mistakes. Indeed, one should not trust a merchant that acts otherwise (p. 54). For Cotrugli, best practices are also ethical practices.

A comparison can be made with another book, the "Summa Arithmetica" written some decades later (1494) by Fra Luca Pacioli. Pacioli was a Franciscan monk, living in Northern Italy, who had been a merchant before taking his religious vows (Sangster, 2018). His book is a pedagogical treatise on arithmetic and geometry that includes a systematic description of double-entry bookkeeping (Thompson, 1991). While this book appeared later than that of Cotrugli, its influence has been so important that Pacioli remains rightly considered as the "Father of Accounting" (Sangster, 2018; Tua, 2017). Similar to Cotrugli, Pacioli is much concerned about ethical issues. For instance, he contends that profits have to be lawful and warns against having two sets of accounting records (Fischer, 2000). While the two books remain different in their pedagogical approach and content, both distill practical considerations for the use of merchants.

Another coincidence for both Cotrugli and Pacioli is their view on religion. For both of them, religious practice is not distinct from the professional life of a merchant. Sangster (2018) claims that Pacioli wanted not only to educate merchants but also to attract them to the faith. For instance, Pacioli prescribes the writing of a pious invocation at the beginning of any accounting book, an indication that Cotrugli also gives in his Chapter XIII. Far from this being a courtesy, or perhaps a legitimation tactic, as Carruthers and Espeland (1991, p. 38) tend to think, one may instead see this indication as consistent with the whole set of prescriptions that both Pacioli and Cotrugli give to merchants, for whom eternal salvation is the horizon of every person, this including the good merchant.

In conclusion, Cotrugli's book is a complex work that admits different readings. It is a description (and prescription) of best trade practices, including the notable chapter on accounting, the first-ever written on the subject. It is also a manual for aspiring merchants, including rich advice on many aspects of their lives, including considerations that we would deem today as "private" (for instance, how to raise children so that they can continue the family trade and spiritual reflections). It is, of course, an invaluable source for historians of business and accounting. Despite the five centuries that separate our time from that of Cotrugli, and all the consequent changes, the contemporary reader can still find this book an insightful read.

While this book is a complex one, a document that we can approach from many viewpoints, it also remains a coherent whole. It presents a complete program for becoming a good merchant in the context of the Italian Renaissance. Consequently, when analyzing this book, one needs to avoid reducing it to its mere technical aspects, valuable and original as those aspects can be. In the next part of this chapter, I will present the book in more detail, highlighting those aspects that are more relevant for our reflections on relational economics.

3 The "Libro del'arte dela mercatura"

The book consists of a short preface and four parts. After a brief preface, the first part presents trade as a subject, bringing definitions and a comprehensive perspective of commercial activities. The second part deals with religious issues. The third part focuses on the civil and political life of the merchant, while the final part deals with the family of the merchant. For a contemporary reader, this choice of issues seems curious, to say the least. We would nowadays consider many of the aforementioned questions as "private", and consequently hardly appropriate for a professional manual. However, in the mind of Cotrugli (and perhaps in the mindset of that time), professional life is not separated from religious, civil and domestic life. Spanning such different issues, the book has some changes in its tone: sometimes recurring to erudite references and the Gospels, sometimes referring to anecdotes that seem known by merchants or citing popular sayings. However, the whole book develops an organized argument, with a clear structure. One may perceive Cotrugli's purpose of providing a condensed, practical tool for aspiring merchants, covering a wide range of issues in a consistent way.

The Preface briefly presents the purpose and aims of the book. Cotrugli explains that when he had to abandon his academic studies, he realized that the state of the merchant profession was far from adequate, and he consequently wanted to write this book for the education of his fellow merchants (p. 24). He claims that there are rules and principles for trade that a good merchant has to master in order to succeed (p. 25).

The first part of the book is the most "academic" one, in the sense that it includes definitions (i.e. what a merchandise is; what is trade), and typologies (i.e. who can be a merchant and who cannot). Thus, this first part is presented in a rigorous, scholarly way. It is also the longest part of the book, comprising 19 different chapters. From the very beginning, ethical considerations are present. For instance, the price has to be fair, and some issues can never be sold (i.e. stolen or pawned goods) (p. 32).

Another curiosity in this book is the emphasis on the qualities of the merchant. Cotrugli devotes the whole Chapter III to the personal characteristics of the merchant. This chapter appears before the more technical chapters, thus emphasizing the primacy of the merchant's character. A young person with a natural inclination to the profession should be educated from the earliest age (p. 37). For Cotrugli, a merchant is above all, an educated and dignified person. Health is also important, as a merchant has to travel frequently by sea, by horse and by foot.

Merchants have to choose a proper location for their activities. A dynamic city, with other merchants, which enjoys peace, would bring more opportunities for a profitable trade. For many reasons, some places may not be so conducive to business and the wise merchant would consequently avoid them. Cotrugli also advises to live in cities where the Lex Mercatoria applies (p. 40) as he considers it to be less prone to legal litigation. This is consistent with Leeson's (2006) claim that the Lex Mercatoria, as a private system, relies on the interactions among trustworthy merchants operating in different ports. In this sense, Cotrugli's insistence on ethical conduct also relates to the merchant's need to maintain a consistent reputation all over different commercial places.

After a description of barter and cash transactions, Cotrugli devotes a relatively long chapter to sales on credit. Far from a mere description, the author justifies the need for credit, as it facilitates transactions that are beneficial in themselves (p. 47). He claims that these transactions are lawful, even if the merchant should prefer to sell by cash. He nevertheless gives a collection of advice on credit selling, putting together practical and ethical considerations. For instance, not to concede credit for large amounts or for long periods (p. 50), or to people who may eventually have trouble in paying back (p. 52). After selling on credit, the merchant has to constantly monitor the accounts receivable so that collections are not delayed (p. 52). By the same token, a merchant has to maintain a reputation for being a good payer (p. 54). One may see that credit remains subservient to the commercial transaction, and it is justified as long as there is a fair trade. In Cotrugli's mind, credit is merely a financial support that facilitates a real transaction.

The author takes a similar stand toward money exchange. Chapter XII describes a sophisticated system of exchanges operating at that time over the main ports in the Mediterranean (e.g. Valence, Barcelona or Venice). This early precedent of today's bureaux de change was useful to travelers and made commercial transactions in different currencies possible. Cotrugli argues for the legitimacy of these transactions, pointing to their usefulness and citing Aquinas. The author takes an apologetic tone at this point, as he is aware of the need of money exchange for economic progress. At the same time, Cotrugli sees financial tools (i.e. credit selling and money exchange) only as subordinate to commercial transactions, and his viewpoint remains far away from any speculation detached from the real economy.

Chapter X is a small treatise in business, and it would merit another essay. Most of his advice sounds incredibly modern. For instance, when he exhorts merchants to become experts, to specialize in a particular activity or line of business, and to diversify among different projects, but not too many of them. He warns against having excess cash positions and buying luxury real estate in the countryside. Besides, he advises merchants not to enter into politics. Cotrugli also gives plenty of advice in Chapter XVIII; this time more on the line of temperance. His idea is that merchants have a public role in the life of the city (p. 79), and in consequence, they have to refrain from any inappropriate behavior. For instance, Cotrugli advises against playing games of chance, doing falsifications or smuggling (p. 80–81). Being a merchant, in Cotrugli's eyes, implies a higher standard of conduct than that of the average person.

Benedetto Cotrugli gained a place in the history of accounting (and in history tout court) because of his Chapter XIII, the first description of double-entry bookkeeping. In the context of the book, this chapter remains a short one, less than 5% of the book length. Despite its brevity, the chapter remains a core element in the book. The author emphasizes the importance of accounting for a merchant, putting forward two arguments. First, keeping accounting records in a proper way would prevent problems with other merchants (p. 70). This advice is consistent with the context of an increasingly complex economy at the time when individual merchants were beginning to have different commercial partnerships. It was not uncommon for a merchant to be simultaneously involved in commercial activities in several cities (p. 65), and consequently, merchants could not rely on their memory alone. According to Adamo et al. (2020), the increased complexity of business relationships at that time implied the need to provide periodical information to business partners.

Second, Cotrugli sees accounting as a powerful learning tool and a way for a better understanding of the business (p. 70). A contemporary reader would see an early intuition about management accounting, and its importance for managerial decisions. While Cotrugli does not present analytical tools (e.g. ratios, key performance indicators), which possibly were not yet developed at the time, he still suggests merchants to read their own accounting, in order to learn. Both arguments (i.e. accounting as records for reliable reporting, and accounting as support for merchants' learning) are central in Cotrugli's mind. Besides, he criticizes those merchants who fail to appropriately record business transactions (p. 70). In a similar fashion, Carruthers and Espeland (1991) argue that record keeping would signal respectability for a merchant.

The author provides a simple procedure for keeping a set of accounting books, bringing simple examples that one can easily understand. The proposed system remains straightforward, with only three books: the Day Book, the Ledger and a Scrapbook. These books can be composed of several volumes, which have to be organized in alphabetical order. However, the author does not enter into much detail, consequently leaving merchants free to adapt the accounting system to their specific needs. We are thus far from contemporary accounting regulation, and its complexity.

Three points strike the contemporary reader of this famous Chapter XIII. The first point is how Cotrugli presents the purpose of accounting. He sees accounting only as a supporting tool for commercial operations, not as a discipline in itself. Thus, there are no professional accountants; there are instead merchants who prepare their own accounting, according to their own needs and following their own criteria. Besides, reporting for external parties is not a key concern at this time. Indeed, Cotrugli does not prescribe models or guidelines for such a reporting, even if we may infer that some kind of disclosure existed, at least to those merchant partners involved in specific commercial projects (Adamo et al., 2020).

Second, the scope of accounting. Carruthers and Espeland (1991) describe how individual projects gradually gave place first to partnerships among merchants, and then to the creation of companies. This process allowed addressing greater-sized projects during longer horizons. However, Cotrugli is not yet there, as his scope remains the individual merchant, and eventually his family. While we can consider his choice a bit narrow, it is consistent with his personal story, and possibly the situation of many of his readers at that time.

Third, the horizon of accounting. Curiously, time is completely absent from Chapter XIII. Cotrugli prescribes a model for recording transactions, and there is no indication about how *and when* to analyze those records. Adamo et al. (2020) explain that there has been a gradual harmonization of reporting horizons from pluri-annual toward annual periods and that this harmonization process is related to the need to provide information to merchant partners. Cotrugli's perspective of business as a personal (or familiar) endeavor leads him to a contrasting view on time. Instead of considering annual periods, he proposes a pluri-annual period of seven years. The seventh year should be a sabbatical year when each merchant should close ongoing operations, collect accounts receivables and analyze the accounting books (p. 82). This period has to be a moment for both reflection and a well-deserved rest. As he usually does, Cotrugli brings numerous citations from the Bible and other respectable sources (i.e. Aristotle, St Augustine) in support of his idea.

This idea of a commercial Sabbath has two implications. First, it confirms Cotrugli's view of accounting having a personal, instead of a corporate scope. This seventh-year cycle supposes the physical and spiritual benefit of the merchant. Such consideration would be meaningless in the context of a legal corporation, by their nature impersonal and abstract, which has no place in Cotrugli's mind. Second, this personal horizon has a purpose, which is the improvement, the development of the merchant as a person, including his relationship with God.

This latter point connects with the second part of Cotrugli's book, which deals with religion. For a contemporary reader, that a manual for merchants includes a whole part devoted to religion seems strange, to say the least. However, in the context of the complete book, this part is consistent, and it illustrates many points raised by the author all over the book. One has to remember that Cotrugli's purpose is to help merchants to become better persons, and in Cotrugli's mind, this necessarily includes their spiritual life. Besides, the content of this chapter would possibly not qualify as "religious literature" by today's standards. Cotrugli intends instead to provide concrete religious advice to merchants, adapted to their situation and lifestyle.

Three important points to note here. First, despite Cotrugli's stated aim of bringing legitimacy to his profession, he does not look for religion as a patina of respectability. He appears to be a sincere believer, and all his advice to merchants seems to be well-intentioned. Merchants should attend the mass (p. 86), pray with fervor and constantly (p. 90) and be generous in giving alms to the poor (p. 92). In Cotrugli's perspective, a merchant can be (indeed, should be) a pious person.

Second, Cotrugli wants the merchant not only to be devout but also to be learned about religion, particularly in issues related to professional practice. For the author, what we call today business ethics is not distinct from religion. Cotrugli devotes a whole chapter to matters of conscience, with practical and concrete examples for the merchant. For instance, a contract that includes penalties for insolvency would not be usury (p. 99), and a profit related to risk-taking would be legitimate (p. 104). Some advice speaks more to today's readers; for instance, when he is against creating cartels (p. 105) or cornering the market (p. 101). Cotrugli goes on to present a distinction between legal and ethical issues, explaining that laws can permit some contracts that are nevertheless illegitimate (p. 104).

Third, when analyzing commercial practices, the author strives to find a middle ground. He acknowledges that contracts need to be flexible and that they have to adapt to the changing realities of trade at that time. He consequently argues for the legitimacy of several business practices (e.g. credit selling, money exchange, forward selling), as these activities make trade possible. At the same time, he firmly set limits to excesses in those practices, and insists that profits have to be fair.

Cotrugli wrote this chapter in a very different time from ours, in the context of Christianity before the Reformation. A contemporary reader may sometimes feel that some of Cotrugli's advice in this second chapter does not apply nowadays, or that at least does not apply to business people who are not Christians. However, the core of his advice to merchants remains valuable to this day, whatever their beliefs may be. Recommendations such as acting in an ethical manner and discerning the ethical implications of business practices are of timeless value.

The third part of the book deals with the civic life of the merchant. Here again Cotrugli makes no distinction between profession and what we could call today "private life". Nothing is private for merchants, being that they hold a public role in the life of the city. Elaborating on the arguments previously raised in the preface, Cotrugli reminds of the importance of the merchant's profession for the city. The merchant has to enjoy a high reputation (p. 115), be reliable and not greedy (p. 127). The merchant has to speak well in public (p. 138) and behave virtuously. According to Cotrugli, the merchant has to be generous, but not as much as noblemen (p. 130). Cotrugli features the Florentine Cosimo de' Medici as a role model for merchants (p. 123), thus proposing a high standard for his merchant readers.

While this third part is sometimes repetitive, and some comments overlap with other pages in the book, the message remains valuable. Cotrugli sees the need to bring legitimacy to a novel profession that he considers necessary for the city's prosperity, and he sets a high bar for merchants, who have to lead an irreproachable life. He presents business as a noble calling and fair profit as a legitimate objective. Far from a being simple endeavor, this new profession calls for intelligent and well-prepared people, with an education that goes beyond mere technical tools.

The book concludes with the fourth part, which is devoted to the merchant's house. Curiously, this part is the second-longest part in the book, a clear indication of how important family life is in the eyes of Cotrugli. Here again, the contemporary reader realizes that for Cotrugli, no distinction between home and business exists. In this fourth part we see, perhaps more than in the other parts of the book, how much the context changed from Cotrugli's times to today. This is particularly the case in what respects to the roles of husbands and wives and parent's expectations toward children. Despite those important changes, some comments remain interesting for the contemporary reader.

First, Cotrugli proposes some initial notions of what we could call today wealth management. For the author, the profits of trade cannot remain forever in the commercial operation. Reinvestment in the business remains of course necessary, but at some moment, profit has to come back to the familiar domain. Cotrugli suggests, for instance, investing in real estate, with some diversification. The merchant should buy two villas, one that generates agricultural income, the other for the family holidays. However, the merchant should not remain much in the latter villa, as this would distract the merchant from taking care of business (p. 144).

Second, the merchant should not postpone retirement, which ideally should happen sometime after being 50 years old. According to Cotrugli, the wise merchant, having cumulated a sizeable wealth, has to liquidate his possessions, in order to assure that his daughters and sons enjoy good situations. The merchant and his wife should maintain some wealth for themselves, in order to retire to one of their villas. There, the merchant should pray, revise his accounting books and his conscience (p. 170).

From these two points, we see again that Cotrugli's scope is the individual entrepreneur, perhaps the family business. He is not considering any organization beyond the family and the modern corporation is alien to his mindset. Consequently, accounting's horizon does not correspond to annual periods, as any standardized horizon would be artificial in Cotrugli's eyes. For the author, the appropriate horizon for accounting is a succession of seven years, based on the biblical tradition and consistent with business projects doable by a single person. Those seven-year horizons, cumulated several times over the lifetime of the merchant, are the central matter of the "examination of conscience" that the merchant will do at the end of his life. This attentive examination of the credits and debits of a lifetime is consistent with the notion of fairness as a central virtue for the good merchant.

4 Some Reflections for the Relational Economics Project

In this chapter, we attempt to use a historical book as an occasion to reflect around the lines of relational economics. The context presented in that book differs much from that of our times; however, we can still make sense of it. Dealing with a story from other times but still comprehensible represents an opportunity to reflect on our time. Thus, a modern reading of a manual for Renaissance merchants can spark some reflections for the relational economics project.

Before going on, I need to clarify two points. First, I refrain from making any value judgment on the historical context of that book. I also abstain from comparing Cotrugli's times to our times, and from discussing whether those times were better or worse. These kinds of judgments are out of the scope of this chapter, and they possibly correspond to historians.

Second, one cannot read Cotrugli's book anachronistically. It is true that this book contains the first written account of what we call today financial accounting, plus some notions of management accounting, and some rudiments of management and business ethics. However, one cannot consider this book as a treatise on any of these fields, as Cotrugli's intent was less to theorize than to present some practical guidelines for his fellow merchants at that time. Consequently, one has to see that book for what it is, a comprehensive illustration of business practices in Italy during the times of the Renaissance, with an elaboration about the highest expectations for merchants. That is, a collection of facts, which are far from us, but we can still use them for our reflection.

In terms of scope, Cotrugli focuses on the merchant's household. Consequently, the accounting process and investment decisions refer to that perimeter. There is no reporting to external parties, while we may imagine some kind of accountability to partners, who are peers to the merchant. We are far from today's central role of shareholders, and their usual place as the main recipients of reporting. Furthermore, and as we saw before, the merchant takes his accounting book with him when he retires. These books remain personal, and they record his story as a merchant. Eventually, some of his children could follow his father's footsteps, as it was the case of Benedetto Cotrugli himself. Nevertheless, the young merchants will be on their own, as there is no notion of company. These new merchants would consequently have their own accounting books.

For relational economics, there is a possible reflection about the scope of our analysis. We, scholars, are much used (and trained for) doing analysis at the level of companies, and we are increasingly aware of the need to make sense of what happens at a higher level, that is when companies develop networks of cooperation. We are perhaps not so much used to this analysis at the lower level of families, and we may ask ourselves if such a level of analysis would cast further light on our understanding of economic processes. We could perhaps look at some economic processes that happen at the level of persons and families, for instance, how wealth is cumulated, diversified, invested and eventually transferred between generations.

Another consideration related to families is how those families prepare the next generation. Cotrugli emphasizes the role of the family as the first educators of the future merchant and the importance of making the young aspiring merchants work in the business as soon as possible. While the "scuole d'abbaco" (the early precedents of our business schools) existed at the time, the author presents the education of the young merchant in a family context.

In terms of horizon, Cotrugli is definitely not thinking of an annual period. This is consequent with his focus on the merchant, and not on companies. For Cotrugli, there is no need to harmonize accounting periods, as the extent of those periods matters only to the merchant. For instance, in that book, investment decisions have two different horizons. When they are in the merchant business, their horizon is the seven-year period. When they are in the family (i.e. real estate), their horizon is instead longer, that is, the active life of the merchant (i.e. until the point when the merchant retires and transmits the family wealth to his children).

For relational economics, one may explore other time horizons, beyond the standard annual period, thus acknowledging that annualized horizons are merely a practical convention. As it happens with conventions, they are not written on the marble, and we would do well in considering other possibilities. Exploring complementary views on time (Quattrone, 2005) may further develop the possibilities of relational economics. For instance, should we (i.e. a person, a company, a community) pursue growth all the time, every year, at the same pace? Should we take sometimes a sabbatical time, as Cotrugli suggested?

In terms of business ethics, it is clear that for Cotrugli, that discipline is an integral part of business, not an appendix or a mere addition. This is in itself an important takeaway for our time, both for research and pedagogy. There is another point about the conceptual basis of business ethics. At that time, and in the context of the Italian Renaissance, Cotrugli could easily bring support from religious sources. We see that he generously cites the scripture, classical philosophers and saints whenever he wants to explore the legitimacy of new business practice. Nowadays, while the need to discern the ethical implications of business remains, we are in a globalized, plural society, with different coexisting beliefs. Thus, a mere call for any religious source, respectable as it may be, would not be universally convincing. There is thus a need to identify general principles that can be widely accepted among different parties.

Particularly in today's dynamic, unpredictable world, the identification of those general principles becomes more urgent. Hopefully, those timeless principles can be applied, similarly as Cotrugli did at his time, in order to discern the changing business situations and the new tools that appear nowadays. Furthermore, one can appreciate Cotrugli's prudent stand toward the "financial innovations" of the time. While he is open to progress, he constantly questions the ethical implications of those innovations, and he only approves them as long as he sees a contribution to the common good. In this sense, his prudent and balanced position is an early precedent for the relational economics concern for "the predominance of financial markets in the economic system…" (Biggiero et al., 2020).

Cotrugli also has the merit of bringing back the viewpoint of the person and her/his conscience. To his mind, business ethics is not a mere issue of compliance. It is not the blind, tick-the-box adherence to this or that guideline or standard. It is instead the realm of the merchant's educated conscience, which allows the merchant to discern the ethical implications of business decisions. While the discernment process that proposes Cotrugli may be done differently today, one may appreciate the idea of businesspersons doing their ethical discernment themselves before (or instead of) "outsourcing" that responsibility to a compliance department. As we may well see, Cotrugli does not underestimate merchants!

Much linked to the former point is a consideration on business education. For Cotrugli, an education for business is part of education as a whole. This education is not limited to technical tools, even if they are necessary, as Cotrugli insists. Furthermore, the author's emphasis on the learned merchant goes far beyond good manners and etiquette. He thinks of a universal person, somebody who can refer to different people in a fair, reliable way. One can easily see here an early precedent to the ongoing reflections on the role of transcultural management in relational economics (Wieland, 2020, p. 105).

Cotrugli highlights the value of a merchant's reputation. One may imagine that the author himself has been a successful merchant, whose creditworthiness was acknowledged in several ports in the Mediterranean. What Cotrugli learned from his experience in the trade, at the level of an individual merchant, is today also relevant at the level of a company. Furthermore, the instant velocity of social networks today can transform a reputational issue anywhere from local to global in a few seconds. This echoes relational economics' interest in "the continuity of relations…(as)…a source of economic and societal value creation in its own…" (Biggiero et al., 2020).

Finally, Cotrugli brings the idea of "enough". After creating enough wealth for his family, the merchant should retire, and devote his last years to preparing for eternal life. While the contemporary reader may (or may not so much) agree with this plan for retirement, to Cotrugli's mind it is clear that business is not an end in itself. Of course, business implies, indeed needs a profit. However, this profit does not need to be too much, but sufficient for living a good life. This kind of reflection can be particularly relevant to the contemporary discussion on the planetary limits, and much connected with the interest of relational economics for sustainable growth.

Relational economics as a nascent theoretical perspective can only profit from looking at different contexts, looking at historical facts as an occasion for scholarly reflection. In this case, a manual for merchants, written more than 500 years ago, becomes an opportunity for some tentative comments around relational economics. It is my hope that these considerations contribute, at least modestly, to the further elaboration of relational economics.

References

Adamo, S., Alexander, D., & Fasiello, R. (2020). Time and accounting in the middle ages: An Italian-based analysis. *Accounting History, 25*(1), 53–68.

Biggiero, L., de Jongh, D., Priddat, B., Wieland, J., & Zicari, A. (2020). Manifesto for a relational economics.

Carruthers, B., & Espeland, W. (1991). Accounting for rationality: Double-entry bookkeeping and the rhetoric of economic rationality. *American Journal of Sociology, 97*(1), 31–69.

Caunedo de Potro , B. (2011). Algunos aspectos de los manuales de mercaduría. El valor del aprendizaje. La pereza es llave de la pobreza. *Anuario de Estudios Medievales, 41*/2, 803–817.

Cotrugli, B. (1458). The book of the art of trade, Eds. Ferraro, C. & Favero G. Palgrave Macmillan.

Falchetta, P. (2013). Benedetto Cotrugli et son traité De navigatione (1464–1465). *The Historical Review/La Revue Historique, 9*, 53–62.
Favero, G. (2017). A new edition of Benedetto Cotrugli's the book of the art of trade, Eds. Carraro and Favero, Benedetto Cotrugli—The Book of the Art of Trade.
Fischer, M. (2000). Luca Pacioli on business profits. *Journal of Business Ethics, 25*(4), 299–312.
Garstka, M. (2018) Ethical issues in the early works of accounting, Annales. *Ethics in Economic Life, 21*(8), Special Issue, 7–15.
Hernández Esteve, E. (1992). Benedetto Cotrugli, precursor de Pacioli en la exposición de la partida doble. *Cuadernos De Estudios Empresariales, 2*, 87–99.
Leeson, P. (2006). Cooperation and conflict, Evidence on self-enforcing arrangements and heterogeneous groups. *American Journal of Economics and Sociology, 65*(4), 891–907.
Perfetto, S. (2017). Nota critica sulla diffusione della partita doppia nei libri mastri delle zecche del Regno di Napoli. *La Firma Di Benedetto Cotrugli, Revista Española De Contabilidad, 26*, 6–26.
Quattrone, P. (2005). Is time spent, passed or counted? The missing link between time and accounting history. *The Accounting Historians Journal, 32*(1), 185–208.
Sangster, A. (2018). Pacioli's lens: God, humanism, Euclid, and the rhetoric of double entry. *The Accounting Review, 93*(2), 299–314.
Sangster, A., & Rossi, F. (2018). Benedetto Cotrugli on double entry bookkeeping. *De computis – Revista Española de Historia de la Contabilidad, 15*(2), 22–38.
Suárez Pineda, J. (2012). Benedetto Cotrugli Raugeo: Padre de la gestión moderna. *Teuken Bidikay, 3*, 99–120.
Thompson, G. (1991). Is accounting rhetorical? Methodology, Luca Pacioli and printing. *Accounting, Organizations and Society, 16*(5/6), 572–599. https://doi.org/10.1016/0361-3682(91)90042-D
Tua, J. (2017). Pacioli continúa vigente quinientos años después. *Revista AECA, Número, 117*, 9–12.
Wieland, J. (2014). *Governance ethics: Global value creation, economic organization and normativity*. Springer.
Wieland, J. (2020). *Relational economics. A political economy*. Springer.

Adrián Zicari is professor in the Accounting and Management Control Department at ESSEC Business School. He is Academic Director of the Council on Business & Society. Born in Argentina, he holds a doctorate from Universidad Nacional de Rosario, Argentina, and an MBA from Universidad Adolfo Ibáñez, Chile. Before entering academia, he was a controller in healthcare organizations in Argentina. He is also honorary representative of Buenos Aires City in Paris. His research interests include measurement systems and management practice in sustainability. His work appears in several academic journals: Journal of Business Ethics, Journal of Cleaner Production, Comptabilité-Contrôle-Audit, Corporate Social Responsibility, and Environmental Management, Social and Environmental Accountability Journal, BMC Health Services Research, and Harvard Business Review—Latin American Edition. He is one of the series editors for the Relational Economics and Organizational Governance book series, Springer.

Shared Value Statement: New Perspectives on Measuring Business Value Creation

Marco Möhrer

Abstract Value creation is the pivotal point in economic analysis and business management. But our current accounting systems only recognize a small part of the values companies actually create for their stakeholders. In this chapter, I will develop some ideas on how we can reimagine the total performance of a business and what this change in perspective means for the measurement of business value creation. I will introduce the shared value statement (SVS) as a reporting instrument that is supposed to give a broader view about the tangible and intangible values that stakeholders can appropriate by participating in a company's value creation network. I will end with some conclusions for the development of a relational accounting of the firm.

Keywords Shared value measurement · Sustainability controlling · Intangibles accounting · Relational accounting · Value-added analysis

1 Introduction

Is a company investment in employee training simply a cost driver for the business? How do you treat company expenses in financial reporting that aim at reducing the ecological footprint of your organization? And what about the costs for safeguarding human rights in the supply chain? In traditional value-added analysis (Arangies et al., 2008; Cox, 1979; Gilchrist, 1971; Machado et al., 2015; Morley, 1978a, b; Renshall et al., 1979; Riahi-Belkaoui, 1992, 1999; Rutherford, 1977; Suojanen, 1954), such transactions are accounted only as input costs of the production process. The result is that their value is not considered part of the calculated value added of a company, although these transactions obviously lead to an increase in value for the affected stakeholders. In other words, we currently measure business value creation without counting for all the *incomes* that have been produced in a firm's value creation network. In this chapter, I will argue that the management of stakeholder relations

M. Möhrer (✉)
Zeppelin University, Friedrichshafen, Germany
e-mail: m.moehrer@zeppelin-university.net

L. Biggiero et al. (eds.), *The Relational View of Economics*, Relational Economics and Organization Governance, https://doi.org/10.1007/978-3-030-86526-9_7

not only creates costs for companies but at the same time also generates economic incomes for stakeholders. A large part of these incomes, however, is intangible (e.g., increased knowledge of employees or greater biodiversity at company locations), which is why to this day, many incomes that stakeholders actually appropriate remain *hidden values* to a company's value-added analysis. This brings me to the following question: what does it take to gain a holistic view in corporate reporting about the tangible and intangible values a company creates for its stakeholders?

In fact, a lot of work has been done in the fields of *intangibles accounting* (Edvinsson & Malone, 1997; Lev, 2001, 2019; Lev & Gu, 2016; Sveiby, 1997; The Konrad Group, 1990) and *sustainability management* (Figge & Hahn, 2004; Figge et al., 2002; IIRC, 2013b; KPMG, 2014; PWC, 2013) to tackle this issue by developing elaborated instruments and frameworks that help companies to better manage their intangibles. However, regardless of this remarkable progress, my impression is that a successful and holistic reporting on tangible and intangible stakeholder incomes presupposes a concept of business value creation that puts the idea of generating values for stakeholders (Freeman, 1984; Freeman et al., 2010; Parmar et al., 2010) at the heart of our thinking about business conduct. The design and set-up of the reporting instruments used to communicate business value creation follow our understanding of the terms and categories we employ to describe the phenomena in the first place (Möhrer, 2021).

To develop my ideas, I will base my argumentation on the grounds of a relational theory of the firm (Wieland, 2018, 2020). In such a theoretical context, the firm is seen as a nexus of stakeholder relations, with the sole purpose of continuing its existence through satisfying stakeholder interests. From a relational point of view, stakeholders invest tangible (capital, payments, infrastructure, etc.) and intangible (know-how, legitimacy, character, integrity, etc.) resources into the cooperation team called *firm* and can therefore expect the allocation of economic incomes in return for this investment. The incomes that stakeholders appropriate as a result of their participation in the value creation network can either be tangible or intangible in nature. They include a tangible factor income (e.g., salaries, taxes, interests, dividends), as well as an intangible and/or tangible cooperation rent (e.g., knowledge, safe working conditions, family-friendly working environment, donations). Factor incomes are part of a legal contract between the firm and its stakeholders, whereas cooperation rents reflect additional income to stakeholders that goes beyond explicit contracting. Together, factor income and cooperation rent make up the total amount of income a stakeholder can gain from its specific relation to a company. For describing this overall economic income of a stakeholder, I will use the term *stakeholder income* (Möhrer, 2021). In this regard, the total performance of a company can then be understood as the sum of all stakeholder incomes created and distributed during a value creation period. In relational terms, this total performance can further be defined as *shared value*.[1] The shared value of a firm is the broadest performance figure for a

[1] The term *shared value* goes back to Porter and Kramer (2011) who used the concept to highlight the simultaneous creation of value for business and society. In fact, I follow Michael Porter and Mark Kramer in many of their arguments. However, I would like to apply the concept of shared

cooperating team of stakeholders, from which all distributable stakeholder incomes must be paid. That is also the reason why we speak of *shared* value in this context.

In the following sections, we will learn more details about the relational approach to business value creation and develop ideas on how to gain a holistic view of the tangible and intangible values a company creates for its stakeholders. To that end, this chapter proceeds as follows: in Sect. 2, I briefly introduce the traditional concept of value creation as it is discussed in economic theory and business management. We will also have a look at the so-called value-added statement (VAS), which is the common reporting instrument used to measure and communicate business value creation. In Sect. 3, this traditional notion is then confronted with a relational view on value creation in which I try to develop arguments that allow us to theorize shared value as the company's total performance for its stakeholders. In this regard, I will sketch the basic assumptions of an *income-based theory of shared value*, before Sect. 4 takes on these thoughts and further elaborates them in the broader context of an *income-based theory of the firm*. Sect. 5 then turns to an accounting perspective and introduces the shared value statement (SVS) as a reporting tool to measure the distribution of economic incomes among company stakeholders. Finally, Sect. 6 concludes with some ideas on the development of a *relational accounting* of the firm.

2 Business Value Creation and the Value-Added Statement

From a historical standpoint, value creation as an economic concept has its roots in macroeconomic theory (Cox, 1979; Haller, 1997; Haller et al., 2018; Morley, 1978a; van Staden, 2000). Here, value creation is reflected in the gross domestic product (GDP) and the national income of an economy. The GDP measures economic value creation from a production point of view, whereas the national income represents the distribution side of the value creation process (Meyer-Merz, 1985). Transferred to a business context, a company's value added can then be understood as its monetary contribution to the creation of the national product (Arangies et al., 2008; Haller et al., 2018; Lehmann, 1954; Rutherford, 1977). In the traditional sense of the word, it stands for the value a company adds to the value of bought-in products and services by applying its production factors, i.e., labor and capital (Haller et al., 2018; Renshall et al., 1979). Especially in the early days of the business management discussion, the close connection between the economic and the business concept of value creation was of great importance (Gilchrist, 1971; Haller, 1997; Lehmann, 1954; Nicklisch, 1932; Suojanen, 1954). In fact, it is possible to historically trace the development of the macroeconomic notion of value creation from its early beginnings in the physiocratic school of economic thought until its current application in business management and accounting (Möhrer, 2021). When it comes to the question of

---

value even stronger to the idea of creating tangible and intangible values (incomes) for company stakeholders.

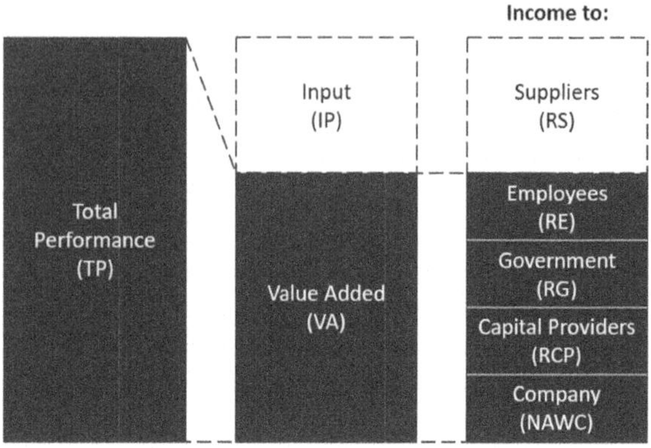

Fig. 1 Basic concept of value creation[2]

measurement, there are two ways to calculate value added. The first is called the indirect (subtractive) method, whereas the second is known as the direct (additive) method of value creation (Haller & van Staden, 2014):

(i) VA = TP – IP (subtractive method)
(ii) VA = RE + RG + RCP + NAWC (additive method).

Following the additive method of value-added analysis, value added (VA) is calculated as the sum of the remunerations generated in a company's value creation process and distributed to employees (RE), the government (RG), and capital providers (RCP). Also part of the value added is the amount that stays within the company, for example, as retained earnings, which can be used by management for future investments (ASSC, 1975; Rutherford, 1977). This part of value added is often called "not appropriated wealth creation" (NAWC) (Haller et al., 2018). Applying the subtractive method, bought-in products and services, i.e., the inputs (IP) of the value creation process, are deducted from the company's total performance (TP) in order to calculate value added. In the traditional idea of economic value creation, the inputs invested in the value creation process are not considered part of a company's value added, although these inputs lead to remuneration for suppliers (RS). Figure 1 shows the basic concept of value creation as it is usually discussed in economic theory and business management.

In an accounting context, the measurement of business value creation is typically conducted by using a value-added statement (Haller, 1997; Haller & van Staden, 2014; Riahi-Belkaoui, 1992, 1999; van Staden, 2000). Like the income statement, the VAS is a financial reporting instrument by which companies can calculate their annual performance in a structured and systematic way (Günther et al., 2016). However, while the income statement measures the net profit of a company, value added reflects a broader performance figure that not only includes economic incomes for shareholders but also for other stakeholder groups such as banks, employees, and the state, as well as values that are not appropriated by one of these groups but stay within the

[2] Own figure. Translated from Möhrer (2021) and based on Haller & van Staden (2014).

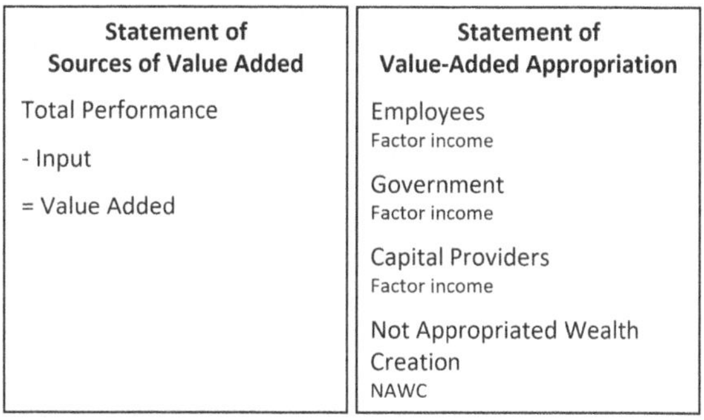

Fig. 2 The value-added statement[3]

company (Haller, 1997; Morley, 1978a; Schäfer, 1951; Weber, 1976). Also, in times of increased awareness of sustainability issues in business management, company investments in society and environmental protection are gaining momentum (Haller & van Staden, 2014; Perera-Aldama & Zicari, 2012; Zicari & Perera-Aldama, 2020). Based on the differentiation between the subtractive and additive method for calculating value added, the VAS can be divided into two separate but complementary statements—the statement of sources of value added and the statement of value-added appropriation (Haller & van Staden, 2014). Figure 2 shows the VAS in its generic form.

There are two aspects with this way of understanding and measuring business value creation that I would like to point out because it brings us back to the argument that many stakeholder incomes generated in a company's value creation network are actually not recorded by a VAS. When we take a closer look at the instrument as it is outlined in Fig. 2, we can see that there are different stakeholder groups participating in a company's value creation process and that they, as a result of this participation, appropriate certain amounts of the generated value added. From the perspective of a relational theory of the firm (Wieland, 2020), it seems that this traditional approach to value creation measurement does not necessarily draw a complete picture of the total economic incomes created and distributed in a company's value creation network. In fact, my impression is that certain stakeholder incomes are not yet counted as such in value-added analysis, either because (i) individual stakeholders are not recognized as legitimate recipients of economic income, and/or because (ii) intangible income allocations have been largely ignored:

Ad (i): Take customers for example. In regular market transactions, customers receive a product or service in exchange for the price they are willing to pay for these goods. One might question, however, if the purchased product or service is really the only thing of value they receive as a result of their relation to the selling company. What about the discounts and allowances that customers get to initiate the purchase in the first place? Or how can we interpret company expenses for after-sales training to improve customer knowledge in terms of product application? It seems fair to say that these benefits represent some sort of tangible (discounts) or intangible (product

[3] Own figure. Translated from Möhrer (2021).

knowledge) income that customers can appropriate as a result of their specific relation to a company. I think the crucial point here is that certain stakeholder groups that stakeholder theory usually sees as valuable elements of a company's stakeholder system (Clarkson, 1995; Donaldson & Preston, 1995; Freeman, 1984) are not recorded yet as legitimate recipients of economic income in value-added analysis, although these stakeholders obviously invest valuable resources into a company's value creation process (Möhrer, 2021; Wieland, 2020).

Ad (ii): For those stakeholders that are actually recorded (mainly employees, government, capital providers), the methodological focus of the VAS lies on the documentation of tangible factor incomes, i.e., mainly salaries, taxes, interests, and dividends, without counting the intangible benefits that stakeholders can gain from their relation to the business. One example for the allocation of intangible income to stakeholders would be an increase in employee health as a result of a company's investments in work safety at its production sites. Another example is company-driven improvements in natural capital as a result of its engagement in climate protection or biodiversity.[4] These and other intangible incomes are not yet part of our accounting approach to measure business value creation, mostly because today's understanding of the term is still determined by a market-based notion of value creation which has its roots in macroeconomic theory, and in which intangible values are usually seen as external effects to the economic system (Möhrer, 2021).

What do these considerations mean for the measurement of business value creation? In fact, I see the fundamental problem in value-added analysis being not primarily in the measurement instrument itself, i.e., the VAS, but rather in the way we understand and conceptualize the idea of business value creation. We should start working on the terms and categories used in value-added analysis before we can draw conclusions for the design and set-up of its reporting instruments. By doing so, we might be able to develop a more holistic view of the different tangible and intangible values a company creates for its stakeholders. To that end, the following section sketches some ideas on an *income-based theory of shared value.*

3 Income-Based Theory of Shared Value

The income-based theory of shared value is a theory of value creation not based on macroeconomics but takes the private business and the specific relations to its diverse stakeholders as a theoretical starting point to explain economic value creation. As such, the normative core of this theory lies in the idea of creating values for stakeholders (Freeman, 2017; Freeman et al., 2010; Parmar et al., 2010; Zollo et al., 2018). As I mentioned early, these values can be tangible or intangible in nature, and they are reframed by an income-based theory of shared value as tangible and intangible incomes that together make up the total economic income a stakeholder

[4] Similar thoughts can also be found in the works of the International Integrated Reporting Council (IIRC), especially in IIRC (2013a) and IIRC (2013c).

can appropriate as a result of its business relation. I introduced the term *stakeholder income* to describe these appropriable incomes. The shared value of a firm can then be defined as the sum of all stakeholder incomes generated in a company's value creation network and distributed to its stakeholders as compensation for their resource investments into the cooperation team. In a very formal notation, which is inspired by the works of Freeman (2017) and Freeman et al. (2020), a firm's shared value can be described as a function consisting of tangible and intangible stakeholder incomes:

$$SV_{FI} = f\left(\underbrace{\frac{SI_{SU}}{SV_{FI}}}_{x_{SU}}, \underbrace{\frac{SI_{EM}}{SV_{FI}}}_{x_{EM}}, \underbrace{\frac{SI_{CO}}{SV_{FI}}}_{x_{CO}}, \underbrace{\frac{SI_{CP}}{SV_{FI}}}_{x_{CP}}, \underbrace{\frac{SI_{CU}}{SV_{FI}}}_{x_{CU}}, \underbrace{\frac{SI_{OR}}{SV_{FI}}}_{x_{OR}}\right)$$

$$SV = Shared\ Value;\ FI = Firm;\ SI = Stakeholder\ Income;$$
$$SU = Suppliers;\ EM = Employees;\ CO = Community/State;$$
$$CP = Capital\ Providers;\ CU = Customers;\ OR = Organisation$$

SV_{FI} stands for the shared value of the firm. It reflects the total monetary performance of a company and results from the tangible and intangible resources invested by stakeholders and processed by the organization. As stated above, a firm's shared value consists of all economic incomes created during a value creation period and distributed to the company's different stakeholder groups. The appropriable income of a stakeholder can either be tangible or intangible in nature and comprises a tangible factor income on the one hand and an intangible and/or tangible cooperation rent on the other. Let's consider the following examples: from the perspective of an income-based theory of shared value, the appropriable income of employees can include annual wages/salaries (factor incomes) as well as an additional income that might take the form of specific knowledge (cooperation rent) that the employee is able to gain as a result of its participation in vocational training. Looking at communities, their total income consists of taxes paid by the company (factor incomes) plus extra income that might result from corporate volunteering activities in local schools (cooperation rent). There are more examples like that, but I think the crucial point here is to understand that such resource allocations by the firm lead to economic incomes from the perspective of their stakeholders. Ultimately, all stakeholder incomes must be paid from the collectively generated shared value of the cooperation team.

SI stands for the stakeholder income distributed by the firm. In the context of an income-based value creation approach, stakeholders are systematically entitled to a share in the company's shared value due to their specific investment of resources. The shared value function outlined above includes the following stakeholder groups[5]: suppliers (SU), employees (EM), community/state (CO), capital providers (CP),

[5] Which stakeholder groups are identified as relevant for the company's income distribution process depends on the company in question and can change over time due to social and political developments or economic disruptions. The shared value function introduced in this chapter is therefore by no means an absolute or static construct, but must be subject to constant reflection and adaptation.

customers (CU), and the organization itself (OR). An income-based theory of shared value considers all stakeholders not only as investors of resources but also as recipients of tangible and intangible incomes. This is an important point and distinguishes the income-based understanding of shared value creation from the macroeconomic notion of value added. Take suppliers for example: while in traditional value-added analysis, suppliers are excluded by definition from the calculation of value added because they are seen as providers of inputs only, they are an integral part of a company's income distribution process from the perspective of an income-based theory of shared value (Möhrer, 2021). In this regard, the operating costs of the focal firm can be interpreted as factor incomes paid in the form of revenues which suppliers appropriate for providing inputs to the production process (GRI, 2018).[6] Also, special attention must be given to the question of why an income-based theory of shared value identifies the organization as a separate stakeholder in the stakeholder system of the firm. With *organization*, I refer to the idea that the organization of companies can be understood as an abstract *going concern* (Commons, 1934, 1990), existing as an *entity in its own* and independently from the interests of a firm's other stakeholder groups (Wieland, 2020). We will get to this point in more detail in the following section because it stands in direct relation to the attributes we use to identify individual and collective actors as stakeholders of a company.

X represents a variable by which it is possible to weigh the stakeholder incomes allocated during a company's income distribution process. It is reported specifically for every stakeholder group and indicates how the collectively generated shared value is paid out by the firm to the stakeholders invested in the cooperation team.[7] By analyzing this variable, accountants and managers can identify current priorities in terms of a company's distribution policy and also recognize future potentials for income allocations based on the firm's strategic objectives. An important aspect regarding the income-based understanding of business value creation is that ultimately, the amount of income (tangible and intangible) distributed to stakeholders must equal the collectively generated shared value of the company. Marvin Lieberman and colleagues chose a similar wording to describe this idea of value creation and distribution by the firm:

> Any rigorous analysis of value creation and appropriation must account for the fact that, by definition, the value created through a firm's activities, and the value distributed to the firm's stakeholders, must be equal. (Lieberman et al., 2017, p. 1194)

I discussed the various aspects of an income-based theory of shared value in more detail in a different setting (Möhrer, 2021). For the purpose of this chapter, I therefore use the following assumptions to summarize its basic ideas:

[6] In recent times, this special interpretation of business value creation has also been mentioned by Haller et al. (2018) and Günther et al. (2016).

[7] Note that the shared value function in the configuration presented here is only valid for $SV_{FI} > 0$, since a division by 0 is mathematically not permissible.

- A firm's shared value is calculated as the sum of all tangible and intangible incomes generated in a company's value creation network and distributed to its stakeholders. It represents the total monetary performance of a firm that results from the tangible and intangible resources invested by stakeholders and processed by the organization.
- Based on its specific resource investments, each stakeholder can claim to appropriate a certain amount of income which is paid from the collectively generated shared value and accrued in the company. The allocation of stakeholder incomes is determined by the stakeholder's contribution to the firm's value creation capacity and safeguarded by the governance structures of the organization.
- An income-based shared value theory is concerned with the stakeholder incomes generated and distributed in a firms' value creation network. Stakeholder incomes include tangible factor incomes as well as intangible and/or tangible cooperation rents which in turn make up the total income a stakeholder can appropriate as a result of its specific relation to the business.
- From an epistemological point of view, an income-based theory of shared value is interested in a descriptive analysis of a firm's income distribution process. It is not about a normative justification for prioritizing stakeholders in terms of their income claims they might have toward a company. Rather, it is about the economic measurement of the generated shared value and its distribution to the stakeholders invested in the firm.
- Analytically, an income-based theory of shared value examines the specific shares of income stakeholders appropriate in relation to the overall performance (shared value) of the firm. Hence, it compares stakeholder groups in terms of the economic incomes they gain from their participation in a cooperation team and thereby identifies current priorities and future allocation potentials for management control.

There is no doubt that the income-based theory of shared value, as it is presented here, is still in its infancy, and much more work has to be done in this field to reach a point in theory building where we are really able "to reexamine the very nature of how we determine firm performance" (Freeman, 2017, p. 7). Thus, the previous consideration can only be understood as one out of many steps toward a more holistic and multidimensional understanding of business value creation—an understanding that allows us to identify and evaluate the values a firm creates for its stakeholders, both in their tangible and intangible configuration. I am aware of the fact that the special treatment of the organization as a separate stakeholder group of the firm can cause serious irritations. For this reason, I will use the following section to build a rationale that enables us to theoretically integrate the organization as an *entity in its own* (Wieland, 2020) into a company's stakeholder system. To that end, it will be necessary to transfer the main ideas of an income-based theory of shared value into the broader setting of an income-based theory of the firm.

4 Notes on an Income-Based Theory of the Firm

Although we are concerned in this chapter with gaining new perspectives on measuring business value creation, it nevertheless seems worthwhile to reflect the accounting part in the wider context of a discussion about the theory of the firm. It was, in fact, Ronald Coase who once stated that "a theory of the accounting system is part of the theory of the firm" (Coase, 1990, p. 12). And indeed, I share the view that both an income-based theory of shared value as well as a shared value statement, which I consider its corresponding reporting instrument, presuppose an understanding of the firm that puts the idea of creating values for stakeholders at the heart of our thinking about business conduct (Freeman, 2017; Freeman et al., 2010; Parmar et al., 2010). I follow Josef Wieland at this point when he concludes that finally, it is the concrete relation between a company and its stakeholders as well as the relations that exist between these exact same stakeholders that build the basis for the creation and distribution of economic incomes by the firm (Wieland, 2018, 2020). That being said, an income-based theory of the firm, at the end of the day, is a relational theory of the firm in the sense as Wieland developed it over the past several years. In fact, it uses its assumptions and applies them to the idea that the total performance of a company (i.e., its shared value) is the result of the many tangible and intangible incomes it distributes to the various stakeholders invested in the cooperation team called *firm*. In addition to that, an income-based theory of the firm argues that a company's organization can be interpreted as a separate stakeholder group in the stakeholder system of the firm. In the following, I will give a brief overview of the main aspects behind this thought.[8] But first, Fig. 3 is supposed to show a vision of the firm as a relation of stakeholder resources and stakeholder incomes.

In an income-based approach to value creation, the purpose of the firm can be defined as the generation of economic incomes for stakeholders. These incomes can either be tangible or intangible in nature. They are appropriated by stakeholders as a result of their specific relation to a company in which they invest resources that also can have a tangible (capital, infrastructure, payments, etc.) or intangible (know-how, legitimacy, skills, etc.) configuration. A very crucial aspect in an income-based theory of the firm is to build a rationale that allows theorizing the organization as a separate stakeholder in the value creation network of a company. The starting point for this is to agree to a theoretical differentiation between the business in general and its organization, which is part of a business' stakeholder system, and which can be identified as an abstract *entity in its own*, existing independently from the interests of the other stakeholders in the system (Wieland, 2020). This idea that the organization of the firm can somehow be designed as a stakeholder in its own, equally existing with other stakeholder groups, is not very common in traditional stakeholder theory (Freeman, 1984, 2010; Freeman et al., 2007, 2011). Here, we usually read about customers, suppliers, financiers, employees, and the broader community who potentially can appropriate incomes as a result of their participation in the company's

[8] Note that a comprehensive discussion about this idea can be found in Möhrer (2021).

Fig. 3 The firm as a relation of stakeholder resources and stakeholder incomes[9]

value creation network. From the perspective of stakeholder theory, this approach is totally sound as long as we consider the organization as the focal point of the stakeholder system (Freeman & Reed, 1983).[10] Taking the organization as a theoretical reference point, economic relationships with stakeholders are established with the goal of creating value for stakeholders.

A relational and income-based theory of the firm in fact shares the idea that the relationships of a company to its stakeholders play a decisive role in creating and

[9] Own figure. Translated from Möhrer (2021) and based on Wieland (2020). The six stakeholder groups we already know from the shared value function introduced earlier are extended here by two more groups, namely the stakeholders *Joint Venture* and *Non-Governmental Organization (NGO)*. We do this, because it shows quite well how broad and complex a company's stakeholder system can be designed. However, for the later development of the SVS, we will work again with a reduced number of stakeholders that also matches the selection we referred to in an income-based theory of shared value.

[10] Freeman and Reed made very clear from the beginning that "the starting point of any stakeholder analysis is identification of the focal organization. It is in relation to this focal point that stakes are established". Freeman and Reed (1983, p. 101).

distributing stakeholder values (Freeman et al., 2020). However, in contrast to traditional stakeholder theory, *relational economics* (Wieland, 2020) does not identify the organization as the focal point of analysis, but the relational transaction (see also Fig. 3). It is important to recognize that relational transactions are not the same as economic transactions in the market-based and purely financial sense of the word. Rather, a relational transaction, with reference to Commons (1934/1990), must be understood as a multidimensional construct to which different tangible and intangible value interests of stakeholders can connect to and thereby influence a company's value creation process (Wieland, 2020).[11] It is only in relation to a specific economic, and in our case multidimensional, transaction as the focal point of stakeholder analysis that the organization is even imaginable as a separate stakeholder group in the stakeholder system of the firm (Möhrer, 2021).

If both are accepted—the idea that the organization is an *entity in its own* and that stakeholders relate to a relational transaction as the focal point of stakeholder analysis—then it is inevitable for our discussion to proceed with the following question: what makes an individual or collective actor a company stakeholder? An income-based theory of the firm identifies two attributes necessary to qualify an economic actor as a company stakeholder: (i) the resources a stakeholder invests into the firm (stakeholder resources) and (ii) the economic incomes appropriated by the stakeholder as a result of this investment (stakeholder incomes). My argument is that both attributes can also be applied to the organization, which in turn would make it a separate stakeholder group in the stakeholder system of the firm:

Ad (i): The resources invested by an organization into the cooperation team is its own governance. With governance, I refer to the formal and informal structures (e.g., policies, procedures, organizational culture, etc.) a company uses to organize its value creation network. In principle, the organization and its governance can exist independently from other stakeholders in the network. We can think of employees who choose to leave the business to work somewhere else, or suppliers who are suddenly substituted because a new market player offers a better fit. Instead, the organizational structure of a firm, i.e., its governance, is something that usually continues to exist, although other stakeholder investments may change over time. In fact, management uses a firm's governance structures to continuously (re-)organize old and new stakeholder resources in a way that is not only beneficial to the invested stakeholders but also to the business as a whole. We know of similar thoughts, for example, from the *dynamic capabilities approach*, in which it is argued that a company's governance can be seen as an economic resource in its own because it increases the productivity of the other resources in the system (Amit & Schoemaker, 1993; Makadok, 2001; Teece et al., 1997).[12] From these arguments, an income-based theory of the firm would conclude that, at the end of the day, it is not exclusively

[11] It is remarkable that Commons (1932/1996) sees the answer to *the problem of correlating law, economics, and ethics* in the concrete economic transaction, which makes it by definition a multidimensional endeavor.

[12] Marshall (1890/2013) was probably one of the first thinkers who introduced the organization as a separate factor of production into the economic discussion.

the invested resources in the traditional sense (e.g., capital, payments, legitimacy, know-how, etc.) that flow into the value creation network of the firm, but it is also the governance structures provided by its organization that would have a relevant contribution to the process of business value creation (Möhrer, 2021).

Ad (ii): For this contribution, the organization can claim a certain share of a company's total performance (i.e., its shared value) for which I suggest the term *organizational income*. With organizational income, I refer to stakeholder incomes that the organization as an *entity in its own* receives from the value creation network in return for its invested resources. As already mentioned earlier, in accounting terms, these incomes are often not considered "real" incomes, but they are called "not appropriated wealth creation" because they include values that are not distributed to stakeholder groups usually referred to in value-added analysis, such as employees, capital providers, or the state. Examples of such income allocations are depreciation and amortization or retained earnings. These incomes are part of the collectively generated shared value of a firm and belong to the organization where they can be used for future investment and development. They exist independently from other stakeholder resources in the system, and their purpose is to safeguard the infinity of the firm as an economic *going concern*.

In the context of an income-based theory of the firm, both the investment of resources and the appropriation of economic incomes are constitutive for qualifying an individual or collective actor as a company stakeholder. It is interesting that in fact, both attributes have always been part of the original definition of a stakeholder given by Freeman (1984). Here, a stakeholder is characterized as "any group or individual who can affect or is affected by the achievement of the organization's objectives" (Freeman, 1984, p. 46). Against the background of an income-based theory of the firm, in the first case ("can affect"), we are dealing with the aspect of providing resources by stakeholders, whereas in the second case ("is affected"), we are talking about the allocation of stakeholder incomes organized by applying organizational governance. Of course, many questions remain open at this point, and much more work will be necessary in the future to develop the income-based approach further to a resilient theory of the firm. However, for the purpose of this chapter, we gained enough insights so far to draw some first conclusions for the design and set-up of a modified value-added statement for which I suggest the term *shared value statement*.

5 The Shared Value Statement

We started this chapter with the observation that the current accounting approach to measuring business value creation seems somehow incomplete because it does not count for all the incomes that have been produced in a company's value creation network. The SVS is meant to tackle this issue by giving a more holistic view of the tangible and intangible incomes a firm creates for its stakeholders. The specific contribution of the SVS is to increase transparency about how a firm distributes the collectively generated shared value to its various stakeholders. It measures in financial terms the income distribution for every single stakeholder group and processes this information for internal and external reporting. Hence, the purpose of a shared value statement is a structured presentation of the tangible and intangible incomes as well as their specific allocation to the company stakeholders. Keeping this purpose in mind is important because it marks a major difference to the macroeconomic-based value-added statement, in which the methodological focus is not on reporting stakeholder incomes, but on measuring a company's contribution to the national product of society. Of course, from a macroeconomic point of view, it still matters to avoid double counting in the process of calculating the GDP (Arangies et al., 2008; Machado et al., 2015; Meek & Gray, 1999), and here is where the VAS stays a relevant reporting instrument for companies. However, in contrast to that, the major interest of an income-based theory of shared value lies in measuring the amount of tangible and intangible incomes generated in the cooperation team, and finally also in the question of how these incomes are actually distributed to stakeholders, either as factor income or in the form of a cooperation rent. In the following, I can only give a brief overview about the major contents of a shared value statement, for which I suggest a division into three main parts, namely (i) a performance statement, (ii) a cost statement, and (iii) a stakeholder income statement (Möhrer, 2021). We will have a closer look at the performance statement first, but before we do that, Fig. 4 gives an impression of how the SVS could be structured in a sample set-up.

Ad (i): The basic structure of the SVS comprises three separate parts: a performance statement, a cost statement, and a stakeholder income statement. The performance statement calculates the total performance of a firm in monetary terms and thereby determines its shared value. The shared value of a cooperation team is the most comprehensive measure of a company's success, from which all distributable incomes to the invested stakeholders must be paid. Besides a company's sales, the performance statement includes additional revenues, such as other operating revenues, revenues from investments or intangible assets, and extraordinary revenues. All these revenues are potential sources of economic income that can benefit the company's stakeholders either in a tangible or intangible way.[13] Employee salaries, payments to suppliers, dividends to shareholders, and also company expenses for vocational training, corporate nutrition programs, or investments in environmental protection are examples of specific income distributions to stakeholders that, at the end of the day, must be paid from the collectively generated shared value of the firm. However, whereas salaries, supplier payments, and dividends reflect tangible factor incomes for stakeholders, the rest can be considered intangible stakeholder income because, in our example, company activities behind these allocations either increase the knowledge of employees (through vocational training), improve employee health (through nutrition programs), or contribute to the preservation of biodiversity (through environmental protection measures). In relational terms, these

[13] Or as Lieberman and colleagues put it in their approach to business value creation: "The lynchpin of this approach is a simple accounting identity that equates the revenues of a firm to the sum of all payments made to its stakeholders" Lieberman et al. (2017, p. 1194).

Shared Value Statement		
Performance Statement		
	Sales	
+	Other operating revenues	
+	Revenues from investments	
+	Revenues from intangible assets	
+	Extraordinary revenues	
=	**Shared Value (Total Performance)**	
Cost Statement		
	Factor costs:	*Company expenses (excluding CSR expenses)*
+	Relational costs:	*CSR expenses*
=	**Organizational Costs**	
Stakeholder Income Statement		
	Suppliers	
	Factor incomes:	*Sales from inputs*
	+ Cooperation rents:	*Benefits from participating in seminars and trainings, e.g., in the areas of environmental protection and human rights, investments in joint CSR projects, etc.*
	= Stakeholder Income Suppliers	
+	**Employees**	
	Factor incomes:	*Net wages, wage taxes withheld, contributions to social security withheld, wage replacement benefits, pension accruals*
	+ Cooperation rents:	*Benefits from vocational training, voluntary social benefits, benefits from programs on employee health and work saftey, investments in family-firiendly working conditions, diversity, etc.*
	= Stakeholder Income Employees	
+	**Community/State**	
	Factor incomes:	*Income taxes, indirect and deferred taxes, other public charges and duties*
	+ Cooperation rents:	*Benefits from corporate social responsibility activities, investments in environmental protection, etc.*
	= Stakeholder Income Community/State	
+	**Capital Providers**	
	Factor incomes:	*Interests paid to banks and other creditors, dividends and other payments to shareholders*
	+ Cooperation rents:	*Benefits from company investments in CSR-related governance structures, ValuesManagementSystems^ZfW^, extended compliance programs, etc.*
	= Stakeholder Income Capital Providers	
+	**Customers**	
	Factor incomes:	*Discounts, allowances or credit notes*
	+ Cooperation rents:	*Benefits from special customer events, dialog platforms, company investments in customer trainings for product safety and application, voluntary non-cash benefits, etc.*
	= Stakeholder Income Customers	
+	**Organization**	
	Factor incomes:	*Retained earnings required by law or company constitution, depreciation and amortization*
	+ Cooperation rents:	*Voluntary retained earnings*
	= Stakeholder Income Organization	
=	**Stakeholer Income**	

◂**Fig. 4** The shared value statement in a sample set-up[14]

intangible incomes are defined as cooperation rents since they reflect additional incomes for stakeholders which result from the specific cooperation between them and the company they are invested in (Möhrer, 2021; Wieland, 2020).

Ad (ii): The cost statement of the SVS calculates the total costs of a company's shared value creation and makes them available for corporate decision-making. In an income-based value creation approach, the organizational costs of a firm include factor costs on the one hand and relational costs on the other. Factor costs accrue because companies use production factors invested by stakeholders, i.e., labor and capital, to create economic value. Factor costs of companies lead to factor incomes for stakeholders. Take again the salaries of employees as an example reflecting a tangible compensation for the workforce they provide to the company. The same is also true for revenues that suppliers earn by delivering inputs to the production process. Both income allocations represent genuine expenses for companies which finally can be measured by applying proper cost accounting. Besides factor costs, a firm's shared value creation also generates so-called relational costs. In *relational economics*, relational costs can be defined as those costs of a company that accrue for allocating intangible values to stakeholders (Wieland, 2020). Giving employees the chance to gain extra knowledge by participating in vocational training, improving work safety in the supply chain, or simply supporting the local community with corporate volunteering activities are examples of company measures that create intangible incomes for stakeholders, but at the same time also generate genuine costs in the organization. These costs, however, are relational in nature because they emerge from the specific relationship between a company and its stakeholders. To put it differently, relational costs are investments of a firm into the long-term cooperation with their stakeholders. They are meant to increase the total amount of income stakeholders can appropriate as a result of their investment into a cooperation team, with the goal of keeping or making them part of a company's stakeholder system (Clarkson, 1995). That is also the reason why a shared value statement measures relational costs in terms of the periodic expenses companies have for performing their *company stakeholder responsibility (CSR)* (Freeman & Velamuri, 2006). At the end of the day, relational costs exist because companies take on the responsibility toward their stakeholders which in fact goes beyond the payments they are obliged to make as a result of legal contracting (Möhrer, 2021). We should be aware, though, that besides such a cost-based approach, there are also various other approaches to measure the intangible values of a company, and all of them have their pros and cons (Working Group "Accounting & Reporting of Intangible Assets", 2013). However, at the same time, I also agree with Laurie Hunter and colleagues who pointed out that in order to develop a proper accounting for intangibles, it might be a good start to

[14] Own figure. Translated from Möhrer (2021). Although the SVS offers a new perspective on business value creation, many contents presented by the instrument can also be found for the VAS, however in a different set-up and theoretical context. See for example Haller & van Staden (2014).

gain a better understanding first of the actual costs that companies have for allocating intangible values to their stakeholders (Hunter et al., 2005, 2012).

Ad (iii): The stakeholder income statement takes the total company costs measured by the cost statement and allocates them to a firm's different stakeholder groups. For every stakeholder, the stakeholder income statement differentiates the total income appropriable by a stakeholder into its factor income as well as a cooperation rent. Factor incomes result from a legal contract that exists between a company and its stakeholder about the specific exchange of resources. Cooperation rents, however, reflect additional benefits for stakeholders which are usually not covered by explicit contracting. Rather, they accrue because companies invest in developing their stakeholder system. In relational terms, the paying of cooperation rents can be understood as an economic incentive for stakeholders to invest their resources into a specific cooperation team (Möhrer, 2021). In this regard, they become necessary income allocations that are supposed to safeguard the continuity of the organization as an economic *going concern* (Commons, 1934/1990; Wieland, 2020). A special feature of the SVS is to provide a detailed view on the various incomes stakeholders can possibly appropriate from their engagement with a cooperation team, and how these incomes are actually distributed in the company's stakeholder system. Take again the factor incomes of customers for example, for which an income-based theory of shared value refers to customer discounts, allowances, or credit notes. In an income-based approach, these measures can be interpreted as stakeholder incomes because they reflect genuine price reductions that either result in a lower market price for the product or service in question or in a refunded payment to the customer. I already mentioned that an income-based theory of shared value identifies the organization as a stakeholder in its own. In the SVS, the organization is therefore listed as a separate stakeholder group that appropriates its own specific income share of the collectively generated shared value. Factor incomes include depreciation and amortization as well as retained earnings required by law or company constitution, whereas cooperation rents cover additional income allocations that are voluntary but nevertheless contribute significantly to the future existence of the organization.

These are only a few examples that show how a shared value statement can increase transparency in the process of measuring a company's income distribution process. Without going too much into detail, the following points are meant to note the most relevant advantages I see when using the SVS in corporate reporting: (1) identification of steering and control potentials for the management with regard to the distribution of stakeholder incomes, (2) transparent presentation of a company's income distribution process over time (historical analysis), and (3) supplementing non-financial sustainability reporting by using a structured monetary reporting framework to communicate the created and distributed values for stakeholders.

6 Concluding Remarks

We are in need of accounting instruments that really account for the specific relations between a company and its stakeholders. Such relations can include tangible and intangible value interests of stakeholders, which makes the firm by definition a multidimensional endeavor of economic value creation. To this day, however, this multidimensionality is only barely recognized in our current accounting systems, therefore leaving room for further development. I see the purpose of a *relational accounting* of the firm being mainly in systematically providing information about the various tangible and intangible values a company creates and manages for its stakeholders. In this regard, the SVS discussed in this chapter can only be one of many instruments that help to gain a better understanding of the actual value creation capacity of a team of cooperating stakeholders. For example, we will also have to think about how we (re-)structure a company's balance sheet so that it tells us about the number of different capitals a firm manages for its stakeholders as well as the development of these capitals over time. In relational terms, such stakeholder capitals can and must include tangible and intangible value categories (e.g., economic capital, natural capital, social capital, etc.) as it has also been suggested years ago by the International Integrated Reporting Council (IIRC, 2013a). In fact, to develop the traditional balance sheet into a *relational balance sheet*, we probably have to change categories from assets and liabilities to stakeholder capitals and stakeholder resources. A corporate balance sheet would then list a company's different stakeholder groups and account for both, that is, their invested resources as well as their multidimensional stock of capital. Of course, all of this will not be possible without having a standardized approach that allows companies to report on their stakeholder capitals in a comparable and transparent way. To that end, I imagine the development of *International Stakeholder Reporting Standards (ISRS)* which in the long run would have to reach the same level of sophistication as we currently know it from the field of financial reporting, but which take the stakeholder relation as their focal point of analysis. No doubt, *relational accounting* is a work in progress, and future research will show where it is heading.

References

Amit, R., & Schoemaker, P. J. H. (1993). Strategic assets and organizational rent. *Strategic Management Journal, 14*(1), 33–46.

Arangies, G., Mlambo, C., Hamman, W. D., & Steyn-Bruwer, B. W. (2008). The value-added statement: An appeal for standardisation. *Management Dynamics, 17*(1), 31–43.

ASSC (1975). The Corporate Report: A discussion paper published for comment by the Accounting Standards Steering Committee. Retrieved from https://www.icaew.com/-/media/corporate/files/library/subjects/corporate-governance/corporate-report.ashx?la=en.

Clarkson, M. B. E. (1995). A stakeholder framework for analyzing and evaluating corporate social performance. *Academy of Management Review, 20*(1), 92–117.

Coase, R. H. (1990). Accounting and the theory of the firm. *The Journal of Accounting and Economics, 12*(1/3), 3–13.
Commons, J. R. (1932/1996). The problem of correlating law, economics and ethics. In M. Rutherford & W. J. Samuels (Eds.), *John R. Commons: Selected essays* (Vol. 2, pp. 453–473). Routledge.
Commons, J. R. (1934/1990). Institutional economics: Its place in political economy (Vol. 1, 2nd ed.). Transaction Publishers.
Cox, B. (1979). *Value added: An appreciation for the accountant concerned with industry.* Heinemann.
Donaldson, T., & Preston, L. E. (1995). The stakeholder theory of the corporation: Concepts, evidence, and implications. *Academy of Management Review, 20*(1), 65–91.
Edvinsson, L., & Malone, M. S. (1997). *Intellectual capital: Realizing your company's true value by finding its hidden brainpower*. Harper Business.
Figge, F., & Hahn, T. (2004). Sustainable value added—Measuring corporate contributions to sustainability beyond eco-efficiency. *Ecological Economics, 48*(2), 173–187.
Figge, F., Hahn, T., Schaltegger, S., & Wagner, M. (2002). The sustainability balanced scorecard—linking sustainability management to business strategy. *Business Strategy and the Environment, 11*(5), 269–284.
Freeman, R. E. (1984). *Strategic management: A stakeholder approach.* Pitman.
Freeman, R. E. (2010). Managing for stakeholders: Trade-offs or value creation. *Journal of Business Ethics, 96*(Supplement 1), 7–9.
Freeman, R. E. (2017). Five challenges to stakeholder theory: A report on research in progress. In D. M. Wasieleski & J. Weber (Eds.), *Stakeholder management* (pp. 1–20). Emerald Publishing.
Freeman, R. E., Harrison, J. S., & Wicks, A. C. (2007). *Managing for stakeholders: Survival, reputation, and success.* Yale University Press.
Freeman, R. E., & Reed, D. L. (1983). Stockholders and stakeholders: A new perspective on corporate governance. *California Management Review, 25*(3), 88–106.
Freeman, R. E., Wicks, A. C., & Parmar, B. L. (2011). Stakeholder theory as a basis for capitalism. In L. Sacconi, M. Blair, R. E. Freeman, & A. Vercelli (Eds.), *Corporate social responsibility and corporate governance: The contribution of economic theory and related disciplines* (pp. 52–72). Macmillan.
Freeman, R. E., Harrison, J. S., Wicks, A. C., Parmar, B. L., & de Colle, S. (2010). *Stakeholder theory: The state of the art.* Cambridge University Press.
Freeman, R. E., Phillips, R., & Sisodia, R. (2020). Tensions in stakeholder theory. *Business & Society, 59*(2), 213–231.
Freeman, R. E., & Velamuri, S. R. (2006). A new approach to CSR: Company stakeholder responsibility. In A. Kakabadse & M. Morsing (Eds.), *Corporate social responsibility: Reconciling aspiration with application* (pp. 9–23). Macmillan.
Gilchrist, R. R. (1971). *Managing for profit: The added value concept.* George, Allen & Unwin.
GRI (2018). GRI 201: Economic performance. Retrieved from https://www.globalreporting.org/standards/gri-standards-downloadcenter/gri-201-economic-performance-2016/?g=8ccf235a-00ab-40b6-a8a2-8506542b5a4b.
Günther, E., Bassen, A., & Haller, A. (2016). Konzept, Aspekte und Herausforderungen des Integrated Reporting. In E. Günther & A. Bassen (Eds.), *Integrated Reporting: Grundlagen, Implementierung, Praxisbeispiele* (pp. 1–197). Schäffer-Poeschel.
Haller, A. (1997). *Wertschöpfungsrechnung: Ein Instrument zur Steigerung der Aussagefähigkeit von Unternehmensabschlüssen im internationalen Kontext.* Schäffer-Poeschel.
Haller, A., & van Staden, C. (2014). The value added statement—An appropriate instrument for integrated reporting. *Accounting, Auditing & Accountability Journal, 27*(7), 1190–1216.
Haller, A., van Staden, C. J., & Landis, C. (2018). Value added as part of sustainability reporting: Reporting on distributional fairness or obfuscation? *Journal of Business Ethics, 152*(3), 763–781.
Hunter, L., Webster, E., & Wyatt, A. (2005). Measuring intangible investment (Working Paper No. 18/05), Melbourne.

Hunter, L., Webster, E., & Wyatt, A. (2012). Accounting for expenditure on intangibles. *Abacus, 48*(1), 104–145.
IIRC (2013a). Capitals: Background paper for <IR>. Retrieved from http://integratedreporting.org/wp-content/uploads/2013/03/IRBackground-Paper-Capitals.pdf.
IIRC (2013b). The international <IR> framework. Retrieved from https://www.integratedreporting.org/resource/international-irframework/.
IIRC (2013c). Value creation: Background paper. Retrieved from http://integratedreporting.org/wp-content/uploads/2013/08/Background-Paper-Value-Creation.pdf.
KPMG. (2014). A new vision of value: Connecting corporate and societal value creation. Retrieved from https://assets.kpmg/content/dam/kpmg/pdf/2014/10/a-new-vision-of-value-v1.pdf.
Lehmann, M. R. (1954). *Leistungsmessung durch Wertschöpfungsrechnung*. Girardet.
Lev, B. (2001). *Intangibles: Management, measurement, and reporting*. Brookings Institution Press.
Lev, B. (2019). Ending the accounting-for-intangibles status quo. *European Accounting Review, 28*(4), 713–736.
Lev, B., & Gu, F. (2016). *The end of accounting and the path forward for investors and managers*. Wiley.
Lieberman, M. B., Garcia-Castro, R., & Balasubramanian, N. (2017). Measuring value creation and appropriation in firms: The VCA model. *Strategic Management Journal, 38*(6), 1193–1211.
Machado, M. A. V., Macedo, M. A. D. S., & Machado, M. R. (2015). Analysis of the relevance of information content of the value added statement in the Brazilian capital markets. *Revista Contabilidade & Finanças, 26*(67), 57–69.
Makadok, R. (2001). Toward a synthesis of the resource-based and dynamic-capability views of rent creation. *Strategic Management Journal, 22*(5), 387–401.
Marshall, A. (1890/2013). *Principles of economics* (8th ed.). Macmillan.
Meek, G. K., & Gray, S. J. (1999). The value added statement: An innovation for U.S. companies. In A. Riahi-Belkaoui (Ed.), *Value added reporting and research: State of the art* (pp. 29–37). Quorum Books.
Meyer-Merz, A. (1985). Die Wertschöpfungsrechnung in Theorie und Praxis. Schulthess.
Möhrer, M. (2021). *Shared Value-Rechnung. Konzeption und Messung betriebswirtschaftlicher Wertschöpfung*. Metropolis.
Morley, M. F. (1978a). *The value added statement: A review of its use in corporate reports*. Gee & Co.
Morley, M. F. (1978b). The value added statement: An innovation in corporate reports. *Certified Accountant*, 165–170.
Nicklisch, H. (1932). *Die Betriebswirtschaft* (7th ed.). Poeschel.
Parmar, B. L., Freeman, R. E., Harrison, J. S., Wicks, A. C., Purnell, L., & de Colle, S. (2010). Stakeholder theory: The state of the art. *The Academy of Management Annals, 4*(1), 403–445.
Perera-Aldama, L., & Zicari, A. (2012). Value-added reporting as a tool for sustainability: A Latin American experience. *Corporate Governance, 12*(4), 485–498.
Porter, M. E., & Kramer, M. R. (2011). Creating shared value: How to reinvent capitalism—And unleash a wave of innovation and growth. *Harvard Business Review, 89*(1/2), 62–77.
PWC (2013). Measuring and managing total impact: A new language for business decisions. Retrieved from https://www.pwc.com/gx/en/sustainability/publications/total-impact-measurement-management/assets/pwc-timm-report.pdf.
Renshall, M., Allan, R., & Nicholson, K. (1979). *Added value in external financial reporting*. The Institute of Chartered Accountants in England and Wales.
Riahi-Belkaoui, A. (1992). *Value added reporting: Lessons for the United States*. Quorum Books.
Riahi-Belkaoui, A. (Ed.). (1999). *Value added reporting and research: State of the art*. Quorum Books.
Rutherford, B. A. (1977). Value added as a focus of attention for financial reporting: Some conceptual problems. *Accounting and Business Research, 7*(27), 215–220.
Schäfer, E. (1951). Vom "Mehrwert" zur "Wertschöpfung." *Zeitschrift für Betriebswirtschaft, 21*(8/9), 449–459.

Suojanen, W. W. (1954). Accounting theory and the large corporation. *Accounting Review, 29*(3), 391–398.
Sveiby, K.-E. (1997). *The new organizational wealth: Managing & measuring knowledge-based assets*. Berrett-Koehler.
Teece, D. J., Pisano, G., & Shuen, A. (1997). Dynamic capabilities and strategic management. *Strategic Management Journal, 18*(7), 509–533.
The Konrad Group (1990). The invisible balance sheet: Key indicators for accounting, control and valuation of know-how companies. Retrieved from https://www.sveiby.com/files/pdf/denosynli gaeng.pdf.
Van Staden, C. J. (2000). The value added statement: Bastion of social reporting or dinosaur of financial reporting? (Working Paper), Palmerston North. Retrieved from https://mro.massey.ac.nz/bitstream/handle/10179/2543/200.pdf.
Weber, H. K. (1976). Die Bedeutung der betrieblichen Wertschöpfungsrechnung. In H.-J. Engeleiter (Ed.), Unternehmen und Gesellschaft: Festschrift zum 75. Geburtstag von Wilhelm Hasenack (pp. 33–59). Neue Wirtschafts-Briefe.
Wieland, J. (2018). *Relational Economics: Ökonomische Theorie der Governance wirtschaftlicher Transaktionen*. Metropolis.
Wieland, J. (2020). *Relational Economics: A political economy*. Springer Nature.
Working Group "Accounting and Reporting of Intangible Assets" (2013). Management control and reporting of intangibles. *Schmalenbach Business Review, 4*(Special Issue), 1–201.
Zicari, A., & Perera-Aldama, L. (2020). Building from scratch: An auto-ethnographic approach for the development of a social reporting model. *Social and Environmental Accountability Journal, 92*, 1–15.
Zollo, M., Minoja, M., & Coda, V. (2018). Toward an integrated theory of strategy. *Strategic Management Journal, 39*(6), 1753–1778.

Marco Möhrer is a sustainability researcher at the Leadership Excellence Institute Zeppelin (LEIZ) at Zeppelin University, where he also wrote his doctoral thesis entitled Shared Value Statement—Concept and Measurement of Business Value Creation. His research concerns the accounting of intangibles, shared value measurement, and value-added analysis. He is the author of several publications on Corporate Social Responsibility and Impact Measurement. Marco Möhrer is also responsible for leading the expert group on Green Controlling for Responsible Business at the International Association of Controllers (ICV).

Managing Global Production Networks: Towards Social Responsibility via Inter-organizational Reliability?

Jörg Sydow, Elke Schüßler, and Markus Helfen

Abstract Taking a whole network perspective, we theorize on whether and how global production networks can enhance their social responsibility by managing the inter-organizational relations that constitute such networks in a more reliable way. Combining insights from the literature on network governance and the management of inter-firm networks, we develop a practice-based perspective on how inter-organizational reliability, understood as the recurrent and effective collaboration of organizations in a network to ensure outcome quality, process stability and work safety, can be extended to issues of social responsibility in the area of labour standards. Our core argument is that creating and nourishing relations between lead firms and suppliers enhances not only inter-organizational reliability but can contribute to a higher degree of social responsibility in global production networks. For network management, i.e. selection, evaluation, allocation and regulation, this means paying more attention to where managing for reliability and responsibility in networks converges in practice. The task at hand for research is to improve our understanding of exactly how and under what conditions inter-organizational reliability contributes to network responsibility.

Keywords Supply chain risks · Inter-firm network · Global production network · Corporate social responsibility · Reliability–responsibility sweet spot · Multi-party work arrangements · Practice perspective · Labour standards

1 Introduction

Countless failures of global industries to ensure the reliability of the operations and deliveries and, at the same time, act in a socially and environmentally responsible way, can be related to work processes being dispersed among a multitude of organizations

J. Sydow (✉) · M. Helfen
Freie Universität Berlin, Berlin, Germany
e-mail: Joerg.Sydow@fu-berlin.de

E. Schüßler
Johannes Kepler Universität Linz, Linz, Austria

L. Biggiero et al. (eds.), *The Relational View of Economics*, Relational Economics and Organization Governance, https://doi.org/10.1007/978-3-030-86526-9_8

acting in and collaborating across different institutional environments. The fact that these environments are characterized not only by diverse government regulations and societal norms, but often also by different levels of economic development, adds to the complications of managerial practice. In the decade before the Covid-19 outbreak, the quintessence of irresponsible supply chain management was to be found in the garment industry where, on April 24, 2013, the collapse of the Rana Plaza factory complex in Bangladesh took the lives of more than 1,100 workers. This accident put the spotlight on the precarious safety of garment workers. Despite a concerted multilateral effort by firms, governments, unions and social movements to improve building safety particularly in Bangladesh (Reinecke & Donaghey, 2015), labour standard violations are still widespread in the industry (Ashwin et al., 2020a, b; Kabeer et al., 2020).

Meanwhile, many incidents in other regions and industries, from mining and shipbreaking to food production and electronics, have received far less public attention—until the outbreak of Covid-19 acted like a magnifying glass. To take just one example, the recurrent scandals around the manipulated off-shore testing of pharmaceuticals have already almost been forgotten, while the pandemic begs the question of under what working conditions personal protective equipment and pharmaceuticals like antibiotics—urgently needed in the current Covid-19 pandemic—are manufactured in and shipped from countries like China, India, Bangladesh or Myanmar (e.g. Gereffi, 2020). Covid-19 has also highlighted substandard working conditions in the heart of Western economies, be it workers in meatpacking plants across Europe, warehouse workers in the United States or textile manufacturers in the UK. These examples are related to a broader question concerning the reliability and responsibility of today's global production networks (GPN), where often sweatshop-like working conditions result from delegating responsibility for workers upstream in the supply chain, not only putting workers' lives at risk, but also destabilizing production and causing significant reputational damage.

Against the background of such "network failures" (Schrank & Whitford, 2011) we ask *whether and how social responsibility in and of GPNs can be enhanced by managing the inter-organizational relations that constitute such networks in a more reliable way*. We do so by favouring a bottom-up perspective which starts from the multi-party work arrangements "on the ground" of GPNs to understand how these increase (or decrease) the reliability of networked operations in global production, possibly thus contributing to improved network responsibility. While reliability and responsibility are often treated as being unrelated, and could even be perceived as conflictive, we argue here that network management is capable of contributing towards shaping GPN in a way that combines increasing demands for reliable operations and deliveries with social responsibility. Hence, it may be worth searching for a "reliability–responsibility sweet spot" at which the interests of firms, customers and workers intersect. In the case of personal protective equipment, for instance, more advanced manufacturing technologies at home and redundant (rather than single) sourcing relations in consequently more extensive production networks could serve the significantly increased demand in end markets (e.g. Gereffi, 2020). In addition, better labour standards, workers' voice and the protection of working conditions (e.g. Anner, 2015) are likely to secure not only the continuous supply of high-quality products, but also a more responsible work environment abroad.

Thus, rather than transferring the responsibility for unreliable and irresponsible GPN to failing regulators (Salminen, 2019), overburdened unions (Fichter et al., 2011), resource-constrained advocacy or consumer groups (Fransen & Burgoon, 2015), or sporadic forms of individual activism (Anner, 2015), we highlight management practices and how they contribute directly to the (ir)responsibility in GPN. Adopting a practice-based perspective that accounts for the duality of structure and agency (Giddens, 1984) and making use of taller rather than a flat ontology (Seidl & Whittington, 2014) allows for a multi-level analysis of how the multi-party work arrangements at the heart of GPN are dynamically shaped by network governance structures and management practices over time and contribute to inter-organizational reliability and network responsibility. For such a perspective it is obviously necessary to take agency and structure into account, such as the (failing) institutions of industrial relations (Helfen et al., 2018).

To answer the research question, we first explain the governance and management of global production networks, paying particular attention to their relational dimension. Then we explore how both network governance structures and management practices can contribute to developing reliable multi-party work arrangements as a basis for (more) social responsibility. We then discuss in greater detail, and with particular respect to managing global production networks, how practices of selection, allocation, regulation and evaluation (cf. Sydow et al., 2016) can contribute to more inter-organizational reliability and thereby increase the scope of choice to improve the standard of network responsibility. We conclude by discussing further implications for studying and managing work and employment arrangements that cross organizational boundaries.

2 Global Production Networks, Their Governance and Management

Inter-organizational networks are generally defined "as a group of three or more organizations connected in ways that facilitate achievement of a common goal" (Provan et al., 2007: 482). When all or at least most of these organizations strive for profit, one may speak of inter-*firm* networks (for a related application to the more or less integrated governance of "networked CSR" see Albareda & Waddock, 2018). More often than not inter-firm networks are strategically led by one or even several "hub firms" (Jarillo, 1988) that are engaged in the orchestration not only of collaborative, multiplex, and long-term vertical client–supplier relationships, but also of horizontal relationships with other business partners (in R&D consortia, for example). Strategic leadership of inter-firm networks, however, does not imply that customers or suppliers, positioned up- and downstream the value chain, have no influence on the structuration of the inter-organizational relationships and practices

(Holmen & Pedersen, 2010; Raj-Reichert, 2020; Sako & Zylberberg, 2019). To the contrary, at least lead customers and first-tier suppliers, many of them transnational actors themselves, are also influential. Obviously, this supplier influence depends upon their managerial capabilities and is moderated—not least with respect to work and employment arrangements (Dallas et al., 2019)—by the involved countries' institutional settings in industrial relations (Brammer et al., 2012; Kano et al., 2020). For instance, lead suppliers may opt for including high value-adding activities (e.g. design or business services) in their portfolio or co-shaping working arrangements by placing CSR requirements on their suppliers (Leppelt et al., 2013).

2.1 Governance of Global Production Networks

"Strategic networks" (Jarillo, 1988), which are strategically led by a hub firm (cf. Müller-Seitz, 2012), have become common for organizing economic activities across national boundaries, complementing the export of goods and services and multinational corporations (MNC) as the market and hierarchical alternative, respectively. When these activities span not only nations but even continents, they are appropriately termed "global production networks" (e.g. Coe & Yeung, 2015, 2019; Henderson et al., 2002) or GPN for short. Sometimes they are more accurately addressed as "global value networks" (Helfen et al., 2018) to avoid (unintended) bias towards manufacturing processes and instead focus on all organizations that are directly involved in the process of value creation, including selling and servicing among others. Typically arranged around and coordinated by large MNC acting as hubs or lead firms (Coe & Yeung, 2015, 2019; Helfen et al., 2018; Levy, 2008; Sydow & Frenkel, 2013), cross-border outsourcing or offshoring to reduce labour cost (rather than transaction cost in the first place) continues to drive the global dissemination of this organizational form of economic activity. In fact, GPN have by now become a ubiquitous phenomenon in the organization of providing almost any kind of goods and services (ILO, 2015; OECD et al., 2014; UNCTAD, 2013) and, with their organizationally fragmented and spatially dispersed but nevertheless reflexively coordinated business, "recognized as the new long-term structural feature of the global economy" (Kano et al., 2020: 579).

Nevertheless, and shifting the focus of analysis somewhat, how to exactly conceptualize the governance of enduring networks of this kind, combining substantial value creation and capturing the capabilities of clients, producers and suppliers, is still a matter of debate (Holmen & Pedersen, 2010; Roberts, 2007; Sako & Zylberberg, 2019). Following Williamson's (1991) seminal characterization of networks as being "hybrids" or intermediary forms between market and hierarchy, Gereffi et al. (2005) have not only applied this typology and Williamson's transaction cost-focused theorizing to GPN—or, in their parlance, "Global Value Chains" (GVC), but also extended it. They did so by splitting up "hybrids" into three types of network governance: modular, relational and captive forms. While modular GVC are based on well-defined interfaces, favour price competition and hence lean to the market form, captive GVC are led by a hub firm orchestrating the network of dependent firms in an almost hierarchical mode of governance. Only relational GVC, to be found, for instance, in the automotive industry, correspond to the ideal of a collaborative, more participative network form of governance (Powell, 1990), though often restricted to the interaction between the original equipment manufacturer (OEM) and its lead customers and key suppliers in the wider centre of GPN.

The importance of the network form, in either of the three modes or types, is now undebated, even by institutional economists who were originally sceptical about the stability of this particular form of governance (Williamson, 1991). In the face of this development, also with an eye on the global scale, Wieland (2020) builds upon institutionalist thought and proposes the development of "relational economics." For this endeavour, he not only points—in contrast to classical institutional economists—to the relevance of collaborative (rather than only transactional) relations, but also to that of relational norms, anchored in compliance with legal regulations, human rights, environmental and social standards, and—last but not least—moral integrity.

With a focus on public organizations, Provan and Kenis (2008) presented their typology of network governance. This typology also distinguishes between a relational or shared form of governance and a lead-organization governance, adding, however, what the authors call "network administrative organizations" (NAO) as an important third type. In contrast to Gereffi and colleagues' typology, these two authors focus not on dyadic buyer–supplier relationships, but explicitly also on the whole network level of analysis (cf. Provan et al., 2007). Most recently, Kenis and colleagues (2019), also concentrating on this level, have specified and extended this typology by allowing NAOs to support both shared and lead-organization forms of network governance. In addition, they now also account for more than one organization to lead complex inter-organizational networks; a complexity that cannot be avoided when, for instance, containing or mitigating a crisis like the present pandemic.

Multiple lead organizations are as important for the power dynamics unfolding in GPN, as is the power asymmetry between client and supplying firms in the captive and the hierarchical modes (Lund-Thomsen & Lindgreen, 2014: 14). For example, important GPN of Japanese origin have always had more than one hub firm orchestrating the network (Lincoln & Shimotani, 2010). In consequence, we would like to add to both typologies that relational types of governance, in one form or the other, dominate the core of GPN, but hierarchical and market forms of coordination continue to matter at the same time.

2.2 *Managing (Strategically Led) Global Production Networks*

Beyond a debate on devising an appropriate typology of network governance, it is important to consider that whatever is the governance structure of whole networks, in the end what matters is the actual management practices deployed. These are both enabled and restrained by more formal governance structures. In turn, as emphasized by quite a diverse range of practice theories (Nicolini, 2012), not least structuration theory (Giddens, 1984) that have already been applied to understand the structuration of strategic networks (Berends et al., 2011; Sydow & Windeler, 1998; Sydow et al., 2016), network management—or more precisely: network management practices—not only produces and reproduces, but may also eventually transform these structures.

We consider in particular four core practices for managing networks: how the members of a network are selected, how resources and responsibilities are allocated, how collaboration is regulated and how participants, relationships and practices are evaluated (Sydow & Windeler, 1998; Sydow et al., 2016). The efficacy of these network management practices is hereby not only influenced by the mode of network governance but also—on a more microlevel—by the (intra-) organizational and—on a more macrolevel—institutional structure in which networks are embedded (Barley & Tolbert, 1997; Vaara & Whittington, 2012). By highlighting management practices, we follow Sako and Zylberberg (2019) and others and incorporate insights from more recent management and organization studies into research on GVC/GPN.

3 Relating Inter-organizational Reliability and Network Responsibility

So far, network governance as well as network management, not to mention their mutual constitution in strategically led GPN, is theoretically underspecified with respect to network responsibility and inter-organizational reliability. This particularly holds for their interplay with work and employment systems and labour standards in GPN (Helfen et al., 2018; Lakhani et al., 2013). Therefore, we focus here on reliability and responsibility in these areas as being two specific network goals that challenge both traditional network governance and network management. Seen as network-level outcomes, inter-organizational reliability and network responsibility may contribute to, but are not identical with, traditional network outcomes discussed in the literature around the notions of "network effectiveness" (Provan & Milward, 1995) or even "relational advantage" (Dyer & Singh, 1998; Roberts, 2007), i.e. additional inter-organizational benefits stemming from joint value creation and the pooling of resources in networks.

When the process of value creation is distributed among various parties, *inter-organizational reliability* can be understood as the recurrent and effective collaboration of organizations in the network to ensure not only outcome quality, process stability and work safety on a continuous basis, but also emergency responsiveness when needed. Such reliability guarantees the undisturbed, ideally error-free value creation and, as far as firms are involved, value appropriation processes by anticipating and containing incidents in the course of its operations (Roberts, 1990; Weick & Sutcliff, 2007; both with reference to high-reliability organizations).

Hence, inter-organizational reliability is a multi-faceted construct. Ramanujam (2018) reviews the meanwhile rather extensive literature on high-reliability and reliability-seeking organizations, listing three aspects that are not mutually exclusive, but seem relevant to conceptualize inter-organizational reliability. The first, reliability as *performance consistency*, has already been alluded to above. In the case of inter-organizational reliability this aspect refers to the ability of organizations "to consistently perform [in their interactions] intended or required function[s] or mission[s], on demand and without degradation or failure" (Ramanujam, 2018: 20). This aspect might be weakly linked to labour standards in GPN, e.g. when the intended function is to consistently and reliably produce cheap goods. The second, which conceives reliability as involving *safety*, is also implied in our definition above. The aspect of safety "emphasizes the avoidance of harm through ongoing management of the risk of injury, danger, or less from routine operations" (Ramanujam, 2018: 20). This aspect is obviously linked particularly closely to labour standards in GPN. The third, finally, translates reliability into *resilience*, thereby focusing on "the organizational response to and recovery from a major shock such as an accident" (Ramanujam, 2018: 22). The same author emphasizes the need not only for a multi-faceted, but also for multi-level consideration of the topic, explicitly mentioning the inter-organizational level.

The extent to which inter-organizational reliability, then, requires—on more micro levels—reliable individuals, teams, organizational subunits or entire organizations and—on more macro levels—reliable whole networks or technical and institutional infrastructures is an important follow-up question. In networks, coordination failure at an interface between single network participants—here: organizations—often has network-wide repercussions for the reliability of service and product delivery (e.g. the regular "call back actions" of faulty products by OEMs; cf. Wowak & Boone, 2015) as well as work safety and employment security. As much as a distinct set of challenges on the network level emerges from risks and uncertainties for individual firms, it also goes beyond that, as the entire networked value creation process may well be disrupted by operational failures, technological breakdowns and natural disasters (Bode et al., 2011).

Network responsibility refers to the expectation that the social and natural environments are prominently considered in practices not only on the level of individual organizations, in particular firms (e.g. Jackson & Brammer, 2014), and in dyadic buyer–supplier relationships (e.g. Crespin-Mazet & Dontenwill, 2012), but also on the whole network level (e.g. Helfen et al., 2018). While the discourse about Corporate Social Responsibility (CSR) has focused for decades on the missions and practices of single corporations (cf. Jackson & Brammer, 2014; Matten & Moon, 2020), the idea to extend responsibility to the level of whole networks is of a more recent origin (cf. Lund-Thomsen, 2020; Lund-Thomsen & Lindgreen, 2014, 2018). With an eye on the network level, and in this particular respect in line with the all-inclusive approach to GPN, we also consider other stakeholders like NGOs, transnational institutions (such as the ILO) and global unions playing a role in the transfer of socially responsible practices within GPN (Fichter et al., 2011; Helfen & Fichter, 2013).

In a similar way to inter-organizational resilience (Datta, 2017), reliability requires increased agility and flexibility, increased training and deference to expertise, consciously created redundancies and risk awareness. Above all, intensive inter-organizational collaboration, as an outcome as well as a means of network-wide information sharing and reflexive coordination, could contribute significantly to increased inter-organizational reliability. If all this applies in practice, then, the question arises as to why should work and employment relations, in particular responsibly designed multi-party work arrangements, not also contribute to increasing the reliability of GPN. Inasmuch as these would, at the same time, decrease violations of labour standards, they reflect a dimension of network responsibility. In other words: Is there a reliability–responsibility sweet spot where the interests of firms and workers in labour standards intersect?

We argue here that, in dealing with socio-technical supply chain risks resulting in the violation of (product) quality standards as well as the interruption of frictionless procedures and process stability (Peck, 2006), work arrangements are indeed key to inter-organizational reliability. This has already been made perfectly clear by various standards and auditing processes, especially in the areas of quality as well as health and safety, and their extension to contractors and personnel service providers (Lim & Prakash, 2017). Apart from such a purely technically motivated approach, which is a rather reactive and indirect one with regards to the wider array of proactive capabilities of human-centred work arrangements, a pre-emptive approach may contribute to coping with major disruptions (Lengnick et al., 2011). Network responsibility goes beyond a focus on technical and processual supply chain risks towards including wider aspects of labour relations and social labour standards, such as those governing the systems for training and skill development, employee satisfaction and worker participation and empowerment through unions and collective bargaining. Our main argument in this paper is that, without the protection, participation and promotion of workers (Sengenberger, 1994), inter-organizational reliability—at least in its most commonly understood facets—remains hollow. Nevertheless, inter-organizational reliability and network (social) responsibility do not always go hand in hand. Rather, it is an important task for management and organization research to explore the potential overlaps and to help managers, worker representatives and policy-makers to identify possible "sweet spots" (Lund-Thomsen & Lindgreen, 2018) between the two network goals, which may occasionally also be in conflict with one another.

4 Managing and Governing Global Production Networks for Reliability and Responsibility

Achieving both reliability and responsibility in a more or less simultaneous management process—or one quality with the help of the other—depends critically on the ways in which work arrangements are managed in GPN, because economic, product quality, regulatory, labour and environmental risks often overlap (Coe & Yeung,

2015, 2019; Sydow & Frenkel, 2013). In these cases, it may be a valid starting point to assume that, as much as responsible practices within and among firms in a network are likely to contribute to inter-organizational reliability, such reliability reinforces socially (and very likely also environmentally) responsible network management practices. However, the goals of reliability and responsibility may also clash. On the network level, suppliers and service providers systematically linked into the GPN face the tension of meeting cost reduction and flexibility demands, while at the same time having to build a reputation as a reliable as well as socially responsible and environmentally sustainable employer. A crucial differentiation from a network perspective in this regard is whether reliability and responsibility refer to properties of the whole network, or whether there is a less ambitious focus on inter-organizational reliability and responsibility, e.g. in single buyer–supplier relations, possibly hardly beyond the core of the network. In our endeavour to clarify the relationship between reliability and responsibility, we concentrate our analysis on the impact of work and employment systems upon inter-organizational reliability and, thereby, network responsibility. The reference to structuration theory, however, sensitizes for recursive co-constitutive processes, including considerations about how the latter may support the former.

Work arrangements in GPN are usually spatially dispersed, organizationally fragmented and institutionally separated. Nevertheless, due to the powerful hands of the lead firm(s), the work arrangements of more often than not far-away suppliers, subcontractors and service providers are influenced by these firms and their (lack of) network management practices that take work and employment arrangements into account. This is due to the fact that multi-party arrangements directly and indirectly involve the (corporate) client(s) in work performance (e.g. Frenkel et al., 1999; Rubery et al., 2003; Kinnie et al., 2005; Marchington et al., 2005, 2011; Bidwell, & Fernandez-Mateo, 2008; Bélanger & Edwards, 2013; Cappelli & Keller, 2013; Weil, 2019). Against this background, it is surprising that the study of work and employment systems and their actual or prospective contribution to social responsibility does not figure prominently in international business research that has increasingly been looking at responsibility issues over the last two decades or so (Leonidou et al., 2019).

A widely accepted and empirically tested framework, explaining consistently how managing multi-party work arrangements in GPN can contribute to inter-organizational reliability and network responsibility, is still to be developed. Figure 1 illustrates a first attempt to systemize the building blocks of such a model, focusing on network social responsibility (Helfen et al., 2018). This model adopts, again in line with structuration theory, a taller (rather than flat) process ontology (Seidl & Whittington, 2014), and acknowledges the interplay between the management practices on a (focal) network level and the firm- (more micro) and field-level structures (more macro) in which they are embedded. It aims to explain how network governance and respective network management practices of selecting, allocating, regulating and evaluating can affect GPN towards social responsibility, here more precisely network responsibility via inter-organizational reliability. It provides the basis for the following discussion on how network governance and network management can influence reliability and responsibility.

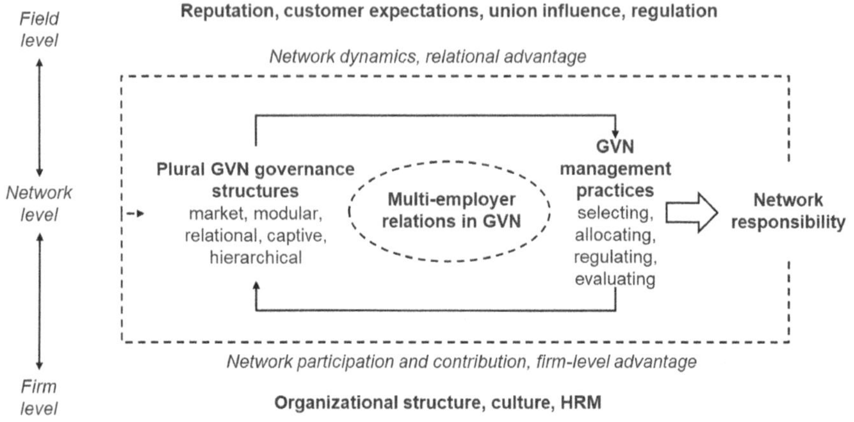

Fig. 1 A network management perspective on employment relations in GPN (Helfen et al., 2018: 1656)

4.1 Network Governance for Reliability and Responsibility

With respect to reliability and responsibility, network governance sets a structural frame for organizing work across organizational boundaries. However, from a practice perspective, it is necessary to understand how work performed inter-organizationally is not only enabled and constrained by these structures, i.e. rules and resources (Giddens, 1984), but in turn shapes network governance structures itself. Actually, it is not well understood how workers and their organizations enact, reproduce and transform network governance, i.e. what their role is in network structuration, and therefore difficult to understand the practice of *governing* whole inter-firm networks, including GPN, with an eye on work and employment.

Only few studies directly link supply chain governance to issues of work and employment across GPN. One fruitful theorization of the structural conditions of employment relations within global production networks is given by Lakhani et al. (2013). Combining Gereffi and colleagues' (2005) GVC governance modes with the criteria on task environments of widely accepted employment systems, Lakhani and colleagues construct a typology on how different value chain configurations produce different outcomes in employment relations as described by skills and knowledge, employment stability and the relevance of the idiosyncrasies of local industrial relations. If one crosses these network governance modes with the criteria of work and employment systems, it is expected that three modes, i.e. relational, modular or market modes, tend towards market governance and provide obstacles for a labour-oriented governance, whereas lead firms in hierarchical and captive configurations will not only be easier to hold accountable, but are also better able to influence working conditions and employment relations in by and large dependent subsidiaries and suppliers. These arguments are further refined by Lund-Thomsen and Lindgren (2018), who find that the mutual dependence of buyers and suppliers in relational modes of governance make it harder to align commercial and worker interests, whereas in captive modes buyers are able to enforce compliance norms. Whether or not compliance regimes lead to better labour standards, however, crucially depends on purchasing practices and whether they reflect concerns for labour standards in their purchasing prices (Amengual et al., 2019; Kuruvilla et al., 2020; Schuessler et al., 2019).

The limited influence in the first three modes originates in an increased degree of independence among suppliers, at least first-tier suppliers, and in an associated increased need for inter-organizational coordination. Additional third-party intermediaries such as buying agents (Oka, 2010) may contribute both to increased independence and to the need for coordination. Several other studies point out that certain relationship qualities may overcome these obstacles, including buying power and long-run, collaborative relationships built around quality issues leading to better labour-related outcomes (e.g. Frenkel & Scott, 2002; Locke, 2013). The rationale here is that within repeated, collaborative and rather long-term relationships, various kinds of safeguards against labour standard violations can be developed and knowledge and other resources exchanged.

Obviously, it is possible to draw a link between the governance of buyer–supplier relations and responsible employment relations in networks. This requires, however, a first step into the direction of a change in perspective from the policies of the single focal firms towards a consideration of network-wide employment relations. Of course, other regulative, normative and cognitive pressures stemming from the institutional field (Scott, 1995) may also be considered key to identifying the formal and informal mechanisms that lead firms might use for governing GPN towards more responsibility.

Irrespective of whether referring to the typology of network governance developed by Gereffi and colleagues (2005) or Provan and Kenis (2008), however, all modes of network governance have distinct implications for organizing work across organizational boundaries and, thereby, for inter-organizational reliability and network responsibility. In the following, we use the Provan and Kenis (2008) typology that was recently expanded by Kenis et al. (2019) because it includes a shared mode of network governance and adds an NAO to each of the modes. While GPN, as argued above, definitively lean more towards the lead-organization mode of governance, the installation of an NAO may add a governance structure that is particularly *able* to support network management practices towards more network responsibility by focusing more on inter-organizational reliability. Whether it is really employed towards this end in practice is a different matter.

(1) The shared (participant) mode of governance is based upon mutual and participative self-organization among all actors in the network. In this case, close collaboration between all network participants, reflected in frequent interaction and multiplex relationships, for instance, has to ensure responsibility and reliability, not least with respect to those roles that carry out the boundary work (Langley et al., 2019). In other words, all of the network participating organizations, more precisely the boundary

spanners acting on their behalf, are needed to care for a network's reliability and share responsibilities for work processes and outcomes. This mode of network governance assumes more than any other that practitioners of more or less all the network participants are in charge and succeed in reaching a consensus. In this type of governance, the work practices of the network participants remain diverse. Given the specific goals, distinct capabilities and high autonomy of the member organizations (the latter also including the decision to participate in the network) diversity is likely to stay, even if the responsible and reliable network actions have become a common concern for network participants. In any case, because of the decentralized nature of the process, the coordination of practices among the network participants and the building of a consensus certainly takes time and needs to overcome short-sighted selfishness. Such an approach without any centralized assistance is indeed presumably, as suggested by Provan and Kenis (2008), more suitable for networks that are, unlike GPN, small in size and coordinate processes that afford only low capital intensity within a regional agglomeration of participants characterized by labour utilization of the professional type.

(2) In the lead-organization mode, one (or a small group of) participant(s) assume(s) the role of a "network orchestrator" (Paquin & Howard-Grenville, 2013). In this case, the lead organization or, in GPN more precisely the hub firm, bears the burden of coordination, although some of the coordinating task may be "delegated" to lead customers and/or key suppliers. In consequence, the lead firm(s) remain(s) de facto (not yet legally) in charge of the responsibility and reliability of network activities. Depending on the work environment, for example, distinguished by asset specificity, task separability and other criteria (Gereffi et al., 2005), centrally placed OEMs might have a higher stake in ensuring some network-wide coordinated work standards than service providers more likely working at the network's periphery. At the same time, the former may have pushed outsourcing and offshoring for a reason that now makes it difficult, if not impossible, to organize for more reliability and/or responsibility. In the case of the lead-organization mode of network governance, quasi-hierarchical forms of authority exist (in particular in the captive mode) and, based upon power asymmetries, open up different possibilities. In this case, the work practices of the lead organization, either a dominant producer like an OEM in car manufacturing (e.g. Dyer & Nobeoka, 2000) or a provider of key services like an airport authority (Helfen et al., 2020), are likely at least to try to set some standards in the network; not least if they wish to secure network responsibility and reliability. Lead organizations are distinguished by their managerial capacity to bring other network participants as well as governance units to support those particular rules for network governance that are aligned with their strategic prerogatives, including those for organizing work and securing labour standards. A firm's reach to exert influence on work practices in the whole network is, however, likely to decline with each step away from the lead organization. Giving relevance to the always prevalent scope of strategic choice (Child, 1972), the lead firm, as is common in many GPN (Sydow & Frenkel, 2013), can also pursue a course of action that, via outsourcing and offshoring, deepens the differences in labour practices among the network participants. This course of action is likely to promote the inequalities between central and

peripheral network organizations, even if they endanger the reliability of the inter-firm network. Within the lead-organization mode, these options of the core firm begin to counteract network responsibility and reliability, as they make such problems arise exactly where a centrally network-wide coordination of work practices may stop short. Examples for pursuing this mode are supplier workshops organized by a hub firm extended to issues of organizing work and managing human resources (e.g. Palmer et al., 2015; Roberts, 2007: 196) or other quasi-externalized solutions organized by core firms to cover issues of work and employment in supply networks (Gospel & Sako, 2010).

(3) The network administrator mode removes the organizational burden of governance to some extent from network participants, by making governing the network the task of a specialized unit, i.e. the NAO. But only in rare cases will an NAO take over all responsibility for the management of the network. In line with the recent expansion of Provan and Kenis' (2008) typology by Kenis and colleagues (2019), we would rather argue that an NAO can be found in inter-organizational networks, including GPN, with a shared as well as a lead-organization governance. What is more, an NAO is likely only to support rather than be a substitute for these two forms of network governance. Nevertheless, the responsibility and reliability of the network may reside to a large extent with the NAO, although the ultimate responsibility may well remain with either the lead organization or all network participants. In this mode, responsibility and reliability *could* be achieved more easily through organizing work across firm boundaries, because this form of governance is, in the long run, better suited to balancing relational advantages with individual contributions than the shared or lead-organization governance modes without an NAO. Of course, much depends upon how the administrating unit is set up, structured, resourced and run; and how much emphasis is, thereby, placed on network responsibility and reliability. Like within organizations, where the separation of responsibilities among a CSR unit on the one hand (mainly symbolic) and the purchasing department on the other (overwhelmingly substantial) is still quite common (Lund-Thomsen & Lindgreen, 2014), much depends on how the NAO is tied into the network. It also matters whether the network administrator is recruited from within the network, or is an external player added to the network.

Interestingly enough, external actors are currently taking over part of this administrator role. That is, gigantic personnel service providers (Manpower, etc.) or other "labor market intermediaries" (Bonet et al., 2013) provide organizations and, increasingly, inter-organizational networks including GPN with manpower. Only in specific cases would one expect this option to contribute to greater responsibility and reliability in the whole network (Coe & Jordhus-Lier, 2011), although, in principle, a network could profit from the specialized capabilities of service providers. But this way of administrating the network typically aims at exploiting the tension of multi-party work arrangements at the expense of (temporary) workers and to the benefit of the (more or less permanent) service provider, i.e. securing the availability of labour and lowering the cost of employment at the same time. The whole network is then confronted with a plethora of reliability and accountability problems stemming from the respective multi-party work arrangements.

(4) Finally, in GPN with more than one hub or lead firm, network responsibility and reliability depend to a large extent upon how this plurality of network orchestrators is willing and able to coordinate the core of the network with regard to work and employment. Only if they succeed in doing so, as in Japanese keiretsu, though with a decreasing rather than increasing emphasis on decent working conditions and employment relations (Lincoln & Shimotani, 2010), or as in the mainly collaborative relationship between an airport authority and its home carrier/airline (Helfen et al., 2020), is it possible to influence the actors of the peripheral network. The coordination of the central actors, however, is at best a necessary but by no means sufficing precondition for organizing for more network responsibility and reliability.

4.2 Network Management for Reliability and Responsibility

The identification of governance types, largely driven by structural considerations such as network size, the heterogeneity of its participants and the organization of its leadership, is just one part of the structuration of whole GPN. The other part is the practices of managers and other individual or collective agents (e.g. states, labour actors or NGOs) to fill in the gaps that remain within a set of structural constraints (or even to change or circumvent these constraints). For example, agents may attempt to select among the diversity of governance modes, apply a mixture of these, or even generate new ones. While network participants often follow programmed scripts embodied in organizational routines in their day-to-day dealings, they are also subject to the idiosyncrasies of situations and contexts and events such as the present Covid-19 crisis, in which they need to adapt, reshape or abandon these very routines. This also holds for GPN managers and management units addressing reliability and responsibility challenges in the buyer–supplier relationships and beyond. In what follows, we discuss how the four key areas of managerial practices that impinge on the quality of networks, i.e. selecting, allocating, regulating, and evaluating, address inter-organizational reliability and can have an impact on network responsibility. We illustrate the respective practices with regard to work organization and employment relations. As is most common for GPN, we assume the existence of a hub firm, possibly supported by an NAO (see Table 1).

Selecting network participants with their domains. Selecting (and also excluding) network participants heavily influences the underlying type and structure of the respective inter-firm network, shaping the buyer–supplier relationships as well as the horizontal inter-organizational relations. This management practice defines the entry points and access rules to a GPN, e.g. whether multiple network memberships (increasingly common for first-tier suppliers in the global automotive industry) are tolerated or not. Selecting firms for network participation by applying criteria that emphasize social responsibility and reliability on the part of the organizational members is also likely to increase the overall responsibility and reliability in a network. Examples for the former are criteria which directly focus on work standards (e.g. the ILO conventions); examples for the latter are those with an indirect

Table 1 Network governance and network management and its impact upon multi-party work arrangements in GPN

Network management practices	Main objects	Generic practices addressing reliability	Generic practices impacting responsibility	Illustrative practices
Selecting	Network participants with their domain of activity	Selecting reliable network members, able to contribute to inter-organizational reliability with an eye on performance consistency, safety, and resilience	Selecting network members with concern for working conditions and labour relations	Reducing the number of subcontractors; using health and safety as well as quality labour-standards as criteria in joint (de-) selection procedures; network-wide sanctioning and corrective action plans in case of violations
Allocating	Tasks, resources and responsibilities	Adapting task, resource and responsibility allocation to available organizational capacities, also to stimulate reliable future development	Adapting task, resource and responsibility allocation to network members in a way that increases network responsibility based upon organizations' (developed) capacities	Allocating resources for network-wide dissemination of information, capacity building, and control; developing management systems (quality, environment, health and safety) focusing business relations (e.g. ISO 45001, SCC, SCP); developing price and incentive systems that allow for responsible work relations (e.g. increasing purchasing prices after the implementation of corrective action plans)

(continued)

Table 1 (continued)

Network management practices	Main objects	Generic practices addressing reliability	Generic practices impacting responsibility	Illustrative practices
Regulating	Network relations and practices	Implementing formal and informal rules that support inter-organizational reliability	Implementing formal and informal rules that support network responsibility	Developing the network towards a more participative and inclusive mix of governance modes by strengthening horizontal relations among buyers, suppliers and worker representatives; enabling collective workers' voice; implementing ILO conventions in standard supply contracts and purchasing practices; signing global framework agreements, accompanied by network-wide information and training
Evaluating	Network participants, relationships and practices	Employing indicators of inter-organizational reliability as evaluation criteria	Employing indicators of CSR and stretching them as evaluation criteria for network responsibility	Linking management evaluations to network performance indicators and joint social responsibility criteria; assessing network risks in supply chain due diligence, inclusion of labour in due diligence process (e.g. OECD Due Diligence Guidelines for the Garment and Footwear Sector)

effect for instance on quality, health and safety, and environmental standards (e.g. ISO family). However, for networks, it may be important to identify and apply these standards in a relational process, also involving external stakeholders (e.g. unions) to lift network-wide practices. Of course, network management of this kind needs to be reflective of place-specific institutional contexts (e.g. influential unions, customer rights) but also be aware of the tension between each network participant's practices and their repercussions in the wider network. This is because—within the context of reliability and responsibility as network goals—practices influencing the interests of network participants and the network as a collective are interdependent. For example, work and employment systems that cut across organizational boundaries need to be reflective of the fact that hub firms, but also first-tier suppliers, even key customers, service providers and other (sub-)contractors, may introduce work and human resource-related practices to the network, thereby altering the coalitions among (sub-)network actors within a network (Holmen & Pedersen, 2010). Acknowledging work and employment systems, and their peculiar network form of multi-party work arrangements as being relevant for reliability and responsibility seems to be easier in dense, quasi-hierarchically integrated networks like the one orchestrated by Toyota in the automotive industry (Aoki & Wilhelm, 2017; Dyer & Nobeoka, 2000; Van Driel & Dolfsma, 2009).

Allocating network tasks, resources and responsibilities. In allocating as a network management practice, the tasks, resources and responsibilities are reflexively distributed among the network's participants but, for this very reason, have also to be brought together to achieve network and participant goals. In this context, the unequal resource endowments of the network firms, especially between the hub firm and the others, are a source of tension for work and employment systems (for SMEs see Edwards et al., 2006). Obviously, different stakeholders, employees, suppliers, clients and members of an inter-firm network may compete over their share in value creation and appropriation (e.g. OEM vs. suppliers) which, depending on institutional conditions inside and outside the system of industrial relations (Brammer et al., 2012), makes a network-wide collaboration in questions of remuneration as well as training and development practices difficult to implement. But there are nevertheless common interests upon which the organization of work and employment across organizational boundaries can be built. This includes the definition of network-wide capacities and competences, for boundary-spanning roles and otherwise, as well as deciding over the employment status of certain groups of workers from the hub firm down to peripheral sub-suppliers. In allocating resources, inter-organizational work and the multi-party work arrangements most likely involved may play their part in deciding over how the firms position themselves in the network and what kind of relationships they develop or maintain in order to ensure inter-organizational reliability with respect to quantitative and qualitative performance continuity, overall work safety, and organizational response and recovery from a major shock. Depending upon the mode of network governance, respective "relationship management" practices could entail deepening horizontal and establishing vertical connections, increasing inclusiveness even in cases where bilateral relationships between network participants are rare, ensuring bottom-up exchange in decentralized networks, and working towards collective self-governance. All these practices, however, would have obvious repercussions for remuneration, work organization and training that may contradict the original interest of a focal firm to outsource or even offshore parts of the value creation process.

Regulating network relations and practices. Regulating focuses on issuing, shaping and enforcing the formal and informal rules of the inter-organizational network. Regulating strategically led inter-firm networks like GPN is, first and foremost, a domain of management decisions, control and prerogatives, typically within the confines of a particular business model imposed on the network by the hub firm from a certain, local institutional environment that influences the organization also of global activities. In our context, and apart from the chosen network governance mode, the question remains as to who effectively controls what resources with the help of which rules in order to organize reliable and responsible production across national boundaries; and who decides in what way over the distribution of earnings and profits in the inter-firm network. This also includes goal setting, as well as decision rights and responsibilities, and involves issues of culture, ideology and power (Vlaar, et al., 2007). As one common feature of inter-firm networks is the fundamental lack of hierarchical authority (Powell, 1990), some management devices for exerting power like hierarchical decision-making and instruments of bureaucratic control are not viable on the whole network level. This is due to the network firms' formal autonomy in making decisions, a limited overview of the whole network, and more or less voluntary conformity to network-wide rules—even in the case of inter-firm networks governed by a captive, not to speak of a relational or modular mode. This lack of hierarchical fiat, which should not be confused with symmetry of power, in particular not within GPN, has severe implications for ensuring network reliability and responsibility by setting formal and informal rules with regard, for instance, to guaranteeing minimum if not decent working and employment conditions. At its core, management has to rely on the more or less voluntary contributions of different actors in the network to formulate and implement rules (including environmental or labour standards), which can be negotiated within a variety of network-internal stakeholder meetings and dialogues (e.g. Palmer et al., 2015). In institutionally diverse contexts, practicing adequate forms of communication (Griffith & Myers, 2005) and building a common identity and language that also integrates peripheral actors are requirements that are not only important for allowing multi-directional knowledge flows across organizational boundaries, but also extremely challenging for network management (Lipparini et al., 2014).

However, the institutional environment also provides for regulatory resources in that some decision rights are subject to stakeholder influence. For example, a key aspect is representation and the voice of workforces. These internal stakeholders obviously, depending upon the respective system of industrial relation in the countries concerned (cf. Bamber et al., 2016), claim a say in the organization of work and employment systems (Rainnie et al., 2011). Apart from labour relations with unions and workers' representatives, ideally supported by bilateral (global framework) agreements instead of unilateral CSR (cf. Fichter et al., 2011), organizing work across firm boundaries takes place within work ethics, professions and labour law, institutions that may either support or undermine respective practices.

As for contributing to network reliability and responsibility, work and employment systems can take on the role of facilitating and stabilizing the interaction among the various organizations participating in the network and, in particular, among the boundary spanners of these organizations. This can be achieved, for instance, by means of deepening relationships and coordinating intervention at the strategic nodes of the network. This also requires an ability to assess the quality of relationships and identify the strategic nodes, i.e. points where it is possible to intervene in multi-party work arrangements with the help of formal or informal, in any case practiced rules to increase reliability and responsibility. For example, intervention in a hub firm such as an OEM in the automotive industry can influence employment relations at not only the subsidiary but also the supplier level, though only to a limited extent. Highly promising in this regard are attempts to collectively regulate work relations through transnational industrial relations agreements that include multiple lead firms as well as union representatives, such as such as the ACT initiative or the Bangladesh Accord in the garment industry (Ashwin et al., 2020a, b) as well as other forms of multi-party bargaining (Blasi & Bair, 2019).

Evaluating network participants, relationships and practices. Regularly, selection, allocation and regulation activities build upon evaluating network participants, relationships and practices; this includes the joint evaluation of respective contributions to achieving network reliability and responsibility. In particular, in the automotive industry evaluation has become a very common practice, not only, but in particular in Japan (Aoki & Wilhelm, 2017). In principle, evaluation criteria or whole evaluation systems could capture network properties including those human resource- and work-related practices that are regarded as being appropriate for addressing reliability and responsibility concerns at the whole network level. Within networks, however, evaluating work systems and employment relations is likely to differ considerably according to different organizational jurisdiction and the diverging high-road or low-road policies and practices for capturing the economic advantages of labour market segmentation. Nevertheless, to ensure network reliability and responsibility, a set of criteria is necessary for evaluating human resource and work-related practices from the network perspective. These aspects are rarely captured by the social auditing practices that dominate to date (Oka et al., 2020).

5 Discussion and Conclusion

Moving further towards a society of networks (Raab & Kenis, 2009) that indeed deserves to be analyzed as a political economy from a relational perspective (Wieland, 2020), inter-organizational reliability as a structural property of GPN may become even more important in the future than it is today. Striving for such reliability, i.e. turning organizations like firms into reliability-seeking organizations (Koch, 1993) and the respective inter-firm networks into reliability-seeking networks (Berthod &

Sydow, 2021), may only be one element in moving from a compliance-based approach towards a "cooperation paradigm" (Lund-Thomsen & Lindgreen, 2014, 2018) in order to promote responsibility in the networks of global production. In other words, increases in network responsibility could be based not only on a more responsible management of single organizations, but also on creating and maintaining collaborative relationships that support this responsibility via increased inter-organizational reliability. For organizing collaboration towards more responsibility as a network-wide goal, the inter-organizational reliability of multi-party work arrangements "on the ground" the critical dimension for network management.

An important step in the direction of a cooperative paradigm is to comprehend GPN as social systems that, at their core as well as their periphery, are not only networks of inter-firm relations but also "systems (of) embodied labour" (Coe & Yeung, 2019: 787, referencing Cumbers et al., 2008). As demonstrated in some detail, network management practices of selecting, allocating, regulating and evaluating—quite like "buffering" and "bridging" as popular strategies to manage supply chain risks (Bode et al., 2011; Manhart et al., 2020)—may all contribute towards these network goals, if used appropriately and collaboratively. However, conflicting demands on suppliers with regard to codes of conduct, continued pressure for low pay and squeeze of margin (Anner, 2015), lack of possibilities to provide continuous employment, and, above all, competitive contexts such as those in the apparel industry in general and fast fashion in particular (e.g. Hammer & Plugor, 2019) make it notoriously difficult to implement a cooperative paradigm.

Lund-Thomsen and Lindgreen (2014: 17) admit themselves that this paradigm, advocated mainly, if at all, by "international brands, Northern-based consultants, academics and NGOs," may not be practicable on the whole network level but only "be feasible with a few selected suppliers, engaged in pilot projects; it appears nearly impossible to replicate such close cooperation across hundreds of suppliers, considering just the logistical challenges." Conceiving GPN as being characterized by a plural rather than only market or hierarchical relational or hybrid/relational form of governance seems to provide a more realistic picture, pointing to the possibilities but also the challenges of organizing for network responsibility via inter-organizational reliability. In consequence, ensuring greater network responsibility via higher inter-organizational reliability may well start at the core of GPN, but remain an unfinished business in institutionally diverse contexts, at least for the years to come. Nevertheless, embracing the networked character of these issues includes taking the kind of governance in GPN and how it is practiced by network management seriously. With regards to the broader issue of human rights (Ruggie, 2003), not only international organizations, but also civil society's networks (for advocacy NGOs' networks, e.g. Zajak et al., 2017; for union networks, e.g. Helfen & Fichter, 2013) as well as corporate social responsibility networks (for business NGOs, e.g. Albareda & Waddock, 2018) have been identified as being relevant for shaping such governance structures and the prevailing practices within these.

Without concrete operational changes in work and employment arrangements that stretch across the system of embodied labour, however, network responsibility via inter-organizational reliability (and vice versa) is unlikely to be achieved, as frictions in distributed work processes and quality problems in products and services will remain untouched due to the divergent work and employment systems operated side-by-side in the network. Conversely, acknowledging an inter-organizational dimension would at least allow human resource management and work organization to manage the fluid and fuzzy structure of multi-party work arrangements. Considering these issues and, in particular, the relationship between inter-organizational reliability and responsibility in networks, a sustainability dimension is added to the currently predominant efficiency- and effectiveness-driven conversation about network governance and network management, not least in the context of GVC (Kano et al., 2020).

Finally, appeals to watch out, not only for the structural details of GPN governance, but also for managerial practices, may sound like pleading for a theoretical shift to the micro-foundations of this organizational form. This is correct from the point of view of the present mainstream treatment of GPN from a more macro perspective, which by and large fails to look at the realized strategies of hub firms and even more so of suppliers in such networks (but see Yeung & Coe, 2015 for explorations in that direction). However, it should not be read as a plea for an individual-level search for behavioural foundations of inter-organizational management. Of course, behavioural aspects are important, but inter-organizational strategy making and structuring are very likely to be better understood in their cross-border institutional context in which value creation and value appropriation is negotiated between capital and labour in developed and developing countries. From a management and organization studies point of view, a practice-based perspective seems to be rather well-equipped for this purpose, because it attempts to understand firm- and network-specific aspects of these undertakings and attributes reliability and responsibility concerns to the organization of systemic forces rather than to individual actors.

References

Albareda, L., & Waddock, S. (2018). Networked CSR governance: A whole network approach to meta-governance. *Business & Society, 57*(4), 636–675.

Amengual, M., Distelhorst, G., & Tobin, D. (2019). Global purchasing as labor regulation: The missing middle. *ILR Review, 73*(4), 817–840.

Anner, M. (2015). Labor control regimes and worker resistance in global supply chains. *Labor History, 56*(3), 292–307.

Aoki, K., & Wilhelm, M. (2017). The role of ambidexterity in managing buyer-supplier relationships: The Toyota case. *Organization Science, 28*(6), 1080–1097.

Ashwin, S., Kabeer, N., & Schüßler, E. (2020a). Contested understandings in the global garment industry after Rana Plaza. *Development and Change, 51*(5), 1296–1305.

Ashwin, S., Oka, C., Schuessler, E., Alexander, R., & Lohmeyer, N. (2020b). Spillover effects across transnational industrial relations agreements: The potential and limits of collective action in global supply chains. *ILR Review, 73*(4), 995–1020.

Bamber, G., Lansbury, R. D., Wailes, N., & Wright, C. F. (Eds.). (2016). *International and comparative employment relations: National Regulation and global changes* (6th ed.). Sage

Barley, S. R., & Tolbert, P. S. (1997). Institutionalization and structuration: Studying the links between action and institution. *Organization Studies, 18*(1), 93–117.

Berends, H., Van Burg, E., & Van Raaj, E. M. (2011). Contacts and contracts: Cross-level network dynamics in the development of an aircraft material. *Organization Science, 22*(4), 940–960.

Berthod, O., & Sydow, J. (2021). Collaborating in high-reliability settings. In J. W. Meek (Ed.), *Handbook of collaborative public management* (pp. 331–348). Elgar.

Bélanger, J., & Edwards, P. (2013). The nature of front-line service work: Distinctive features and continuity in the employment relationship. *Work, Employment and Society, 27*(3), 433–450.

Bidwell, M., & Fernandez-Mateo, I. (2008). Three's a crowd? Understanding triadic employment relationships. In P. Capelli (Ed.), *Employment relationships* (pp. 142–178). Cambridge University Press.

Blasi, J., & Bair, J. (2019). An analysis of multiparty bargaining models for global supply chains. Conditions of Work and Employment Series No. 105. International Labour Organization (ILO).

Bode, C., Wagner, S. M., Petersen, K. J., & Ellram, L. M. (2011). Understanding responses to supply chain disruptions: Insights from information processing and resource dependence perspectives. *Academy of Management Journal, 54*(4), 833–865.

Bonet, R., Cappelli, P., & Hamori, M. (2013). Labor market intermediaries and the new paradigm for human resources. *Academy of Management Annals, 7*(1), 341–392.

Brammer, S., Jackson, G., & Matten, D. (2012). Corporate social responsibility and institutional theory: New perspectives on private governance. *Socio-Economic Review, 10*(1), 3–28.

Cappelli, P., & Keller, J. R. (2013). Classifying work in the new economy. *Academy of Management Review, 38*(4), 575–596.

Child, J. (1972). Organizational structure, environment and performance: The role of strategic choice. *Sociology, 6*(1), 1–22.

Coe, N. M., & Yeung, H. W. (2015). *Global production networks*. Oxford University Press.

Coe, N. M., & Yeung, H. W. (2019). Global production networks: Mapping recent conceptual developments. *Journal of Economic Geography, 19*, 775–801.

Coe, N. M., & Jordhus-Lier, D. C. (2011). Constrained agency? Re-evaluating the geographies of labour. *Progress in Human Geography, 35*(2), 211–233.

Crespin-Mazet, F., & Dontenwill, E. (2012). Sustainable procurement: Building legitimacy in the supply network. *Journal of Purchasing & Supply Management, 18*, 207–217.

Cumbers, A., Nativel, C., & Routledge, P. (2008). Labour agency and union positionalities in global production networks. *Journal of Economic Geography, 8*, 369–387.

Dallas, M. P., Ponte, S., & Sturgeon, T. J. (2019). Power in global value chains. *Review of International Political Economy, 26*(4), 666–694.

Datta, P. (2017). Supply network resilience: A systematic literature review and future research. *International Journal of Logistics Management, 28*(4), 1387–1424.

Dyer, J. H., & Nobeoka, K. (2000). Creating and managing a high performance knowledge-sharing network: The Toyota case. *Strategic Management Journal, 21*(3), 345–367.

Dyer, J. H., & Singh, H. (1998). The relational view: Cooperative strategy and sources of interorganizational competitive advantage. *Academy of Management Review, 23*(4), 660–679.

Edwards, P., Ram, M., Sen Gupta, S., & Tsai, C. (2006). The structuring of working relationships in small firms: Towards a formal framework. *Organization, 13*(5), 701–724.

Fichter, M., Helfen, M., & Sydow, J. (2011). Employment relations in global production networks—Initiating transfer of practices via union involvement. *Human Relations, 64*(4), 599–624.

Fransen, L., & Burgoon, B. (2015). Global labour-standards advocacy by European civil society organizations: Trends and Developments. *British Journal of Industrial Relations, 53*(2), 204–230.

Frenkel, S. J., Korcynzski, M., Shire, K. A., & Tam, M. (1999). *On the front line. Organization of work in the information economy*. Cornell University Press.

Frenkel, S. J., & Scott, D. (2002). Compliance, collaboration, and codes of labor practice: The Adidas connection. *California Management Review, 45*(1), 29-49.

Gereffi, G. (2020). What does the COVID-19 pandemic teach us about global value chains? The case of medical supplies. *Journal of International Business, 3*, 287–301.

Gereffi, G., Humphrey, J., & Sturgeon, T. (2005). The governance of global value chains. *Review of International Political Economy, 12*(1), 78–104.

Giddens, A. (1984). *The constitution of society*. Polity.

Gospel, H., & Sako, M. (2010). The unbundling of corporate functions: The evolution of shared services and outsourcing in human resource management. *Industrial and Corporate Change, 19*(5), 1367–1396.

Griffith, D. A., & Myers, M. B. (2005). The performance implications of strategic fit or relational norm governance strategies in global supply chain relationships. *Journal of International Business Studies, 36*(3), 254–269.

Hammer, N., & Plugor, R. (2019). Disconnecting labour? The labour process in the UK fast fashion value chain. *Work, Employment and Society, 33*(6), 913–928.

Helfen, M., & Fichter, M. (2013). Building transnational union networks across global production networks: Conceptualising a new arena of labour-management relations. *British Journal of Industrial Relations, 51*(3), 553–576.

Helfen, M., Schüßler, E., & Sydow, J. (2018). How can employment relations in global value networks be managed towards social responsibility. *Human Relations, 71*(12), 1640–1665.

Helfen, M., Sydow, J., & Wirth, C. (2020). Service delivery networks and employment relations at German airports: Jeopardizing industrial peace on the ground? *British Journal of Industrial Relations, 58*(1), 168–198.

Henderson, J., Dicken, P., Hess, M., Coe, N., & Yeung, H. W. C. (2002). Global production networks and the analysis of economic development. *Review of International Political Economy, 9*(3), 436–464.

Holmen, E., & Pedersen, A. C. (2010). How do suppliers strategise in relation to a customer's supply network initiative? *Journal of Purchasing & Supply Management, 16*, 264–278.

International Labour Office (ILO). (2015). World employment and social outlook: The changing nature of jobs. ILO.

Jackson, G., & Brammer, S. (2014). Introducing grey areas: The unexpectedly weak link between corporate irresponsibility and reputation. *Socio-Economic Review, 12*, 154–166.

Jarillo, J. C. (1988). On strategic networks. *Strategic Management Journal, 9*(1), 31–41.

Kabeer, N., Huq, L., & Sulaiman, M. (2020). Paradigm shift or business as usual? Workers' perspectives on multi–stakeholder initiatives in Bangladesh after Rana Plaza. *Development and Change, 51*(5), 1360–1398.

Kano, L., Tsang, E. W. K., & Yeung, H. W. (2020). Global value chains: A review of the multidisciplinary literature. *Journal of International Business Studies, 51*(4), 577–622.

Kenis, P., Schol, L. G. C., Kraaij-Dirkzwager, M. M., & Timen, A. (2019). Appropriate governance responses to infectious disease threats: Developing working hypotheses. *Risks, Hazwards, and Crisis in Public Policy, 10*(3), 275–293.

Kinnie, N. J., Swart, J., & Purcell, J. (2005). Influences on the choice of HR system: The network organization perspective. *International Journal of Human Resource Management, 16*(6), 1004–1028.

Koch, B. A. (1993). Differentiating reliability seeking organizations from other organizations: Development and validation of an assessment device. In K. H. Roberts (Ed.), *New challenges to understanding organizations* (pp. 75–97). Macmillan.

Kuruvilla, S., Liu, M., Li, C., & Chen, W. (2020). Field opacity and practice-outcome decoupling: Private regulation of labor standards in global supply chains. *ILR Review, 73*(4), 841–872.

Lakhani, T., Kuruvilla, S., & Avgar, A. (2013). From the firm to the network: Global value chains and employment relations theory. *British Journal of Industrial Relations, 51*(3), 440–472.

Langley, A., Lindberg, K., Mørk, B. E., Nicolini, D., Raviola, E., & Walter, L. (2019). Boundary work among groups, occupations, and organizations: From cartography to process. *Academy of Management Annals, 13*, 704–736.

Lengnick, C. A., Beck, T. A., & Lengnick-Hall, M. L. (2011). Developing capacity for organizational resilience through strategic human resource management. *Human Resource Management Review, 21*, 243–255.

Leonidou, L. C., Katsikas, C. S., Samiee, S., & Leonidou, C. N. (2019). Socially responsible international business: Review, synthesis, and directions. In L. C. Leonidou, C. S. Katsikas, S. Samiee, & C. N. Leonidou (Eds.), *Socially responsible international business: Critical issues and the way forward* (pp. 6–28). Elgar.

Leppelt, T., Foerstl, K., & Hartmann, E. (2013). Corporate social responsibility in buyer-supplier relationships. Is it beneficial for top-tier suppliers to market their capabilities to ensure a responsible supply chain? *Business Research, 6*(2), 126–152.

Levy, D. L. (2008). Political contestation in global production networks. *Academy of Management Review, 33*(4), 943–963.

Lim, S., & Prakash, A. (2017). From quality control to labor protection: ISO 9001 and workplace safety, 1993–2012. *Global Policy, 8*(Suppl. 3), 66–77.

Lincoln, J. R., & Shimotani, M. (2010). Business networks in postwar Japan: Whither the keiretsu? In A. M. Colpan, T. Hikino, & J. R. Lincoln (Eds.), *The Oxford handbook of business groups* (pp. 127–156). Oxford University Press.

Lipparini, A., Lorenzoni, G., & Ferriani, S. (2014). From core to periphery and back: A study on the deliberate shaping of knowledge flows in interfirm dyads and networks. *Strategic Management Journal, 35*(4), 578–595.

Locke, R. M. (2013). *The promise and limits of private power: Promoting labor standards in global economy*. Cambridge University Press.

Lund-Thomsen, P. (2020). Corporate social responsibility in global value chains. In S. Ponte, G. Gereffi, & G. Raj-Reichert (Eds.), *Handbook on global value chains* (pp. 285–295). Elgar.

Lund-Thomsen, P., & Lindgreen, A. (2014). Corporate social responsibility in global value chains: Where are we now and where are we going? *Journal of Business Ethics, 123*(1), 11–22.

Lund-Thomsen, P., & Lindgreen, A. (2018). Is there a sweet spot in ethical trade? A critical appraisal of the potential for aligning buyer, supplier and worker interests in global production networks. *Geoforum, 90*, 84–90.

Marchington, M., Grimshaw, D., Rubery, J., & Willmott, H. (2005). *Fragmenting work. Blurring organizational boundaries and disordering hierarchies*. Oxford University Press.

Marchington, M., Rubery, J., & Grimshaw, D. (2011). Alignment, integration and consistency in HRM across multi-party networks. *Human Resource Management, 50*(3), 313–339.

Manhart, P., Summers, J. K., & Blackhurst, J. (2020). A meta-analytical review of supply chain risk management: Assessing buffering and bridging strategies and firm performance. *Journal of Supply Chain Management, 56*(3), 66–87.

Matten, D., & Moon, J. (2020). Reflections on the 2018 decade award: The meaning and dynamics of corporate social responsibility. *Academy of Management Review, 45*(1), 7–28.

Müller-Seitz, G. (2012). Leadership in interorganizational networks: A literature review and suggestions for future research. *International Journal of Management Reviews, 14*(4), 428–443.

Nicolini, D. (2012). *Practice theory, work, & organization: An introduction*. Oxford University Press.

Oka, C. (2010). Channels of buyer influence and labor standard compliance: The case of Cambodia's garment sector. *Advances in Industrial and Labor Relations, 17*, 153–183.

Oka, C., Egels-Zandén, N., & Alexander, R. (2020). Buyer engagement and labour conditions in global supply chains: The Bangladesh Accord and beyond. *Development and Change, 51*(5), 1306–1330.

OECD, Wto, and World Bank Group. (2014). *Global value chains: Challenges, opportunities, and implications for policy*. OECD.

Paquin, R. L., & Howard-Grenville, J. (2013). Blind dates and arranged marriages: Longitudinal processes of network orchestration. *Organization Studies, 34*(11), 1623–1653.

Palmer, M., Simmons, G., Robinson, P. K., & Fearne, A. (2015). Institutional maintenance work and power preservation in business exchanges: Insights from industrial supplier workshops. *Industrial Marketing Management, 48*, 214–225.

Peck, H. (2006). Reconciling supply chain vulnerability, risk and supply chain management. *International Journal of Logistics, 9*(2), 127–142.

Powell, W. W. (1990). Neither market nor hierarchy: Network forms of organization. *Research in Organizational Behavior, 12*, 295–336.

Provan, K. G., Fish, A., & Sydow, J. (2007). Interorganizational networks at the network level: A review of the empirical literature on whole networks. *Journal of Management, 33*(3), 479–516.

Provan, K.G., & Milward, H.B. (1995). A preliminary theory of interorganizational network effectiveness. A comparative study of four community mental health systems. Administrative Science Quarterly, 40(1): 1–33.

Provan, K. G., & Kenis, P. (2008). Modes of network governance: Structure, management, and effectiveness. *Journal of Public Administration Research and Theory, 18*, 229–252.

Raab, J., & Kenis, P. (2009). Heading toward a society of networks: Empirical developments and theoretical challenges. *Journal of Management Inquiry, 18*(3), 198–210.

Rainnie, A., Herod, A., & McGrath-Champ, S. (2011). Review and positions: Global production networks and labour. *Competition and Change, 15*(2), 155–169.

Raj-Reichert, G. (2020). The role of transnational first-tier suppliers in GVC governance. In S. Ponte, G. Gereffi, & G. Raj-Reichert (Eds.), *Handbook on global value chains* (pp. 354–369). Elgar.

Ramanujam, R. (2018). The multiple meanings and models of reliability in organizational research. In R. Ramanujam & K. H. Roberts (Eds.), *Organizing for reliability: A guide for research and practice* (pp. 17–33). Stanfort University Press.

Reinecke, J., & Donaghey, J. (2015). After Rana Plaza: Building coalitional power for labour rights between unions and (consumption-based) social movement organisations. *Organization, 22*(5), 720–740.

Roberts, K. H. (1990). Some characteristics of one type of high reliability organization. *Organization Science, 1*, 160–176.

Roberts, J. (2007). The modern firm. Organizational design for performance and growth. Oxford University Press.

Rubery, J., Cooke, F. L., Earnshaw, J., & Marchington, M. (2003). Inter-organizational relations and employment in a multi-party environment. *British Journal of Industrial Relations, 41*(2), 265–289.

Ruggie, J. G. (2003). The United Nations and globalization: Patterns and limits of institutional adaptation. *Global Governance, 9*, 301–321.

Sako, M., & Zylberberg, E. (2019). Supplier strategy in global value chains: shaping governance and profiting from upgrading. *Socio-Economic Review, 17*(3), 687–707.

Salminen, J. (2019). From product liability to production liability: Modelling a response to the liability deficit in global value chains on historical transformations of production. *Competition & Change, 23*(4), 420–438.

Schrank, A., & Whitford, J. (2011). The anatomy of network failure. *Sociological Theory, 29*(3), 151–177.

Schuessler, E., Frenkel, S., Ashwin, S., Kabeer, N., Egels-Zandén, N., Alexander, R., Huq, L., Oka, C., Lohmeyer, N., Rahman, S., & Rahman, K. M. (2019). Garment supply chains since Rana Plaza: Governance & worker outcomes. Garment Supply Chain Governance Project Final Report. Freie Universität: https://www.wiwiss.fu-berlin.de/forschung/Garments/Medien/04-09-Changes-in-the-Governance-final.pdf.

Scott, R. W. (1995). *Organizations and institutions*. Sage.

Seidl, D., & Whittington, R. (2014). Enlarging the strategy-as-practice research agenda: Towards taller and flatter ontologies. *Organization Studies, 35*(10), 1407–1421.

Sengenberger, W. (1994). Protection—Participation—Promotion: The systemic nature and effects of labour standards. In W. Sengenberger & D. Campbell (Eds.), *Creating economic opportunities: The role of labour standards in industrial restructuring* (pp. 45–60). ILO.

Sydow, J., & Frenkel, S. (2013). Labor, risk and uncertainty in global supply networks—Exploratory insights. *Journal of Business Logistics, 34*(3), 233–242.

Sydow, J., & Windeler, A. (1998). Organizing and evaluating interfirm networks: A structurationist perspective on network processes and effectiveness. *Organization Science, 9*(3), 265–284.

Sydow, J., Schüßler, E., & Müller-Seitz, G. (2016). *Managing inter-organizational relations: Debates and cases*. Palgrave Macmillan.
UNCTAD. (2013). World investment report 2013: Global value chains. Investment and trade for development. United Nations.
Vaara, E., & Whittington, R. (2012). Strategy-as-practice: Taking social practices seriously. *Academy of Management Annals, 6*(1), 285–336.
Van Driel, H., & Dolfsma, W. (2009). Path dependence, initial conditions, and routines in organizations: The Toyota production system re-examined. *Journal of Organizational Change Management, 22*(1), 49–72.
Vlaar, P. W. L., Van den Bosch, F. A. J., & Volberda, H. W. (2007). Towards a dialectic perspective on formalization in interorganizational relationships: How alliance managers capitalize on the duality inherent in contracts, rules and procedures. *Organization Studies, 28*(4), 437–466.
Weick, K. E., & Sutcliffe, K. M. (2007). *Managing the unexpected: Resilient rformance in an age of uncertainty* (2nd ed.). Jossey-Bass.
Weil, D. (2019). Understanding the present and future of work in the fissured workplace context. *Russell Sage Foundation Journal of the Social Sciences, 5*(5), 147–165.
Wieland, J. (2020). *Relational economics—A political economy*. Springer Nature.
Williamson, O. E. (1991). Comparative economic organization: The analysis of discrete structural alternatives. *Administrative Science Quarterly, 36*(2), 269–296.
Wowak, K. D., & Boone, C. A. (2015). So many recalls, so little research: A review of the literature and road map for future research. *Journal of Supply Chain Management, 51*(4), 54–72.
Yeung, H. W., & Coe, N. (2015). Toward a dynamic theory of global production networks. *Economic Geography, 91*(1), 29–58.
Zajak, S., Egels-Zandén, N., & Piper, N. (2017). Networks of labour activism: Collective action across Asia and beyond. *Development and Change, 48*(5), 899–921.

Jörg Sydow is a Professor of Management and Chair for Inter-firm Cooperation at the School of Business & Economics at Freie Universität Berlin, Germany. He serves or served on the editorial boards of many leading academic journals including Organization Science, Academy of Management Journal, Academy of Management Review, and Journal of Management Studies, and is currently a Senior Editor of Organization Studies. He recently co-edited, with Hans Berends, a volume of Research in the Sociology of Organizations on Managing Inter-organizational Collaborations—Process Views. Bingley, UK: Emerald, 2019.

Elke Schüßler is Professor for Business Administration and Head of the Institute of Organization Science at Johannes Kepler University Linz, Austria. She does research on social and environmental challenges and uses theories of organizational creativity, institutional innovation, collective action and path dependence to understand how these challenges can be addressed. Elke has published in leading management and industrial relations journals like Academy of Management Journal, Human Relations or Industrial and Labor Relations Review.

Markus Helfen is a research fellow in the Department of Management in the School of Business & Economics, Freie Universität Berlin, Germany. He does research in the fields of employment relations, HRM and organization theory with a focus on collective action and institutional work. Current topics and projects include global labour standards, HRM and employment relations in interorganizational settings as well as sustainability studies. Markus has published in leading management and industrial relations journals like Organization Studies, Human Relations, and the British Journal of Industrial Relations.

Incentives, Autonomous Motivation, and Bank Managers' Socially Responsible Behavior

Vincent Bouchet, Stefan Linder, and Nicolas Mottis

Abstract For fostering Socially Responsible Behavior (SRB) of their managers, firms increasingly consider tying managers' bonuses to the achievement of certain environmental, social, or societal objectives. Yet, we still know very little about the actual effects of such incentives for SRB. In particular, it is unclear whether such incentives are effective or whether they risk to (partially) "crowd-out" individuals' autonomous motivation for SRB. Based on two vignette experiments with managers, we provide first empirical evidence on this matter. Financial rewards seem inefficient for enhancing managers' engagement in SRB, but do not seem to crowd-out their autonomous motivation to engage in SRB. Therefore, top managers who wish to foster SRB are better served by focusing on attracting and retaining individuals who are autonomously motivated for SRB rather than on to trying to foster SRB by implementing SRB-related remuneration systems.

Keywords Socially responsible behavior · Corporate social responsibility · Motivation · Incentives · Rewards · Crowding-out

1 Introduction

Increasingly, firms face demands by consumers, non-governmental organizations, and the general public to conduct business in a more socially responsible manner. This has triggered both a broad stream of research on this matter (e.g., Bénabou & Tirole, 2010; Carroll, 1999; Porter & Kramer, 2006) and efforts by many firms to foster Socially Responsible Behavior (SRB) by their managers and employees.

SRB can take many forms and relates to the "discretionary decisions and actions taken by individuals in organizations to enhance societal well-being (do good) or to avoid harmful consequences for society (do no harm)" (Crilly et al., 2008: 176).

V. Bouchet (✉) · N. Mottis
Ecole Polytechnique, Palaiseau, France

S. Linder
ESSEC Business School, Cergy, France
e-mail: linder@essec.edu

L. Biggiero et al. (eds.), *The Relational View of Economics*, Relational Economics and Organization Governance, https://doi.org/10.1007/978-3-030-86526-9_9

Thus, SRB is a specific type of pro-social behavior, occurring in the specific social setting of business and related to the corporate social responsibility of the firm. Most humans exhibit a certain degree of pro-social behaviors, such as donating to charities, supplying their blood, or giving their time for good causes (Bénabou & Tirole, 2010). It thus seems likely that managers and employees will engage in SRB without their firms installing reward systems that incentivize such behaviors. Yet, there is also some evidence that suggests that pro-social behavior might not be due to autonomous motivation alone: donations to charities are larger if tax deductible and a number of experiments show that "buying social prestige is part of the incentive to engage in pro-social behavior" (Bénabou & Tirole, 2010: 3). This evidence suggests that financial and non-financial incentives might be an important factor to consider for fostering engagement in SRB within firms.

Given the conflicting views on pro-social behaviors of humans in general, it is surprising that extant research pays fairly little attention to the role of rewards, characteristics of individual managers and employees, and their motivations in triggering engagement in SRB (Crilly et al., 2008; a notable exception being Holmås et al., 2010). The overwhelming majority of scholarly work so far has concentrated on a firm- or organizational-level of analysis (Aguinis & Glavas, 2012; Bansal & Song, 2017; Bansal & Song, 2017; Crilly et al., 2008; Post et al., 2002). Research has greatly enhanced our understanding of firm-level intentions, initiatives, and outcomes, and established legitimacy of Corporate Social Responsibility (CSR) and related constructs. But it is individuals who act, not organizations (Coleman, 1990; Felin & Foss, 2005) and "management ultimately means intervening at the level of individuals" (Foss, 2009: 21).

Thus, for now, we can only try to infer the effects of reward policies on SRB by transferring insights from related phenomena, such as pro-social behavior more generally or organizational citizenship behavior. Yet, while these are related phenomena, important differences exist. Thus, extant research does not provide guidance to practitioners on whether and how they should incentivize SRB within their firms. However, increasingly firms start including SRB-related objectives in the remuneration package of their managers. In France, the number of CAC 40 companies that incorporate CSR criteria has increased from 10% in 2006 to more than 70% at the end of 2015 (e.g., Morgan ORSE, 2012, 2017; Stanley, 2016). Consequently, whether such reward policies truly foster engagement in SRB is a highly topical question.

Based on two experimental studies with managers, we aim to narrow this gap in research. We focus on whether tying managers' bonuses to the achievement of non-financial, environmentally, or socially oriented performance measures interacts with managers' pre-existing autonomous motivation and whether it fosters their engagement in socially responsible behavior, that is, their engagement in projects promising to promote the environmental or social performance of their organizations. For fostering generalizability of our findings and since SRB is a multi-faceted phenomenon, our two studies draw on a set of five different projects for which we also manipulate whether the societal benefits achieved by implementing these projects are likely to translate into financial benefits that (largely) cover the projects' costs or not.

We contribute to extant literature in a number of ways: first, to our best knowledge, we are the first to explore the effects of alternative reward systems on motivation and engagement in SRB on an individual level of analysis. Moreover, in contrast to the overwhelming majority of studies so far conducted on a potential interaction between rewards and autonomous types of motivation, our study relies on active managers and a real business setting. Our results thus likely are more readily applicable to business practice than studies relying on non-business settings or student samples. Moreover, it equally responds to Huang et al. (2003) who suggested that extant evidence on the interaction of incentives with motivation that typically stem from a North-American context may not easily translate to other cultural contexts. By providing evidence gathered with managers in France, we contribute to an internationally more balanced set of evidence.

2 Background

2.1 Corporate Social Responsibility: From a Firm Perspective to Micro-corporate Social Responsibility

Firms today face an increasing pressure from numerous sides, including, but not limited to the media, customers, governments, and non-governmental organizations, for what may be broadly described as "corporate social responsibility" (Garriga & Melé, 2004; McWilliams & Siegel, 2001). Companies respond to this pressure for CSR by engaging in various actions such as, for example, donating money to charities, supporting local communities, or committing publicly to respect of and fair treatment of employees, suppliers, and other stakeholders.

The overwhelming majority of extant research into corporate social responsibility (CSR) takes an organizational- or firm-level perspective and studies such topics, as for example, the study of issues in environmental or sustainability reporting (e.g., Cooper & Owen, 2007; Gray, 2006), reputation-building through CSR (Cho et al., 2012), firm's motivations for engaging in CSR (Albinger & Freeman, 2000; Besley & Ghatak, 2007; Campbell, 2007), organizational-level performance effects of CSR (e.g., Crifo & Forget, 2014; Porter & Kramer, 2006), or definitional questions (e.g., Carroll, 1999; Matten & Moon, 2008).

Yet, ontologically seen it is individuals who act, not organizations (Coleman, 1990; Felin & Foss, 2005; Foss & Linder, 2019; Johnson et al., 2007). As "management ultimately means intervening at the level of individuals" (Foss, 2009, p. 21), developing insights at the level of individual managers and employees and their socially responsible behavior is thus important for advising practitioners on how to foster their firms' CSR performance. Whereas Aguinis and Glavas (2012) pointed out that a minority of CSR research has focused on the individual level of analysis, recent research, analyzing the psychological microfoundations of CSR (or micro-CSR) in research domains such as human resource management and organizational behavior, has grown these last 5 years (Foss & Linder, 2019). Among the limited micro-level work on CSR, Gond et al. (2017) identify three streams : (1) the individual drivers of CSR engagement, (2) people's evaluations of CSR initiatives, and (3) reactions to CSR initiatives. They also highlight that studies have typically focused on the third steam and neglected individual drivers of CSR. Our study contributes to fill this gap in literature.

2.2 *Theoretical Framework*

2.2.1 Socially Responsible Behavior as a Specific Social Behavior

SRB denotes the "discretionary decisions and actions taken by individuals in organizations to enhance societal well-being (do good) or to avoid harmful consequences for society (do no harm)" (Crilly et al., 2008: 176). Such behaviors may target the well-being of stakeholders inside the organization just as much as outside it (ibid.). SRB seems similar to organizational citizenship behavior or pro-social organizational behavior and. Yet, in contrast to SRB, these, however, focus primarily on activities beneficial to the organization but not necessarily to society (Crilly et al., 2008; Deckop et al., 1999). Gond et al. (2017) consider four types of CSR engagement at the individual level: (i) CSR-related attitudes (e.g., what do employees think about the global CSR strategy of the firm?) (ii) decisions (e.g., do executives invest in CSR initiatives?) (iii) appraisals (e.g., do managers see CSR positively?) (iv) behaviors (e.g., eco-friendly behaviors). Then, we consider SRB as a subfield of pro-social behavior, focusing on behavior related to the corporate social responsibility of the firm. SRB is more specific than pro-social behavior as it takes place in the specific social setting of business. Moreover, when engaging in SRB, an employee or a manager does so on behalf of the firm whereas he would engage in pro-social behavior on behalf of him/herself or other charity organizations.[1]

2.2.2 An Agency-Theoretical View on the Role of Incentives

Much of economics-based literature assumes humans to incur disutility from engaging in work (Fehr & Falk, 2002; Kunz & Pfaff, 2002) and, hence, sees the danger that they will not show the desired actions if not incentivized to do so or pressured by the external context in some form (Lazear, 2000; Milgrom & Roberts, 1992). Agency-theoretical views submit a need for incentivizing individuals based on multiple dimensions of their work, if their principals wish them to sufficiently consider all dimensions. As most current reward systems focus on managers' or

[1] We are indebted to the reviewers for suggesting this distinction.

employees' performance on economic criteria, agency theory would thus recommend extending incentives to include outcomes of socially responsible behavior in order to motivate individuals to devote sufficient attention and effort to these outcomes besides the economic ones (Holmström & Milgrom, 1994). This can be done by adjusting an organization's remuneration scheme to include a bonus for attaining CSR-related objectives. It is thus not surprising, that more and more firms include CSR-related objectives in the remuneration package of their executives and managers (e.g., Morgan ORSE, 2012, 2017; Stanley, 2016). This would suggest that financial and non-financial incentives provided by a firm's reward systems might be an important factor to consider for fostering engagement in socially responsible behaviors within firms.

2.2.3 The Role of Incentives for Pro-social Behavior

There is a rich stream of literature studying the role of incentives for pro-social and altruistic behaviors of individuals (e.g., Bénabou & Tirole, 2006; Deci, 1975; Lacetera & Macis, 2010; Mellstrom & Johannesson, 2008; Titmuss, 1971) and for (un-)ethical behavior (e.g., Hegarty and Sims, 1978). Thus, for example, it is now well-established that most humans exhibit a certain degree of pro-social behavior, such as donating to charities, supplying their blood, or giving their time for good causes (Bénabou & Tirole, 2010). Thus, it seems possible that managers and employees will engage in socially responsible business behavior without their firms installing reward systems that incentivize such behaviors. Yet, there is also some evidence that suggests that pro-social behavior might not be due to autonomous motivation alone: donations to charities are larger if tax deductible and a number of experiments show that "buying social prestige is part of the incentive to engage in pro-social behavior" (Bénabou & Tirole, 2010: 3).

Whereas these lines of research can help us in understanding potential factors relevant for SRB, their insights need not necessarily translate to SRB. Donating blood, volunteering, or charitable giving, and similar altruistic activities in turn differ quite markedly from common business settings and SRB therein (Kunz & Linder, 2012). Compensation, remuneration, and rewards are a "natural" feature of common business settings as individuals largely engage in jobs for earning money. Hence, the situational framing of SRB is a quite different one than, for example, in volunteering or donating blood. The link between rewards and SRB thus clearly merits scholarly attention.

2.2.4 Self-determination Theory

Self-Determination Theory (SDT) "*represents a broad framework for the study of human motivation and personality*" (e.g., Deci & Ryan, 1985; Deci and Ryan, 2000a, b). SDT and its sub-theories highlight that a particular behavior can be driven by different (types of) motivations as summarized in Table 1.

Table 1 Self determination theory and its sub theories

<table>
<tr><td rowspan="3">Goal Contents Theory Reasons</td><td colspan="4">Extrinsic motivation</td><td>Intrinsic motivation</td></tr>
<tr><td colspan="4">For instrumental reasons</td><td>For its own sake</td></tr>
<tr><td colspan="2"></td><td colspan="2">Driven by values and goals</td><td>Driven by emotions</td></tr>
<tr><td rowspan="3">Organismic Integration Theory</td><td>External</td><td>Introjected</td><td>Identified</td><td>Integrated</td><td rowspan="3"></td></tr>
<tr><td>"Obtain reward of avoid punishment"</td><td>"Ego involvement or guilt"</td><td>"Identifies with the project values or meanings"</td><td>"Part of the person's sense of self"</td></tr>
<tr><td colspan="4">-Internalization +</td></tr>
<tr><td>Causality Orientation Theory</td><td colspan="2">Controlled motivation</td><td colspan="3">Autonomous motivation</td></tr>
</table>

One important and quite widely received distinction is between extrinsic motivation (for instrumental reasons) and intrinsic motivation (i.e., motivation resulting from the interplay of an individual's innate psychological needs and the degree to which the nature of the activities at hand allows satisfying these needs) (Hackman and Oldham, 1976; Lindenberg, 2001; Ryan & Deci, 2000). Regarding extrinsic motivation, Organismic Integration Theory states that instrumental reasons can be more or less internalized, and lead to four different types of regulation: external (e.g., a financial bonus, a malus, career progression, or awards), introjected (e.g., to feel guilty), identified (e.g., to understand and accept a project), or integrated (e.g., when norms are fully internalized, Frey, 1997; Lindenberg, 2001; Weibel et al., 2010). These different types of motivation in turn lie on a spectrum of causal orientations ranging from controlled to autonomous.

SDT submits that financial incentives (controlled motivation) may undermine pre-existing autonomous motivation. In other words: trying to heighten an individual's engagement in certain behaviors by means of giving rewards may be ineffective as it might simply correspond to replacing one motivation—pre-existing autonomous motivation for the behavior—by another one, namely: controlled motivation, thus leaving overall the "amount" of motivation unchanged. Such a "crowding-out" (Frey, 1997) of autonomous motivation by incentives is claimed for both tangible rewards (e.g., a monetary bonus) and non-tangible factors (e.g., deadlines, directives, pressured evaluations, or imposed goals) (Ryan & Deci, 2000). The underlying reasoning for this claim is that the administration of extrinsic incentives that are perceived as controlling shifts the locus of causality from an internal to an external one (Gagné & Deci, 2005).

2.3 A Review of Empirical and Experimental Studies on Socially Responsible Behavior

Gond et al., (2017) systematically analyze CSR drivers' studies by the lens of the multiple needs model of justice (Cropanzano et al., 2001). According to this model, CSR engagement results from three types of drivers: instrumental, relational, and moral drivers. In order to remain consistent with the SDT framework, we will present some of these studies using the SDT distinction between controlled and autonomous motivation.

2.3.1 Controlled Motivation and the Role of Financial Incentives

Norris and O'Dwyer (2004) report on the tensions experienced in a U.K. company, where performance measurement and financial reward systems worked against socially responsive decision-making. Their rich account of the practices and difficulties at that firm greatly help to better understand the challenges in the relations between management control systems, rewards, and SRB. Yet, their study is explorative in nature and due to the single case not suited for generalizing results. Moreover, it does not truly address the role of different motivations for SRB and potential interactions of rewards with these motivations.

Another range of studies focuses on the role of traditional financial incentives in the sense of agency theory (alignment of the CEO's and shareholders' interests) on CSR. Based on an empirical work on 600 U.S. firms over the period 2005–2009, Fabrizi et al. (2014) show that traditional financial incentives have a negative effect on CSR whereas non-monetary incentives have a positive effect on CSR. But this does not address the role of variable income indexed on CSR performance.

The study by Holmås et al. (2010) more closely addresses the question of how incentives are linked to engagement in SRB. Their findings suggest that fines crowd-out agents' autonomous motivation, leading to a reduction in effort for SRB. In typical settings within firms, however, fines are not the most common form of incentives. While some firms may operate a kind of malus system, bonus, or pay-for-performance schemes are clearly more common. Findings on the relation of a malus system for autonomous motivation may not directly translate to the case of bonus schemes: the "mental frame" created of a malus system may be quite different from that under a bonus system.

Graves et al. (2013) used a survey on Chinese employees from retail, manufacturing, information technology, and energy firms. They focuses on the impact of a clear environmental vision ("environmental transformational leadership") on controlled motivation and autonomous motivation of employees . But they also use the SDT framework to study the impact of the two types of motivation on pro-environmental behavior. They conclude that an increase in autonomous motivation was associated with an increase in pro-environmental behavior. While this study could support our first hypothesis, it remains different in many ways: the type of employees observed, the geography as the type of experiment. Hence, the scarce available empirical evidence does not allow advising practitioners on whether including SRB-related objectives in the remuneration package of managers and/or employees truly fosters engagement in socially responsible behaviors.

2.3.2 Autonomous Motivation

Among the drivers related to autonomous motivation, Gond et al. (2017) make a distinction between relational drivers and moral drivers. By relational, they mean a need for recognition ("social networking"), at the level of the firm but also with respect to the outside world. Glavas (2016) suggests that CSR engagement might be driven by more personal drivers such as a need for positive self-regard and self-esteem. Moral values are related to employee's care concerns (Rupp & Mallory, 2015). In the sense of SDT, all these drivers can be related to identified or integrated regulation (both corresponding to autonomous motivation). According to Gond et al. (2017), moral drivers have been subject of more research: environmental concern (Graves et al., 2013), as social preoccupations (Tongo, 2015) have highlighted as important individual driver of SRB.

2.3.3 Lack of Analysis at the Middle Level Management

The link between rewards and SRB may exist at three levels in organizations: on the level of top managers and their behavior, on the level of middle- and front-line managers, and on the level of ordinary employees. Given different resources available to these individuals and decision rights, the possibilities and thus the effectiveness of rewards for attaining desired CSR outcomes may differ. Managers below the level of top management and "ordinary" employees frequently develop tacit knowledge about market and stakeholder needs as well as about the perception of certain business behaviors by various local stakeholders. Likewise, middle- and lower-level managers, and in particular employees, are likely to be exposed most prominently in their daily operational work to the strengths and weaknesses of existing business practices and processes within firms (Burnss and Vaivio, 2001). Thus, middle and lower levels within an organization are arguably in a particular pivotal position for turning "talk about CSR" into "action" (Graves et al., 2013). Hence, understanding the role of rewards in fostering engagement in socially responsible behaviors within firms' middle and lower ranks is a topic of great interest to practitioners.

Consequently, looking at the current state of knowledge, Norris and O'Dwyer's (2004) conclusion that there is a lack of research exploring "the systems that influence managerial decision making in a socially responsive vein," remains valid today. Gond et al. (2017) point that "*despite the likely importance of values to middle managers, relatively few studies focus particularly on this group.*"[2] In part, this

[2] We would like to thank greatly one of the reviewers for suggesting this excellent point.

status mirrors a general lack of "empirical investigations of the effects of incentive compensation on managerial behavior" (Chang et al., 2012: 1349). Drawing on Self-Determination Theory (SDT) and two vignette experiments with managers, we aim to narrow this gap. We focus on middle and lower level managers in the present study and concentrate on what is called within the literature on SDT a "crowding-out" (Frey, 1997) of autonomous motivation by external incentives (controlled motivation).

3 Hypotheses

Protecting the environment, furthering social causes, or creating a better place to work at—to mention just a few examples—of CSR-related SRB, are likely to closely correspond to many individual's personal desires. Thus, it seems highly likely that many managers and employees engage in the behaviors implied by SRB for their autonomous motivation. This leads to our first hypothesis:

Hypothesis 1: Autonomous motivation is a driver behind the engagement in SRB.

Paying managers and employees a flat salary is unlikely to influence the level of autonomous motivation for SRB. Since their income is independent of their actions, they may freely engage in SRB or refrain from doing so. In contrast to a flat salary structure, performance-contingent monetary rewards introduce a pressure on the individual (external motivation) to perform a certain task or show a particular behavior (Gagné & Deci, 2005). They thus shift the perceived locus of causality to one external to the individual (ibid.). Therefore, paying managers or employees for achieving certain business targets related to CSR (e.g., lower CO2 emissions, higher employee satisfaction, less stress among employees) or rewarding them in some other manner for achievement of SRB-related goals, pressures them to engage in activities that promise to attain these targets. This can be explained by the fact that individuals have to meet (or exceed) a standard to get (maximize) the reward (Deci et al., 2001). Based on SDT, if individuals who had a propensity to engage in these behaviors due to their needs and internalized norms, can be expected to experience a (partial) crowding-out of autonomous motivation by the external incentive. Provided that autonomous motivation is an important driver behind managers' or employees' SRB, switching from a flat salary system to one that provides incentives for SRB—for example, through the inclusion of environmental or societal objectives within the bonus formula used—SDT would predict that such (monetary) rewards for achieving CSR-related outcomes will undermine the pre-existing autonomous motivation for these behaviors. This leads to our second hypothesis:

Hypothesis 2: Tying managers' bonuses at least partially to the achievement of certain societal or environmental performance objectives crowds-out autonomous motivation for engaging in SRB.

Our hypotheses imply directional claims. Testing such claims calls for either longitudinal evidence or data gathered by means of an experiment. We rely on two vignette experiment studies. These experiments rely on short case scenarios containing the situational variables of interest to the experimenter and collect participants' reactions to these scenarios—in our case: engagement in SRB—and a set of control variables or moderator variables on scales similar to a conventional survey (Alexander & Becker, 1978; Hartmann & Maas, 2010; Robertson, 1993).

Vignette experiments seem particularly suited to our study as they allow examining not directly observable aspects, such as motivation, and have been highlighted as especially appropriate for analyzing the influence of social context on individual decisions and behaviors (Taylor, 2006). Vignette experiments encourage the participants to interpret the situation as being close to real life (Hughes, 1998) as they can present quite a rich situational context to participants by providing several independent situational elements in a coherent scenario (Fehr & Gächter, 2002; Robertson, 1993). Since vignette experiments imply a controlled and isolated alteration of the selected factors (Alexander & Becker, 1978; Rossi & Anderson, 1982; Starmer, 1999), they provide the same capacity to infer causality as other experimental methods. They thus offer a significant advantage over cross-sectional field studies (cf. Burney and Widener, 2007; Schwenk, 1982). Since the experimenter controls most of the independent variables, vignette experiments also suffer less from dangers of common-method bias requiring particular caution and remedies in field surveys (Podsakoff et al., 2003). Moreover, several studies found results obtained in vignette experiments to closely mirror results found by other methods (e.g., Hainmueller et al., 2015). Therefore, vignette experiments seem a well-suited method for testing the incentive-SRB relation. It is not surprisingly thus, that vignette experiments have been both repeatedly proposed (e.g., Robertson, 1993) or used by scholars for studying issues in ethical and socially responsible decision-making and behavior (e.g., Crilly et al., 2008; Fritzsche & Becker, 1983) and incentive effects (e.g., Belle & Cantarelli, 2015; Kunz & Linder, 2012; Weibel et al., 2010; Wolfe & Loraas, 2008).

4 Study 1

4.1 Method

4.1.1 Subjects

For testing our hypotheses we chose the setting of a bank manager responsible for one or several branches of a retail bank. Banks have seen themselves increasingly exposed to criticism lately and the question of rewarding SRB is very topical, which facilitates ensuring that participants perceive the scenarios not as hypothetical, but as "real." Chng et al. (2012), we rely on participants from a training program carried out at a major metropolitan French business school for our main sample. The participants are all managers from the banking industry and have considerable job experience (average is 8 years). In the following we rely on data from 165 decisions made by 58 participants (we dropped some answers from incompletely filled-in questionnaires). Two pretests—one with 28 Master of Science students, the second with 15 experienced managers (aged from 30 to 45)—served for scale development purposes (caused by the need to translate scales from English into the local language) and for refining the survey instrument.

4.1.2 Design of Scenarios

To further enhance the quality of our results, we test the impact of alternative SRBs, since SRB can be manifold. Prior research suggests that issue characteristics may play a role in explaining managers' behaviors (Jones, 1991). For example, Fritzsche and Becker (1983) found that marketing managers reacted differently to various categories of ethical problems. Our scenarios are informed by the practices that one of the authors has seen in place in some of the countries' largest companies and aligned with studies on French companies using variable incentive on CSR performance (Morgan ORSE, 2012, 2017; Stanley, 2016).

To account for the potential effects of issue characteristics, we use a set of three different types of socially responsible behavior that the individual might engage in (1) the decision about organizing a training for ones' subordinates about eco-friendly driving thus likely reducing the CO_2 emissions of the unit's (note: that can be one or a group of branches) employees while visiting clients, (2) the decision to hire a substitute for a parent that will go on maternity/paternity leave which facilitates the transition and allows containing the work-stress of the remaining employees, and (3) the possibility to hire an additional part-time employee who would help in better taking care of the needs of customers with disabilities and/or senior citizens with special needs.

Some authors claim that the benefits of living up to CSR cover the additional costs incurred (e.g., Porter and Kramer, 2002). As so often, debate about whether this is truly the case persists in academia. Therefore, we decided to deliberately allow for both "win–win" as well as "win–lose" situations by varying the impact that the alternative behaviors have on financial performance of the bank branch. Each alternative was thus presented to the participating managers both as "paying" for its costs through a corresponding increase in financial performance of the branch and as the respective behaviors paying at best part of their costs.

In manipulating the reward system, we relied on three alternative versions: a flat salary system, a salary plus variable bonus component of 15% depending on the attainment of social and environmental performance objectives, and the same salary plus bonus system but with a bonus component of 30%. By varying the size of the bonus, we account for the recurrent claims that the size of the incentive plays a significant role for the consequence's effort bonus scheme (e.g., Pokorny, 2008). The cues for our independent variable (incentives) were provided by means of short descriptions inspired by Kunz and Linder (2012) and Weibel et al. (2010). Appendix 1 provides the exact wording of the text cues used. In order to keep response-burden for participants within acceptable limits and thus to avoid effects of fatigue likely linked to lengthy experiments, we employed a mixed design for collecting data on the 3 (different SRB-related projects) × 2 (the project "paying for its own costs" vs. SRB being costly) × 3 reward systems (fixed, 15% bonus based on non-financial indicators; 30% bonus based on non-financial indicators) full factorial similar to previous vignette experiments into the reward-motivation relation (e.g., Kunz & Linder, 2012). Each participant thus faced the three different SRB-related projects, but their characteristics (paying for its own costs and the reward system) were chosen randomly. Then they could differ for the same participant.

4.2 Measure of Engagement in SRB and Motivation

Whenever possible, we relied on pre-existing scales (sometimes translated).

4.2.1 Motivation

Measurement of individuals' autonomous and controlled motivation draws on items adapted from Kunz and Linder (2012) and Reinholt et al. (2011). Both studies are based on an instrument originally developed by Ryan and Connell (1989). Items from this scale have been used before in vignette experiments (e.g., Kunz, 2015; Kunz & Linder, 2012; Linder, 2016; Weibel et al., 2010). Since our study took place in France and in order to ensure language issues, we decided to rely on translated items, rather than the original items in English. As the original scale was developed for studies within an education/school context and with a business setting in mind, some items had to be adjusted so as to make them fit with our context. For example, minor adaptations of some items, notably those used to measure controlled motivation were done so that they would fit a business context—for example, by referring an item to the impact on the remuneration or the bonus the person can receive. Cronbach's alpha was 0.71 for autonomous motivation and 0.77 for controlled motivation. Appendix 4 provides the exact wording of the items used.

4.2.2 Engagement in SRB

Given the paucity of research on SRB, no scale fitting our experiment was readily available. Scale development started out from prior interviews of the authors with managers in French firms and from the description of SRB given in Crilly et al. (2008) by asking individuals about their willingness to support financially (based on their own resources), to rally support for, and to battle themselves for the SRB-related projects proposed in the vignettes. The pre-tests served to refine the items and drop some. See Appendix 3 for details on the final scale. Cronbach's alpha of the scale with our main sample was 0.64, thus slightly below the common threshold of 0.70, yet seem acceptable for a newly constructed scale.

4.2.3 Control Variables

Work experience and age facilitate putting oneself into the respective situations described in the vignettes as the repertoire of situations already experienced in their own lives is larger for older and more experienced individuals. Moreover, experience, as George and Jones (2005) note, is related to an individual's abilities.

Gender was included as Schwartz and Rubel (2005) found that men are more likely to value power, while women value benevolence more than men do. This might lead women to show higher values for the intentions to foster the SRB-related projects than men (Hatch & Stephen, 2015). Risk-aversion might play a role for how strong individuals react to (uncertain) performance-contingent incentives. Hence, we included a short instrument to assess risk aversion. Since Crilly et al. (2008) found self-transcendence values (universalism and benevolence) of individuals to influence the level of SRB that they exhibited, we included the instrument used by Schwartz (2007), which is a short version of the one employed by Crilly et al. (2008).

Two dummy variables (SRBTyB and SRBTyC) serve to control the fact that we use three different SRBs in our vignettes (see Appendix 2). Since each of these SRBs may be either "paying" for its costs through a corresponding increase in financial performance of the branch or paying at best part of their costs, we include a third dummy variable (SELFPAY) for control.

No further controls were included, as the random allocation of the vignettes to participants can be expected to take care of self-selection issues present in normal field surveys that scholars using such surveys try to (partially) control for by adding control variables about the respondent's personality and organization.

4.2.4 Manipulation Checks

Following Pablo (1994) we employed short questions to check whether participants perceived the situations as intended by the experimenters, that is: to check the success of our experimental manipulation of the independent variables. The manipulation checks correlate significantly ($p < 0.01$) with our experimental variables, which suggest that the experimental manipulation worked as intended.

4.3 Descriptive Results

Table 2 provides the descriptive statistics. Some 65% of respondents were male and work experience in paying jobs ranged between 8 and 33 years with an average of about 20 years. Respondents on average are 44 years old.

Pair-wise correlations—as shown in Table 2—suggest that the control variables are mostly insignificant, with the exception of the type of SRB project—that is whether it "pays for itself" or not, the work-experience, and the "universalism" values an individual holds. Since age and work experience are highly correlated (pairwise correlation = 0.92 at $p < 0.01$), we rely on work experience in the following multivariate analyses and exclude age to counter dangers of multi-collinearity.

4.4 Multivariate Results

Table 3 reports the results of the multivariate analysis to identify the relations between incentives and SRB. Since each respondent replied to multiple vignettes, the answers to these vignettes might not be fully independent. They might thus violate an important assumption underlying ordinary least squares regression: the independence of the observations from each other. In order to account for this possibility, we used clustered regression analysis with robust standard errors. We constructed four models. Model 1 includes only the control variables, Model 2 adds the direct effects of individuals' motivation for SRB, Model 3 also includes the direct effect of providing a bonus contingent upon non-financial performance, and Model 4 finally shows the interaction effects of rewards with autonomous and controlled motivation. Based on previous research, we model the undermining effect of incentives as interaction terms of incentives with autonomous motivations (Kunz, 2015; Kunz & Linder, 2012; Linder, 2016; Sauermann & Cohen, 2010; Weibel et al., 2010) and follow common recommendations in literature to construct the interaction, such as mean-centering (e.g., Aiken & West, 1993; Jaccard & Turrisi, 2003). Mean Variance Inflation Factor (VIF) in all models is below 1.62 suggesting that multi-collinearity is not a major issue of concern.

As Model 1 shows, work-experience, universalism, SELFPAY, and the type of project contribute significantly to explaining the engagement in SRB. Model 2 identifies autonomous motivation to be a statistically significant (at $p < 0.01$) driver of the level of SRB. Thus, hypothesis 1 cannot be rejected based on the present data. Adding in the rewards for achieving CSR-related outcomes in Model 3 in turn does not materially affect the picture, as the rewards do not show up significant at common threshold levels. When adding-in also the interaction terms of integrated motivation with rewards and extrinsic motivation with rewards (Model 4), they show the expected signs, yet neither of these interaction effects attains statistical significance. Results are materially unchanged when running instead of a clustered regression a normal OLS regression.

4.5 Discussion

The first experiment suggests that financial incentives for socially responsible behavior are inefficient, while autonomous is a significant driver of SRB. In order to consolidate these results, we built a second study, which extends the Study 1 in two ways: (a) the type of decision scenarios used and (b) the measurement of motivation.

Table 2 Descriptive statistics of Study 1

Variable	Mean	SD	Min	Max	1	2	3	4	5	6	7	8	9	10	11	12
1. Inclination to engage in SRB[a]	0.00	1.00	−3.02	1.61	*0.64*											
2. Autonomous movation[a]	0.00	1.00	−3.04	1.30	**0.58*****	*0.71*										
3. Controlled movation[a]	0.00	1.00	−1.54	2.36	**0.24*****	0.03	*0.77*									
4. CSR-contingent pay	0.79	0.82	0.00	2.00	0.10	0.08	**0.24*****									
5. Gender	1.65	0.48	1.00	2.00	−0.01	**−0.14***	0.03	0.07								
6. Work experience	20.05	5.41	8.00	33.00	**0.14***	**0.19****	**−0.13***	0.06	**−0.19*****							
7. Risk aversion	1.30	0.46	1.00	2.00	−0.09	**−0.16****	−0.01	**−0.20*****	**0.18*****	**−0.30*****						
8. Universalism	4.77	0.76	2.67	6.00	**0.28*****	**0.54*****	**−0.15****	0.03	**-0.15****	**0.14***	-0.08					
9. Benevolence	4.91	0.83	3.00	6.00	0.10	**0.19*****	**−0.15****	0.12	**0.14****	0.01	**-0.13***	**0.39*****				
10. SELFPAY	0.51	0.50	0.00	1.00	**0.25*****	0.14	**0.14**	−0.03	−0.04	−0.05	0.12	−0.07	−0.10			
11. SRBTyB	0.33	0.47	0.00	1.00	0.03	**0.11***	0.07	−0.03	0.00	0.00	0.00	0.00	0.00	0.04		
12. SRBTyC	0.33	0.47	0.00	1.00	−0.09	**−0.17****	0.06	0.00	0.00	0.00	0.00	0.00	0.00	−0.08	**−0.50*****	

(continued)

Table 2 (continued)

Variable	Mean	SD	Min	Max	1	2	3	4	5	6	7	8	9	10	11	12
13. Age	43.57	4.50	35.00	56.00	0.12	**0.14***	−0.13	0.00	**−0.29*****	**0.92*****	**−0.26*****	0.08	−0.08	−0.07	0.00	0.00

$n = 165$. Significance of correlations: ***$p < 0.01$; ** $p < 0.05$; *$p < 0.10$ (two-tailed test}
[a]Factor based on multiple items; alpha on the diagonal

5 Study 2

5.1 *Subjects*

For the second study, we used a similar panel than from study 1. We rely on data from 126 decisions made by 42 participants. The participants are all managers from the banking industry and have considerable job experience (average is 18 years).

5.2 *Design of Scenarios*

To further enhance the quality of our results, we changed two of our three different types of socially responsible behavior that the individual might engage in (1) the decision to organize a training for their team about eco-friendly driving thus likely reducing the CO_2 emissions of the unit's (same as in Study 1) (2) the possibility to hire an additional employee in a region where unemployment is high (3) the decision to renovate the buildings of the agency.

As in experiment 1, we allow both "win–win" as well as "win–lose" situations by varying the impact that the alternative behaviors have on financial performance of the bank branch and relied on three alternative versions of salary system.

5.3 *Measure of Engagement in SRB and Motivation*

5.3.1 Autonomous and Controlled Motivation

For measuring individual's motivation, we used an adapted version of Gagné et al. (2010). Their Motivation at Work Scale is based on Ryan and Connell's (1989) but has been adapted to a business context and translated in different languages, including French. Four items are used to measure autonomous motivation (corresponding to "identified regulation" in the original table of Gagné et al., 2010) and four items are used to measure controlled motivation (corresponding to "external regulation—material"). Appendix 5 provides the exact wording of the items used. Cronbach's alpha was 0.90 for autonomous motivation and controlled motivation.

5.3.2 Engagement in SRB

We add one question to the ones used for Study 1 (see Appendix 3). Cronbach's alpha of the scale with our sample was 0.79, thus above the common threshold of 0.70.

5.3.3 Control Variables

We keep all the control variables used in Study 1.

5.3.4 Manipulation Checks

Like in Study 1, we employed manipulation check questions as in Pablo (1994) to verify that our manipulations worked as intended. The items used correspond to those used in Study 1 and the correlations of participants' responses to them with our experimental variables are all significant ($p < 0.01$), thus suggesting that the manipulations were successful.

5.4 *Descriptive Results*

A total of 42 participants (corresponding to 126 vignettes) provided useable data. Table 1 provides the descriptive statistics. As in Study 1, some 64% of respondents were male and work experience in paying jobs ranged between 8 and 33 years with an average of about 18 years. Respondents on average are 42 years old.

Pair-wise correlations—as shown in Table 4—suggest that some control variables are significant: the type of SRB project—that is whether it "pays for itself" or not, universalism and benevolence values, as the type of scenario. As on Study 1, since age and work experience are highly correlated (pairwise correlation = 0.81 at $p < 0.01$), we rely on work experience in the following multivariate analyses and exclude age to counter dangers of multi-collinearity (Table 4).

5.5 *Multivariate Results*

Table 5 reports the results of the multivariate analysis to identify the relations between incentives and SRB. Since each respondent replied to multiple vignettes, the answers to these vignettes might not be fully independent. As for Study 1, we used four clustered regression analysis with robust standard errors. Mean Variance Inflation Factor (VIF) in all models is below 1.78 suggesting that multi-collinearity is not a major issue of concern.

In Model 1, self-transcendence value, SELFPAY, and the nature of the project (type of scenario) contribute significantly to explaining the engagement in SRB. Model 2 identifies autonomous motivation to be a statistically significant (at $p < 0.01$) driver of the level of SRB. Thus, in line with the Study 1 results, hypothesis 1 cannot be rejected based on the present data. Adding in the rewards for achieving CSR-related outcomes in Model 3 in turn does not materially affect the picture, as the rewards do not show up significant at common threshold levels. When adding-in also

Table 3 Multivariate analyses of Study 1

	Model 1		Model 2		Model 3		Model 4	
	coef	se	coef	se	coef	se	coef	se
Gender	0.016	0.171	0.081	0.172	0.084	0.173	0.088	0.170
Work Experience (in years)	**0.025***	0.013	**0.020***	0.012	**0.021***	0.012	**0.020***	0.012
Risk aversion	−0.160	0.174	−0.021	0.148	−0.034	0.155	−0.031	0.160
Universalism	**0.289****	0.139	0.011	0.133	0.011	0.133	0.001	0.133
Benevolence	0.018	0.105	0.016	0.086	0.020	0.086	0.034	0.085
SELFPAY	**0.482*****	0.115	**0.264****	0.114	**0.262****	0.115	**0.261****	0.120
SRBTvB	-0.017	0.172	−0.146	0.144	−0.156	0.146	−0.159	0.147
SRBTvC	-0.249*	0.148	−0.156	0.129	−0.165	0.130	−0.171	0.131
Autonomous motivation			**0.508*****	0.109	**0.507*****	0.109	**0.512*****	0.155
Controlled motivation			**0.202****	0.078	**0.210****	0.079	**0.150***	0.089
CSR-contingent pay					−0.044	0.073	−0.042	0.075
Reward x autonomous motivation							−0.017	0.092
Reward x controlled motivation							0.080	0.067
Observations	173		169		169		169	
N clust	58		58		58		58	
F	4.81		10.23		9.90		16.44	
Prob > F	0.000		0.000		0.000		0.000	
R2	0.171		0.405		0.406		0.409	
Adjuster R2	0.130		0.367		0.364		0.360	
Root MSE	0.888		0.761		0.762		0.765	
Mean time VIF	1.24		1.32		1.31		1.62	
Max time VIF	1.38		1.78		1.78		2.71	

Robust standard errors in parentheses
*** $p < 0.01$, ** $p < 0.05$, * $p < 0.1$

the interaction terms of integrated motivation with rewards and extrinsic motivation with rewards (Model 4), they show the expected signs, but only the interaction effect between reward and controlled motivation attains statistical significance. Results are materially unchanged when running instead of a clustered regression a normal OLS regression.

Table 4 Descriptive statistics of Study 2

Variable	Mean	SD	Min	Max	1	2	3	4	5	6	7	8	9	10	11	12
1 Inclination to engage in SRB[a]	0.00	1.00	−3.02	1.70	*0.79*											
2 Autonomous movation[a]	0.00	1.00	−2.66	1.48	**0.69*****	*0.90*										
3 Controlled movation[a]	0.00	1.00	−1.36	2.09	**0.29*****	**0.26*****y	*0.90*									
4 CSR-contingent pay	0.99	1.00	0	2	0.11	0.02	**0.36*****									
5 Gender	1.65	0.48	1	2	−0.01	0.01	**0.15***	−0.01								
6 Work experience	18.13	4.82	8	33	0.02	0.12	0.01	−0.01	0.01							
7 Risk aversion	1.37	0.48	1	2	−0.03	0.06	**−0.17***	0.01	0.01	0.01						

(continued)

Table 4 (continued)

Variable	Mean	SD	Min	Max	1	2	3	4	5	6	7	8	9	10	11	12
8 Universalism	4.87	0.85	2.33	6	**0.17***	**0.31*****	−0.09	−0.02	−0.03	**0.16***	**0.32*****					
9 Benevolence	4.92	0.89	2.5	6	**0.21****	**0.28*****	0.02	0.00	**−0.17***	**−0.16**	**0.19****	**0.22****				
10 SELFPAY	0.52	0.50	0	1	**0.22*****	**0.16****	0.08	0.02	0.01	−0.00	−0.04	0.09	0.04			
11 SRBTyB	0.33	0.47	0	1	**0.14***	0.10	0.10	0.05	0.00	0.00	0.00	0.00	0.00	−0.01		
12 SRBTyD	0.33	0.47	0	1	**−0.22*****	−0.09	−0.12	−0.01	0.00	0.00	0.00	0.00	0.00	0.02	**−0.50*****	
13 Age	41.63	5.45	31	59	−0.00	0.08	0.01	−0.00	**−0.20****	**0.81**	0.14	**0.24*****	**−0.21****	0.01	0.01	0.00

$n = 126$. Significance of correlations: $^{***}p < 0.01$; $^{**}p < 0.05$; $^{*}p < 0.10$ (two tailed test)
[a]Factor based on multiple items; alpha on the diagonal

Table 5 Multivariate analyses of Study 2

	Model 1		Model 2		Model 3		Model 4	
	coef	se	coef	se	coef	se	coef	se
Gender	0.166	0.257	−0.148	0.173	−0.137	0.176	−0.179	0.179
Work experience (in years)	0.011	0.025	−0.016	0.012	−0.016	0.012	**−0.021***	0.012
Risk aversion	−0.205	0.228	*−0.062*	*0.147*	0.072	0.150	−0.048	0.152
Universalism	0.152	0.118	*0.027*	*0.098*	0.024	0.099	0.043	0.098
Benevolence	0.244*	0.122	*−0.025*	*0.092*	−0.024	0.093	−0.016	0.087
SELFPAY	**0.393*****	0.192	0.217*	*0.128*	0.218	0.129	0.200	0.133
SRBTvB	0.135	0.184	*0.012*	*0.181*	0.006	0.184	0.052	0.182
SRBTvD	**−0.410****	0.188	*−0.178*	*0.158*	−0.183	0.157	−0.120	0.173
Autonomous motivation			0.631***	*0.063*	**0.634*****	0.064	**0.778*****	0.146
Controlled motivation			*0.112*	*0.096*	0.095	0.092	−0.102	0.096
CSR-contingent pay					0.038	0.071	0.062	0.074
Reward x autonomous motivation							−0.127	0.111
Reward x controlled motivation							**0.158****	0.078
Observations	126		116		116		116	
N clust	42		*42*		42		42	
F	3.65		*19.29*		18.05		19.72	
Prob > F	0.003		*0.000*		0.000		0.000	
R2	0.161		*0.508*		0.509		0.535	
Adjusted R2	0.104		*0.461*		0.457		0.476	
Root MSE	0.974		*0.717*		0.720		0.707	
Mean time VIF	1.21		*1.29*		1.31		1.78	
Max time VIF	1.34		*1.4*		1.44		3.52	

Robust standard errors in parentheses
$^{***}p < 0.01$, $^{**}p < 0.05$, $^{*}p < 0.1$

5.6 Discussion

Overall, the results of Study 2 confirm the results previously found on Study 1, namely that hypothesis 1 cannot be rejected with a new set of SRB scenarios and a different measure of autonomous and controlled motivation. We observe a significant interaction between reward and controlled motivation, which is coherent as our controlled motivation items focused on material external regulation. But as on Study 1, our data does not support a crowding-out of autonomous norm-based motivation by controlled motivation. These results are unchanged when running a path analysis.

6 Concluding Discussion

Firms increasingly face pressure from many sides to conduct business in a more socially responsible manner (e.g., Bénabou & Tirole, 2010). This raises the question of how firms can foster socially responsible decision-making by their managers and employees. Resorting to financial incentives, such as a bonus, for attaining certain social targets seems a possible solution. Little, however, is known about the effectiveness and efficiency of such reward systems in fostering socially responsible behavior.

Our two vignette experiment studies suggest that such financial incentives for socially responsible behavior are at best of limited help for fostering SRB. Whereas our data does not support a crowding-out of autonomous norm-based motivation for SRB by controlled motivation such as financial incentives, it equally does not show much impact of such incentives on the level of intentions to engage in SRB. Study 1 suggests that they have no impact on the level of SRB. Study 2, in turn, seems to suggest that at best their impact is much smaller than that of autonomous motivation. Hence, our studies do not support upholding the often debated, yet rarely empirically studied effect of a "crowding-out" of autonomous motivation by extrinsic incentives. Yet, ur studies clearly show that autonomous motivation is a significative driver of SRB. Top managers interested in fostering the SRB exhibited by the members of their organization should, therefore, focus on attracting and retaining individuals who are autonomously motivated for SRB rather than on to trying to foster SRB by implementing SRB-related remuneration systems.

Some limitations of our study though call for further research into the matter of incentives for SRB. Besides the fact that we do not observe actual engagement in SRB, but only the inclination or tendency to undertake SRB, vignette experiments require resorting to rather "black-and-white" situational descriptions—that is: binary or variables with only three or four different levels—in order to keep the universe of combinations to a manageable level. In reality, however, there are many different reward systems and a plethora of SRB. The measured effects might also depend on participants' perceptions of attaining certain performance targets that allow getting a bonus (e.g., Heath et al., 1999). While we control for work experience which likely influences an individual's perceptions of how well certain targets can be achieved, and while we equally control for participants' core self-evaluations, the experiment does not fully account for differences in individuals' perception regarding the achievability of the non-financial targets that would give right to a bonus. Finally, whereas convenience samples are not uncommon in research (Van der Stede et al., 2005), the kind of convenience sampling approach used to recruit participants in the experiment and the modest sample size of samples (respectively 165 and 142 cases) calls for some caution in the interpretation and generalization of results. To limit this potential issue, we performed two studies with similar design, but varying the type of scenarios and the measures of motivation. Whereas these limitations thus call for further research into the relation of rewards and motivation for SRB, our study contributes to existing literature in a number of ways.

To our best knowledge, we are the first to explore the effects of alternative reward systems on the motivation and engagement in socially responsible behavior on an individual level of analysis. Moreover, as opposed to the overwhelming majority of studies so far conducted on a potential interaction between rewards and autonomous types of motivation, our study relies on managers. Moreover, it draws on a business setting and thus promises to yield results that are more readily applicable to business practice than previous findings, which typically rely on non-business settings or student samples. Finally, our study responds to the remark by Huang et al. (2003) that insights on autonomous motivation which so far have predominantly been generated within a North-American context may not easily translate to other cultural contexts. We thus contribute to a more balanced international set of evidence on the interaction between incentives, motivations, and behaviors.

Appendices

Appendix 1: Vignette Cues Used for the Independent Variables*

Cues regarding remuneration and reward practices.

- **Fix**: The remuneration package of your company only includes a fixed salary (no variable part).
- **15% bonus**: The remuneration package of your company includes a fixed salary and an individual bonus capped at 15% of your base salary and based on the attainment of CSR objectives (social or environmental) set for each manager.
- **30% bonus**: The remuneration package of your company includes a fixed salary and an individual bonus capped at 30% of your base salary and based on the attainment of CSR objectives (social or environmental) set for each manager.

*Cues were provided without any separating headings, subheadings, or bullet points. Original vignettes in French, translated by the authors.

Appendix 2: Descriptions of Alternative SRB Projects*

Project A

One part of the commercial team makes an intensive use of cars to go and visit clients. A contractor is proposing you an eco-friendly driving training program. It would reduce the CO_2 emissions of your fleet and cost 15.000 euro for the whole team. The experience of other companies has demonstrated that this kind of education program has a real impact on CO_2 emissions.

Project Aa	*Project Ab*
They would diminish by 10% and the corresponding fuel savings would provide an 18-month payback for the program	They would diminish by 10%, thanks to substantial fuel savings, but these savings would be absorbed by the higher cost due to faster modernization and renewal of the car fleet

Project B

An analysis of operations has shown that the quality of clients' processing could be optimized through a 5% cost increase: recruitment of part-time employees for peak hours, payment of extra-hours to other employees. It would notably improve the quality of elderly and handicapped people reception.

Project Ba	*Project Bb*
It is clear that these additional costs would be almost covered by a sales increase and a better customer loyalty	It is clear that these additional costs would contribute to improve your image, but will not be compensated by equivalent revenues

Project C

A maternity leave is expected in your team for the next term. There are good chances that the person will continue with a parent leave of at least a year. For a smoother transition and a stress reduction of her colleagues, you consider recruiting a successor right now. It would generate an additional cost of 30 000 euro for this year. The other option is to wait until the HR department addresses the issue in spring.

Project Ca	*Project Cb*
Moreover, the corresponding productivity gains and the safeguarding of the turnover favored by this anticipated recruitment would by and large cover the additional cost, within a 12 to 18 months period though	Nevertheless, the corresponding productivity gains and the positive impact on the turnover generated by this anticipated recruitment would only compensate for one third of the additional cost

It is clear that this action would reduce the stress of your team and improve the quality of its working environment.

Project D

One of the challenges of your retail banking network is the relationship with the territories in which you are located; You are in an area where there is unemployment among young people, especially among those of immigrant origin. One possibility for your agency would be to contribute to the resolution of this unemployment problem by opening an additional position, even if the needs of your agency in terms of staffing are already covered.

Project Da	*Project Db*
Even if it is primarily an action for local development, you estimate that the additional costs generated by this recruitment will be covered in 18 to 24 months by net product increases through customer development	It is clear that this is primarily a development action and that it will not generate additional net banking income (PBN), the additional cost being roughly equivalent to that of an beginner employee

Project E

Your agency is installed in buildings built in the 1970s, whose energy performance is lower than what can be achieved with recent technologies; You could therefore launch a thermal and electrical renovation project (lighting, office equipment).

Project Ea	*Project Eb*
You have estimated the overall cost of this operation: it will be 70% covered by energy savings over the next 4 years	You have estimated the overall cost of this operation and, although it will be possible to bring the building up to the best technical standards of the moment, it will probably take more than 10 years to recover the costs incurred in energy savings

*Cues were provided without separating headings, subheadings, or bullet points. Original vignettes in French, translated into English by the authors.

Appendix 3: Items Used to Measure Engagement in SRB

Given the organizational situation that you just read, how will you behave?

Give your position on your willingness to defend the proposed action for the next budget	*Strongly disagree*	*Strongly agree*
I will convince other colleagues to support me	*1 – 2 – 3 – 4 – 5 – 6 – 7*	
I will try to convince my hierarchy to support this project	*1 – 2 – 3 – 4 – 5 – 6 – 7*	
I will directly finance this project myself by reallocating some resources of my own budget which had already been allocated elsewhere	*1 – 2 – 3 – 4 – 5 – 6 – 7*	
I will request funding from the group's Sustainable Development Department (it has a specific budget for this type of initiative).[a]	*1 – 2 – 3 – 4 – 5 – 6 – 7*	

[a]This fourth question was only used in Study 2

Appendix 4: Items Used to Measure Motivation for SRB in Study 1**

Could you also tell us what is motivating your previous replies ***I am committed to doing this because…***	*Strongly disagree*	*Strongly agree*
… I believe this project is a good thing to do. It reflects my own personal beliefs.[a]	*1 – 2 – 3 – 4 – 5 – 6 – 7*	
… it enables me to get a remuneration.[b]	*1 – 2 – 3 – 4 – 5 – 6 – 7*	
… it will have a positive impact on my career.[b]	*1 – 2 – 3 – 4 – 5 – 6 – 7*	
… caring about the others and the environment is an integral part of who I am.[a]	*1 – 2 – 3 – 4 – 5 – 6 – 7*	
… it will be considered favorably for the calculation of my annual bonus.[b]	*1 – 2 – 3 – 4 – 5 – 6 – 7*	
… I will be less well evaluated than my colleagues if I do not do it.[b]	*1 – 2 – 3 – 4 – 5 – 6 – 7*	

**Original items in French, Items taken from Kunz and Linder (2012) and Reinholt et al. (2011) (in English) who adapted items from an instrument originally developed by Ryan and Connell (1989)

[a]Item used to measure autonomous motivation

[b]Item used to measure controlled motivation

Appendix 5: Items Used to Measure Motivation for SRB* in Study 2

Could you also tell us what is motivating your previous replies ***I am committed to doing this because…***	*Strongly disagree*	*Strongly agree*
… it allows me to get compensation	1 – 2 – 3 – 4 – 5 – 6 – 7	
… this will be taken into account when calculating my annual bonus	1 – 2 – 3 – 4 – 5 – 6 – 7	
… it will help me maximize my personal income	1 – 2 – 3 – 4 – 5 – 6 – 7	
… it will have a positive impact on my career	1 – 2 – 3 – 4 – 5 – 6 – 7	
… I consider it important to make efforts corresponding to the proposed action	1 – 2 – 3 – 4 – 5 – 6 – 7	
… this project is in line with my personal values	1 – 2 – 3 – 4 – 5 – 6 – 7	
… I think this project is a good thing. It reflects my beliefs and personal values	1 – 2 – 3 – 4 – 5 – 6 – 7	
… this project has a personal meaning for me	1 – 2 – 3 – 4 – 5 – 6 – 7	

***Original items in French, taken with minor adjustments from Gagné et al. (2010) The first four items are used to capture controlled motivation; the last four items to measure autonomous motivation

References

Aguinis, H., & Glavas, A. (2012). What we know and don't know about corporate social responsibility: A review and research agenda. *Journal of Management, 38*(4), 932–968.

Aiken, L. S., & West, S. G. (1993). Multiple regression: Testing and interpreting interactions (2nd printing). Sage Publishing.

Albinger, H. S., & Freeman, S. J. (2000). Corporate social performance and attractiveness as an employer to different job seeking populations. *Journal of Business Ethics, 28*, 243–253.

Alexander, C. S., & Becker, H. J. (1978). The use of vignettes in survey research. *Public Opinion Quarterly, 42*, 93–104.

Bansal, P., & Song, H. C. (2017). Similar but not the same: Differentiating corporate responsibility from sustainability. *Academy of Management Annals, 11*, 105–149.

Belle, N., & Cantarelli, P. (2015). Monetary incentives, motivation, and job effort in the public sector: An experimental study with Italian government executives. *Review of Public Personnel Administration, 35*(2), 99–123.

Bénabou, R., & Tirole, J. (2006). Incentives and pro-social behavior. *American Economic Review, 96*(5), 1652–1678.

Bénabou, R., & Tirole, J. (2010). Individual and corporate social responsibility. *Economica, 77*, 1–19.

Besley, T., & Ghatak, M. (2007). Retailing public goods: The economics of corporate social responsibility. *Journal of Public Economics, 91*, 1645–1663.

Burney, L. & Widener, S.K. (2007). Strategic performance measurement systems, job-relevant information, and managerial behavioral responses – role stress and performance. Behavioral Research in Accounting, 19(1), 43-69.

Burnss, J., Vaivio, J. (2001). Management accounting change. *Management Accounting Research, 12*(4):389–402

Campbell, J. L. (2007). Why would corporations behave in socially responsible ways? An institutional theory of corporate social responsibility. *Academy of Management Review, 32*(3), 946–967.

Carroll, A. (1999). Corporate social responsibility: Evolution of a definitional construct. *Business and Society, 38*(3), 268–295.

Chng, D. H. M., Rodgers, M. S., Shih, E., & Song, X.-B. (2012). When does incentive compensation motivate managerial behaviors? An experimental investigation of the fit between incentive compensation, executive core self-evaluations, and firm performance. *Strategic Management Journal, 33*, 1343–1362.

Cho, C. H., Guidry, R. G., Hagemann, A. M., & Patten, D. (2012). Do actions speak louder than words? An empirical investigation of corporate environmental reputation. *Accounting, Organizations and Society, 37*(1), 14–25.

Coleman, J. S. (1990). *Foundations of social theory*. The Belknap Press of Harvard University Press.

Cooper, S. M., & Owen, D. L. (2007). Corporate social reporting and stakeholder accountability: The missing link. *Accounting, Organization and Society, 32*, 649–667.

Crifo, P., & Forget, V. (2014). The economics of corporate social responsibility: A firm level perspective survey. *Journal of Economic Surveys, 29*, 112–130.

Crilly, D., Schneider, S. C., & Zollo, M. (2008). Psychological antecedents to socially responsible behavior. *European Management Review, 5*, 175–190.

Cropanzano, R., Byrne, Z. S., Bobocel, D. R., & Rupp, D. R. (2001). Moral virtues, fairness heuristics, social entities, and other denizens of organizational justice. *Journal of Vocational Behavior, 58*, 164–209.

Deci, E. L. (1975). *Intrinsic motivation*. Plenum Press.

Deci, E. L., & Ryan, R. M. (1985). *Intrinsic motivation and self-determination in human behavior*. Plenum Press.

Deci, E. L., & Ryan, R. M. (2000a). Self-determination theory and the facilitation of intrinsic motivation, social development, and well-being. *American Psychologist, 55*, 68–78.

Deci, E. L., & Ryan, R. M. (2000b). The "what" and "why" of goal pursuits: Human needs and the self-determination of behavior. *Psychological Inquiry, 11*, 227–268.

Deci, E. L., Koestner, R., Ryan, R. M. (2001). Extrinsic rewards and intrinsic motivation in education: Reconsidered once again. *Review of Education Research, 71*, 1–27.

Deckop, J. R., Mangel, R., & Cirka, C. C. (1999). Research notes. Getting more than you pay for: Organizational citizenship behavior and pay-for-performance plans. *Academy of Management Journal, 42*(4), 420–428.

Fabrizi, M., Mallin, C., & Michelon, G. (2014). The role of CEO's personal incentives in driving corporate social responsibility. *Journal of Business Ethics, 124*(2), 311–326.

Fehr, E., & Falk, A. (2002). Psychological foundations of incentives. *European Economic Review, 46*, 687–724.

Fehr, E., & Gächter, S. (2002). Altruistic punishment in humans. *Nature, 415*, 137–140.

Felin, T., & Foss, N. J. (2005). Strategic organization: A field in search of micro-foundations. *Strategic Organization, 3*, 441–455.

Foss, N. J. (2009). Alternative research strategies in the knowledge movement: From macro bias to micro-foundations and multi-level explanation. *European Management Review, 6*, 16–28.

Foss, N. J., & Linder, S. (2019). *Microfoundations: Nature, debate and promises*. Cambridge University Press.

Frey, B. S. (1997). *Not just for the money: An economic theory of personal motivation*. Edward Elgar Publishing.

Fritzsche, D. J., & Becker, H. (1983). Ethical behavior in marketing managers. *Journal of Business Ethics, 2*, 291–299.

Gagné, M., & Deci, E. L. (2005). Self-determination theory and work motivation. *Journal of Organizational Behavior, 26*, 331–362.

Gagné, M., Forest, J., Gilbert, M.-H., & al. (2010). The motivation at work scale: Validation evidence in two languages. *Educational and Psychological Measurement, 70*(4), 628–646.

Garriga, E., & Melé, D. (2004). Corporate social responsibility theories: Mapping the territory. *Journal of Business Ethics, 53*, 51–71.

George, M., & Jones, G.R. (2005). Understanding and managing organizational behavior, 5th Edition. Pearson.

Glavas, A. (2016). Corporate social responsibility and organizational psychology: An integrative review. *Frontiers in Psychology*. https://doi.org/10.3389/fpsyg.2016.00144.

Gond, J.-P., El Akremi, A., Swaen, V., & Babu, N. (2017). The psychological microfoundations of corporate social responsibility: A person-centric systematic review: Micro-CSR: A systematic review. *Journal of Organizational Behavior, 38*(2), 225–246.

Graves, L. M., Sarkis, J., & Zhu, Q. (2013). How transformational leadership and employee motivation combine to predict employee proenvironmental behaviors in China. *Journal of Environmental Psychology, 35*, 81–91.

Gray, R. (2006). Social, environmental and sustainability reporting and organizational value creation? Whose value? Whose creation? *Accounting, Auditing and Accountability Journal, 19*(6), 793–819.

Hackman, J. R., & Oldham, G. R. (1976). Motivation through the design of work: Test of a theory. *Organizational Behavior and Human Performance, 16*, 250–279.

Hainmueller, J., Hangartner, D., & Yamamoto, T. (2015). Validating vignette and conjoint survey experiments against real-world behavior. *Proceedings of the National Academy of Sciences, 112*(8), 2395–2400.

Hartmann, F. G. H., & Maas, V. S. (2010). Why business unit controllers create budget slack: Involvement in management, social pressure, and machiavellianism. *Behavioral Research in Accounting, 22*(2), 27–49.

Hatch, C. D., & Stephen, S.-A. (2015). Gender effects on perceptions of individual and corporate social responsibility. *Journal of Applied Business and Economics, 17*, 63–71.

Heath, C., Larrick, R. P., & Wu, G. (1999). Goals as reference points. *Cognitive Psychology, 38*, 79–109.

Hegarty, W. J., Sims jr, H. P. (1978) Organizational philosophy, policies and objectives related to unethical decision behavior: A laboratory experiment. *Journal of Applied Psychology, 64*, 331–338

Holmås, T., Kjerstad, E., Lurås, H., & Straume, O. R. (2010). Does monetary punishment crowd out pro-social motivation? A natural experiment on hospital length of stay. *Journal of Economic Behavior & Organization, 75*(2), 261–267.

Holmström, B., & Milgrom, P. (1994). The firm as an incentive system. *American Economic Review, 84*, 972–991.

Huang, X., & Van de Vliert, E. (2003). Where intrinsic job satisfaction fails to work: National moderators of intrinsic motivation. *Journal of Organizational Behavior, 24*, 159–179.

Hughes, R. (1998). Considering the vignette technique and its application to a study of drug injecting and HIV risk and safer behaviour. *Sociology of Health & Illness, 20*, 381–400.

Jaccard, J., & Turrisi, R. (2003). *Interaction effects in multiple regression* (2nd ed.). Sage Publishing.

Johnson, G., Langley, A., Melin, L., & Whittington, R. (2007). *Strategy as practice: Research directions and resources*. Cambridge University Press.

Jones, T. M. (1991). Ethical decision making by individuals in organizations: An issue-content model. *Academy of Management Review, 16*(2), 336–395.

Kunz, J. (2015). Objectivity and subjectivity in performance evaluation and autonomous motivation: An exploratory study. *Management Accounting Research, 27*, 27–46.

Kunz, J., & Linder, S. (2012). Organizational control and work effort: Another look at the interplay of rewards and motivation. *European Accounting Review, 21*(3), 591–621.

Kunz, A. H., & Pfaff, D. (2002). Agency theory, performance evaluation, and the hypothetical construct of intrinsic motivation. *Accounting, Organizations and Society, 27*, 227–295.

Lacetera, N., & Macis, M. (2010). Do all material incentives for pro-social activities backfire? The response to cash and non-cash incentives for blood donations. *Journal of Economic Psychology, 31*, 738–748.

Lazear, E. P. (2000). Performance pay and productivity. *American Economic Review, 90*, 1346–1361.
Lindenberg, S. (2001). Intrinsic motivation in a new light. *Kyklos, 54*, 317–342.
Linder, S. (2016). Fostering strategic renewal: Monetary incentives, merit-based promotions, and engagement in autonomous strategic action. *Journal of Management Control, 27*(2), 251–280.
Matten, D., & Moon, J. (2008). Implicit and explicit CSR: A conceptual framework for a comparative understanding of corporate social responsibility. *Academy of Management Review, 33*(2), 404–424.
McWilliams, A., & Siegel, D. (2001). Corporate social responsibility: A theory of the firm perspective. *Academy of Management Review, 26*(1), 117–127.
Mellstrom, C., & Johannesson, M. (2008). Crowding out in blood donation. Was Titmuss right? *Journal of the European Economic Association, 6*(4), 845–863.
Milgrom, P., & Roberts, J. (1992). *Economics, organization & management*. Prentice-Hall.
Norris, G., & O'Dwyer, B. (2004). Motivating socially responsive decision making: The operation of management controls in a socially responsive organization. *British Accounting Review, 36*, 173–196.
ORSE (2012). Etude sur l'intégration de critères RSE dans la part variable de la rémuneration des dirigeants et des managers.
ORSE (2017) Critères RSE et rémunération - Guide sur l'intégration de critères RSE dans la rémunération variable des dirigeants et Managers.
Pablo, A. L. (1994). Determinants of acquisition integration level: A decision-making perspective. *Academy of Management Journal, 37*, 803–836.
Podsakoff, P. M., MacKenzie, S. B., Lee, J. Y., & Podsakoff, N. P. (2003). Common method bias in behavioral research: A critical review of the literature and recommended remedies. *Journal of Applied Psychology, 88*, 879–903.
Pokorny, K. (2008). Pay-but do not pay too much: An experimental study on the impact of incentives. *Journal of Economic Behavior & Organization, 66*(2), 251–264.
Porter, M., & Kramer, M. (2006). Strategy and society. *Harvard Business Review, 84*(12), 78–92.
Porter, M. E., & Kramer, M. R. (2011). Creating shared value: How to reinvent capitalism – and unleash a wave of innovation and growth. *Harvard Business Review*, Jan–Feb: 62–77.
Reinholt, M., Pedersen, T., & Foss, N. (2011). Why a central network position isn't enough: The role of motivation and ability for knowledge sharing in employee networks. *The Academy of Management Journal, 54*(6), 1277–1297.
Robertson, D. C. (1993). Empiricism in business ethics–suggested research directions. *Journal of Business Ethics, 12*, 585–599.
Rossi, P. H., & Anderson, A. B. (1982). The factorial survey approach: An introduction. In P. H. Rossi & S. L. Nock (Eds.), *Measuring social jugements: The factorial survey approach* (pp. 15–67). Sage.
Rupp, D. E., & Mallory, D. B. (2015). Corporate social responsibility: Psychological, person-centric, and progressing. *Annual Review of Organizational Psychology and Organizational Behavior, 2*(1), 211–236.
Ryan, R. M., & Connell, J. P. (1989). Perceived locus of causality and internalization—Examining reasons for acting in 2 domains. *Journal of Personality and Social Psychology, 57*, 749–761.
Ryan, R. M., & Deci, E. L. (2000). Intrinsic and extrinsic motivations: Classic definitions and new directions. *Contemporary Educational Psychology, 25*, 54–67.
Sauermann, H., & Cohen, W. M. (2010). What makes them tick? Employee motives and firm innovation. *Management Science, 56*(12), 2134–2153.
Schwartz, S. H. (2007). Universalism values and the inclusiveness of our moral universe. *Journal of Cross-Cultural Psychology, 38*, 711–728.
Schwartz, S. H., & Rubel, T. (2005). Sex difference in value priorities: Cross-cultural and multimethod studies. *Journal of Personality and Social Psychology, 89*(6), 1010–1028.
Schwenk, C. R. (1982). Why sacrifice rigour for relevance? A proposal for combining laboratory and field research in strategic management. *Strategic Management Journal, 3*, 213–225.
Stanley, M (2016). S+R Soundbite: How can ESG be embedded into executive compensation?

Starmer, C. (1999). Experimental economics: Hard science or wasteful tinkering? *Economic Journal, 109*, 5–15.
Taylor, B. J. (2006). Factorial surveys: Using vignettes to study professional judgment. *British Journal of Social Work, 36*, 1187–1207.
Titmuss, R. M. (1971). *The gift relationship*. Allen & Unwin.
Tongo, C. I. (2015). Social responsibility, quality of work life and motivation to contribute in the nigerian society. *Journal of Business Ethics, 126*(2), 219–233.
Van der Stede, W. A., Young, S. M., & Chen, C. X. (2005). Assessing the quality of evidence in empirical management accounting research: The case of survey studies. *Accounting, Organizations and Society, 30*, 655–684.
Weibel, A., Rost, K., & Osterloh, M. (2010). Pay for performance in the public sector–benefits and (hidden) costs. *Journal of Public Administration Research and Theory, 20*, 387–412.
Wolfe, C., & Loraas, T. (2008). Knowledge sharing: The effects of incentives, environment, and person. *Journal of Information Systems, 22*(2), 53–76.

Vincent Bouchet holds a PhD in management science from the Institut Polytechnique de Paris, and is a member of the Energy and Prosperity Chair. He completed his PhD at the Management Research Centre of the École polytechnique, in partnership with the Caisse des Dépôts Group. His research focuses on the integration of climate issues in finance.

Stefan Linder is associate professor of accounting and management control at ESSEC Business School in Paris. He holds a Ph.D. from Copenhagen Business School. He studies the role of organizational control and incentive systems for managerial behavior and firm-level outcomes. His work has been published among others in European Accounting Review, IEEE Transactions on Engineering Management, Journal of Business Ethics, Journal of Banking & Finance, Journal of Management, and Small Business Management.

Nicolas Mottis is professor at Ecole Polytechnique and Director of the Executive Master. His research projects cover, first, the links between strategy and control (governance models, strategic planning, business plan, value creation, incentives systems, key performance indicators, scorecards, socially responsible investment, corporate social responsibility…); and second, innovation and entrepreneurship in high tech sectors (project management, creation of startups, development of new ventures in existing firms…). He has published many articles and several books on these topics.

Part IV
Global Value Networks and Relational Contracts

Transcultural Cooperation in Global Networks. A Contribution to the Research Program of Relational Economics

Julika Baumann Montecinos

Abstract This paper analyzes the manifold and far-reaching implications of considering cultural factors as resources for cooperation. Building on the theory of Relational Economics, it proposes a paradigm shift toward a transcultural approach which is understood to focus on commonalities in contexts of cultural diversity and to highlight the requisite conditions for generating local and transcultural cooperation rents. The success of cooperative value creation in regio-global inter-, intra-, and extra-firm networks depends not least on the individual and organizational abilities to engage in transcultural learning processes and to establish communities of practice across cultural boundaries. In addressing these issues, this paper focuses on analyzing the relevance of cultural factors for economic performance by conceptualizing them in terms of their potential to serve as transcultural commons, which includes deriving a consistent conception of culture that is conducive to such an endeavor, and contributing to an understanding of the relationship between transculturality and diversity. Ultimately, the aim is to more accurately depict volatile, uncertain, complex, and ambiguous economic realities, and to open up new perspectives for successful transcultural cooperation in value creation networks of organizations.

Keywords Relational economics · Transculturality · Transcultural management · Cooperation in global networks · Cultural economics · Transcultural commons · Cultural capital

The world being interconnected is nothing new. Rather, trends such as the globalization of value chains or increasing digitalization serve to reinforce a phenomenon that has existed for a very long time, at least since people started trading with each other. The image of caravans travelling along the old Silk Road can be seen as a metaphor not only for the early exchange of goods, but also for connections between people and cultures. In the same sense, dealing with the role of culture and considering its relevance in global exchange constellations is nothing new, either. Back in 1928, Robert Ezra Park claimed in his article "Human migration and the marginal man"

J. Baumann Montecinos (✉)
Zeppelin University, Friedrichshafen, Germany
e-mail: Julika.Montecinos@zu.de

L. Biggiero et al. (eds.), *The Relational View of Economics*, Relational Economics and Organization Governance, https://doi.org/10.1007/978-3-030-86526-9_10

that "[i]n the long run, [...] people and races who live together, sharing in the same economy, inevitably interbreed, and in this way if in no other, the relations which were merely co-operative and economic become social and cultural" (Park, 1928, p. 891).

Two aspects mentioned by Park appear particularly interesting here: on the one hand, the inevitability of cultural exchange; on the other, the observation that social and cultural relations arise from cooperation, that is, from shared practices and experiences. Such a perspective on approaching culture as both a setting for and a result of cooperation, however, received little attention in the further economic debate: while standard economics has not generally been concerned with questions on the relevance of culture for the economy, approaches such as New Institutional Economics focused more on the principal classification of cultural factors as informal institutions than on a consideration of the complex reciprocities between culture and concrete economic activity (see Baumann Montecinos, 2019, pp. 97ff.).

Against this backdrop, two current impulses now offer an occasion to rethink the long-standing existence of global cooperation networks and to identify the corresponding implications for research and practice: one impulse is provided by the United Nations' Sustainable Development Goals (SDGs) with their paradigm-shifting objective of "Transforming our World" (United Nations, 2015). The SDGs combine the call for a cooperative effort across cultures and sectors to shape mutually beneficial economic and social development on the one hand with the recognition of country-specific, local solution-finding competence on the other (see Baumann Montecinos, 2019, p. 1 and p. 47; Wieland & Baumann Montecinos, 2018, pp. 18ff.). A second impulse accompanies and reflects this paradigm shift in the economic debate, and focuses on the success factors and relevance of cooperation in complex multivalent networks: the elaboration of a theory of Relational Economics (see Wieland, 2018, 2020, 2022), which serves as both a point of departure and frame of reference for this paper. Here, the implications that this theoretical stance has for the consideration and integration of cultural factors in the analysis of real-life cooperation, especially with regard to their role in identifying and expanding potential cooperation corridors in networks of value creation, will be of particular interest.

The consequences of this shift in the scientific consideration of cultural-economic correlations are manifold and far-reaching: it involves the further elaboration of the traditional intercultural concept into one of transcultural competence[1] and thus the shift from a classic, static model of culture to a dynamic one that focuses on joint learning and creative processes in the course of concrete experiences of cooperation—experiences which, as has already been mentioned, have long been part of the history of human cross-cultural interaction. All these contributions that the relational view can make to a revised understanding of the role of cultural factors in economics can only be outlined here, as will be done in the pages that follow.

[1] For the current discussion on relevant trends regarding concepts of competence for dealing with cultural diversity, see, among others, Bennett (2020), Bolten (2020), Deardorff (2020), Henze (2020) and Nazarkiewicz (2020).

1 A Relational View on Cooperative Value Creation

In order to recognize the significance and nature of the transcultural approach, particularly with regard to its contributions to understanding the prerequisites of cooperation in global networks, it is useful to take a closer look at the two aforementioned impulses behind this orientation.

The first of these impulses stems from the UN's Sustainable Development Goals (SDGs), which—and this is particularly significant for our purposes—are formulated as common goals for all countries and entail obligations for all. Demanding global cooperation on an equal level is not a well-intentioned afterthought; rather, it is positioned at the heart of the agenda as a starting point and prerequisite for achieving shared goals. In contrast to the previous Millennium Development Goals, which focused in particular on addressing problems such as hunger and poverty in so-called developing countries, the SDGs also include goals that especially require the participation of more prosperous countries, for example, in the areas of climate protection or waste avoidance (see Wieland & Baumann Montecinos, 2018, p. 18).[2] One could even claim that in this manner every country becomes a developing country with regard to certain goals. At the very least, it is clear to see that the ideas of meeting on an equal footing, and of viewing the existing challenges as shared ones, actually seems to be taken seriously. The fact that Goal 17 explicitly calls for a global pact between all countries and especially between representatives of different sectors, including the private sector, to achieve inclusive economic and social development, underscores the spirit of "Transforming our World" (United Nations, 2015). The call to cooperate across cultural and sectoral borders for mutual benefit thereby takes center stage. What seems particularly important here is that the perception of the world as being *our* world not only inherently presupposes a willingness to recognize each other as cooperation partners, but that it also implies a process of transformation to which all parties are exposed, and to which they are called upon to productively contribute. This emphasis on commonalities and the common purpose of cooperating productively corresponds to the basic assumptions of a transcultural approach, as will be further elaborated on in the course of this paper.

This is all the more applicable since the SDGs also reflect the fact that such a transcultural approach, in its emphasis on commonalities, always immanently considers the simultaneous importance of cultural diversity. This is reflected in the fact that the respective contributions of the individual countries are not uniform; rather, each country is expected to make its own specific contribution. This is particularly noteworthy, and is an expression of the necessary dialectic of commonality and diversity, which is described for the SDGs as follows: "[A] common understanding has emerged that there must be a universal agenda. […] Universality implies that all countries will need to change, each with its own approach, but each with a sense of the global common good" (United Nations, 2014, p. 14).

---

[2] For a discussion of the SDGs from this type of perspective, and considering a variety of approaches and implications, see Fetzer &Baumann Montecinos, 2016.

In this context, transforming *our* world also means being dependent on the cooperative effort to plan and facilitate inclusive development and to engage in joint learning processes (see Wieland & Baumann Montecinos, 2018, p. 19). Accordingly, the call for a "Global Partnership for Sustainable Development" as formulated in Goal 17 (United Nations, 2015) is accompanied by the insight that the SDGs "require an unprecedented level of cooperation and collaboration among civil society, business, government, NGOs, foundations and others for their achievement" (Stibbe et al., 2018, p. 6) and makes all these actors part of a global cooperation network (see Wieland & Baumann Montecinos, 2018, p. 20).

This is precisely where the second impulse comes in, giving new momentum to the current debate on the conditions for successful global cooperation, and this is where we move from the field of international development and politics to economic theory, namely to Josef Wieland's theory of Relational Economics (2018, 2020; 2022). The main focus here is on the theory's explanatory power with regard to the realities of globally operating organizations, which are illustrated in Fig. 1.

This figure shows that, in keeping with the theory of Relational Economics, we understand the framework conditions for the actions of globally operating companies to be characterized by the complexity, dynamics, connectedness, and dependencies of regio-global value chains as polyvalent intra-, inter-, and extra-firm networks.

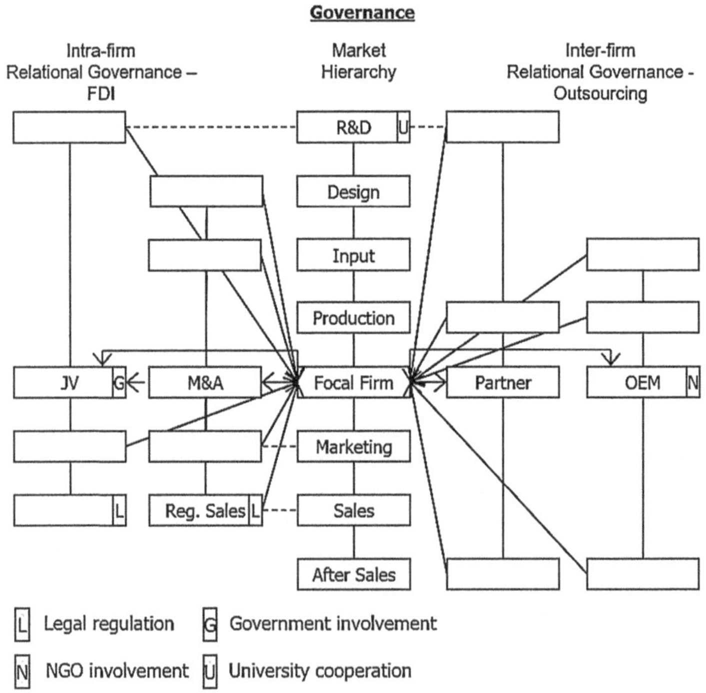

Fig. 1 The firm as a nexus of transcultural stakeholder relations (from Wieland, 2020, p. 79)

Wieland describes such networks as minisocieties that organize and execute relational transactions as dynamic attractors for multiple actors and decision logics (Wieland, 2022) and thereby in their role concerning the relationalization of polyvalent events (ibid.). In a nutshell, this approach views every organization as a nexus of stakeholder relations and analyzes the implications this relational perspective holds for theory and practice. With regard to the epistemological interest of the present paper, it is essential to point out that the complex realities of globally operating organizations as relational constructs offer fertile soil for transcultural cooperation, and at the same time justify a thorough academic investigation of the conditions for successful cooperation. This refers in particular to the requirements that this complexity imposes on individuals and organizations to continuously and consistently develop their willingness and ability to cooperate across cultural borders and to engage in corresponding learning processes. Our research program on transcultural competence deals with such questions, which also form the basis for the following considerations, focusing on cultural factors and their relevance for the use and expansion of cooperation corridors, and thus for economic performance. Essentially, the following sections present the findings of a study on the conception of cultural aspects as potentially cooperation-enabling and economically effective factors (see Baumann Montecinos, 2019) and combine them with the current academic and practical discourses on Relational Economics.

When dealing with complex and dynamic global and cross-sectoral challenges—and this has been confirmed by reviewing the SDGs and the realities of globally operating organizations—addressing cultural diversity seems to be crucial to meeting these challenges. Even if we acknowledge that cultural diversity is not a new phenomenon, the challenge remains to approach it in a way that can productively address the previously described concerns. Accordingly, and in the spirit of Relational Economics, it will be argued in the following that culture is a resource that can have an impact on the generation of cooperation rents both locally and potentially globally. Cultural resources function as commons and hold the potential to become transcultural commons in the sense of shared initial capital for developing and expanding cooperation corridors in contexts of cultural diversity. Such a view of culture as a resource for cooperation must also address the interrelationships between commonality and diversity itself, as the following sections will show.

2 Culture as a Resource for Cooperation

In order to specify the role of cultural factors for achieving political, societal, and/or economic goals, it is first necessary to approach the concept of culture from a definitional standpoint. The fact that there are innumerable cultural concepts (see Keller, 1982) and that Helmut Leipold accordingly states that "the difficulties of all research programs oriented toward cultural economics begin with the understanding of culture" (Leipold, 2006, p. 3, translated by the author) should not discourage us at this point, but rather encourage us to arrive at a definition of culture that is oriented on the present endeavor, and to then apply it consistently. Such a focused working definition of culture can be achieved in ten steps, paving the way for considering the relevance of culture for economic cooperation as comprehensively as possible:

Ten steps to defining culture	
Firstly	Culture is human made (although basic prosocial skills such as empathy are part of the physiological make-up of human beings) (see Annen, 2004; Tomasello, 2016)
Secondly	Culture comprises all forms of thinking, feeling, acting, and creating (see Taylor, 1871; Hofstede & Hofstede, 2005)
Thirdly	Culture has a constructive function: our cultural "eyeglasses" shape our subjective perception of the world and prescribe meanings, evaluations, categories, and patterns of action (see Weber, 1922/1988; Berger & Luckmann, 1966; Bennett, 2017, 2020)
Fourthly	Culture has a governance function: through its constructive function; it has both an enabling and limiting effect and thus provides a cultural "framework" for action (see North, 1990; Hofstede & Hofstede, 2005)
Fifthly	Culture is shared by a group of people and has an identity-building effect among them (see Park, 1950/2005; Baecker, 2003)
Sixthly	Culture is not uniform. Each individual internalizes his or her own characteristics and has his or her own cultural "toolbox" with elements from multiple cultures (see Swidler, 1986; DiMaggio, 1994; Boyacigiller et al., 2004)
Seventhly	Culture is acquired through learning processes in the course of socialization (see Hurrelmann, 2002; Tomasello, 1999)
Eighthly	Culture is constantly changing (see Denzau & North, 1994; Tomasello, 1999; Appiah, 2006; Bolten, 2020)
Ninthly	Culture develops in a path-dependent manner (see North, 1990)
Tenthly	There is therefore not one culture; there are many.

(Based on Baumann Montecinos, 2019, p. 83, translated by the author)

It is the cultural diversity thus identified, or, to put it more pointedly in keeping with Schramm (2008, p. 11), the observation that the world is and will remain "colorful," that determines the starting conditions for transcultural cooperation and transcultural learning processes aimed at creating relations and commonalities. Pursuing a transcultural approach, understood in this sense, means focusing on the conditions for successful cooperation in a setting of cultural diversity. Here, the prefix "trans" stands for something connective, which permeates different cultures and beyond. Our approach builds on the classic works of Ortiz (1940/1983) and Welsch (1999), among others, and follows the call for "positive cross-cultural scholarship" (Barmeyer & Franklin, 2016, p. 200; Stahl & Tung, 2015) that has come to widely shape the field. This shift in perspective toward the productive potentials of cultural diversity is reflected, for example, in research on strategies for reconciling cultural differences (see Trompenaars & Hampden-Turner, 2012) or for achieving complementarity and synergy (see Barmeyer & Franklin, 2016). It is in the context of this shift toward "positive cross-cultural scholarship" that we seek to introduce and further develop the relational approach's proposal to focus on commonalities and conditions for cooperation, as a consistent paradigm using the term transculturality.

The two cultural functions defined above as an immanent part of our present understanding of culture play a decisive role here: both the constructive function and the governance function of culture characterize the prevailing atmosphere of cooperation and may thus influence the size of existing and potential cooperation corridors in relational transactions. Building on Wieland's earlier concept of Cooperation Economics, according to which the cooperation atmosphere concerns the "formation of shared and lived values and culture" in the sense of "informal incentives and constraints" (Wieland, 1998, p. 15), I have previously argued that taking a closer look at the two cultural functions can yield important insights (see Baumann Montecinos, 2019, p. 134): through the constructive function of culture as "eyeglasses" for the subjective perception and interpretation of the world, the preferences, incentive structures, utility calculations, and thereby the decision logics of the actors involved in a transaction are influenced and thus their actions are shaped. At the same time, through its governance function, culture coordinates and simplifies interactions between people by providing a "framework" and the "rules of the game," thus lending economic activities an order that can reduce frictions and thus facilitate mutually beneficial interaction. In this way both cultural functions—the constructive function and governance function—contribute to the prevailing atmosphere of cooperation and shape the size of cooperation corridors in multivalent networks of relations. Thus, both are essential to understanding the role of culture in economic performance and at the same time to justifying the classification of cultural factors as informal institutions, as has been conceptualized by Ostrom (1986, 1990), North (1990, 1991) and others. Strictly speaking, only those cultural aspects that are considered to be economically relevant are called informal institutions, and only they are of interest to us here.

By shaping the cooperation atmosphere through their constructive and governance functions, informal institutions enable cooperation and thus potentially the generation of cooperation rents (see Wieland, 1998, 2020), defined as "those incomes that are generated when individual resources are pooled into team production and that are greater than the sum of individual incomes from the separate use of resources and their coordination through the market" (Wieland, 1998, p. 24, translated by the author, citing Alchian & Demsetz, 1972). If we further assume with Wieland that "[t]he performance capability of an economic system depends on the amount of its cooperation opportunities" (Wieland, 1998, p. 24, translated by the author), then this also applies at a global level and we may expect both local and transcultural cooperation rents to be generated—a promising aspect that will be discussed in more detail later.

On an important note, Relational Economics employs individual transactions as its unit of analysis and thus emphasizes the temporality and context dependency of cooperation, which, however, may lead to the development of communities of practice (see Wenger et al., 2002) if continued over time. Precisely describing the preconditions and implications of the formation of such communities of practice is an important component of our work on the concept of transculturality as part of the research program of Relational Economics (see Wieland & Baumann Montecinos, 2019). It ties directly into the change in perspective that the Sustainable

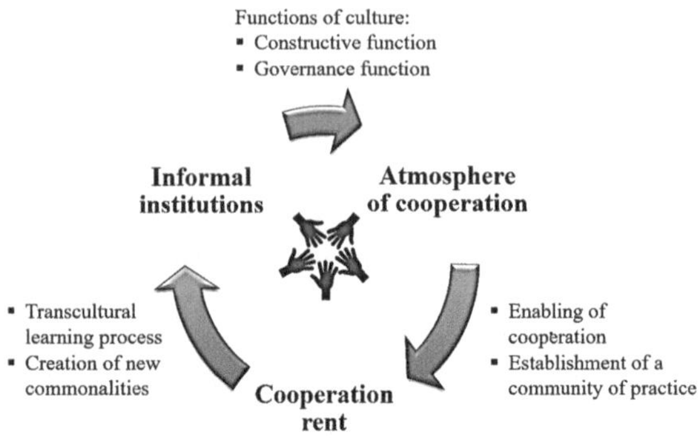

Fig. 2 Culture as a resource for cooperation

Development Goals, as well as the realities of companies in their role as regio-global intra-, inter-, and extra-firm networks, have triggered with regard to cooperative relationships and the conditions for their success. The same applies to the investigation of the transcultural learning processes that are at work in cooperation constellations that can generate new commonalities. It can be further assumed that these new commonalities, which may arise from shared cooperation practices, in turn shape the atmosphere of future cooperation and so on. Figure 2 is intended to illustrate this process as a continuously unfolding and self-reproducing cycle. It emphasizes the role of cultural factors as resources that can keep the generation of cooperation rents going and continuously provide opportunities for mutually beneficial cooperation.

In light of these interrelationships, the following explanations will take a closer look at two essential aspects. On the one hand, a model for describing transcultural learning processes for the development of new commonalities will be discussed. On the other, a proposal will be made to clarify the questions of which cultural factors have an impact on economic performance, and of how they can do so, especially at a global level.

3 Transcultural Learning

Given our understanding of culture as a resource for cooperation and the corresponding discussions above, learning processes play a significant part. They accompany relational transactions from the very beginning and can lead to new commonalities to thus further develop the pool of informal institutions as a fertile basis for long-term cooperation. Against this backdrop, above all working on a relational understanding of individual and organizational learning processes,[3] as well as refining the concept of commonalities and describing the corresponding competencies to identify

[3] For a valuable contribution to understanding organizational learning processes and their importance for transcultural cooperation, see Geraldo Schwengber & Beretta Kindlein, 2021.

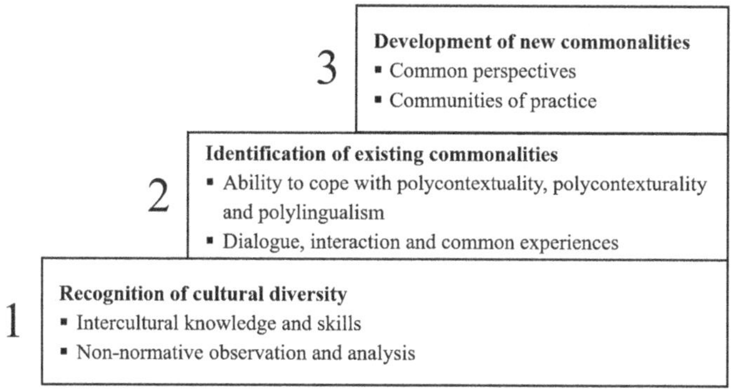

Fig. 3 3-step Model of Transcultural Learning (based on Baumann Montecinos et al., 2019, p. 221; Wieland, 2019, p. 38)

and create them, offer promising paths for further research in order to understand the success factors of cooperation even better.

As a point of departure for such research and as an invitation for further academic and practical debate, we have developed a 3-step transcultural learning model (Fig. 3), which offers a possible framework of the conditions for enabling new commonalities and thus new cooperation resources.

As a first step, the model describes the need to recognize and acknowledge cultural diversity. This is where traditional intercultural concepts come into play, whose focus is often used to provide knowledge about other cultures and arrive at corresponding interaction strategies. When encountering people from other cultures, the model then suggests that the adoption of a non-normative observer's attitude might be helpful in terms of starting a collaborative process. This means, on the one hand, that one does not always have to comment on or judge the differences between their and other cultures and, on the other, that one does not have to make overcoming diversity in the sense of adopting the position of the other a precondition for cooperation (see Wieland, 2019). At the same time, however, this does not rule out the possibility that, with regard to distinct transactions, for example, when there are allegations of human rights violations involved, cooperation may be terminated or not take place. Generally speaking, the recommendation to approach cultural diversity with a non-normative attitude means one should first of all listen, observe, and seek to understand others in order to evaluate potential sources of conflict and commonalities. Here, awareness of one's own cultural attachment and possible unconscious biases is just as important as the recognition of the possibility that one is not the (only) expert oneself. The goal is to recognize that the option that can be considered preferential in a given transaction can, if at all, only be achieved through the relationalization of the cooperation partners involved and their resources. Thereby, the cultural diversity that characterizes the configuration of resources in cooperative settings can be complex, particularly in globally oriented projects. In such projects, different national cultures represent only one dimension, whereas many other layers of cultural affiliation, such as professional cultures, industry cultures, corporate cultures, generation-specific cultural characteristics, or factors such as sociocultural or religious backgrounds may also be relevant determinants of a specific interaction. Instead of the dominance of nation-state influences, which one might seek to describe using static comparative national schemata, such a learning model is instead concerned with a dynamic "micro-cultural diversity" (Bolten, 2020, p. 64), which is characterized by the affiliations of individuals and organizations with pluralistic cultural contexts—a circumstance that is thoroughly addressed in the research on the multiple cultures perspective and its implications for cross-cultural management (see Phillipps & Sackmann, 2015; Boyacigiller et al., 2004).

In the terminology of Relational Economics, the cultural setup can be described as a temporary and polyvalent event, and the cooperation partners are continuously called upon to approach polycontextual, polycontextural, and polylingual constellations with an attitude of openness toward finding productive solutions. Accordingly, step 2, the identification of existing commonalities, depends on this ability in order to enable dialogue, interaction, and common experiences. The polycontextuality, polycontexturality, and polylingualism of a given cooperation situation characterize its complexity and shape the starting setting for possible approaches to finding common ground for cooperation and exploiting and expanding the existing cooperation corridor. Possible starting points for the identification of commonalities and thus for dialogue and cooperation can be found in the contexts of action of the stakeholders involved (polycontextuality), in their decision logics (polycontexturality), and in the language games that are used (polylingualism) (see for these three terms in more detail Wieland, 2020, p. 11f). In relational transactions, these common starting conditions are always local and temporary events. They result from the combination of the individual and collective actors involved and their specific contexts, decision logics, and language games, as well as from the relationalization of these aspects as resources. Table 1 attempts to systematize some of these possibilities on the basis of the four cultural dimensions of relational transactions as described by Wieland (2020, p. 114)—nation, profession, organization and individual—and to illustrate their role as cultural resources for cooperation, by giving some examples of transaction-specific settings.

Here, it becomes apparent that enabling dialogue, interaction, and common experience can start at many different levels of cultural affiliation and is linked to the ability to cope with polycontextual, polycontextural, and polylingual realities. At the same time, it should be emphasized that this matrix does not claim to fully capture possible starting points for commonalities: in addition to the fact that cultural diversity is much more complex—for example, generational cultures or industry cultures as well as factors such as religion or sociocultural background have already been mentioned—it must also be borne in mind that commonalities can indeed arise across cultural boundaries through shared practical experience. From and between these polycontextual, polycontextural, and polylingual constellations, commonalities can emerge and be developed to further foster a mutual learning process as well as the exploitation and expansion of existing cooperation corridors. Accordingly, one of the central assumptions in Relational Economics is that commonalities manifest precisely in

Table 1 Cultural resources in polycontextual, polycontextural, and polylingual settings

		Examples of transaction-specific settings for dialogue, interaction, and shared experience		
		Polycontextuality	Polycontexturality	Polylingualism
Cultural resources	Nation	For example, Indian and German stakeholders both come from democratic countries	For example, Chinese and German cultures generally both exhibit a tendency toward relatively pronounced long-term orientation (see Hofstede Insights, 2020)	For example, the US and German cultures generally both stand for more direct communication; they are so-called low context cultures (see Hall, 1990)
	Profession	For example, engineers are usually entrusted with technical tasks and/or technological development tasks	For example, for engineers, technical feasibility and the pursuit of innovation are mostly relevant decision-making criteria	For example, engineers understand the meaning of technical drawings and understand the language of mathematics
	Organization	For example, automotive companies are usually part of complex global value chains and depend on the respective emissions legislation in local markets	For example, companies with a strong corporate culture may tend to make more centralized decisions (see Wieland, 2016)	For example, a company's code of ethics specifies certain communication values for the organization as a whole
	Individual	For example, two individuals may have similar personal and professional experience horizons, which influence their perspectives on a particular transaction	For example, two individuals may base their decisions on certain interpretations of moral values	For example, two individuals may have similar communicative reference systems

practical, concrete transactions as temporary and context-dependent relational events and can take on manifold forms in the process. Following Alfred N. Whitehead's process philosophy and its groundbreaking statement that "apart from the experiences of subjects there is nothing, nothing, nothing, bare nothingness" (Whitehead, 1929/1985, p. 167), the ability to cope with polycontextuality, polycontexturality, and polylingualism and to engage in dialogue, interaction, and shared experience across cultural borders becomes a crucial enabler of transcultural learning processes and essential to finding common ground for cooperation.

As a next step, such shared practices and experiences may lead to the creation of new common perspectives over time (step 3). In this way, so-called communities of practice provide patterns and structures for ongoing transcultural learning processes, including the development of their own commonalities, for example, in terms of shared habits, customs, practices, routines, or, more generally, shared attributions of meaning. Importantly, this is not a question of the formation of a new cultural identity—the existence of which can also principally be debated (cf. Jullien, 2021)—but of belonging to a community of practice as something new that is more than the sum of its individual parts, and which always remains linked to a specific transaction.

To briefly summarize, these initial suggestions for a transcultural learning model should have shown that the focus on real-life transactions and a long-term perspective on cooperation require a corresponding understanding of culture, namely a relational one. In this context, transcultural learning processes seek to establish and continuously develop cooperative relationships in complex and polyvalent networks in order to achieve larger potential cooperation corridors for the generation of cooperation rents. These considerations make it clear that the relational approach has far-reaching consequences not only for our understanding of culture and cultural commonalities, but also for our understanding of what it takes to cooperate successfully across cultural borders. The logical follow-up questions of which cultural factors are particularly relevant and beneficial, and of how exactly they influence the generation of cooperation rents, will be addressed in the next section. There we will find further confirmation of the understanding of culture as a resource and the importance of learning processes and cooperation experiences, helping us to further contextualize and refine these findings.

4 From Cultural Capital to Transcultural Commons

The fact that cultural factors shape the conditions of cooperation has hopefully been made clear by the previous elaborations. Moreover, several representatives of different schools of economic theory have since acknowledged the relevance of culture for economic performance. However, there have been very few attempts to specify which cultural aspects are important for economic value creation, or how they work. In this regard, I have previously proposed a concept of capital (see Baumann Montecinos, 2019). This concept, which has been termed Moral Capital and includes a total of six sub-forms (Fig. 4), understands them as bundles of resources, each of

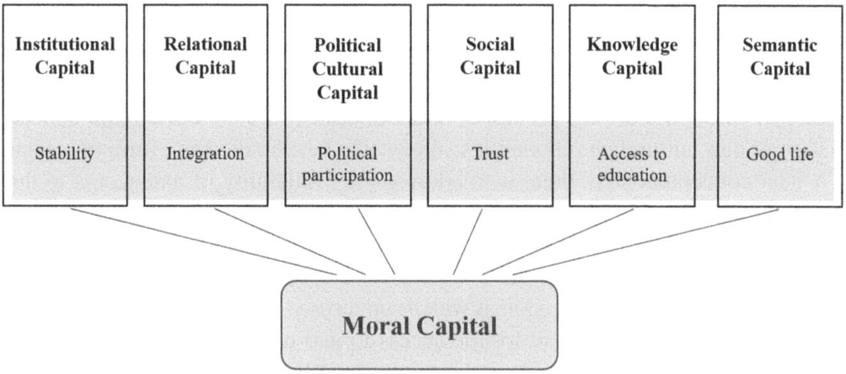

Fig. 4 Moral Capital Concept (from Baumann Montecinos, 2019, p. 250, translated by the author)

which has the potential to enable learning processes and cooperation for mutual benefit, and thus the generation of cooperation rents.

In this context, the six manifestations of capital, with their respective "moral-cultural dimensions" that have been narrowed down to the notions of "stability," "integration," "political participation," "trust," "access to education," and "good life," are to be understood as categories for the influence of culture on perception and behavior via its constructive and governance function, and in terms of their potential connection to economic performance. When specifying the determinants of the cooperative atmosphere, this concept includes the recognition that each of these categories contains the relevant factors to increase the respective form of capital through the outlined learning processes and thus to expand cooperation corridors. These forms of capital and their respective economic relevance have been described and justified in detail elsewhere (see Baumann Montecinos, 2019). Therefore, here we will focus on a total of three aspects of this proposal for the conceptual specification of the role of culture for cooperation-economic performance. First, the identified factors' nature as capital will be substantiated. Second, these forms of capital will then be conceptualized as representing commons, before third, the local and transcultural dimensions of the argument are discussed in more detail.

Thus, with regard to the nature of the cultural factors outlined in Fig. 4 as capital, they can be described as non-material resources that have both an input and an output side and thus fulfill the usual criteria for being classified as capital (see Baumann Montecinos, 2019; Grootaert & Bastelaer, 2002; Lin, 2001): while the input side refers to the investments needed in order to build up this capital, for example, through learning processes as outlined in the previous section and which can be considered a cost factor here, a look at the output side shows that future returns can be expected in the form of cooperation rents. As already noted, they can arise from the shaping of the cooperation atmosphere by culture through its constructive function and governance function. Moreover, if the continuous development of cultural assets and the creation of new commonalities through shared cooperation practices are assumed, it can also be assumed that this form of capital accumulates with increasing use, thereby following the postulate of path dependency as a characteristic of informal institutions (see North, 1990, pp. 92ff.). It thus becomes clear that the main tenet of a relational perspective on culture, namely the concept of culture as a resource that is (further) developed through learning processes and can lead to cooperation rents and the creation of new cultural commonalities, allows it to be classified as a form of capital.

A next conceptual step, then, is to address the availability of and access to this form of capital. Here it soon becomes apparent that cultural capital is characterized neither by excludability nor by rivalry in its use, and that these classifications are not particularly helpful at this point (see Wieland, 2012).[4] Rather, it can be said that there is a danger of insufficient provision as well as underuse—similar to what has already been diagnosed in the literature for the access to and use of knowledge: "Overuse of intangible assets is impossible in principle. [...] Rather, the more people have access to existing knowledge, the more new ideas and innovations can arise from the recombination of this knowledge" (Dobusch & Quack, 2011, p. 41, translated by the author). A similar situation can be assumed for the forms of cultural capital identified here, and questions about the realization of chances for cooperation take on central prominence (see Baumann Montecinos, 2019, pp. 147f.). We can thus describe these non-material resources as commons, where the aim is to maximize their acceptance, spread, and use (see ibid., p. 150), in order to exploit and expand the existing and potential cooperation corridors as much as possible. Such an understanding is in line, for example, with Elinor Ostrom's approach of describing shared "generalized norms of reciprocity and trust" as "initial social capital" (Ostrom, 1990, p. 211) that can enhance the well-being of the group. If we then employ the concept of transculturality outlined above, according to which new commonalities can be created in the course of shared cooperative experiences and learning processes, then these assumptions can also be applied to cross-cultural constellations and include the option of continuous and context-specific development of new common resources as relational events. Accordingly, cultural capital can be seen as a shared potential to unfold its economically relevant effects, also in the form of transcultural commons (see Baumann Montecinos, 2019, p. 330). In this context, transcultural commons consist of dynamic enabling processes for additional cooperation opportunities stemming from shared cooperation practices in settings of cultural diversity (see ibid., p. 333).

Thus, the idea of describing culture as a resource can be further differentiated at this point, and it can be said that corresponding cooperation rents can be generated both within a cultural group (local cooperation rent) and across cultural lines (transcultural cooperation rent). Both forms of cooperation rent can be traced back to the constructive function and governance function of culture, and the described correlations of effects between the input and output side can be observed in a comparable way in both cases, although they refer to different cooperation contexts (see ibid., p. 335). Accordingly, the specification of economically relevant cultural factors and their mode of action as commons, presented in this section, could concretize the

[4] For a concept of global public goods, see Kaul et al. (1999).

relational perspective on cultural diversity and support the elaboration of a corresponding concept of transculturality. Some central questions in this theoretical and practical discourse on the cultural conditions for exploiting the potentials of cooperation have now been addressed. What remains is the clarification of the correlation between transculturality and diversity, which will be attempted in the following, closing section.

5 Transculturality and Diversity: A Relation—What Else?

All this raises the important question, especially with regard to the relational perspective, of what contributions the models and assumptions discussed here can make when the level of concrete practice and learning that is so relevant to this approach is always local and thus highly polyvalent. The recognition that such conceptual frameworks are at first always abstract, while their actual application takes place in real life, is therefore central and requires further elaboration in terms of its implications. In this context, however, one might go so far as to claim that one of the strengths of the transcultural approach is that it views the coexistence and mutual conditionality of commonalities and diversity as a relational construct, and thus focuses on the productive side of their relationalization. In this regard, the distinction between thin and thick descriptions as proposed by Ryle (2009), Geertz (1973/1993), Walzer (1994), and others is particularly helpful. If one follows their argumentation and applies it to the subject at hand, then culture in its concrete application is initially always to be understood as a local, context-specific, and therefore thick description. When cooperation is extended to broader, further contexts, thin values are then abstracted, which can serve as cooperation resources in the form of shared interests or cultural assumptions or goals, around which concrete, thick experiences are grouped—as steps in a continuous learning process. More precisely, thin shared values remain abstract until they are applied to a concrete local situation and become "thick" through their implementation. It is in this concrete application at the level of a thick description that local manifestations of cultural resources may emerge that are context-dependent and thus may lead to real-life diversity. In turn, this diversity of local expressions of shared cultural attributions provides the starting point for learning processes that enable the formation of new commonalities, which are themselves capable of increasing thickness at the transcultural level over time. Accordingly, Fig. 5 portrays transculturality and diversity as elements of a recursive process of mutual conditionality and enabling, including the subsumption of this interrelation through the lens of the categories of thin and thick description.

If we consider the recursive cycle itself, it first illustrates the coexistence of transculturality and diversity as already outlined above, each of which represents both the precondition and the consequence of its counterpart. The left arrow indicates how, through adaptation and further development processes, existing thin commonalities are applied to concrete context-specific implementations and thus produce a possible diversity of variations. The right arrow then takes this diversity as its starting

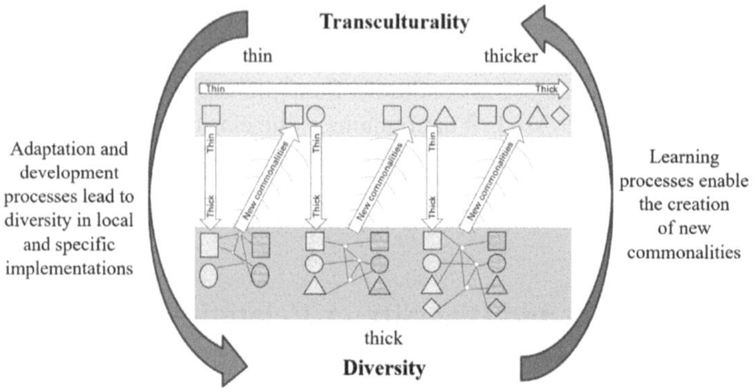

Fig. 5 Relational process model of diversity and transculturality (based on Baumann Montecinos, 2019, pp. 336f.)

point and reflects learning processes that allow new commonalities to emerge and communities of practice to be established. In this regard, the diverse local adaptations are always to be understood as temporary events in a continuous process of creating commonalities and new starting conditions for cooperation. The fact that new forms always arise from shared practical experience is illustrated in the interior of the cycle, although in view of the sheer complexity of reality, the depiction is admittedly limited. In any case, the recognition of this dialectic connection between transculturality and diversity, and of the possibility of creating new transcultural commonalities from shared practice in contexts of diversity, represents an important contribution to our understanding of transcultural leadership and paves the way for various interesting applications.

Below, one such possible application is presented in the form of the Transcultural Values Management System (Fig. 6).

The figure shows how, in globally operating organizations, strategic management decisions are derived in the context of existing, thick business realities. These normative decisions represent thin values that are formulated, for example, in an organization-wide code of ethics. In a next step, the figure illustrates how conveying thin values specified as strategic management decisions can be achieved in a variety of ways when rolled out at the local or regional level, and how opportunities for learning from and with each other enable a shared global interpretation of the respective value. This is illustrated using the example of a company's normative strategic decision to commit to diversity in terms of a "Preference for Plurality" embedded in its code of ethics, which then—via internal process steps involving different local prioritizations and implementations and enabling a context for sharing and learning—leads to a thicker understanding of diversity as "Living Plurality" (see Wieland & Baumann Montecinos, 2018, p. 28). This example provides some initial insights into how transcultural learning can be described not only at the individual level, but also as an

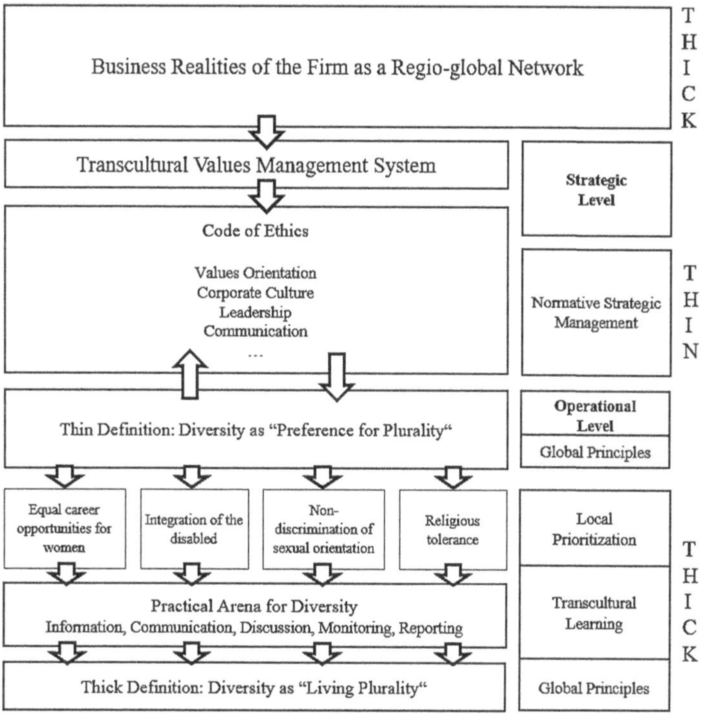

Fig. 6 Transcultural Values Management System, illustrated by the example of "Diversity" (based on Wieland & Baumann Montecinos 2018, p. 28)

organizational process. The fact that the interplay between these two is particularly interesting can be understood as a key incentive for pursuing further research.

If we accept the challenges and opportunities presented to us by the SDGs in terms of their far-reaching call for worldwide partnerships on equal footing, and by the realities of globally operating companies as regio-global inter-, intra-, and extra-firm networks of polyvalent relations, and if we further assume that understanding and using culture as a resource has always been important in times of complexity and dynamic processes of change, then perhaps the ideas suggested here can contribute to better prospects of cooperation for all. If these elaborations have succeeded in specifying those cultural resources that, as commons, are suited to being jointly used and developed, and which can thus play an important part in generating both local and transcultural cooperation rents in a relational economy, then this paper has achieved its goal.

References

Alchian, A. A., & Demsetz, H. (1972). Production, information costs, and economic organization. *American Economic Review, 62*(5), 777–795.

Annen, K. (2004). Kulturelle Ökonomik am Beispiel von Sozialkapital. In G. Blümle, N. Goldschmidt, R. Klump, B. Schauenberg, & H. V. Senger (Eds.), *Perspektiven einer kulturellen Ökonomik* (pp. 29–43). LIT.

Appiah, K. A. (2006). *Cosmopolitanism: Ethics in a world of strangers*. W. W. Norton.

Baecker, D. (2003). *Wozu Kultur?* Kulturverlag Kadmos.

Barmeyer, C., & Franklin, P. (2016). Achieving complementarity and synergy: The third step to leveraging diversity in intercultural management. In C. Barmeyer & P. Franklin (Eds.), *Intercultural management. A case-based approach to achieving complementarity and synergy* (pp. 199–213). Palgrave Macmillan.

Baumann Montecinos, J. (2019). *Moralkapital und wirtschaftliche Performance. Informelle Institutionen, Kooperation, Transkulturalität*. Springer Gabler.

Baumann Montecinos, J., Hunzinger, E., Singh, P., & Wiesmüller, S. (2019). Transcultural management in global firms. In J. Wieland & J. Baumann Montecinos (Eds.), *Transcultural leadership and transcultural competence* (pp. 181–223). Metropolis.

Bennett, M. J. (2017). Constructivist approach to intercultural communication. In Y. Kim (Ed.), *International encyclopedia of intercultural communication*. Wiley.

Bennett, M. J. (2020). A constructivist approach to assessing intercultural communication competence. In G. Rings & S. Rasinger (Eds.), *The Cambridge handbook of intercultural communication* (pp. 521–535). Cambridge University Press.

Berger, P. L., & Luckmann, Th. (1966). *The Social Construction of Reality: A Treatise in the Sociology of Knowledge*. Penguin Books.

Bolten, J. (2020). Rethinking intercultural competence. In G. Rings & S. Rasinger (Eds.), *The Cambridge handbook of intercultural communication* (pp. 56–67). Cambridge University Press.

Boyacigiller, N. A., Kleinberg, M. J., Phillips, M. E., & Sackmann, S. A. (2004). Conceptualizing culture: Elucidating the streams of research in international cross-cultural management. In B. J. Punnett & O. Shenkar (Eds.), *Handbook of international management research* (2nd ed., pp. 99–167). University of Michigan Press.

Deardorff, D. K. (2020). Defining, developing and assessing intercultural competence. In G. Rings & S. Rasinger (Eds.), *The Cambridge handbook of intercultural communication* (pp. 493–503). Cambridge University Press.

Denzau, A. T., & North, D. C. (1994). Shared mental models: Ideologies and institutions. *Kyklos: International review for social sciences* (Vol. 47, pp. 3–31). Blackwell Publ.

DiMaggio, P. (1994). Culture and economy. In N. J. Smelser & R. Swedberg (Eds.), *The Handbook of economic sociology* (pp. 27–57). Princeton University Press.

Dobusch, L., & Quack, S. (2011). Auf dem Weg zu einer Wissensallmende? *Gemeingüter, Aus Politik und Zeitgeschichte* (Vol. 61, 28-30/2011, pp. 41–46). Bundeszentrale für politische Bildung.

Fetzer, J. & Baumann Montecinos, J. (Eds.) (2016). Ziele – Werte – Wege. Die Sustainable Development Goals als Agenda 2030? *Forum Wirtschaftsethik, Jahresschrift des DNWE* (2015 ed., Vol. 23). Deutsches Netzwerk Wirtschaftsethik – EBEN Deutschland e.V..

Geertz, C. (1973/1993). Thick description: Toward an interpretive theory of culture. In Ibid. *The interpretation of cultures. Selected essays* (pp. 3–31). Fontana Press.

Geraldo Schwengber, J., & Beretta Kindlein, B. (2021). Building bridges not silos: Organisational learning processes and the role of a shared lingua franca as an a priori requirement for transcultural cooperation. In J. Baumann Montecinos, J. Geraldo Schwengber, & J. Wieland (Eds.), *Relational leadership—Case studies from Brazil* (pp. 243–265). Metropolis.

Grootaert, C., & Bastelaer, T. V. (2002). *The role of social capital in development. An empirical assessment*. Cambridge University Press.

Hall, E. T. (1990). *Understanding cultural differences*. Intercultural Press.

Henze, J. (2020). Horizonte der interkulturellen Kompetenzdiskussion. In A. Moosmüller (Ed.), *Interkulturelle Kompetenz. Kritische Perspektiven* (pp. 57–97). Waxmann.
Hofstede, G., & Hofstede, G. J. (2005). *Cultures and organizations: Software of the mind*. McGraw-Hill.
Hofstede Insights (2020). Compare countries. Retrieved December 14, 2020, from https://www.hofstede-insights.com.
Hurrelmann, K. (2002). *Einführung in die Sozialisationstheorie* (8th ed.). Beltz.
Jullien, F. (2021). *There is no such thing as cultural identity*. Polity Press.
Kaul, I., Gruneberg, I., & Stern, M. A. (1999). *Global public goods. International cooperation in the 21st century*. Oxford University Press.
Keller, E. v. (1982). *Management in fremden Kulturen: Ziele, Ergebnisse und methodische Probleme der kulturvergleichenden Managementforschung* (Vol. 10). Haupt.
Leipold, H. (2006). *Kulturvergleichende Institutionenökonomik: Studien zur kulturellen, institutionellen und wirtschaftlichen Entwicklung* (Vol. 2749). Lucius & Lucius.
Lin, N. (2001). *Social Capital. A Theory of Social Structure and Action*. Cambridge University Press.
Nazarkiewicz, K. (2020). Zwischen Problemanzeige und Lösung: das Dilemma der interkulturellen Kompetenz. In A. Moosmüller (Ed.), *Interkulturelle Kompetenz. Kritische Perspektiven* (pp. 301–320). Waxmann.
North, D. C. (1990). *Institutions*. Cambridge University Press.
North, D. C. (1991). Institutions. *The journal of economic perspectives*, *5*(1), 97–112. American Economic Association.
Ortiz, F. (1940/1983). *Contrapunteo cubano del tabaco y el azúcar*. Editorial de Ciencias Sociales.
Ostrom, E. (1986). An agenda for the study of institutions. *Public choice* (Vol. 48, pp. 3–25). Martinus Nijhoff Publishers.
Ostrom, E. (1990). *Governing the commons. The evolution of institutions for collective action*. Cambridge University Press.
Park, R. E. (1928). Human migration and the marginal man. *The American Journal of Sociology, 33*(6), 881–893. University of Chicago Press.
Park, R. E. (1950/2005). *Race and culture. Essays in the sociology of contemporary man*. The Free Press.
Phillips, M. E., & Sackmann, S. A. (2015). Cross cultural management rising. In N. Holden, S. Michailova, & S. Tietze (Eds.), *The Routledge companion of cross-cultural management* (pp. 8–18). Routledge.
Ryle, G. (2009). The thinking of thoughts: What is "le Penseur" doing? *Collected essays 1929–1968* (Vol. 2, pp. 494–510). Routledge.
Schramm, M. (2008). *Ökonomische Moralkulturen: die Ethik differenter Interessen und der plurale Kapitalismus*. Metropolis.
Stahl, G. K., & Tung, R. L. (2015). Towards a more balanced treatment of culture in international business studies: The need for positive cross-cultural scholarship. *Journal of International Business Studies, 46*(6), 391–414.
Stibbe, F. T., Reid, S., & Gilbert, J. (2018). *Maximising the Impact of Partnerships for the SDGs. A Practical Guide to Partnership Value Creation*. The Partnering Initiative and UNDESA.
Swidler, A. (1986). Culture in Action: Symbols and Strategies. *American Sociological Review, 51*, 273–286.
Taylor, E. B. (1871). *Primitive Culture: Researches into the Development of Mythology, Philosophy, Religion, Art, and Custom* (Vol. 1). John Murray.
Tomasello, M. (1999). *The Cultural Origins of Human Cognition*. Harvard University Press.
Tomasello, M. (2016). *A Natural History of Human Morality*. Harvard University Press.
Trompenaars, F., & Hampden-Turner, C. (2012). *Riding the waves of culture. Understanding diversity in global business* (3rd ed.). Nicholas Brealey Publishing.
United Nations (2014). The road to dignity by 2030: Ending poverty, transforming all lives and protecting the planet. Synthesis Report of the Secretary-General on the Post-2015 Agenda. United

Nations. Retrieved December 14, 2020, from http://www.un.org/disabilities/documents/reports/SG_Synthesis_Report_Road_to_Dignity_by_2030.pdf.
United Nations (2015). Resolution adopted by the General Assemby on 25 September 2015, 70/1. Transforming our world: the 2030 Agenda for Sustainable Development. Retrieved December 14, 2020, from http://www.un.org/ga/search/view_doc.asp?symbol=A/RES/70/1&Lang=E.
Walzer, M. (1994). *Thick and thin: Moral argument at home and abroad*. University of Notre Dame Press.
Weber, M. (1922/1988). Die "Objektivität" sozialwissenschaftlicher und sozialpolitischer Erkenntnis. In J.Winckelmann (Ed.), *Max Weber: Gesammelte Aufsätze zur Wissenschaftslehre* (7th ed., pp. 146–214). J.C.B. Mohr (Paul Siebeck).
Welsch, W. (1999). Transculturality—The puzzling form of cultures today. In M. Featherstone & S. Lash (Eds.), *Spaces of culture: City, nation, world* (pp. 194–213). Sage.
Wenger, E., McDermott, R. A., & Snyder, W. (2002). *Cultivating communities of practice: A guide to managing knowledge*. Harvard Business Press.
Whitehead, A. N. (1929/1985). *Process and reality, Gifford lectures 1927–28*. Macmillan.
Wieland, J. (1998). Kooperationsökonomie. Die Ökonomie der Diversität, Abhängigkeit und Atmosphäre. In G. Wegner & J. Wieland (Eds.), *Formelle und informelle Institutionen. Genese, Interaktion und Wandel* (pp. 9–33). Metropolis.
Wieland, J. (2012). Globale Standards als globale öffentliche Güter. In M. Maring (Ed.), *Globale öffentliche Güter in interdisziplinären Perspektiven, Schriftenreihe des Zentrums für Technik- und Wirtschaftsethik am Karlsruher Institut für Technologie* (Vol. 5, pp. 235–250). KIT Scientific Publishing.
Wieland, J. (2016). Transculturality and economic governance. In J. Wieland & K. M. Leisinger (Eds.), *Transculturality—Leadership, management and governance* (pp. 12–32). Metropolis.
Wieland, J. (2018). *Relational Economics. Ökonomische Theorie der Governance wirtschaftlicher Transaktionen*. Metropolis.
Wieland, J. (2019). Transculturality as a leadership style—a relational approach. In J. Wieland & J. Baumann Montecinos (Eds.), *Transcultural leadership and transcultural competence* (pp. 21-41). Metropolis.
Wieland, J. (2020). *Relational economics. A political economy*. Springer.
Wieland, J. (2022). Relational Economics: Theoretical Framework and Managerial Implications—A Short Introduction. In L. Biggiero, D. de Jongh, B. Priddat, J. Wieland, A. Zicari & D. Fischer (Eds.), *The Relational View of Economics* (pp. 17-41). Springer.
Wieland. J. & Baumann Montecinos, J. (2018). Transculturality and global value creation. In J. Wieland & J. Baumann Montecinos (Eds.), *Transcultural leadership. Learning about Sub-Saharan Africa* (pp. 17–39). Metropolis.
Wieland, J., & Baumann Montecinos, J. (Eds.). (2019). *Transcultural leadership and transcultural competence*. Metropolis.

Julika Baumann Montecinos is post-doctoral researcher in the research group on Transcultural Competence and member of the steering team of the Transcultural Caravan, a hub for global thinking, teaching and research (https://www.transcultural-caravan.org), at Zeppelin University's Leadership Excellence Institute. Since September 2021, she has been professor of Intercultural Management at the Business School of Furtwangen University, Germany.

Leadership in Multi-stakeholder Partnerships (MSPs) that Address the SDGs: Relational Leadership and Ubuntu in Dialogue

Yolande Steenkamp, Dominik Fischer, and Derick de Jongh

Abstract In the interest of advancing our understanding of leadership in multi-sector partnerships (MSPs) that address the Sustainable Development Goals (SDGs), this chapter brings the relational leadership approach of Uhl-Bien (2006) and Wieland (2017, 2020) in dialogue with the African relational ontology of Ubuntu. The introduction describes the urgent need to analyze leadership in MSPs that achieve the SDGs, given the advantage of collaboration between sectors by sharing resources to maximize effectiveness in SDG-related activities. By showing that relationships (individual, collective, and organizational) are a determining component of MSPs, a case is made for relational leadership as an appropriate lens to consider leadership in MSPs. In light of increasing scholarly attention on the African ontology of Ubuntu in the context of business and leadership studies, the chapter then considers Ubuntu from the perspective of Wieland (2017, 2020) relational leadership and relational leadership from the perspective of Ubuntu, keeping the MSP-context and the global need for collaboration in mind as the context which the dialogue is aimed to address. While the authors point out several promising implications and avenues for further exploration, they close by highlighting the need for empirical studies in Ubuntu research to prevent romanticizing the African ontology and nullifying the contributions it could make.

Keywords Relational leadership · Responsible leadership · MSPs · Ubuntu

1 A Introduction: The Importance of Rationality in Addressing the Sustainable Development Goals (SDGs)

Along with a growing awareness of the complex and adaptive, or "wicked" (Rittel & Webber, 1973) problems facing the global community and biosphere, multi-sector

Y. Steenkamp (✉) · D. de Jongh
Department of Business Management, University of Pretoria, Hatfield, South Africa
e-mail: yolande.steenkamp@up.ac.za

D. Fischer
Zeppelin University, Friedrichshafen, Germany

L. Biggiero et al. (eds.), *The Relational View of Economics*, Relational Economics and Organization Governance, https://doi.org/10.1007/978-3-030-86526-9_11

partnerships (MSPs) have likewise risen in prominence (Dentoni et al., 2018:333). This is due in part to the hope that the collaborative structures and practices that characterize MSPs may uniquely position them to contribute to both a breadth ("interconnected change across multiple spheres") as well as to a depth ("a power shift among actors in society and a related redistribution of resources in a system") of systemic change (Dentoni et al., 2018:334), resulting in alleviation of these complex and global problems. The United Nations (UN) Agenda 2030 has given official recognition in SDG 17 to the critical role of MSPs in achieving the SDGs, specifying in Target 17.16 that "multi-stakeholder partnerships[1]" are to "mobilize and share knowledge, expertise, technology and financial resources, to support the achievement of the Sustainable Development Goals in all countries, in particular developing countries" (UN General Assembly, 2015:32).

As the excerpt above highlights, and similar to any partnership between firms operating primarily based on an economic system, access to resources is a critical motivating factor for MSPs aiming to contribute to the SDGs (see Stibbe, Reid, & Gilbert, 2019:6). Examples of resources critical to multi-stakeholder partnerships for the SDGs are financial resources (Stenberg et al., 2017) or knowledge required by collaborative projects involving actors from multiple sectors (Clark et al., 2016:4570). Individual sectors acting alone, such as the political, economic, or governmental domains, lack the capacity to sufficiently contribute to the SDGs, making collaboration a necessary means for their achievement.

The urgent need for MSPs makes the skills for collaboration across these sectors critical (see ibid., p. 4574). Nevertheless, partnering is a considerable challenge for the actors involved, with limited coverage in the literature (Stibbe et al., 2019:7). Similarly, current management and leadership theories do not yet provide a satisfactory answer to the challenges arising from such cooperation. With transaction costs playing a determining role in many such partnerships, the question of relationality between MSP partners is usually not the point of departure in the analysis of either MSPs or their leadership. This chapter, in contrast, prioritizes a relational approach to leadership in MSPs. After arguing in favor of analyzing leadership in MSPs from a relational perspective, the relational leadership theories of Uhl-Bien (2006) and Wieland (2017, 2020) are reviewed and brought into dialogue with Ubuntu, a word that describes an African relational ontology of personhood. The question driving this approach is how the European-American theory of relational leadership and the African concept of Ubuntu might inform each other, perhaps opening new avenues to "enhance the Global Partnership for Sustainable Development" (UN National Assembly, 2015:32).

[1] The UN Agenda 2030 refers to multi-stakeholder partnerships rather than to multi-sector partnerships, both of which can be denoted by the abbreviation MSPs. However, when referring to multi-stakeholder partnerships, Agenda 2030 qualifies these as promoting "effective public, public–private and civil society partnership" (UN General Assembly, 2015:32), thereby indicating that these stakeholders represent different sectors. This chapter therefore consistently refer to MSPs as multi-sector partnerships, in order to avoid any misunderstanding of the partnerships we have in mind. In essence, we understand these to be the same as those specified in Agenda 2030.

2 Toward a Relational Leadership Approach to Multi-sector Partnerships (MSPs) Addressing the SDGs

Relationality is a central component in the success of MSPs (Wieland, 2020), and therefore also in the analysis of its leadership. Partnerships require relationships between the stakeholders in terms of the involved organizations and their individual actors. As such, leadership in MSPs is a complex phenomenon, which is why multiple perspectives are necessary to describe it (Armistead et al., 2007:225). Thus far, leadership studies have addressed partnerships from the perspective of strategy (Hitt & Ireland, 2002) and also from the perspective of responsible leadership for the "common good" (Maak, 2007:329), stressing the importance of stakeholder social capital (ibid.:330; see also MacDonald et al., 2019: 411) and the notion of building on relational phenomena, which is not as well captured by classical approaches to leadership (Maak, 2007: 329). That all partnerships for the SDGs are based on relations—both personal and organizational—offers a unifying perspective on the contexts in which leadership in such MSPs emerges, suggesting relational leadership theory as the best-suited approach to describing and analyzing leadership in MSPs.

Relational leadership (Uhl-Bien, 2006; Uhl-Bien and Ospian, 2012) describes leadership not only in terms of input affecting desired goals, but also rather as an outcome that emerges from a relational process. This perspective sees leadership as "a social influence process through which emergent coordination (e.g., evolving social order) and change (e.g., new approaches, values, attitudes, behaviors, ideologies) are constructed and produced" (Uhl-Bien, 2006:668). Uhl-Bien (2006) distinguished between the entity perspective and the relational perspective in relational leadership. For both of these, the relational approach radically alters the view that leadership is seated in an individual who possesses certain traits, replacing it instead with the constructionist understanding that leadership is "embedded in the everyday interactions and conversations—the relational practices—of leaders" (Cunliffe and Eriksen, 2011:1428) . Strengthening this argument, Hunt and Dodge (2000:448) discuss that relational perspectives go beyond the classical approaches on leader/follower relations, observing leadership "wherever it occurs" (see Uhl-Bien, 2006 from where we adopted this reference and discussion). Relational leadership has a social dimension, as it is seen as a process to influence coordination and change (see Uhl-Bien, 2006:654). Uhl-Bien (2006:661) further discusses Rost (1995), seeing leadership as leading a relationship where stakeholders preferably hold equal positions.

Wieland (2020)[2] has likewise taken a relational approach to leadership as part of his broader research agenda on relational economics (see also, e.g., Wieland, 2017), which is still being further developed. Wieland (2017:241; 2020) stresses the importance of leadership in a relational view for integrating stakeholders into collaborative partnerships, as it is the case for MSPs that address the SDGs, mainly as seen from

[2] This book is the revised and translated version of Wieland (2018).

a resource perspective. In the following, we would like to briefly discuss and build on Wieland's (2017, 2020) perspective on relational leadership from leadership in MSPs.

Similar to Stibbe et al., (2019:7), when discussing multi-stakeholder transactions of organizations arising from different sectors to address social issues, Wieland (2020:106) distinguishes between the individual level in terms of motivation (*micro-level*) and organizational level in terms of structure (*meso-level*) (ibid.). Echoing Uhl-Bien (2006), he stresses processes and relationships instead of individual actors (Wieland, 2020:107). As a result, for MSPs, relational leadership is a process that impacts the structures of organizations and the motivation of individuals over time to build a beneficial partnership between organizations (see also Nicholson and Kurucz, 2019:29). However, MSPs are also influenced by an overarching structure at the *macro-level* (e.g., legal framework and culture).[3] Relational leadership therein is a resource for value creation, asset-specific to a transaction, and a governance structure to balance resources (Wieland, 2017:241; 2020:108).

In this perspective, relational leadership is defined as the process of relationing the resources of different stakeholders, as the following definition demonstrates:

> Relational leadership is the art of creating adaptive processes, informal (character, values, organizational culture) and formal (rules, procedures, organizational structures) governance structures for a learning process in which all relations between the stakeholders involved and their resources can have their best possible effect concerning a specific transaction. [own translation] (Wieland, 2017:249)

Many actors from different sectors can agree that the need to realize the SDGs serves as a common basis for collaboration (Florini & Pauli, 2018, p. 584) , yet various decision logics guide the decisions and behavior of the actors arising from different sectors (Wieland, 2020:58). To address these challenges, for the stakeholders of a cooperation project such as an MSP to contribute to the SDGs, three building blocks are indispensable to the success of the project, each on an individual and organizational level (Wieland, 2017:250). These three building blocks of relational leadership are (i) willingness to cooperate, (ii) ability to cooperate, and (iii) cooperation rent—for each on both an individual and organizational level (Wieland, 2017:249–251, also for a detailed elaboration; Wieland, 2020:94–97).

The willingness to cooperate encompasses interest, discourse, and bond (see Wieland, 2017:250, 252 for a detailed elaboration, also on the following outlines). Actors must be interested in joint goals and activities as Wieland (2017) discusses and cites Clarke & Fuller (2010:86) to justify the existence of the MSP. Therefore, they need to find solutions to navigate problems (ibid.) despite the different decision logics according to which they operate (Wieland, 2020, p. 58). Specifically, the shared goal to work toward realizing the SDGs might be a potential base for all actors, but these must by necessity be translated into their unique decision logics, or into an emerging decision logic for the MSPs, if the collaboration is to be successful. For this reason, discourse is a critical aspect for MSPs needing to navigate micropolitics

[3] See Wieland (2020:50–53) for a discussion on micro-, meso-, and macro-level influencing transactions.

and power imbalances and to find ways for reaching consensus (Arévalo & Ros-Tonen, 2009:733). This often requires negotiations (ibid.:734), particularly when actors have different perspectives on the aims and/or operations of the MSP. Actors must be willing to engage in a bond or type of connection with other stakeholders because this determines whether the relationship outcome is successful or not (see Uhl-Bien, 2006:669).

If the willingness for cooperation is prevalent among the actors (individual and organizational) of the MSP, the ability to cooperate is the second critical pillar (Wieland, 2017:249–251 for a detailed discussion). It too has three subcategories, namely stakeholder orientation, communication, and learning (ibid.). Stakeholder orientation is critical in MSPs (Rod & Paliwoda, 2003) because, as stated above, stakeholders provide critical resources for the overall partnership. Wieland (2017:250) summarizes that stakeholders should be evaluated according to the resources they contribute. The resources then qualify individual stakeholders for the partnership and indicate the importance of each stakeholder for the overall partnership. Also, learning is emphasized (ibid.), with relational leadership itself understood to be a learning process.

As Wieland (2017:250–251) describes, the goal of relational leadership in MSPs is, on the one hand, relational rent (e.g., Lavie, 2006; Dyer and Singh, 1998) among the stakeholders, which, on the other hand, must go further in order to achieve specific common goals—in the case of the SDGs, for example, societal value. Wieland (2017:250–251) identifies recognition and trustworthiness as critical components. As a critical element, trust is critical for MSPs if they are to be effective (Armistead et al., 2007, p. 219). Examples of building trust are personal accountability, listening well, or speaking the truth (ibid.).

As stated, these building blocks of Wieland's (2017) relational leadership have to be applied on the individual and the organizational level. However, relational leadership as a complex phenomenon is also impacted by multiple levels. Therefore, considering individual and collective levels is not enough since the overall institutional environment, such as culture and societal rules, also influences relational leadership (see Wieland, 2020). These necessarily differ between regions or, increasingly, in multinational and/or multi-cultural working environments, and are therefore highlighted when MSPs are constituted by members representing different socioeconomic, national, and/or cultural contexts. Cultural contexts constitute several fundamental tenets, including values, traditions, rituals, and practices, including different levels of the individual (micro-level), the interpersonal (meso-level), and the social world (macro).

Nevertheless, in the context of global collaboration—not limited to but including partnerships for realizing the SDGs—such local expressions of culture are confronted with increasing complexity. For this reason, this chapter explores the potential for dialogue between a cultural relational ontology (Ubuntu) and the relational points of departure for economics and leadership, described above, with the former representing an African and the latter predominantly Western points of departure. Through this exploration, we illustrate our agreement with Wieland that the institutional, meso-level of culture plays a decisive role as co-determinants of success in MSPs that realize the SDGs. In the next section, we provide an overview of Ubuntu before outlining a few points for dialogue that we suggest should be explored in further research.

3 A Relational Ontology of Personhood (Ubuntu) and the Macro-level of Multi-sector Partnerships

The critical emphasis of relational leadership as a learning process between stakeholders (Wieland, 2017:249) implies that all partners in such relations must be respected actors in their own right and contribute their experience and resources. That this is often not the case where international relations with Africa are concerned is not a historical curiosity, but, as postcolonial studies continue to make clear, a contemporary reality. The massive gap in the literature around African leadership reflects a bias toward Western approaches and philosophical traditions—what Nkomo has called "the ideological coding of Western (primarily USA) conceptions of leadership and management" (2011:366). For this reason, this chapter is exploring the sub-Saharan context as a dialogue partner to contemplate the potential of the institutional (macro-) context in contributing to successful collaboration in MSPs. This section reflects relationality from an African perspective, namely that of Ubuntu, as a contribution to the primarily Western theory of relational leadership. In doing this, we offer some critical suggestions in moving forward toward constructing an African approach to relational leadership. We also attempt to de-couple leadership theory from a predominantly Western scholarly tradition, offering epistemological diversity by recognizing Ubuntu as an alternative ontology.

Ubuntu describes a collective understanding of personhood that gives expression to collective moralities. Explicitly described in sub-Saharan Africa, Ubuntu has been popularized in the field of management through publications of Mbigi (1997, 2005) and Mbigi and Maree (1995), and in the popular imagination by Archbishop Desmond Tutu and more recently his granddaughter Nompumelelo Mungi Ngomane (2020). Ubuntu, translated as "I exist because we exist," denotes a vision of personhood that understands the individual fundamentally through her or his social relationships with other persons (Gobodo-Madikizela, 2018: xxiii). In this view of human existence, belonging to community constitutes "the very essence of being human … It is not 'I think therefore I am.' It says rather 'I am human, therefore I belong, I participate, I share'" (Tutu, 1999:31). Emphasizing consensus, Ubuntu expresses a collectivistic orientation of mutuality and communal relationships based on harmony and fellowship, forming "the foundation for the basic values that manifest themselves in the ways African people think and behave towards each other and everyone else they encounter" (Mangaliso, 2001:24).

Ubuntu is more than a value or ethical stance but indeed describes an ontology of the human person. Metz and Gaie (2010) illustrated the similarity of sub-Saharan morality with Aristotelian teleology, namely that human existence is oriented toward a goal of self-realization. The difference with Aristotelianism lies in the fact that the only way "to develop one's humanness is to relate to others positively. One becomes a person solely 'through other persons', which means that one cannot realize one's true self in opposition to others or even in isolation from them" (Metz & Gaie, 2010:275). Secondly, positive relations with others are defined in strictly communal terms. Rather than simply implying that the will of the majority holds sway, "developing or respecting community (harmony) is an objectively desirable kind of interaction that should instead guide what majorities want or which norms become dominant" (Metz & Gaie, 2010:275–276).

Scholarly literature on Ubuntu is limited, yet it has been put forward as a value or philosophy endemic to Africa that holds great potential for management, leadership studies, and business, both generally and especially in the inter- or transcultural context (Mutwarasibo, 2019:27). Our guiding question in the following section is whether anything new emerges when relational leadership and Ubuntu dialogues on the notion of relationality, specifically in the collaboration context exemplified by MSPs.

4 Relational Leadership and Ubuntu: A Dialogue

4.1 Questions to Ubuntu from the Perspective of Relational Leadership

How can Ubuntu help shape stakeholder relations in complex multi-cultural and (often) global collaborations, such as in MSPs?
If one considers *Ubuntu* as describing "the intrinsic connection between humanity and the eco-system in which communal responsibility sustains life" (Jimoh, 2017: 40), then even in the absence of abstract theories of the firm, the idea of the interdependence of the actors in an economy was endemic to (parts of) Africa, arguably long before Freeman (1984) formulated stakeholder theory. One way that might be explored is by considering communal approaches to personhood as a narrative rather than the descriptive or analytical approaches often preferred in individualistic traditions. Instead of analyzing the different parts that constitute a human person, the narrative approach elucidates the person's social relations (Jimoh, 2017:41) so that identity becomes a story of *being together*. The question here is how the tendency of typically Western approaches to MSPs, such as analyzing their structures, governance, leadership, and individual responsibilities, might be complemented by approaching MSPs as forms of belonging to a shared purpose and as stories that continue to unfold through the relations that constitute them. Perhaps future research may be surprised to find that studying MSPs as art—as drama or performance—may reveal hitherto unimagined dimensions of their leadership.

How might Ubuntu find expression in non-personal formal and informal processes that govern long-term economic relations and collaborative partnerships, both national and international?

Ubuntu is traditionally seated in human relations (Mutwarasibo, 2019:27), yet globalized business relationships often take the shape of impersonal processes, contracts, and governance practices. As the renowned intercultural researcher Darla Deardorff (2020:1–4) noted recently in reference to the education sector, the "challenge … is to explore how these principles of loving one's neighbor translate into programs and practices." Wieland's definition of relational leadership concerns how an African relational ontology might contribute to adaptive processes and informal and formal governance structures that result in processes of learning together how to optimize the efficacy of all stakeholders to realize a common goal. How to translate the person-oriented notion of Ubuntu into practice in contexts utilizing abstract, conceptual language processes remains unclear. One urgent area to consider is how the cultural practices of Ubuntu might be translated into governance practices that are more endemic to particular African contexts to determine whether this might contribute to the effectiveness of MSPs. However, this remains unexplored in Ubuntu scholarship; however, well-established ways of ensuring harmony in African communities would be a necessary starting place. The field is open for research to explore how traditional communal processes (both formal and informal) ensure harmony between stakeholders in sub-Saharan contexts and address conflict when it arises. The guiding principle in this would remain the notion of belonging to a community, with such formal and informal processes aimed at guarding against disharmony and disintegration by restoring balance in relationships where this becomes threatened. It is crucial to note Jimoh's (2017:41) description of the "interpenetrating" communitarian person as exercising.

> rationality, the capacity for virtue, evaluating and making moral judgments and therefore capable of making a choice. These are not attributes that the community bestows on the individual rather, the individual develops them, and they are nurtured within the community

From this perspective, the "art of creating adaptive processes and informal and formal governance structures for a learning process" [own translation] (Wieland, 2017:249) would be translated as a leadership of belonging—creating processes and structures that enhance belonging and harmony among all stakeholders.

4.2 Questions to Relational Leadership from the Perspective of Relational Ontology

Should we continue to prioritize transactions? Wieland's definition structures the components of relational leadership around particular transactions, whereas the African logic is to structure transactions around personal relationships. The benefit of relational economics is that it moves away from the vantage point of individual "deals" to focusing on the continuity of relationships. *Ubuntu* might contribute to conceptualizing stakeholders as relation holders—or those who belong—in view of the interconnections that knot human beings and communities together (Woermann & Engelbrecht, 2017). In this sense, Wieland's relational leadership, with its emphasis on stakeholder relations, finds a ready dialogue partner in Southern Africa, in that Ubuntu recognizes how interrelated human interests are, suggesting working toward the greater good of others as a goal of ethical leadership (Tavernaro-Haidarian 2018).

In-between individuals and organizations? Wieland distinguishes between the micro-, meso-, and macro-levels influencing transactions (individual, organizational, and cultural). However, in the African mind, the individual is not conceived apart from the community. African conceptions of personhood see social relationships as not contingent but necessary, since humans cannot live in isolation from other humans (Jimoh, 2017:41–42). The question now becomes whether a relational leadership model can be conceived that gives the same prevalence to the communal that collectivistic cultures do?

The fact that Wieland's own relational approach to economics and leadership has been strongly influenced by the process-relational philosophy of Alfred North Whitehead promises much in terms of possibilities for dialogue with *Ubuntu*, since Wieland's relational approach springs from the recognition that being in relation is fundamental to the existence of humans, and that their economic systems must reflect this. In dialoguing with *Ubuntu*, relational economics and relational leadership will have to explore how the very notion of *relation* is understood by both thought traditions. The question of whether individuals are ontologically more fundamental than relationality, or relationality ontologically more fundamental than individuals, does not have to be definitively settled, however. Instead, the different light that various approaches might cast on the ideas and experiences is one of the most valuable contributions of the transcultural approach.

4.3 Can a Critical Reading of Ubuntu Emerge?

Much of the literature on Ubuntu is guilty of "essentialism," or portraying African values (and in this case leadership) as homogenous and generalizing it as though it were the same everywhere. In addition, there is a tendency toward romantic and exotic portrayals of so-called "African" values that can be offered as a cure to all ills. We do well to remember that discovering certain "authentic" expressions of African culture that have remained cocooned from Western influence is a fantasy after centuries of colonization. This begs the question of just where we hope to find the so-called "African" values that we are so eagerly describing as binary opposites to Western values (Mbembe, 2002; cf. Nkomo, 2011:377)? Furthermore, in considering the ancient problem of the one and the many as an encounter between individualism and collectivism, we must ask whether the greater good (harmony and continuity of the community) is in all cases the highest good, even if this should come at the cost of the individual. Is Louw's description of Ubuntu's "we" as "an overarching notion that both supersedes and honors the individual identities within it" (Louw,

2010, in Tavernaro-Haidarian 2018:18) just another instance of romanticism, or are individuals at times sacrificed for the sake of safeguarding communal harmony at all cost?

Another point that begs for critical reflection lies at the intersection of Ubuntu and patriarchal culture, and here African female scholars are beginning to lead the way. Duvenage argued that *Ubuntu* might enable gendered polarizations and that in the Black Consciousness Movement and South Africa's Truth and Reconciliation Commission, during a time when nationalist agenda ran rampant, "Ubuntu—as a tool for a cohesive social and moral order—worked to legitimize the oppression of women and upheld a patriarchal ideology" (Duvenage, 2020:2). The way that this functions is that women are expected to exemplify traditional culture, existing as women-in-community, while men are allowed to become men-in-themselves, with popular fiction upholding "the 'moral arrival' of men" (Duvenage, 2020:2). One study (Chisale, 2018:1–2) has problematized the supposed gender connotations of *Ubuntu* in the context of social, communal unpaid care, finding based on empirical data collected among the elderly in the Greater KwaZulu-Natal, South Africa, that *Ubuntu* is conceptualized "in a context of caregiving" as not exclusively feminine, with men also displaying caring behavior in traditional African communities. Similarly, and based on empirical data, Luvalo (2019) found that *Ubuntu* could address the victimization of women and children. Interestingly, however, this was because the isiXhosa-speaking elders considered a patriarchy based on *Ubuntu* as enabling a caring society that protected the vulnerable—a view that many will doubtlessly find highly problematic. Perhaps Manyonganise's (2015) reflection on the ambivalence of *Ubuntu* in the lives of women serves as a fitting conclusion, for now, elucidating both the oppressive and the liberating nature of *Ubuntu*, which points to the need for focused research to gain a deeper understanding into this ambiguity, on the one hand, as well as the need to engage in further deconstruction and reconstruction to reimagine *Ubuntu* as affirming the value and moral freedom of all humans regardless of gender, or for that matter regardless of sexuality, race, or religion.

Finally, instances of corruption and violence on the continent beg the question of Ubuntu's reach—something that Asamoah and Yeboah-Assiamah (2019:317) perhaps solve too easily by claiming that leaders who perpetrate such acts "are not true Africans by deeds but merely profess to be." Romantic imaginings of relational personhood collapse in view of repetitive eruptions of xenophobic attacks in South Africa, for example. If *Ubuntu* is really, as Mangaliso asserts, "humaneness—a pervasive spirit of caring and community, harmony and hospitality, respect and responsiveness—that individuals and groups display for one another," and "the foundation for the basic values that manifest themselves in the ways African people think and behave towards each other and everyone else they encounter," (2001:24), how does one make sense of such dehumanizing acts? Before scholars are willing to engage in these critical questions, any contribution of Ubuntu to global leadership studies will be idealistic at best or, at worst, just another case of "othering" Africa. Utilizing Ubuntu in leadership studies will require rigorous hermeneutics, deconstruction as well as reconstruction, and empirical research in order to create: (i) descriptions of contextual expressions of Ubuntu as it is experienced in concrete locations and situations (e.g., Buqa, 2015; Müller et al., 2019), and (ii) an understanding of how Ubuntu functions (again, in specific contexts) in relation to in-group/out-group boundaries on the one hand (cf. Staszak, 2009), and in relation to tensions between individual and collective interests, on the other. Finally, the apparent ambivalence of *Ubuntu* concerning gender equality needs urgent exploration. In short, we need descriptions of Ubuntu leadership that reveal variation and complexity rather than objectifying simplifications.

5 Conclusion: Toward Co-responsibility

Mangaliso (2001:24), who defined *Ubuntu* as "humaneness—a pervasive spirit of caring and community, harmony and hospitality, respect and responsiveness—that individuals and groups display for one another," held that organizations that incorporate such values would "enjoy a more sustainable competitive advantage" (2001:32). While we agree with this notion, this chapter has expanded the dominant organizational focus in Ubuntu literature in the business field to point out possibilities for international dialogue in relational leadership and relational economics. As we look toward a future of international collaboration and economic relations with Africa as both an agent in her own right as well as a partner in addressing global challenges, "co-responsibility" invites thinking along the lines of relational leadership, and Ubuntu indeed holds great promise as a platform from which such relational approaches can be co-constructed in international relationships with the West. However, the "semantic innovation" of an inclusive *Ubuntu* logic needs to be based on much more representative research than a few descriptions generalized in leadership literature to supposedly represent the entire African continent (cf. Nkomo, 2011:377). As things stand in business literature, this is mostly still just a claim calling for further research, specifically to provide empirical data to respond to the many conceptual papers arguing for Ubuntu's potential to make a positive contribution to various contexts. A critical methodological access point to such descriptions is story-telling. Pérezts et al. (2019) have illustrated how relationality can be developed through story-telling and an African experiential pedagogy to benefit ethical leadership education. Research into relationality between Africa and the West will have to be dialogical across cultures, multidisciplinary, and make room for mutual enrichment. Perpetually speaking about Ubuntu in general, unspecified terms undermines its empirical relevance. Much research is needed to address this from a relational leadership perspective.

To return to relational leadership theory as put forward by Uhl-Bien (2006) and especially Wieland (2017), empirical research that describes how leadership in African organizations and MSPs in sub-Saharan Africa expresses itself through formal and informal governance processes will be particularly helpful, specifically in revealing how Ubuntu may or may not be found as determining factor in this regard. Due to the different decision logics and diverse institutional cultures that characterize partnerships across sectors, MSPs are by nature multi-cultural. Wieland's (2017) recognition of the macro-, or institutional level, which includes the importance of cultural logic, clarifies that local contexts must be taken into account. Therefore, it is crucial to harness the skill to collaborate transculturally, even if participants should represent the same national or regional cultures.

We have entered into the dialogue of this chapter with this conviction in mind, embracing the opportunity to interrogate the idea of relationality from two perspectives; as a result, various new areas for research have emerged. To close, let us return to Wieland's (2017) definition of relational leadership:

> Relational leadership is the art of creating adaptive processes, informal (character, values, organizational culture) and formal (rules, procedures, organizational structures) governance structures for a learning process in which all relations between the stakeholders involved and their resources can have their best possible effect concerning a specific transaction [own translation] (Wieland, 2017:249).

At the end of our dialogue, and as an invitation to continue this engagement, we offer a possible suggestion of how Wieland's definition above may be expressed from the perspective of a relational ontology. Giving voice to an *Ubuntu* that might be reconstructed to open up new possibilities of sustainable being-in-relation, we might suggest based on Wieland that relational leadership is.

> … the art of creating adaptive processes, informal (character, values, organizational culture) and formal (rules, procedures, organizational structures) governance structures for a learning process in which all transactions may have their best possible effect concerning specific relations (Adapted from Wieland, 2017:249).

References

Arévalo, E. B., & Ros-Tonen, M. A. (2009). Discourses, power negotiations and indigenous political organization in forest partnerships: The case of Selva de Matavén Colombia. *Human Ecology, 37*(6), 733–747.

Armistead, C., Pettigrew, P., & Aves, S. (2007). Exploring leadership in multi-stakeholder partnerships. *Leadership, 3*(2), 211–230.

Asamoah, K., & Yeboah-Assiamah, E. (2019). Ubuntu Philosophy for Public Leadership and Governance Praxis: Revisiting the Ethos of Africa's Collectivism. *Journal of Global Responsibility, 10*(4), 307–321.

Buqa, W. (2015). Storying Ubuntu as a Rainbow Nation. *Verbum et Ecclesia* 36(2), 8, 1434. https://doi.org/10.4102/ve.v36i2.1434

Clarke, A., & Fuller, M. (2010). Collaborative strategic management: Strategy formulation and implementation by multi-organizational cross-sector social partnerships. *Journal of Business Ethics, 94*(1), 85–101.

Clark, W. C., Van Kerkhoff, L., Lebel, L., & Gallopin, G. C. (2016). Crafting usable knowledge for sustainable development. In *Proceedings of the National Academy of Sciences*, 113(17), 4570–4578.

Cunliffe, A. L., & Eriksen, M. (2011). Relational leadership. *Human relations, 64*(11), 1425–1449.

Deardorff, D. K., (Re)Learning to live together in 2020. *Journal of International Students* 10(4):15–18. doi: https://doi.org/10.32674/jis.v10i4.3169.

Dentoni, D., Bitzer, V., & Schouten, G. (2018). Harnessing wicked problems in multi-stakeholder partnerships. *Journal of Business Ethics, 150*, 333–356. https://doi.org/10.1007/s10551-018-3858-6

Duvenage, A. (2020). Patriarchal forms of national community in post-apartheid literature: Re-examining ubuntu and gender in Sindiwe Magona's Mother to Mother (1998) and Zakes Mda's The Heart of Redness (2000). *The Journal of Commonwealth Literature*, 1–12. https://doi.org/10.1177/0021989420908049.

Dyer, J. H., & Singh, H. (1998). The relational view: Cooperative strategy and sources of interorganizational competitive advantage. *The Academy of Management Review, 23*(4), 660–679.

Florini, A., & Pauli, M. (2018). Collaborative governance for the sustainable development goals. *Asia & the Pacific Policy Studies, 5*(3), 583–598.

Freeman, R. E. (1984). *Strategic management: A stakeholder approach*. Boston, MA: Pitman.

Gobodo-Madikizela, P. (2018) Human moments. In D.P. Veldsman & Y. Steenkamp (Eds.), *Debating otherness with Richard Kearney: Perspectives from South Africa* (pp. 21–26), AOSIS, Cape Town. https://doi.org/10.4102/aosis.2018.BK94.00f

Hitt, M. A., & Ireland, D. R. (2002). The essence of strategic leadership: Managing human and social capital. *Journal of Leadership & Organizational Studies, 9*(1), 3–14.

Hunt, J. G., & Dodge, G. E. (2000). Leadership déjà vu all over again. *The Leadership Quarterly, 11*(4), 435–458.

Jimoh, A. K. (2017). Ubuntu, Ibuanyindanda: Harnessing African philosophy of personhood for peaceful co-existence in Nigeria. *Ewanlen: A Journal of Philosophical Inquiry* 1(1):40–49.

Lavie, D. (2006). The competitive advantage of interconnected firms: An extension of the resource-based view. *Academy of Management Review, 31*(3), 638–658.

Louw, D. J. (2010). *Power sharing and the challenge of ubuntu ethics*. Paper presented at the forum for religious dialogue symposium of the research institute for theology and religion at the University of South Africa, January 2010, Pretoria, South Africa.

Luvalo, L. M. (2019). Patriarchy and Ubuntu philosophy: The views of community elders in the Eastern Cape Province. *e-Bangi: Journal of Social Sciences and Humanities* 16(7):1–10.

Maak, T. (2007). Responsible leadership, stakeholder engagement, and the emergence of social capital. *Journal of Business Ethics, 74*(4), 329–343.

MacDonald, A., Clarke, A., & Huang, L. (2019). Multi-stakeholder partnerships for sustainability: Designing decision-making processes for partnership capacity. *Journal of Business Ethics, 160*(2), 409–426.

MacDonald, A., Clarke, A., Huang, L., Roseland, M., & Seitanidi, M. M. (2017). Multi-stakeholder Partnerships (SDG #17) as a Means of Achieving Sustainable Communities and Cities (SDG #11). In W. Leal Filho (Ed.), *Handbook of Sustainability Science and Research* (pp. 193–209). Springer International Publishing. https://doi.org/10.1007/978-3-319-63007-6_12

Mangaliso, M. P. (2001). Building Competitive Advantage from Ubuntu: Management Lessons from South Africa. *Academy of Management Executive, 15*(3), 23–32.

Manyonganise, M. (2015). Oppressive and liberative: A Zimbabwean woman's reflections on Ubuntu. Verbum et Ecclesia 36(2), 1438, 7. https://doi.org/10.4102/ve.v36i2.1438

Mbembe, A. (2002). African Modes of Self-Writing, trans S. Rendall. *Public Culture, 14*(1), 239–273.

Mbigi, L. (1997) *Ubuntu: The african dream in management*. Pretoria: Knowledge Resources.

Mbigi, L. (2005) *The spirit of african leadership*. Johannesburg: Knowledge Resources.

Mbigi, L. and Maree, J. (1995) *Ubuntu: The spirit of african transformation management*. Johannesburg, Knowledge Resources.

Metz, T., & Gaie, J. B. R. (2010). The African ethic of Ubuntu/Botho: Implications for research on morality. *Journal of Moral Education, 39*(3), 273–290.

Müller, J., Eliastam, J., and Trahar, S. (2019). *Unfolding narratives of ubuntu in Southern Africa*. Routledge Contemporary Africa Series. New York: Routledge

Mutwarasibo, F. (2019). I am because we are—the contribution of the ubuntu philosophy to intercultural management thinking. *Interculture Journal, 18*(32), 15–32.

Ngomane, N. M. 2019. *Everyday ubuntu: Living better together, the African way*. London: Bantam Press
Nicholson, J., & Kurucz, E. (2019). Relational leadership for sustainability: Building an ethical framework from the moral theory of 'ethics of care.' *Journal of Business Ethics, 156*(1), 25–43.
Nkomo, S. M. (2011). A postcolonial and anti-colonial reading of African leadership and management in organization studies: Tensions, contradictions and possibilities. *Organization, 18*(3), 365–386. https://doi.org/10.1177/1350508411398731
Pérezts, M., Russon, J.-A., & Painter, M. (2019). This time from Africa: Developing a relational approach to values-driven leadership. *Journal of Business Ethics*. https://doi.org/10.1007/s10551-019-04343-0
Rittel, H. W., & Webber, M. M. (1973). Dilemmas in a general theory of planning. *Policy Sciences, 4*(2), 155–169.
Rod, M. R., & Paliwoda, S. J. (2003). Multi-sector collaboration: A stakeholder perspective on a government, industry and university collaborative venture. *Science and Public Policy, 30*(4), 273–284.
Rost, J. C. (1995). Leadership: A discussion about ethics. *Business Ethics Quarterly, 5*(1), 129–142.
Staszak J-F (2009) Other/Otherness. In Kitchin R and Thrift N (Eds), *International encyclopedia of human geography* (Vol. 12, pp. 43–47). Oxford: Elsevier Science.
Stenberg, K., Hanssen, O., Edejer, T.T.-T., Bertram, M., Brindley, C., Meshreky, A., & Soucat, A. (2017). Financing transformative health systems towards achievement of the health sustainable development goals: A model for projected resource needs in 67 low-income and middle-income countries. *The Lancet Global Health, 5*(9), e875–e887.
Stibbe, D., Reid, S., & Gilbert, J. (2019). *Maximising the impact of partnerships for the SDGs. A practical guide to partnership value creation. Oxford, UK: The Partnering Initiative and UN DESA*. Retrieved July 13,2020, from: https://www.thepartneringinitiative.org/wp-content/uploads/2018/07/Maximising-partnership-value-for-the-SDGs.pdf.
Tavernaro-Haidarian, L. (2018). A relational model of public discourse: The African philosophy of Ubuntu. Oxon: Routledge
Tutu, D. (1999). *No future without forgiveness*. NY: Doubleday.
Ubuntu as care: Deconstructing the gendered Ubuntu. Verbum et Ecclesia 39(1), a1790. https://doi.org/10.4102/ve.v39i1.1790
Uhl-Bien, M. (2006). relational leadership theory: Exploring the social processes of leadership and organizing. *The Leadership Quarterly* 17(6): 654–676
Uhl-Bien, M., and Sonia O. (Eds.) (2012). *Advancing Relational Leadership Research: A Dialogue Among Perspectives*. New York: Information Age Publishing
UN General Assembly, (2015). Transforming our world: the 2030 Agenda for Sustainable Development, 21 October 2015, A/RES/70/1, https://sustainabledevelopment.un.org/post2015/transformingourworld. Accessed 2 Nov. 2020.
Wieland, J. (2017). Relationale Führung und intersektorale Governance. In Lehmann, M. & Tyrell, M., Komplexe Freiheit (Eds.), *Wie ist Demokratie möglich? Komplexität und Kontingenz* (pp. 237–257). Wiesbaden: Springer. https://doi.org/10.1007/978-3-658-14969-7_11.
Wieland, J. (2018). Relational Economics: Ökonomische Theorie der Governance wirtschaftlicher Transaktionen. Marburg, DE: Metropolis.
Wieland, J. (2020) *Relational economics: A political economy*. Cham, CH: Springer
Woermann, M., & Engelbrecht, S. (2017). The Ubuntu challenge to business: From stakeholders to relationholders. *Journal of Business Ethics*. https://doi.org/10.1007/s10551-017-3680-6

Yolande Steenkamp is a post-doctoral researcher and senior lecturer at the Albert Luthuli Leadership Institute, University of Pretoria, South Africa, and network manager of SDSN South Africa. She has a background in Theology and Ancient Cultural Studies and specializes in transdisciplinary research on leadership that addresses contemporary challenges. She explores the ethical dimensions of the imagination, narrative, and hospitality to the O/other and contributes to questions of ethics, meaning, value, and collaboration for sustainable development. In 2020, she spent five months at Zeppelin University, Germany, to collaborate on the joint research project between the University of Pretoria and Zeppelin University: Relational Leadership for the SDGs: Implications for a developed and a developing economy. She also collaborates with Zeppelin University on a project that studies the effect of storytelling on transcultural and social entrepreneurial learning in previously colonized, developing contexts.

Dominik Fischer is post-doctoral researcher at the Chair of Institutional Economics at Zeppelin University. His research focuses on strategy and governance in global value chains with an emphasis on emerging markets based on relational economics. He also focuses on innovation and cooperation in stakeholder networks.

Derick de Jongh is professor and director of the Albert Luthuli Leadership Institute, University of Pretoria, South Africa, specializing in corporate citizenship and responsible leadership. He is passionate about creating learning opportunities through research and education that build individual and institutional capacity. He contributes to the emerging responsible leadership approach through relevant research aimed at informing strategy and policy, and by influencing and shaping undergraduate and postgraduate curricula to be more responsive to and relevant in broader society. He has been collaborating with the Leadership Excellence Institute Zeppelin (LEIZ) at Zeppelin University in their Transcultural Leadership and their Relational Economics projects since 2018. He is a co-author of the Manifesto for Relational Economics initiated by Josef Wieland.

Relational Contracting in Practice: A Route to Relational Economics?

Tim Cummins and Sally Guyer

Abstract In 2016, when awarding the Nobel prize for Economic Sciences, the awarding committee observed that 'Modern economies are held together by innumerable contracts'. It, therefore, seems logical that relational economics could be supported—and perhaps enabled—by relational contracts. In this chapter, we suggest that the emergence of the networked world has in essence already created the core framework for a relational economy, but this shift is currently frustrated by the lack of institutions, procedures and rules necessary for its management. Relational contracting may provide the missing link and prove to be a catalyst for change, but first we must be clear about what is meant by relational contracting. The definition of 'relational contracts' remains imprecise and traditional legal and economic theory appears to recognize that this may take several forms. This chapter explores the current state of relational contracts (an artefact) and relational contracting (a process) and suggests that emerging technologies provide an opportunity for new thinking and to turn relational economics from theory to practice.

Keywords Collaboration · Ecosystems · Transparency · Industry codes · Governance

1 Introduction

In 2018, the European Commission initiated an exploratory project to 'model the European economy[1] as an ecosystem of contracts'.[2] In releasing the initial feasibility study, the Commission observed: 'With the evolution of today's economy from

[1] See https://www.nobelprize.org/prizes/economic-sciences/2016/press-release/.

[2] See https://op.europa.eu/en/publication-detail/-/publication/38673158-6411-11ea-b735-01aa75ed71a1.

T. Cummins (✉)
Leeds University Business School, Leeds, UK
e-mail: tcummins@worldcc.com

S. Guyer
Durham University Business School, Durham, UK

L. Biggiero et al. (eds.), *The Relational View of Economics*, Relational Economics and Organization Governance, https://doi.org/10.1007/978-3-030-86526-9_12

industry and manufacturing to services, information and networks, Gross Domestic Product ("GDP") and similar economic measurement approaches struggle to account for the intangible structures and assets of today's economy. The modern economy is increasingly based on networks, services and insights'.

Whether consciously or not, the Commission had recognised the fundamental weakness of transactional economics as the foundation for measures of relative wealth or production. Concepts such as Gross Domestic Product are no longer providing accurate insights in a world where economic exchange is increasingly across multiple borders, often involving services, and frequently digital in form.

Then, COVID-19 struck and created dramatic levels of economic and social disruption around the world. Among its many impacts, it revealed fundamental weaknesses in critical data flows, the absence of visibility into complex supply chains and the fragmented nature of organisational design.[3] For business and commerce, it widened cracks that were already becoming visible, but in many cases had been ignored or dismissed as too difficult to fix. Indeed, it may even be argued that the emergence of the networked world has in essence already created a relational economy, but without the core institutions, procedures and rules that are necessary for its management. The fact that these core enablers have not yet caught up is resulting in confusion and conflict. It was this confusion and conflict that the pandemic cruelly exposed.

COVID-19, therefore, has the potential to be the catalyst that forces us to think more deeply about the way that businesses and society operate and—more importantly—to implement meaningful change. Among the changes may be a shift away from the predominant transactional approach to contracting, instead of adopting relational terms and frameworks. However, while such a move would be transformational in the way we observe and manage interconnections, it would not in itself bring about the relational economy.

In this chapter, we will explore the form and purpose of relational contracts, the benefits they bring, the structural implications of their use and the barriers to adoption, while at the same time examining the far greater impact that would arise from technologically enabled relational contracting platforms.

2 Why Contracts Matter

'Modern economies are held together by innumerable contracts'.[4]

As the awards committee for the Nobel prize in Economic Sciences recognised in making this statement, 'contracts' are foundational artefacts for the structuring and organisation of our world. They set rights and obligations. They define economic

[3] See for example 'COVID-19: Catalyst for Change' at https://theloadstar.com/covid-19-catalyst-for-change-and-the-key-to-unlocking-supply-chain-visibility/.

[4] See previous citation.

outcomes. They influence behaviours. As research has indicated,[5] contracts serve many purposes—and in consequence, they may become confused and confusing, or they may be used by particular groups to support their specific interests. Indeed, research by World Commerce and Contracting has found that almost 90% of business users find contracts difficult or impossible to understand—meaning that they are often ignored for operational purposes.[6]

The belief that politics, society and economics are out of balance is not new. Concepts such as 'the triple bottom line' of people, planet and profit go back more than 25 years,[7] yet have made a limited impact. In spite of compelling arguments for change, it has proven impossible to overcome the embedded measurements of profitability and growth as the primary indicators of business success and the consequential focus on transactional costs as a way of maximising returns. When the triple bottom line was first advocated by John Elkington in 1994, the forces of technology-led globalisation were in their infancy. If adopted, this framework could have led us down a very different path, towards a broader sense of business value and a more balanced distribution of wealth and benefits. Instead, 'globalisation' rapidly became a source of enhanced corporate profits through creative off-shoring and outsourcing models that took advantage of tax havens and low-cost sources of production and labour. Underpinning all of these activities were contracts, which rapidly became more prolific and more expansive in their content. Increasingly, they were designed as instruments to assert legal rights, transfer risk and drive down input costs. In becoming transactional, contracts steadily lost any moral dimension and have become instruments of power.[8] Businesses were encouraged to pursue 'commoditisation' of supply and to adopt the belief that relationships were expendable. This belief was embedded in theories such as strategic sourcing, which treated relationships as a source of avoidable expense and promoted arm's-length transactional purchasing, often using methods such as blind auctions to prevent possible loyalty or preferential treatment towards a particular supplier. Corporate management saw suppliers as expendable and encouraged regular use of competitive bidding to maintain pressure on the supply market.

While these strategies certainly contributed to a fall in input prices and an age of relative plenty for many, others remained invisible and were left behind.[9] It is from

[5] See IACCM report: 'The Purpose of a Contract' (October 2017) https://www.worldcc.com/Portals/IACCM/resources/files/9876_j18069-iaccm-purpose-of-contract-a4-2017-11-14-v1-webready.pdf.

[6] Foss, K. 'Why are agreements so hard to understand?' published in Contracting Excellence Journal (April 2019) at https://journal.iaccm.com/contracting-excellence-journal/why-are-agreements-so-hard-to-understand.

[7] Sitnikov C. S. (2013) Triple Bottom Line. In: Idowu S.O., Capaldi N., Zu L., Gupta A.D. (eds) Encyclopedia of Corporate Social Responsibility. Springer, Berlin, Heidelberg. https://doi.org/10.1007/978-3-642-28036-8_465.

[8] See for example Handfield, R and Hasan, R: 'Breaching contracts, cutting lifelines for innocent workers' Contracting Excellence Journal (May 2020) https://journal.iaccm.com/contracting-excellence-journal/slow-down-at-startup-allow-for-transition-0.

[9] Rodrik, D: 'Global Poverty Amid Global Plenty', Americas Quarterly (Spring 2012).

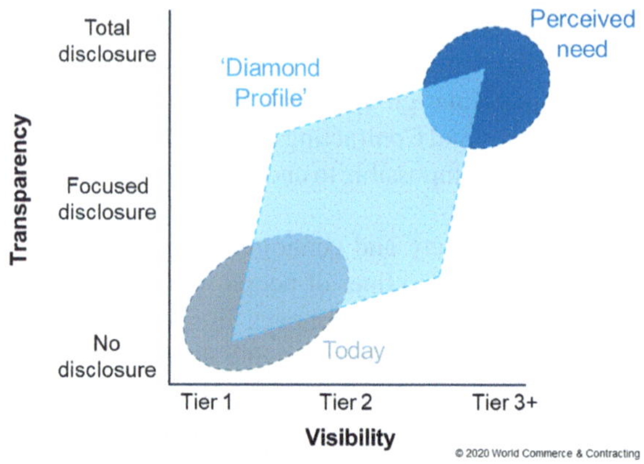

Fig. 1 The current state of supply chain visibility

ruthless, narrow value systems such as these that we now seek to recover, but in general, our contracting systems and models have not caught up. They remain based on standards and templates more suited to an inward-looking, transactional model that operates in denial of external dependencies. This approach has a direct link to the weaknesses exposed by the pandemic. For example, the extent of risk transfer has a direct impact on the extent and nature of communication and transparency. A focus on low cost results in suppliers seeking out the cheapest viable sources of supply—and then keeping them as secret as possible. It is forces such as these that operate in direct conflict with the principles of an open, sharing economy, an economy designed to ensure fairness and integrity in the distribution of risks and rewards.[10]

The chart above illustrates the consequences of today's contracting models. The drive for the lowest cost has resulted in extended supply chains—essentially following a path predicted by Nobel prize-winning economist Ronald Coase in his work 'The Nature of the Firm'[11] and subsequently developed in the transaction cost theories of academics such as Oliver Williamson.[12] When driven by low-cost considerations, organizations have typically outsourced more and more of their production and, since the late 1990s, also outsourced many of their business processes. According to the consultants, Bain, external purchasing averages 43% of an organization's costs.[13] McKinsey, a strategic advisory firm, suggests it is often higher,

[10] Cummins, T. Furner, A. and Guyer, S: 'Enhancing the Value of Extended Supply Ecosystems' World Commerce & Contracting (March 2020) https://www.worldcc.com/Resources/Content-Hub/View/ArticleId/9685/Enhancing-the-Value-of-Extended-Supply-Ecosystems.

[11] Coase, R: 'The Nature of the Firm' (November 1937) available at https://onlinelibrary.wiley.com/doi/full/10.1111/j.1468-0335.1937.tb00002.x.

[12] Williamson, O and Winter, S (ed.): 'The Nature of the Firm: Origins, Evolution & Development', Oxford University Press, July 1993 ISBN: 9,780,195,083,569.

[13] Bain & Company: 'Unearthing the Hidden Treasure of Procurement' (October 2016) https://www.bain.com/insights/david-schannon-unearthing-treasure-of-procurement-video/.

2020	Term
1	Limitation of Liability
2	Price / Charge / Price Changes
3	Indemnification
4	Delivery / Acceptance
5	Scope and Goals / Specification
6	Termination
7	Payment
8	Responsibilities of the Parties
9	Warranty
10	Liquidated Damages

Fig. 2 The most negotiated terms

representing up to 70% of a company's total expenditure.[14] The days of the integrated enterprise, where all or most activities were undertaken by internal staff, are long gone.

As previously observed, these cost pressures, except in the case of strategic or regulated activities, have consistently resulted in many organisations seeking cheaper sources of supply. They also lead to contract terms that maximise the ease of switching between suppliers. In consequence, supply chains have grown longer, while trust and loyalty have eroded. Contracts, rather than building relationships, often operate in denial of them. This point is illustrated by regular studies[15] of the contract terms that are most regularly negotiated in business-to-business transactions (see Figs. 1 and 2 below). These findings, based on input representing negotiators in almost 1,000 multi-national, cross-industry organisations, indicate a strong focus on asset protection and risk transfer. The terms in the top ten are heavily weighted towards the economic and business consequences of failure, rather than those that might support and encourage success.

[14] Mckinsey & Company: Using a rapid procurement transformation to generate cash quickly ((September 2017) https://www.mckinsey.com/business-functions/operations/our-insights/using-a-rapid-procurement-transformation-to-generate-cash-quickly.

[15] World Commerce and Contracting has undertaken these studies since 2004. The latest report is 'Most Negotiated Terms 2020', (October 2020) https://www.worldcc.com/Portals/IACCM/Resources/9937_1_Most%20Negotiated%20Terms%202020.pdf.

	Most Important term 2020
1	Delivery/Acceptance
2	Scope and Goals / Specification
3	Responsibilities of the Parties
4	Price / Charge / Price Changes
5	Data Privacy / Data security / Cybersecurity
6	Service Levels
7	Limitation of Liability
8	Change Management
9	Warranty
10	Termination

Fig. 3 The most important terms (from World Commerce & Contracting, 'Most Negotiated Terms 2020')

This focus is in large part explained by predominant organisational measurement systems, which are geared to support revenue growth and profit margins, often within relatively short measurement periods. In consequence, contract negotiators are mostly motivated to avoid risks that could damage financial performance and (in the case of buyers) to minimise input costs through notional savings. Such an approach often results in missed opportunities and does not promote thought about the wider economic and social implications of the relationship or transaction being negotiated.[16] A study conducted by researchers from the University of California, Irvine, concluded that many contract negotiators are 'preventist' in their behaviour.[17] In other words, they see success primarily in terms of preventing unwanted consequences—even though this may in fact undermine the value of the outcome achieved, with a consequent negative impact on revenue and profit.

However, there is a marked contrast between the topics that predominate in so many negotiations and those which negotiators appreciate to be most important (see Fig. 3).

Here, we see a greater understanding of the need for relational elements, ensuring clarity over goals and responsibilities—perhaps driven by the awareness of the things that typically go wrong (Fig. 4).

[16] There are some signs that this may change with the introduction of wider goals, such as the ESG principles, social value contracting and growing concerns over reputational risk. See for example '181 CEOs have realized companies need a purpose beyond profit' (Harvard Business Review, August 2019) https://hbr.org/2019/08/181-top-ceos-have-realized-companies-need-a-purpose-beyond-profit.

[17] Bauman et al., Optimism and Prevention in Contracting, IACCM (November 2019) https://www.worldcc.com/Portals/IACCM/resources/files/10916_iaccm-optimismprevention.pdf.

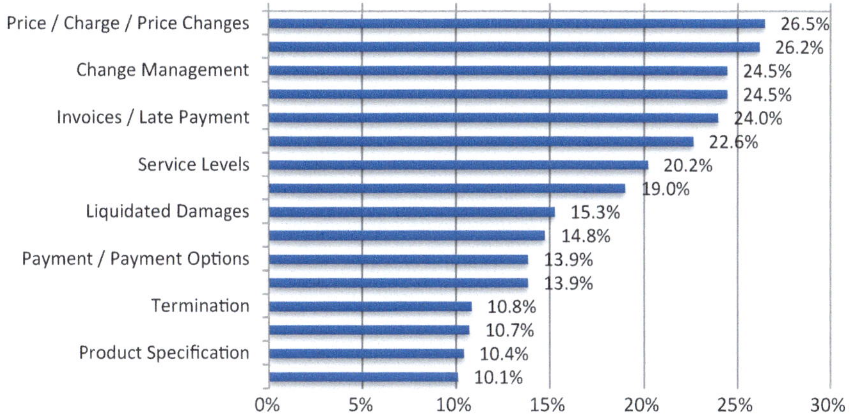

Fig. 4 The most frequent source of disagreement or dispute ('Most Negotiated Terms 2020')

The lists in Figs. 3 and 4 each offer a stark contrast to the terms that are most negotiated and illustrate a depth of understanding among negotiators that their actions may be sub-optimal in terms of contract outcomes. Yet despite this understanding, and (according to the survey) a declared wish to alter the focus, there continues to be no change. According to the negotiators, this is because of perceived resistance by their counter-party and also by others within their own organisation.

All of this data points to the conclusion that contracts today are commonly anti-relational. They are not designed to encourage positive behaviours or high-quality data flows or communications. They are not even seen as operational guides for those who will be charged with overseeing performance. Instead, their over-arching purpose seems to be to ensure mutual understanding on a relatively narrow set of performance parameters and to distribute the risks of failure based on the power dynamics that exist between the parties. Given this predominant model, it is not surprising that the overall interdependencies of supply and outcomes are given limited attention, even though warnings of supply fragility go back more than a decade.[18] It is this approach that left organisations blinded to the consequences of the pandemic, unable to predict supply disruptions or anticipate the supply chain frailties that have become an urgent threat to business performance and capability. In the words of an article published by The Atlantic, 'The coronavirus exposes the fragility of an economy built on outsourcing and just-in-time delivery'.[19]

---

[18] See for example Stonebraker, Goldhar & Nassos 'Weak links in the supply chain: measuring fragility and sustainability' (Journal of Manufacturing Technology Management, Vol. 20, Issue 2, February 2009).

[19] Lizzie O'Leary, 'The Modern Supply Chain Is Snapping', (The Atlantic, March 2020).

In summary: contract and relationship practices in a transactional context.

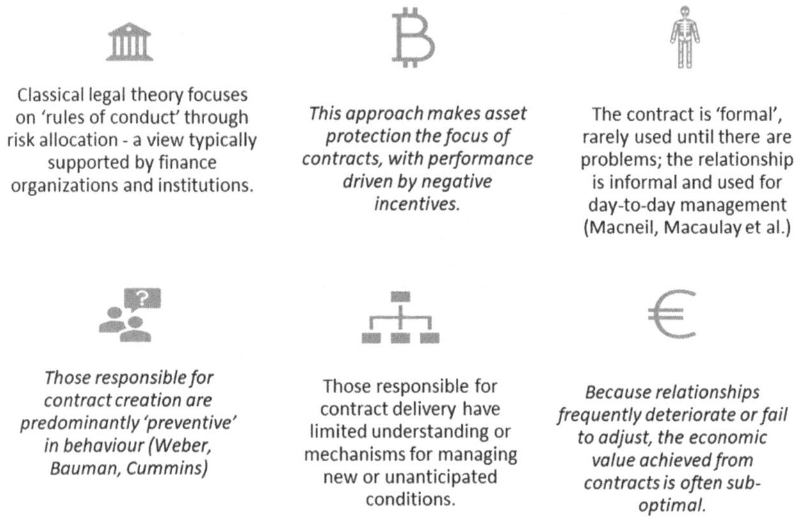

3 Relational Contracts: How They Differ

The concepts behind relational contracts go back to the 1960s and the writings of legal theorists Ian Macneil and Stewart Macaulay.[20] Macneil, in particular, recognised that classical forms of contract typically ignored what he termed 'the administrative' aspects of any contracting process—the areas that today we may call governance and performance management. In 'The Many Futures of Contract',[21] he developed his ideas to argue that contracts should be seen as 'relations' rather than the discrete transactions envisaged by neo-classical contract theory. Thus, even a simple transaction operates in a wider social and economic context, involving more than the parties involved in the specific act of exchange. To support his ideas, Macneil subsequently developed a set of 14 relational 'norms' that influence exchange relations.[22]

The critical point in Macneil's work is his acknowledgement that contracts occur within a complex and interconnected web of relationships and it is the integrity of this overall web on which success depends.

[20] See, for example, Galetti, S: 'Contract Interpretation and Relational Contract Theory', The Comparative and International Law Journal of Southern Africa, Vol. 47, No. 2 (JULY 2014), pp. 248–275, Published By: Institute of Foreign and Comparative Law.

[21] I R Macneil, 'The Many Futures of Contract' (Southern California Law Review, Vol 47, 1974).

[22] I R Macneil, 'Contracting Worlds and Essential Contract Theory' (Social and Legal Studies, Volume 9, 2000).

Macaulay's early work was rather different, in that he questioned the value and relevance of contracts to the average business executive. In 1963, following a limited set of interviews with business owners, he wrote: "Businessmen often fail to plan exchange relationships completely, and seldom use legal sanctions to adjust these relationships or to settle disputes".[23] It was this perceived 'irrelevance' of contracts that was subsequently picked up by economists. Oliver Hart and others then started to draw distinctions between formal, court-enforceable contracts and the more typical informal contracts, where enforcement largely depends on the threat of losing a long-term relationship, or potentially suffering reputational damage (two possibilities, it should be noted, that were somewhat weakened by the erosion of loyalty and commitment that has been discussed earlier in this chapter).[24]

This thinking can have the effect of reducing the purpose of a contract to being solely or primarily directed at formal enforcement through the courts—a narrow purpose that helps explain the typical content of a contract, as noted in the previous section when discussing 'The Most Negotiated Terms'.

Gillian Hadfield revisited and broadly confirmed Macaulay's findings, at least in the case of well-established, long-term relationships. However, in cases where innovation was involved or a loss of intellectual property was possible, attitudes changed. For Hadfield, a formal contract 'serves to coordinate beliefs about what constitutes a breach of a highly ambiguous set of obligations'.[25]

Together, these numerous studies led to the increased understanding that different forms of transaction require different forms of relationship for their success and that those relationships have varying levels of dependency on formal contracts. This was further developed by the recognition that contracts are, by their nature, 'incomplete'—they cannot realistically or efficiently anticipate every event that could potentially disrupt their performance.[26] This means that there is always a possibility that renegotiation will be required and, according to the work of economist Oliver Hart, this introduces a 'hold-up problem', whereby the parties may be reluctant to invest due to the uncertainty of the eventual reward.[27]

Collectively, these works advanced the theories of contracting, but had little impact in practice. The number and size of contracts saw exponential growth in the period 1980—2020, accompanied by a rapid increase in the number of qualified lawyers and their presence within most large firms.[28] Those contracts continued to be driven

---

[23] S Macaulay, 'Non-Contractual Relations in Business: A Preliminary Study' (American Sociological Review, Vol. 28, No. 1, Feb. 1963).

[24] In reality, very few disputes proceed to the courts. Not only is the result often unpredictable, but it is potentially damaging to the reputation of both parties. The potential for litigation is therefore in many respects 'phantom menace'.

[25] G K Hadfield and I Bozovic, 'Scaffolding: Using Formal Contracts to Build Informal Relations to Support Innovation' (Wisconsin Law Review, Vol. 5, 2016).

[26] See for example the works of …

[27] O Hart, published in 'The Hold-Up Problem and Incomplete Contracts: A Survey of Recent Topics in Contract Theory' (Bulletin of Economic Research, 53.1, 2001).

[28] For example, in the period 1980–2020, the number of practicing attorneys in the United States grew from 574,000 to 1,350,000 (Source: American Bar Association 'Profile of the

by concepts of enforcement through the courts, or through legally-driven dispute resolution methods. The idea that contracts should somehow shape or frame relationships, or acknowledge their dependence on a broader network of stakeholders, was typically ignored, dismissed as too vague or seen as too risky. In consequence, except for some examples in the field of alliances and teaming agreements, 'relational contracting' has largely been dismissed.

At this point, it is important to note that a major reason for legal concern is the potential implication of 'good faith' that a relational contract will introduce. This will be further discussed in the section on barriers to adoption.

Given this limited practical use, differences of opinion regarding the characteristics and precise purposes of a relational agreement persist. For some, it operates within the confines of a specific contract and builds on traditional content with prescribed rules, practices and behavioural norms that would normally be deemed informal, and therefore a component of 'relationship management'. Under this model, it might be argued that the term 'relational' is misleading and that it is in fact no more than an integrated approach to formalised contract governance (or, in the words of Macneil, 'administration').

The nine principles of a relational contract

1. Communication—an established protocol,
2. Risk allocation—mutually accepted and balanced,
3. Problem-solving—established forums and techniques,
4. Culture of accountability, not blame,
5. Joint working—mechanisms to identify need and methods,
6. Balanced incentives and consequences,
7. Mutual objectives and sense of purpose,
8. Performance measurement,
9. Continuous improvement.

The list above shows one view of the nine principles or norms that need to be addressed in a relational contract. These have been used and successfully tested in establishing a number of relational frameworks and were incorporated in a paper, 'Unpacking Relational Contracts', published in 2017.[29] While these principles may be formally embedded within the contract (as in the model cited above), they can also be adopted through a form of Charter (see Fig. 5). One benefit of the Charter approach is that it can be used as a consistent framework for interactions and norms across a network of independent and interdependent parties.

In this model, there is an appreciation of the fact that performance depends on a wider sense of 'relational clarity' that extends across the stakeholder community. Several examples of this broader thinking come from programs developed

Legal Profession', July 2020) https://www.americanbar.org/news/reporter_resources/profile-of-profession/.

[29] Frydlinger, Cummins, Vitasek and Bergman, 'Unpacking Relational Contracts: The Practitioner's Go-To Guide for Understanding relational Contracts' (https://www.vestedway.com/wp-content/uploads/2016/10/Unpacking-Relational-Contracting_v19.pdf).

Fig. 5 Example of a relational charter, developed by the Australian Department of Defence to provide an operational framework for a long-term sustainment contract (Courtesy of Australian DoD)

by the Australian Department of Defence, which viewed the participants in major programs as essentially 'an enterprise' in its own right and developed 'Relational Charters' (such as that in Fig. 5) which were adopted by multiple parties. Through their commitment to share data and information, this model clearly becomes closer to the principles of relational economics, yet still it does not recognise the full extent of the interconnections.

A further variant arises in the context of 'industry codes', a potential direction being given momentum by the COVID-19 pandemic. The lack of transparency in today's supply chains (noted earlier in this chapter) has generated heightened concern about the potential for economic fragility. In industries where demand has been especially hard-hit, such as aerospace and oil and gas, there is a push[30] for increased collaboration and greater openness, a recognition that the industry needs to monitor its overall health and resilience by having the greater insight into the economic condition of its members. With many programs operating for 30 years or more, this requires a major departure from the transactional, arms-length approach of the past.

Yet even this would take us only part of the way towards a truly relational economy and it is through initiatives such as that being explored by the European Commission that we may see the true shift come about. In this case, it would not so much be through the introduction and use of individual relational contracts, but rather that contracting in its entirety becomes relational—that the use of technology platforms enables us to understand and evaluate the interconnections between the innumerable

[30] As reported by World Commerce & Contracting in 'Negotiation: it's not what it used to be ', Commitment Matters blog (September 2020) https://commitmentmatters.com/2020/09/21/negotiation-its-not-what-it-used-to-be/.

contracts that were noted by the Nobel prize committee. In this instance, a technology platform might not only capture the existence and ongoing performance data related to a contract, but could also gather information from other sources (such as company reports or credit rating agencies) to enable timely and reliable insight into both the contract and the economic resilience of the parties on which its outcome depends.

4 Relational Contracts: The Benefits

The most obvious and immediate benefit that comes from a relational contract is that it creates a heightened degree of clarity and certainty in the way that performance will be managed and the principles for governance. This provides better-defined mechanisms to handle change and uncertainty, or to reconcile differences that arise over the course of the agreement. As such, it represents an effective way to tackle the issues of 'incompleteness' identified by Hart et al.

When viewed in this context, relational terms and principles operate across a spectrum. The need for a formal definition, mutual agreement and structured implementation depends on various factors which might include some or all of the following:

- The overall duration and complexity of the relationship and hence the likelihood of significant change in circumstances or needs;
- The extent to which there is underlying uncertainty over the deliverables or how they will be delivered;
- The degree to which the parties have a propensity for misunderstandings, for example, due to culture or language;
- The requirement for joint working and collaboration across multiple parties.

In practice, there is growing evidence of the benefits that accrue from a disciplined approach to relational contracts. These include the previously cited examples from the Australian Department of Defence,[31] as well as a variety of case studies that made use of the 'Vested' approach developed by Kate Vitasek and the University of Tennessee.[32] These examples have common features of cost savings, improved profitability, increased innovation, and more adaptive relationships based on principles of mutual interest, rather than self-interest. However, it has to be acknowledged that these success stories are essentially anecdotal. Few organisations have adopted and delivered relational approaches on a consistent basis.

[31] See for example https://journal.iaccm.com/contracting-excellence-journal/how-australias-department-of-defence-harnessed-the-power-of-the-relationship.

[32] Vitasek, K. and Manrodt, K: 'Vested', Palgrave McMillan (2012).

5 Relational Contracts: Structural Implications

Relational contracting does not come naturally. Organisations have been designed to manage transactional contracts. While many operate with a basic form of relational agreement—for example, Master Services Agreements—this is to drive greater efficiency and to avoid a need for case-by-case negotiation. A review of these agreements quickly reveals that the relational content described in the previous section is typically minimal or absent. In other words, contracts are in most cases not designed to manage relationships and rarely address any issues associated with the wider network impacted by the agreement, unless perhaps related to control issues, such as terms that must flow through to sub-contractors.

As previously explained, today's contracts are mostly seen as the formal record of exchange, the obligations associated with that exchange and the consequences of failure. While this may include some details related to administration or performance, for any agreement of an ongoing nature it is typically assumed that day-to-day management will be handled informally, via the relationship. This includes not only specific issues of performance, but also more fundamental topics such as arrangements for joint working, handling altered requirements or incremental opportunities. This informality often works well if operations are smooth and relatively stable; it can be more problematic when there are significant performance issues or if overall business conditions are volatile.

Few organisations have developed tools or systems that are effective at anticipating risks or designed to manage disruptive events. COVID-19 offered insights into organisational readiness. For example, in a study by World Commerce and Contracting, 81% of respondents acknowledged the weaknesses in their contract management systems.[33] Even those who had a consolidated online repository for their agreements often struggled to find key data points. Contract performance data was typically scattered across multiple independent systems which meant that the terms or status of those agreements was hard to find and involved extensive manual effort.

The most streamlined environments are found in businesses that deal in commodities and where transactional agreements are therefore relatively complete. Amazon is an example of such a business and operates systems that not only automate most elements of contract performance, but also link interdependent agreements—for example, a customer order with the availability of supply and the logistics of delivery and payment.

The aim of most businesses has been to standardise and commoditise to the greatest possible extent. Where this is not possible, they have invested in relationship managers and deployed operational resources to manage performance. Relational contracting challenges this thinking. It is more prescriptive in the way that the relationship will be managed and requires two or more parties to adopt common

[33] World Commerce & Contracting: 'Managing Contracts Under COVID-19: What Have We Learnt?' (April 2020) https://www.worldcc.com/Portals/IACCM/resources/files/11079_managing-contracts-covid-19-report.pdf.

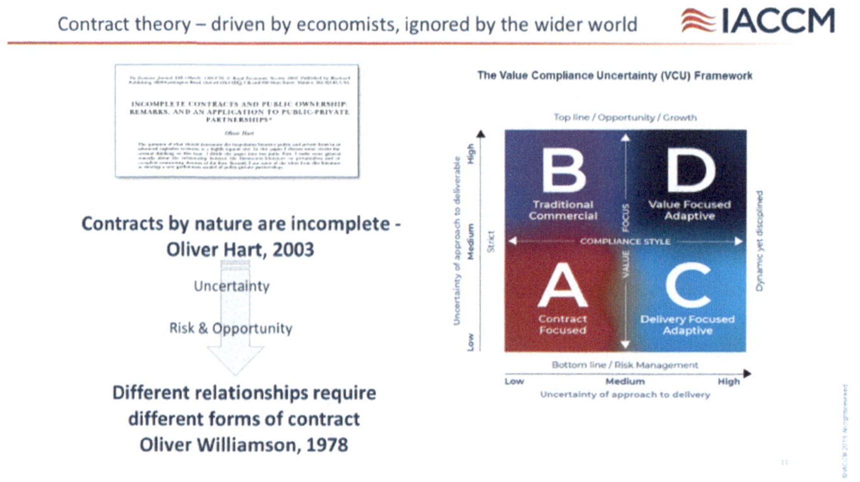

Fig. 6 Risk, compliance and uncertainty management (Courtesy of World Commerce & Contracting)

approaches, which are likely to be an exception to normal methods and procedures. This leads to a perception of increased cost and complexity, even though the opposite may be true. In general, organisations have no data to calculate the typical cost of managing their existing contracts, nor of the economic gains or losses that may result from their current approach.

In a 2019 study, World Commerce and Contracting examined current practices in post-award contract management.[34] The purpose was to identify the best approaches to achieving optimum and mutual economic value. The study was unable to identify any organisation that could demonstrate such a capability on a repetitive basis. The main reason for this was that today's transactional approach to contracting means that there is rarely an analysis of the contract terms or structure needed to deliver the best results. The procurement and sales models discussed throughout this chapter have led to most business being conducted under standardised forms of agreement that operate within box A of Fig. 6 below. This is essentially a commodity model, where the parties seek to minimise the cost associated with oversight and make little provision for ongoing change or its management. By contrast, a relational model establishes a requirement to collaborate and to be more transparent in data and information sharing. This typically means there is a need for larger, dedicated teams, especially at the outset of the agreement when detailed procedures and working methods must be defined. Especially for those who are new to relational models, this feels like a fundamental change to organisational structure and demands. It also

[34] Cummins, T. and Guyer, S: 'Improving the Performance of Contracts Post-Award', World Commerce & Contracting (November 2019) https://www.worldcc.com/Portals/IACCM/resources/files/10991_iaccm-post-award-summary-report.pdf.

acknowledges the likelihood of change and possible renegotiation, which does not sit well within today's rigid budgeting and cost management systems.

These same structural challenges apply whether the relational agreement is one-to-one, one-to-many or many-to-many. If relational frameworks are adopted at an industry level, the scale of that disruption will initially be far greater, but of course, this is only until it stabilises and becomes an operational norm.

6 Relational Contracts: Barriers to Adoption and Use

In a recent webinar,[35] two partners from international law firm CMS opined that many lawyers are reluctant to promote relational contracting because they do not believe organisations are capable of adapting to their delivery requirements.

As indicated in the previous section, the norms and behaviours of a relational contract are not consistent with the typical operating model and management systems of today's businesses. Hence, they represent an exception and exceptions represent a risk of unexpected costs or non-performance. From a legal perspective, it would be seen as irresponsible to enter into an agreement that created obligations that were unlikely to be met. This is one factor that has led many relational agreements to follow the Charter approach previously mentioned, thereby avoiding the need to engage with lawyers.

Another common concern with relational contracting is the belief that it will cost more to administer. It is certainly true that the participants in a relational agreement need to designate dedicated resources and that specific activities—such as establishing the relational terms or the charter—require incremental workload. The real point here is again that organisations prefer contracts to fit within their standard processes. Exceptions are viewed as expensive. This view takes no account of the downstream benefits that flow from a more collaborative contracting model and which have been spelled out in some of the earlier referenced case studies—the reduced costs of tensions or disputes over performance, the added value from ongoing improvements or innovation. Since organisations rarely have systems that can monitor or measure these benefits, the reaction that 'relational contracting costs more' is hard to challenge with more than anecdotal data and is therefore unlikely to disappear unless or until there is a far more extensive body of examples.

Relational contracts may also be seen as challenging established power structures and therefore result in opposition from managers who feel threatened by a loss of authority. As previously noted, a relational approach creates 'an enterprise within an enterprise'. This implies a shift from normal authority and control mechanisms.

[35] 'Relational Contracting: A Risk Too Far?' World Commerce & Contracting (October 2020) https://www.worldcc.com/Resources/Content-Hub/View/ArticleId/9945/Ask-the-Expert-Relational-Contracting-a-risk-too-far.

Finally, the fact that relational contracting is today the exception means that it can rarely develop or succeed without the support of at least one executive sponsor—someone with the power and authority to make it happen. This sponsorship must be replicated in each of the partner organisations and may need to be sustained throughout the life of the agreement.

In combination, these barriers represent a formidable obstacle to the progress of relational contracting—similar in many ways to the challenges that have faced relational economics or, indeed, any other fundamental shift in the way we form, govern or measure economic activity and the distribution of wealth.

7 Concluding Remarks

Given the limited adoption of relational contracts and the significant barriers to their development, is there any hope for progress?

Contract negotiators consistently state their preference for 'win–win' solutions, leading to mutual gain.[36] They also believe that the COVID-19 pandemic may be the catalyst for change.[37] There are encouraging signs of progress, especially among the industries hardest hit by the pandemic. Supply chain fragility, a consolidation of the supply base, the urgency of innovation may combine to generate increased cooperation and the development of industry codes and practices that include behavioural norms and relational codes.

There are also broader social and political pressures for business and governments to change the way that they measure success, in particular with regard to the sort of sustainability principles embedded in the environmental, social and corporate governance (ESG) guidelines promoted through the United Nations Global Compact. Already, elements of these principles are finding their way into contracts and regulations, for example in areas such as social value and diversity requirements. In order to monitor and report on levels of compliance or achievement, organisations are being forced to re-think the challenges of transparency, visibility and data flows highlighted in this chapter. This can only be achieved through an expanded approach to monitoring and reporting, extending beyond single contracts and their limited transactional view.

Hence there are reasons for optimism that contracts will increasingly be seen as critical tools in the structuring and management of ecosystems—that these 'innumerable contracts' which are holding together our modern economies will themselves become linked through the very technologies that initially led to fragmentation and transactional thinking.

Such a development would break down many of the barriers that have constrained relational economics—in particular, increased transparency of data and more open

[36] 'Most Negotiated Terms 2020'–previous citation.

[37] Id.

information flows across relational partners, networks and ecosystems. Yet this development alone is not enough since it does not address the need for such data to be consolidated, to provide holistic indicators of economic performance. It is here that the initiative being promoted by the European Commission is truly exciting and transformational, offering the possibility of a regulatory and governance framework that would not only capture, but also mandate, the collection of the data that would make relational economics a reality.

Tim Cummins is professor of International Commercial & Contract Management, University of Leeds, School of Law, where he leads the development of inter-disciplinary commercial programs. He is the founder and president of World Commerce & Contracting and built a worldwide non-profit association that increasingly influences commercial policies and contracting practices in major corporations and governments. In September 2019, he was presented with the Financial Times 'Market Shaper of the Year' Award. Before founding World Commerce & Contracting, Tim Cummins was on the Chairman's staff at IBM Corporation. His early career included management roles in the banking, automotive, and aerospace industries.

Sally Guyer is Chief Executive Officer of World Commerce & Contracting, leading and supporting her global team and the association's members to pursue excellence in commercial and contract management. Sally is an experienced and accomplished commercial professional, having held senior positions at various corporate and multi-national organizations, primarily in the Telecoms and IT industries. With a background in Law, Sally worked in-house before establishing her own legal and commercial consultancy, focused on support for Small and Medium Enterprise. Recruited initially as Chief Operating Officer in 2014, Sally was appointed CEO in 2018. In 2019, Sally was invited to become Chair of the Board for the Open Contracting Partnership, a silo-busting collaboration across governments, businesses, civil society, and technologists, committed to opening up and transforming government contracting worldwide. In May of 2021, Sally was appointed Professor in Practice in Strategy and Innovation at the University of Durham Business School.

Part V
Epistemology and Relational Economics

Relational Processes in Whitehead's Metaphysics and Commons' Economics. The Relevance of Cosmology for Economic Theory

Michael Schramm

Abstract Scientific methodologies are faced with two problems. On the one hand, they have to decide whether to proceed macro- or microanalytically. This paper deals with several microanalytical conceptions (Whitehead, Commons, Wieland, etc.) that have chosen this approach because the basic units (events, transactions) are the only "things" that actually exist. In this sense, these microanalytical approaches are "reductive" (they concentrate on the most basic units). On the other hand, scientific theories have to deal with the problem of complexity reduction. Because it is the nature of scientific theories to come up with models which are abstractions from the "messy" reality, science must always be confronted with the question of how much complexity reduction is appropriate. While radical "reductionist" methods declare that all things are actually "nothing but ...", the mentioned conceptions are not "reductionist" because they conceptually take into account the polydimensionality of the real. In this view, the concrete world of business presents itself as a network evolving out of countless transactions with a polydimensional (and not: monodimensional) nature.

Keywords Scientific methodology · Abstraction · Macroanalytic · Microanalytic · Reductive · Reductionist · Natural ontology · Social ontology · Cosmology · Process philosophy · Event · Net-work · Polydimensionality · Transaction · Going concern

With his "Relational Economics", Josef Wieland has presented a theoretical offer. And theoretical concepts are always faced with a fundamental question: How much abstraction should theory allow? The physicist Brian Greene formulates the challenge as follows:

M. Schramm (✉)
University of Hohenheim, Stuttgart, Germany
e-mail: michael.schramm@uni-hohenheim.de

L. Biggiero et al. (eds.), *The Relational View of Economics*, Relational Economics and Organization Governance, https://doi.org/10.1007/978-3-030-86526-9_13

> The art of science [...] lies in making judicious simplifications that render problems tractable while retaining enough of their essence to ensure that the conclusions drawn are relevant.[1]

Inevitably, scientific theories are therefore of a reductive nature, because one cannot think without abstractions at all. But the crucial question is how much abstraction is allowed on the one hand and how much of the 'essence' (Greene) is retained on the other. The mathematician, physicist and philosopher Alfred North Whitehead names the problem behind it:

> The disadvantage of exclusive attention to a group of abstractions [...] is that [...] you have abstracted from the remainder of things. In so far as the excluded things are important [...], your modes of [abstract] thought are not fitted to deal with them.[2]

It is not simply a matter of any theory having a "blind spot". The crucial problem is how big this "blind spot" is. In other words, how much complexity reduction is appropriate? This is precisely where Josef Wieland's theory programme comes in. Of course, the reductionism of conventional mainstream economics did not come about by chance:

> there are good methodological reasons in every theory for the reduction of complexity which first renders an object capable of theoretical treatment.[3]

Wieland is fully aware of the fact that his theoretical offerings ("Governance Ethics" or "Relational Economics"), in contrast, are associated with an increase in complexity:

> his basic conceptual suggestion "consequently amounts [...] to an increase in complexity—with the corresponding follow-up problems".[4]

These follow-up problems arise from the fact that a theory that is less reductionist, i.e. allows for more complexity, cannot of course be quite as elegant as a theory that simplifies (reduces) much more radically. That is the price to pay. But the strongly reductionist mainstream economics also pays a high price, a probably even higher prize, which Nobel Prize winner Richard Thaler sums up as follows:

> Economic theory [neoclassical mainstream economics] is elegant and simple—and wrong![5]

In this sense, Wieland accepts an increase in complexity in his theory because without it important things would remain hidden. He accepts that his theoretical

---

[1] Greene (2020, p. 117). Previously, he described the problem in this way: "[T]he art [...] lies in simplifying the horrendously complex so as to preserve essential [...] features while making the theoretical analysis tractable." (Greene 2011, p. 17).

[2] Whitehead (1925/1967), p. 59.

[3] Wieland (2014), p. 127.

[4] Wieland (2014), p. 127.

[5] Thaler (2010); time code: 19:55 Min. The term "elegance" (of a scientific theory) reminds me of a saying by physicist Ludwig Boltzmann: one should leave elegance to the tailors and shoemakers (cit. Einstein, 1917/2009, p. v: "man solle die Eleganz Sache der Schneider und Schuster sein lassen").

approach is more "messy" than conventional mainstream economics,[6] because the things excluded in neoclassical economics actually are important if one wants to aim for a conception that is appropriate to reality.

Science always thinks in abstractions. But precisely for this reason, science must always be confronted with the question of how much complexity reduction is appropriate. Otherwise, there is a risk of the 'fallacy of misplaced concreteness', as Whitehead calls it. This is the mistake of confusing one's own abstracting model with concrete actuality.[7] The ability of a theory to depict the essential components of the dynamic network of economic transactions, is the crucial point here.

1 Economics of Transaction. The Microanalytical Theory Decision

Josef Wieland's "Relational Economics" is a microanalytical economics (and ethics). Its basic unit is the economic transaction. This is particularly evident in his (early) "governance function" from 2001[8]:

$$\text{Tmij} = \text{f}(\text{aISij}, \text{bFIij}, \text{cIFij}, \text{dOKKij})$$
$$(\text{a} \ldots \text{d} = -1, 0, 1; \text{i} = \text{specific transaction}; \text{j} = \text{specific place})$$

This function maps the factors influencing the moral dimension (m) of a distinct transaction (T).[9] In Wieland's concept, transaction analysis forms the basis for the ultimate goal: the governance of moral-economic transactions.[10]

Probably, Wieland's most important source for this orientation towards transaction and governance is Oliver E. Williamson's Transaction Cost Economics. His economics can be seen as a continuation of the transaction cost approach, which Ronald Coase had already founded in 1937 in his famous essay on The Nature of the

[6] In this sense, Nobel Prize winner Paul Krugman also encouraged his own discipline shortly after the financial crisis: "[E]conomists will have to learn to live with messiness." (Krugman, 2009).

[7] Whitehead sees the job of philosophy or metaphysics in confronting the sciences with this "fallacy of misplaced concreteness" and making itself useful as a "critique of abstractions": "You cannot think without abstractions; accordingly, it is of the utmost importance to be vigilant in critically revising your modes of abstraction. It is here that philosophy finds its niche as essential to the healthy progress of society. It is the critic of abstractions." (Whitehead, 1925/1967, p. 59 f.). So, considering "the 'fallacy of misplaced concreteness' […] [i]t is the office of metaphysics to determine the limits of the applicability of such abstract notions." (Whitehead, 1929/1979, p. 93).

[8] This "governance function" can be found for the first time in Wieland (2001), p. 9, and then of course in subsequent applications, such as Wieland (2005), p. 29, or Wieland (2014), p. 16.

[9] We do not need to go into the details of this governance function here. But the influencing factors are: "individual self-commitment" (IS), "formal institutions" (FI), "informal institutions" (IF), and "the mechanisms of coordination and cooperation of a certain organization" (OCC). This governance function shows that Wieland advocates a polydimensional or "comprehensive concept of governance as its starting point" (2014, p. 7).

[10] Cf. Wieland (2014), pp. 8 f.

Firm.[11] However, for the microanalytical theory decision to regard the distinct transaction as the basic unit of analysis, Williamson always referred to another economist, namely John R. Commons. As was to be expected, Williamson started his 2009 Nobel Prize speech with a famous quote from Commons. Williamson declared:

> John R. Commons, who was a leading institutional economist during the first half of the twentieth century, formulated the problem of economic organization as follows: 'The ultimate unit of activity … must contain in itself the three principles of conflict, mutuality, and order. This unit is a transaction' (Commons 1932, 4).[12]

Except in his early years, Williamson referred to this quote from Commons in all his important works and in many papers, and consequently made the distinct transaction the ultimate unit of further investigation:

> [T]he transaction is made the basic unit of analysis.[13]

But now two things attract attention. Firstly, as far as I can see, Williamson never really explained what has been the theoretical-strategic reason for him to place the transaction at the centre of his governance analyses, i.e. to proceed microanalytically.[14] On the other hand, it is striking that Williamson always made an omission in the Commons quote, which is indicated by the three dots.[15] In checking what Williamson has omitted, one will find a surprise. For the complete original passage in John R. Commons is the following (I've put in italics what Williamson has omitted):

> Thus the ultimate unit of activity which correlates law, economics and ethics must contain in itself the three principles of conflict, mutuality, and order. This unit is a transaction.[16]

If we now look at the title of the original essay, we see that it was dedicated to precisely this problem (which Williamson omitted), namely the "Problem of Correlating Law, Economics, and Ethics". What Williamson "achieved" with his omission was a reductionist economization of the transaction, which Commons wanted to reconstruct precisely as a polydimensional event—in which the legal, economic and ethical dimensions meet. It must be said that Williamson made his reductionist

[11] Cf. Coase (1937).

[12] Williamson (2009), p. 673.

[13] Williamson (2009), p. 674.

[14] This was probably simply because he had previously worked with the transaction *cost* approach.

[15] The typical omission is found in Williamson (1995a), p. 187; Williamson (1995d), p. 36; Williamson (1996a), p. 12; Williamson (1999), p. 1088; Williamson (2000), p. 599; Williamson (2002a), p. 438; Williamson (2002b), p. 175; Williamson (2005a), p. 3; Williamson (2005b), p. 25; Williamson (2005c), p. 371; and in the Nobel Prize speech: Williamson (2009), p. 673. More generally, Williamson refers to Commons in: Williamson (1975), p. 3. 254; Williamson (1981), p. 1543; Williamson (1985), p. 3. 6; Williamson (1991a), p. 281; Williamson (1991b), p. 8 (in W./Sidney); Williamson (1991c), p. 93 (in W./Sidney); Williamson (1991d), p. 79; Williamson (1995a), p. 225; Williamson (1995c), p. 34; Williamson (1996a), p. 26. 45. 58. 105. 175. 234. 371; Williamson (1996b), p. 390. In Williamson (1996a), p. 251, he at least takes up the keyword "law" ("To be sure, John R. Commons deserves credit for his early recognition that 'law and economics' was a combined enterprise (Commons, 1924, 1925)." But "ethics" remains banned here too.

[16] Commons (1932/1996), p. 454 (emphasis mine).

omission directly against Commons' systematic intention.[17] And it is probably no exaggeration to say that Wieland's conceptual focus is not least of all to reverse this omission by Williamson and to start precisely with the problem that Commons formulated at the time: the relational analysis business of correlating law, economics and ethics in a transaction. So it applies: back to Commons!

If one turns to the original writings of John R. Commons in this sense, one finds that after his decision—already made in 1924—to make the transaction the ultimate basic unit of his conception, he discovered that a philosophical metaphysician had made a very similar theory-strategic decision for his cosmology. And this metaphysician was the mathematician, physicist and philosopher Alfred North Whitehead. Commons wrote:

> These [...] transactions are to economics what Whitehead's [...] 'event[s]' are to physics.[18]

The parallels between Commons' economics and Whitehead's cosmology suggest that a decision of metaphysical significance is involved here: in the effort to clarify "how the (business) world really works (in general)", it is theoretically strategically appropriate to proceed both microanalytically and polydimensionally, in other words: to use a "reductive" but not "reductionist" method (I will come to this terminology shortly). So, first of all, the question (not further discussed by Williamson) must be clarified, what exactly are the reasons for regarding the transaction as the "ultimate unit of activity", as the micro-analytical basic unit for the economic analysis.

In a sense, my paper is actually "only" discussing one single sentence of John R. Commons ontologically and metaphysically, namely the following sentence (already quoted):

> [T]he ultimate unit of activity which correlates law, economics and ethics [...] is a transaction.[19]

[17] There is an interesting passage in his Nobel Prize Lecture that is no longer found in the published version. There Williamson declares: "It 's not clear, that this is the way he meant it, but it 's the way that I employ it." (https://www.nobelprize.org/prizes/economic-sciences/2009/williamson/lecture/; time code: 00:06:40 Min.) I think it's pretty clear that Williamson's reductionism—which turns the polydimensional transaction of Commons into a purely economic event—is *not* "the way he meant it". Williamson actually only takes over from Commons the microanalytical approach to transactions. He writes about it: "My debts to Commons are principally that he defined the economic problem in a spirit that is very much akin to my own. I do not borrow more in detail from what he did because his is a highly personalized analysis" (Williamson, 1975, p. 6). But Commons had just seen "the economic problem" in "Correlating Law, Economics, and Ethics".

[18] Commons (1934/2009), p. 96.

[19] Commons (1932/1996), p. 454. It is not difficult to see that I have also made an omission in this quotation on my part. However, this omission does not serve the purpose of retouching a systematic problem (as Williamson did with Commons' "Problem of Correlating Law, Economics, and Ethics"). The reason for the omission is simply that the so-called "Commons Triple" ("conflict, mutuality, and order") is not relevant to the topic of my paper.

2 Natural Ontology and Social Ontology of Actual Transactions. Living in Exactly One, but Complex Universe

Why does Commons declare the transaction to be the basic microanalytical unit? The answer is: because in the economy the transactions are the only "things" that actually exist. And the philosophical discipline that deals with this question of what kinds of "things" there are in our universe, i.e. "what exists",[20] is called "Ontology". Of course, philosophers argue about how to classify what exists.[21]

(1) "*Natural* Ontology". One possible (and traditional) division is the tripartite division into physical, mental and abstract "things". There are very different events in our universe: the formation of a star, the birth of a child, the decay of an elementary particle, a chemical reaction, thinking an idea, or, at the very beginning, the Big Bang. If, on the other hand, we look at the content of a thought or feeling, for example, then these "things" are of a different nature: although a thought or feeling is produced—according to a common understanding—by something physical (the brain), but they themselves are not physical, but mental. And finally—somehow—there are also "things" that are again of a different nature: numbers, for example, or the laws of logic are in themselves neither physical nor mental, but abstract. This traditional tripartite division can be called the "Ontology of the Natural".

(2) "*Social* Ontology". Now the philosopher John R. Searle has convincingly argued that besides this traditional (three-part) "natural ontology", another type of existing reality should be distinguished, which he calls "social ontology". The first decisive characteristic of social ontology is that it exists only because it was simply invented by human beings:

> we are inventing a reality out of nothing.[22]

These are, therefore "imagined orders [...] existing only in our imagination".[23] For example, paper money is such an invention of a social reality. It was not nature ("natural ontology") that created banknotes, but human society ("social ontology"). The same is true for political offices, football games or companies:

> God can create light by saying 'Let there be light!' Well, we cannot create light but we have a similar remarkable capacity. We can create [...] corporations by saying [...] 'Let there be a corporation!' [24]

[20] See Searle (1998/1999), p. 5: "ontology (what exists)". "Ontology [...] is concerned to answer existence questions." (Thomasson 2015, p. 1).

[21] For current introductions to this ontological question see Urbich & Zimmer (2020); Thomasson (2015).

[22] Searle (2010/2011), p. 105.

[23] Harari (2015/2018), p. 143.

[24] Searle (2010/2011), p. 100.

So, "social ontology" is a remarkable matter. The existence of money is something objectively real, but at the same time money is real money only because we subjectively think it is money. In Searle's philosophy this "puzzling character of social ontology"[25] is clarified in the following way:

Basically, Searle considers his concept of "social ontology" as part of a "metaphysics of [...] social relations".[26] More specifically, Searle has worked out that the strange ontology of social reality can only be dealt with through a double conceptual distinction:

First of all: Mount Everest is a mountain that physically is objectively there; and it would be there objectively even if there were not a single person on earth who would say: "There's a mountain!" Money, on the other hand, is only money because we think it is money and we accept it as money.[27] The question arises: How can money be an objective reality if it is money only because we subjectively think it is money? The three traditional ontological "drawers" are "things" which—in Searle's terminology—are "ontologically objective": their existence does not depend on someone else thinking them. Mount Everest is there as a physical fact, even if nobody would think that there is a mountain. If someone has an idea, then that thought would be there in the mind of that person as a mental fact even if nobody else knew about it. The number 3 would exist as an abstract fact even if nobody would think that the number of the apples here is exactly 3.[28] All these "things" are "ontologically objective". Money, on the other hand, is "ontologically subjective": if nobody would think that the piece of paper here is money, it would not be money.[29] Our thoughts obviously have the power to make something else (money) out of a thing (a physical piece of paper). We can create money, so to speak, "out of nothing".[30]

But now Searle makes a second distinction, namely the one between "*epistemically* objective" and "*epistemically* subjective".[31]

For example, the statement that the *Lehman Brothers* went bankrupt on 15 September 2008 is an "epistemically *objective*", i.e. objectively (acknowledged) fact.

---

[25] Searle (2010/2011), p. ix.

[26] Searle (1995), p. 3.

[27] Money "is money only if we think it is money " (Searle 1998/1999, p. 112).

[28] However, the ontological objectivity of numbers is controversial. But I myself think that they exist in any universe in an ontologically objective way. But that is a separate question. It should be noted that, despite this ontological objectivity, the number 3, for instance, is of an *abstract* nature; there is nothing concrete about it.

[29] "If everyone forgot what money was, there wouldn't be any money anymore". (Dennett, 1991, p. 24).

[30] See Searle (2010/2011), p. 105: "we are inventing a reality out of nothing". So, we "have created a remarkably potent object, a limited liability corporation, so to speak out of thin air." (Searle, 2010/2011, p. 98).

[31] The term "epistemology" he explains briefly and to the point: "epistemology (how we know)" (Searle, 1998/1999, p. 5).

> This statement "is epistemically objective, because its truth or falsity can be ascertained independently of the attitudes and opinions of observers".[32]

In contrast, the assessment of whether Apple or Samsung smartphones have the more beautiful design has an "epistemically *subjective*" character.

Money—and this is what makes it so remarkable as an example of an entity of "social ontology"—is "ontologically *subjective*", but at the same time "epistemically *objective*": although this euro note is only money if we *subjectively* think it's money ("ontological subjectivity"), but if I were to tear a 200 € note in front of you now, you would think in horror: "This moron has just destroyed 200 €!" So, anyone who does not realise that this € note is *objectively* money ("epistemic objectivity") has a problem of perception.

(3) Living in A *Physical* Universe. After this double conceptual distinction, another point is important: like all other things, social-ontological realities only gain concrete actuality in physical actions (in the economy: transactions). *Example 1*: In our traffic system there exists the rule "Stop at red (lights)" This traffic rule as such is of an *abstract* nature. It only becomes reality when—and only when—people actually adhere to it in their *concrete* behaviour. However, this is not always the case: some people actually stop; others overlook the red because they are dreaming; yet others knowingly ignore it because their self-interest in getting quickly now from A to B outweighs the situation. The fact that the *concrete* reality at the red traffic light often looks different from the (in itself) only virtual or abstract traffic rule is again based on the (ontological) fact that reality is more diverse or *poly*dimensional than the *mono*dimensional traffic rule. There are innumerable possibilities that can determine real action, not just traffic regulations. *Example 2*: Most legal systems have provided for a criminal prohibition of bribes. However, the actual reality does not at all correspond to the legal rules: for many years, a considerable dark field of at least 95% has been expected here.[33] This means that in this case, the legal system remains largely *abstract* (merely virtual). The prohibition of bribes is an "epistemically *objective*" fact: it is important to know that bribery is prohibited, and therefore if discovered, sanctions are to be expected. Nevertheless, the rules of the game regarding the criminal prohibition of bribes remain "ontologically *subjective*": you must not have to follow them! And the estimated darkfield of at least 95% shows that most economic actors apparently do not actually do so. The more actors ignore this rule, the clearer its inherently *abstract* nature becomes. The "incentive arrangement" enshrined in criminal law only becomes *reality* if the actors are concretely guided by the incentives and do follow the rule. If absolutely nobody would recognise this rule as guiding real action, the rule would remain completely *virtual* or *abstract* even as an incentive arrangement. In terms of its reality content, it would then be practically *non-existent* (any

[32] Searle (2010/2011), p. 18.

[33] Bannenberg/Schaupensteiner (2004/2007), p. 40.

longer).[34] This possibility that a rule can remain completely abstract depends precisely on its "ontological *subjectivity*". However, if the abstract social ontological realities are to become *actuality*, they must be concretised into physical *actions* (actual stopping at the traffic lights; economic: *transactions*). We invent money by assigning a function to a piece of paper (namely to function as money),

> but that function is manifested only in actual transactions; hence, our interest is not in the object but in the processes and events where the functions are manifested.[35]

In this way the "*social* ontology" is bound back to the "*natural* ontology". Although we live in a complex world which has not only a "natural" but also a "social ontology", we still "live in exactly one world, not two or three or seventeen".[36] And it is one of the characteristics of this one world that there is no actuality without physical concreteness.[37] Note, that this does not mean that everything is merely physical. But all things that are actual must have a physical dimension. This also applies to "social ontology".[38] The relevance of the natural cosmology for the economy lies fundamentally in the fact that the "social ontology" of the economy can only be realised in physically concrete transaction processes.

> [M]oney has to exist in some physical form or other. [...] Most money is now in the form of magnetic traces on computer disks. It does not matter what the form is as long as it can function as money, but money must come in some physical form or other. [...] [T]here must be some physical realization. [...] Institutional facts exist, so to speak, on top of brute physical facts.[39]

Thus, on the one hand, Commons' transaction is characterised in two respects by "social ontology", i.e. institutional rules, namely in its *economic* and in its *legal* dimension. But on the other hand, these two social-ontological codes only

---

[34] "There are at least two different senses of the objective/subjective distinction: an epistemic sense and an ontological sense. The epistemic sense has to do with knowledge. The ontological sense has to do with existence." (Searle, 2010/2011, p. 18).

[35] Searle (1995), p. 57.

[36] Searle (1995), p. xi.

[37] "[A]part from things that are actual, there is nothing—nothing either in fact or in efficacy. [...] This general principle will be termed the 'ontological principle.' [...] The ontological principle declares that [...] in separation from actual entities there is nothing, merely nonentity—'The rest is silence". (Whitehead, 1929/1979, p. 40 & 43).

[38] Searle basically assumes that this one world is characterised by certain "basic facts", namely the physical facts which are investigated by natural sciences (cf. Searle, 2010/2011, p. 4). This is the "basic ontology" (Searle, 2010/2011, p. 108). Hence its "basic requirement" that—in *one* world—everything must also be related to the "basic facts" or "basic ontology". So, "social ontology" must also be connected with "basic ontology"—in my terminology: with "natural ontology": "On the conception of basic ontology [...] it should be impossible for anything in the real world not to be grounded in the basic facts [...]. Money, corporations, and blindfold chess cannot just float on thin air". (Searle, 2010/2011, pp. 108 f.).

[39] Searle (1995), p. 34 f.

gain actuality in the concrete *transaction*. And that is why Commons made the *transaction* the basic "unit of investigation in economics".[40]

3 Reductive" or "Reductionist? An Important Methodological Difference for Microanalytical Approaches

The "basic idea" of Josef Wieland 's Governance Ethics and his Relational Economics is the hypothesis that all the problems of Economics and Business Ethics "can be described microanalytically as the immanent [...] dimension[s] of distinct economic transactions".[41] In order not to misconceive this microanalytical theory strategy that links Wieland with Commons as well as Whitehead (and myself), it is important to remember a terminological distinction: Wieland's microanalytical approach is "reductive" but not "reductionist".

This useful distinction was proposed by the philosopher Thomas Nagel. Usually, only the term "reductionist" is used to describe the methodical approach of the sciences. A well-known plea for a strictly "reductionist" methodology is made by the physicist and Nobel Prize winner Steven Weinberg in the chapter "Two Cheers for Reductionism" of his book Dreams of a Final Theory[42]:

> [O]ne common feature of everyone's idea of reductionism is a sense of hierarchy, that some truths are less fundamental than others to which they may be reduced, as chemistry may be reduced to physics.[43]

Human beings are less fundamental than biology, biology is less fundamental than chemistry, and chemistry is less fundamental than physics. So, in the end, everything is reducible to physics. The "reductionist" method is a "nothing but ..." approach: there may be many different things, but at the end of the day all things that exist, all our lives are nothing but physical particles thrown together:

> The reason we give the impression that we think that elementary particle physics is more fundamental than other branches of physics is because it is.[44]

---

[40] Commons (1950/1956), p. 52.

[41] Wieland (2014), p. 15. "The basic idea of Governance Ethics is the consideration that all of the questions discussed nowadays in regard to the role and performative capacity of the economy in the realization of the moral claims and concepts of a society and, vice versa, of ethics in economic and entrepreneurial transactions can be described microanalytically as the immanent moral dimension of distinct eco-nomic transactions." (Wieland, 2014, p. 15) "In [...] Relational Economics, [...] transactions [...] *sui generis* have a normative, legal, political, moral and sundry other dimensions." (Wieland, 2018/2020, p. 85).

[42] Weinberg (1992/1993), p. 51–64.

[43] Weinberg (1992/1993), p. 51.

[44] Weinberg (1992/1993), p. 55.

This may seem bleak to many people, but, according to Weinberg, it is simply the scientific truth:

> The reductionist worldview is chilling and impersonal. It has to be accepted as it is, not because we like it, but because that is the way the world works.[45]

The "reductionist" method and worldview is best summarised in the following quotation from Weinberg:

> All the explanatory arrows point downward, from societies to people, to organs, to cells, to biochemistry, to chemistry, and ultimately to physics.[46]

Now, Thomas Nagel makes an important differentiation: he distinguishes this "reductionist" approach from a conception which he calls "reductive":

> I will use 'reductive' as the general term for theories that analyze the properties of complex wholes into the properties of their most basic elements. I will continue to use 'reductionist' for the more specific type of reductive theory that analyzes higher-level phenomena exclusively in terms of physical elements and their physical properties. […] The point to keep in mind is that it is possible for an antireductionist theory to be reductive, provided that the elements to which it reduces higher-level phenomena are not exclusively physical. That is the kind of reductive theory I am talking about here.[47]

A "*reductive*" approach is, therefore, one that proceeds *micro*analytically and assumes that our entire concrete reality is built up from basic units—in physics, for example, from elementary particles or elementary events, in economics from transactions. Such a "reductive" approach can also be "reductionist": Weinberg's physical reductionism, for example, claims that these basic units are ultimately "nothing more than" physical entities and thus all the realities of the cosmos of purely physical nature. And an economistic reductionism declares these basic units of the economy, the transactions, to be "nothing else than" economic processes, that is, they are of a purely economic nature. An example of such an economistic reductionism is the theory of Oliver Williamson already mentioned. But there are also, as Nagel points out, "reductive" theories which are at the same time "*antireductionist*" and do not claim that the basic units are exclusively monodimensional. The economic conceptions of John R. Commons, of Josef Wieland, of myself and also—as we will see in a moment—the cosmological metaphysics of Alfred North Whitehead are such theories, which are "reductive" but not "reductionist". They rather assume that the ultimate units are polydimensional in nature.

In the following two sections, I would like to introduce the two "reductive", but not "reductionist" conceptions most important for my subject, namely the cosmology of Alfred North Whitehead on the one hand and the economics of John R. Commons on

---

[45] Weinberg (1992/1993), p. 53.

[46] I could not find this "quote", which is attributed to Steven Weinberg in numerous publications, in the writings of Weinberg. So, I e-mailed him, and an hour later he answered: "No, I never said the sentence you quote, and I have no idea where it comes from. This is not an uncommon occurrence. Some of the best quotes of me are things I never said. Best, Steven Weinberg " (e-mail October 08, 2019).

[47] Nagel (2012), p. 54, fn. 14.

Table 1 Whitehead's Metaphysics and Commons' Economics

Whitehead's cosmology	Commons' economics
"Creativity"	"Activity"
"Reductive"	
"Event" ("actual occasion" ...)	"Transaction"
"Society" (existing in its occasions) with "defining characteristic"	"Going concern" ("existing in its transactions") with "working rules"
Not "reductionist"	
Polydimensionality of "events" ("physical and mental poles")	Polydimensionality of "transactions" ("law, economics and ethics")

the other. The cosmology of Whitehead is relevant to Commons' economics because economic transactions are also events in this cosmos and therefore the way the world (the cosmos) works determines how the transactions of the economy are working. The relationships are summarised in the following table (Table 1).

4 Cosmological Process Metaphysics. Alfred North Whitehead

Alfred North Whitehead (*1861; †1947) was a British mathematician and physicist who, at the age of 63, accepted a chair of Philosophy at Harvard University (Cambridge, USA) and wrote several metaphysical works there, including his major work Process and Reality.[48] Because Whitehead called his cosmology a "metaphysical" one, then, against the usual misunderstandings, it should be pointed out that metaphysics here has nothing to do with absurd speculations, such as how many angels fit on the tip of a needle. Rather, Whitehead understood his "metaphysics" in the strict sense of philosophy of science, namely as the philosophical endeavour of finding out "how the world works (in general)"[49]:

[48] Whitehead's books are not easy to understand. For example, the then young student James Wilkinson Miller (documented in: Lowe, 1990, p. 142) reports on Whitehead's first lecture in the USA: "the opening lecture plunged us into a morass of absolutely unintelligible metaphysics". About the "Gifford Lectures" which Whitehead held in Edinburgh (Scotland) in 1928 and which then became the basis of his major work *Process and Reality*, one of the visitors, a Dr. J. M. Whittaker, reports that due to the very successful previous Gifford Lectures offered by the physicist Arthur Stanley Eddington, many people came to Whitehead's first lecture: "Eddington [...] was a marvellous popular lecturer who had enthralled an audience of 600 for his entire course. The same audience turned up to Whitehead's first lecture but it was completely unintelligible [...]. The audience at subsequent lectures was only about half a dozen in all, so I am told, for I fear that I myself was one of the backsliders". (cit. Lowe, 1990, p. 250). There is even a rumour that in the end there were only two listeners left (cf. Lowe, 1990, p. 250).

[49] This wording ("how the world works") is not Whitehead's, but Alan Greenspan's, who used it to explain the term "ideology": "Well, remember that what an ideology is. It's a conceptual framework

> By 'metaphysics' I mean the science which seeks to discover the general ideas which are indispensably relevant to the analysis of everything that happens.[50]

It was chiefly with his main work Process and Reality that Alfred North Whitehead presented a cosmological metaphysics which he himself has mostly called a "Philosophy of Organism" but which has now become better known as "Process Philosophy". And it's a good term, because the idea of "process" is indeed central to Whitehead:

> '[P]rocess' is the fundamental idea.[51] So, a most important metaphysical [...] principle is that the very essence of real actuality—that is of the completely real—is process. [...] There is no halt.[52]

But the systematically even more ultimate term in Whitehead's cosmology is "*creativity*". As quantum physics views energy as the raw material of the universe and elementary particles as concrete embodiments of this energy, so does Whitehead's metaphysics describe the universal basic character of the world with the term

---

with the way people deal with reality. Everyone has one. […] To exist, you need an ideology. The question is whether it is accurate or not. And what I'm saying to you is, yes, I've found a flaw […] in the model that I perceived is the critical functioning structure that defines how the world works, so to speak." (Greenspan in 2008, see, for example, https://www.pbs.org/newshour/show/greenspan-admits-flaw-to-congress-predicts-more-economic-problems). If we replace Greenspan's ambiguous term "ideology" with the term "*metaphysics*", we can firstly say that "metaphysics" focuses on the conceptual frameworks with which we *generally* deal with reality. "Metaphysics" turns on the question of how the world works *in general*—whereas the different fields of science deal with the question of how the world works *in detail*. Secondly, we are faced with the fact that metaphysics is *inevitable* ("everyone has one"). And thirdly, we always have to ask if the metaphysical worldview in question is reasonable or "*accurate*", that is, if it is really problem-solving. In Karl R. Popper's Philosophy of Science the status of metaphysical theories is further clarified. He distinguished between three types of theory: "*First*, logical and mathematical theories. *Second*, empirical and scientific theories. *Third*, philosophical or metaphysical theories". (Popper, 1963/1985, p. 197) It is the empirical falsifiability which distinguishes scientific theories (natural sciences) from metaphysical theories: "According to this view […] a system is to be considered as scientific only if it makes assertions which may clash with observations" (Popper, 1963/1985, p. 256). While the theories of the sciences are, therefore, empirically falsifiable, it is the characteristic of metaphysical theories that they are not falsifiable empirically: "[N]on-testable theories […] may be described as metaphysical." (Popper, 1963/1985, p. 257) But that does not mean that they are senseless or useless. Quite contrary to any positivistic rejection of metaphysical statements, Popper considers them as very important: "But metaphysical hypotheses are important for science in at least two ways. First of all, in order to have a general picture of the world we need metaphysical hypotheses. Secondly, in the actual preparation of our research we are guided by what I have called 'metaphysical research programmes'". (Popper in: Popper/Eccles 1977/2003, p. 442).

[50] Whitehead (1926/2007), p. 84.

[51] Whitehead (1919/1925/2011), p. 202. Cf. Whitehead (1926/2007), p. 112; Whitehead (1929/1979), p. 22; Whitehead (1936/1968), p. 140.

[52] Whitehead (1933/1967), p. 274.

"creativity" [53] (which was presumably coined by himself![54]). With this term, Whitehead is aiming to express the fact that we live in a universe of activity and precisely not in a universe of the dead and passive matter:

> 'Creativity' is [...] divested of the notion of passive receptivity [...]; it is the pure notion of the activity [...]. It is that ultimate notion of the highest generality at the base of actuality.[55]

Due to this creative basic character of reality/ies things are made fluid and become dynamic in an evolutionary way: everything is in flow (cf. Heraklits πάντα ῥεῖ = "everything flows"). New things are "born", grow and decay again.

4.1 *"Reductive". A Cosmos of Relational Events*

(1) "*Events*". With reference to quantum physics, Whitehead initially assumes, micro-analytically, the existence of many realities which are linked in processual relativity, and energetic process-droplets that he calls "*events*", "*actual entities*", or "*actual* occasions":

> This epoch is characterized by electronic and protonic actual entities, and by yet more ultimate actual entities which can be dimly discerned in the quanta of energy.[56]

In terms of *metaphysics*, it is important, at this point, that the universe is made up of entities that have the character of *process droplets* that are *genetically relative* and exist in a *minute temporal period* (maybe on billionth of a second).

> 'Actual entities'—also termed 'actual occasions'—are the final real things of which the world is made up.[57]

These "events" or "occasions" are also the basic units of the, thus, the micro-analytical conception of Whitehead's "Process Philosophy".[58]

---

[53] The completely elementary and foundational meaning of the term "creativity" in Whitehead's metaphysics can already be seen by the fact that he calls "creativity" "the ultimate" (Whitehead, 1929/1979, p. 20), the "universal of universals characterizing ultimate matter of fact" (Whitehead, 1929/1979, p. 21), the "ultimate principle" (Whitehead, 1929/1979, p. 21) or "that ultimate notion of the highest generality at the base of actuality" (Whitehead, 1929/1979, p. 31).

[54] Ford (1987), p. 179, wrote: "Alfred North Whitehead introduced the term 'creativity' [...] He appears to have coined this neologism". Meyer (2005), p. 2, also said: "Whitehead did invent 'creativity'".

[55] Whitehead (1929/1979), p. 31.

[56] Whitehead (1929/1979), p. 91. In his earlier books on natural philosophy he calls the basic units of the universe "events": "The fundamental assumption to be elaborated in the course of this enquiry is that the ultimate facts of nature [...] are events" (Whitehead, 1919/1925/2011, p. 4). Space and time are built out of them: "Time and space [...] express relations between events" (ibid., p. 61). In his later metaphysical works he usually used the terms "actual entities" or "actual occasions".

[57] Whitehead (1929/1979), p. 18.

[58] "*How* an actual entity *becomes* constitutes *what* that actual entity *is* [...]. Its 'being' is constituted by its 'becoming'. This is the 'principle of process'" (Whitehead, 1929/1979, p. 23).

(2) "*Societies*". At the *micro*-level, the universe consists, according to Whitehead, of such process droplets ("events", "occasions"), while all bigger formations—such as atoms, water drops, ants, stones, trees, people or plants—are more lasting things. These things consist of "actual occasions" which, in a manner of speaking, "cooperate" more closely and, in this, achieve a *certain stability* of the structure. Whitehead calls these more complex and more lasting things of this world at the *macro-cosmic* level "*societies*":

> The real actual things that endure are all societies. They are not actual occasions.[59]

"Societies" are, accordingly, *complex* structures. As (contingently) separate complexes of "events" they depend on a shared characteristic which then defines them as a "society" belonging to each other and which differentiates them from other "societies". Whitehead calls this element of identity, which is common to all elements of a "society" a "*defining characteristic*":

> A society has an essential character, whereby it is the society that it is.[60] The common form is the ‚defining characteristic' of the society.[61] The self-identity of a society is founded upon the self-identity of its defining characteristic, and upon the mutual immanence of its occasions.[62]

Whitehead's "societies" are, in any case, "organic" forms which (have to) reproduce their "defining characteristic" every day in an evolutionary "life"-process. A "society" is existing in its occasions.

I do not want to expand on the system of "societies" at this point, but I do want to point out, in advance, that organisations—such as business enterprises—can be imagined, metaphysically, as "societies". (The German word for stock corporation—"*Aktiengesellschaft*" = "society of shareholders", is telling.).

In Whitehead's cosmology all things—the "actual occasions" at the micro-level, the "societies" on the meso-level, and finally the universe on the macro level—are seen as dynamic "organisms":

> Science is [...] becoming the study of organisms. Biology is the study of the larger organisms; whereas physics is the study of the smaller organisms.[63]

The "final real things of which the world is made up" are not "particles", not dead billiard balls, but "waves". Nothing in nature is like a static machine. Even the whole universe is "growing". And all things within the universe are growing, changing their form, ageing, dying … So, consequently, Whitehead explicitly called his metaphysical concept the "Philosophy of Organism".[64] Actuality is an "organic" fabric or network of myriads of events. The philosopher Ludwig Wittgenstein suggested—in

[59] Whitehead (1933/1967), p. 204.

[60] Whitehead (1933/1967), p. 204.

[61] Whitehead (1929/1979), p. 34.

[62] Whitehead (1933/1967), p. 204.

[63] Whitehead (1925/1967), p. 103.

[64] e.g., Whitehead (1929/1979), p. xi. 7. 18 and so on.

Fig. 1 Ludwig Wittgenstein's "*thread*" and "*fibres*"

a completely different context—a metaphor that expresses this organic "spinning" of the truth quite well (Fig. 1):

> ... as in spinning a thread we twist fibre on fibre. And the strength of the thread resides not in the fact that some one fibre runs through its whole length, but in the overlapping of many fibres.[65]

.

So, just like the "thread" develops out of the "spinning" and the "overlapping of many fibres" in an evolutionary way, the thread of a human life is also spun from a vast number of individual events. The thread of life has to *reproduce* itself with every new day. The continuing, ongoing spinning represents, in this, the distinctive *identity* of this person from their conception to their death, in which, however, nothing remains the same "sub-stantially" but where this human being—this human "society" of "actual occasions"—continually changes over the course of his life, gains experiences, starts turning grey, and at some point this human "society" dissolves. All things in the universe have the same "organic" character—from the atom to the business enterprise, and also a galaxy.

4.2 Not "Reductionist". Not Everything in the Physical Cosmos is Physical

Whitehead's theory is "reductive"—the "societies" are existing in their "events"—but not "reductionist". Within the framework of his cosmology, this antireductionist character is particularly evident in his rejection of the view that everything in the physical cosmos ultimately has a purely physical nature (this was Weinberg's thesis, as reported). Coming from mathematical physics, Whitehead, as a philosophical

---

[65] Wittgenstein (1953/2009), p. 36 (§ 67). Interestingly, there is a quite similar passage in John R. Commons: "Of course, [...] we mean not a substance nor entity, but a principle of similarity running through all the changing parts" (1934/2009, p. 620).

metaphysician, developed a cosmology that also claimed the mental as a fundamental characteristic of all things. This must be explained briefly.

When we look at the world, we see that there are some "societies" that do have something very interesting that other "societies" do not have: namely mind or even consciousness. Obviously, one has to distinguish (at least) two different types of "societies"[66]:

- On the one hand, there are "societies", which are mere aggregates, like stones or clouds (in process philosophy they are called mere "aggregational societies");
- However, on the other hand, there are those "societies" that incorporate a complex structure, namely, a central nervous system (with a brain) that allows for mind and consciousness (process philosophy here speaks of "compound individuals").

And so, a metaphysical question arises: what has to be the nature of these elementary "actual occasions"—of those "final real things of which the world is made up"—, so that mind or consciousness can arise (given the required structuring of a "compound individual": central nervous system, brain)?

And the answer Whitehead's cosmological metaphysics gives to this question is the following: beyond their physical nature the elementary "building blocks" of the universe ("actual occasions") must have a kind of mental nature, a "potential for mentality" or a kind of "protomentality". The emergence of the mind from completely mindless matter would be nothing but magic, nothing but a miracle![67] So, Whitehead declares that the elementary "building blocks" of the world must be ontologically polydimensional (physical and "mental"):

> Thus an actual entity is essentially dipolar, with its physical and mental poles.[68] Each actuality is essentially bipolar, physical and mental.[69]

This polydimensionality does "not necessarily involve consciousness".[70] On the level of the elementary particles, it is merely a "mental" potential.

Whitehead called his metaphysical hypothesis, that there is a kind of "protomentality" all the way down, the "*reformed subjectivist principle*",[71] because "actual occasions" which have a kind of "protomentality" are also something like "subjects"

---

[66] See Hartshorne (1936/1967).

[67] "Why aren't we zombies? I think the answer lies in the nature of the building blocks of organisms. If science acknowledges human experience at all, it must ask from what it has evolved. If it is acknowledged that it has evolved from animal experience, the question is pushed further back. At some point, does experience, mentality, or subjectivity emerge from entities that are totally lacking in these properties, entities that are simply objects for other subjects? If the basic constituents of the physical world are purely material, then the answer must be yes. But to believe this is to affirm a miracle. Unless you believe in miracles, you would expect mindless atoms to evolve into zombies. But this does not seem to happen. Griffin provides cogent and detailed arguments against the common view that mentality evolves from that which has no mentality at all" (Birch, 2008, p. 253).

[68] Whitehead (1929/1979), p. 239.

[69] Whitehead (1929/1979), p. 108.

[70] Whitehead (1929/1979), p. 239.

[71] See Whitehead (1929/1979), pp. 79–80, 157, 160, 167, 189, 196–197.

or "agents". Physicist Freeman Dyson answers the question about empirical evidence for (a rudimentary form of) "mind" in an elementary particle as follows:

> Well, simply that it seems to make choices. […] So the atom seems to have a freedom to choose. That's something which characterizes quantum processes […] It's spontaneous that to my mind implies that the thing makes a choice. […] This freedom that the individual atom has to have […] seems to be an indication of some rudimentary form of mind.[72] Matter in quantum mechanics is not an inert substance but an active agent, constantly making choices between alternative possibilities according to probabilistic laws. [...] It appears that mind, as manifested by the capacity to make choices, is to some extent inherent in every electron.[73]

And maybe our brain is a kind of amplifier that is using this rudimentary form of mind to produce full-fledged conscious agency. In contemporary philosophy, this metaphysical hypothesis is called "panpsychism" (πᾶν = everything + ψυχή = mind).[74]

5 Transaction Economics. John R. Commons

"Metaphysics" is concerned with the question of how the world works in general whereas the natural sciences are dealing with the question of how the world works in detail. If we transfer this approach to human society and especially to economy, it is possible to say the following. "Business Metaphysics" is concerned with the question of "how the business world works in general",[75] whereas the specialised discipline of economics is dealing with the question of how the business world works *in detail.*

Nevertheless, specialised economics can also contain conceptual elements that are more or less *metaphysical.* For example, a discussion on the "essence" or the "nature of the firm" is actually such a metaphysical question.[76] An economist who gave such

[72] Robert Wright interviews Freeman Dyson, Complete Interview. Download: https://meaningoflife.tv/videos/40595 (time code: 13:09 min.) Similarly Bohm & Hiley (1993), P. 387: "Even an electron has at least a rudimentary mental pole, represented mathematically by the quantum potential".

[73] Dyson (1988/2004), p. 297. Whitehead usually uses the word "decision": "The word 'decision' does not here imply conscious judgment […]. But 'decision' cannot be construed as a casual adjunct of an actual entity. It constitutes the very meaning of actuality. An actual entity arises from decisions *for* it, and by its very existence provides decisions *for* other actual entities which supersede it" (Whitehead, 1929/1979, p. 43).

[74] Here are some advocates of this "crazy" idea of panpsychism: Charles S. Peirce, John Dewey, William James, Ernst Haeckel, Henri Bergson, Bertrand Russell, Arthur Eddington, Carl Gustav Jung, Alfred North Whitehead, Pierre Teilhard de Chardin, Freeman Dyson, Roger Penrose, Bernard Haisch, Rupert Sheldrake, Thomas Nagel, David Chalmers, Galen Strawson, Giulio Tononi, Christof Koch and Gregory Matloff. On the subject of "panpsychism" see my own documentation: https://www.youtube.com/watch?v=6Uy5-mOGgC8.

[75] See Schramm (2016); Schramm (2017); Schramm (2019); Wagner (2019).

[76] The phrase "The Nature of the Firm" immediately brings to mind the essay by Ronald H. Coase from 1937 (Coase 1937). Despite the title, the problem Coase set himself in this famous essay was

metaphysical questions a relatively large space in his work was the aforementioned John Rogers Commons (*1862; †1945). For example, his answer to the question of the "nature of the firm" reveals a "*reductive*" and thus *metaphysical* concept:

> [A] corporation [...] became an economic going concern existing in its transactions.[77]

As Commons has conceived the transactions in a *poly*dimensional way ("correlating law, economics, and ethics"), his "Business Metaphysics" is not only "reductive" but also anti- "reductionist"—similar to the metaphysics of Whitehead, which he has cited in agreement several times. In the same way that I have used Alfred North Whitehead as an example to affix the idea of an appropriate "Metaphysics", it is also possible, in my opinion, to use John R. Commons as an example for an appropriate "Business Metaphysics".[78] This is matched by the fact that Commons like Whitehead placed concrete events at the centre of the analysis from the outset. At the core of Commons 's conception is the question about "the ultimate unit of activity".[79] As, with Whitehead, the universal fundamental character of the world is described by the term "creativity ", so Commons calls—metaphorically speaking—the fundamental "stuff" of which the business world is made up "activity".

> Economics should be a science of activity.[80] Economics is a science of activity.[81]

What *really* happens in business are forms of this (business) *activity*. Commons is not about some equilibrium model—quite the opposite: it is about the economic *activities*, the economic *events*, the *transactions*.

5.1 "Reductive". An Economy of Relational Transactions

Commons represented a *microanalytical* approach that sought an "ultimate unit of activity". From the outset, Commons' conception is thus reductive in nature.

---

not the *metaphysical* question concerning the "nature of the firm" as opposed to the "nature of the market". Rather, he was concerned with a purely *economic* explanation for the existence of firms in the context of a market economy. And his explanation relies on the quantitative level of "transaction costs"! Posing this question, however, he clearly started from the premise that the qualitative nature of the firm is ontologically identical to the nature of the market and that the "language" used in both cases is that of transaction *costs*.

[77] Commons (1934/2009), p. 53 (emphasis mine). The historical background with Commons is a reform of the way companies were valued in the eyes of the (tax) law in 1893 in Indiana, which is, however, not particularly relevant for our context.

[78] What Ronald H. Coase said about the older institutional economics does not, in my opinion, apply to Commons: "The American institutionalists were not theoretical but anti-theoretical, particularly where classical economic theory was concerned. Without a theory they had nothing to pass on" (1984, p. 230). This derogatory judgment is not only "too harshly" (Williamson 1996a, p. 251, fn. 2), but simply wrong.

[79] Commons (1934/2009), p. 58 (emphasis mine).

[80] Commons (1950/1956), p. 34.

[81] Commons (1950/1956), p. 203.

(1) "*Transactions*". Already in the first of his three major works, i.e. in the *Legal Foundations of Capitalism* from 1924, Commons defined the transaction as the basic unit of economics:

> A transaction [...] is the ultimate unit of economics, ethics and law.[82]

Just like Whitehead metaphysically sees "actual occasions" ("events", "actual entities") as concrete occurrences of "creativity", so the "transactions" function, with Commons, as microanalytical concrete occurrences of "activity":

> I made the transaction the ultimate unit of economic investigation.[83] Thus the ultimate unit of activity [...] is a Transaction. A transaction [...] is the smallest unit of institutional economics.[84]

In this, he makes explicit references to the metaphysics of Whitehead:

> These [...] transactions are to economics what Whitehead's [...] ‚event[s]' are to physics.[85]

For his own theoretical decision to start from the transactions in a microanalytical way, Commons explicitly refers to the cosmology of Alfred North Whitehead. However, Whitehead was not the cause of his theory decision—which was already made in 1924[86]—but a metaphysical confirmation of his theory strategy. Commons' "transactions" function, accordingly, like Whitehead's "actual occasions". Because of this, it is possible to also describe Commons' position by paraphrasing a Whitehead quote: "Transactions" are the final real things of which the world of economy is made up.[87] What is metaphysically meaningful in this is that, in the world of economics, it is only these transactions that are real. Economic actors exist economically only in their transactions, regardless of whether they are individual (manager, consumers) or corporate economic actors (companies).

> Thus the unit of investigation in economics is not an individual, it is a transaction.[88] I make transactions the units of economic science.[89]

---

[82] Commons (1924/2012), p. 68. To refrain from this polydimensionality means to think "abstract" (Commons 1924/2012, p. 387).

[83] Commons (1934/2009), p. 4.

[84] Commons (1934/2009), p. 58 (emphasis mine).

[85] Commons (1934/2009), p. 96. That Commons takes a *metaphysical* strategic decision with using this micro-analytical foundation of his economic of institutes can be seen in the numerous parallels he draws in his economics to physics, chemistry, biology and astronomy (cf. Commons 1934/2009, p. 55). Because we live precisely in *one* and only in one real universe, Commons is able to word his basis for a *metaphysical* conceptualisation, "how the *economic* world works (in general)", in analogy to Whitehead's cosmological concept of metaphysics, "how the *physical* world works (in general)".

[86] Whitehead did not publish metaphysical books until 1925.

[87] See Whitehead (1929/1979), p. 18.

[88] Commons (1950/1956), p. 52.

[89] Commons (1950/1956), p. 57.

In the same way, economic "laws" or "game rules" only *concretely* exists in corresponding transactions which give life to these "laws". This is because these "laws" or "game rules" remain *abstract* precisely until they reproduce in *concrete* transactions, "become incarnate", become concrete. He put this point into quite philosophical terms:

> The actual is always acting. [...] Not-acting is nothing.[90]

(2) "*Going Concerns*". Just like Whitehead differentiates between "events" ("actual occasions") on the one hand and "societies" (as "cooperations" or "cooperations" of "events") on the other, so the concept of John R. Commons has, on the one hand, the "transaction" and on the other that which he calls a "going concern".[91] In this, too, he explicitly follows Whitehead:

> These going concerns and transactions are to economics what Whitehead's 'organic mechanism' [later called: "society"; M.S.[92]] and 'event' are to physics.[93] [T]ransactions [...] are functionally interdependent, and their interdependence constitutes the whole which, following American usage, we name a going concern. [...] This going concern is itself a larger unit, and is analogous to that which in biology is an 'organism,' or in physics a 'mechanism.' But its components are not living cells, nor electrons, nor atoms—they are transactions.[94]

Metaphysically decisive is, here, the theory's strategy to construct "going concern" in a way that only its actual (real) transaction has concrete existence:

> [W]e must perceive that the true unit of economic theory is not an individual but a going concern composed of individuals in their many transactions,[95] a going concern with its constituent transactions.[96] It is an economic going concern existing in its transactions.[97]

A further point that is conceptionally important is that the transactions that build up to a "going concern" need a shared characteristic that turns them into transactions of *this* "going concern". And like Whitehead's "societies" are marked by a "defining characteristic", so the "going concern" is, with Commons, *structured* by that which he calls "*working rules*":

---

[90] Commons (1924/2012), p. 70. The sentence could well be written by Whitehead, for whom the "actual entities" or "actual occasions" were the only real things.

[91] Commons also provides a German translation of the term „Going Concern ": "The German equivalent, *gutgehendes Geschäft*." (Commons 1934/2009, p. 69, fn. 102).

[92] In Whitehead (1925/1967, p. 106 f.) "organic mechanism" means "some larger, deeper, more complete pattern" in the sense of what in Whitehead (1929/1979) is then called "society".

[93] Commons (1934/2009), p. 96.

[94] Commons (1932/1996), p. 454.

[95] Commons (1932/1996), p. 335.

[96] Commons (1950/1956), p. 118.

[97] Commons (1934/2009), p. 53 (emphasis mine).

> A going concern is a joint expectation of beneficial bargaining, managerial and rationing transactions, kept together by 'working rules.' When the expectations cease, then the concern quits going.[98] It is these going concerns, with the working rules that keep them agoing.[99]

A "going concern" exists in the becoming and perishing of transactions that are "spinning" (Wittgenstein) a dynamic network or web as the concrete reality of the corporation.

> A transaction occurs at a point of time. But transactions flow one into another over a period of time, and this flow is a process. The courts have fully developed the notion of this process in the concept of a 'going concern' .[100]

Like Whitehead, Commons sees all "things" (transactions; "going concerns") as dynamic "*organisms*":

> Whitehead has observed that the Eighteenth Century method of science had no notion of the organic unity of the whole in a changing relation of the parts to the whole. [...] But the mechanism [of an 'organic unity' or an 'going concern'] itself is 'organic' in that it is a kind of prolonged interweaving of changing events [or 'transactions'], having, as Whitehead says, a past, a present realization, and a future life in its present events.[101]

This "organic" character shapes all sorts of things on earth. In the same way that human beings are born, grow, age, and die, so companies—Commons' "going concerns"—too, can be "born" (emerge), they can grow, they can shrink or "die". But there is a significant difference: while biological creatures have to die, companies *can* also die, but do *not have to*. In principle they can "live" forever:

> a corporation in one respect may even be said to have a higher status than the individual, for it may be endowed with that legal perpetuity which is pictured as 'immortality'.[102]

This "legal perpetuity" is an—in itself—abstract possibility of "social ontology"; in concrete terms, of course, the company only survives if it succeeds in reproducing itself in concrete transactions on and on:

> The "going [...] concern 'goes' as long as the participants earn a living or a profit through collective action; it may die by bankruptcy, be dissolved, or be absorbed [eaten] by another corporation. Individuals come and go, but the concern goes on, if not in one form, then in

---

[98] Commons (1932/1996), p. 454 (emphasis mine). "Thus the going concern may be looked upon as a person with a composite will, but this so-called 'will' is none other than the working rules of the concern operating through the actions and transactions of those who observe the rules" (Commons, 1924/2012, p. 147).

[99] Commons (1934/2009), p. 69.

[100] Commons (1924/2012), p. 7 f.

[101] Commons (1934/2009), p. 619 (emphasis mine). However, it must be acknowledged that Commons has come up with somewhat idiosyncratic distinctions between "mechanism", "machine" or "machinism" and "organism" (cf. Commons 1934/2009, p. 119. 635). However, he rejected the machine thinking ("machinism") of neoclassical economics just as Whitehead rejected the metaphysics of the machine in classical physics: "The main criticism to be directed against the economists and technicians is their mechanistic imitation of the physical sciences" (Commons, 1950/1956, p. 287).

[102] Commons (1924/2012), p. 144.

another. Hence our 'institutions' are, in reality, 'going concerns.' A going concern is an organization".[103]

Organisations are not "simply *legal fictions*",[104] they are not invisible legal entities existing only in contemplation of law, but "*economic going concern[s] existing in its transactions*".[105] Viewed as actualities, organisations are—to use Wittgenstein's metaphor cited above—"threads" existing in the ongoing "spinning" of "fibres" ("transactions").

5.2 Not "Reductionist". Not Everything in the Economy is Economic

Commons' theory is "reductive", but decidedly *not* "reductionist". From the beginning, the *poly*dimensionality of his transactions was even the decisive problem for him (the "Problem of Correlating Law, Economics and Ethics "), not the so-called "Commons Triple" ("conflict, mutuality, and order"), to which Williamson refers. This problem of how to deal with the *poly*dimensionality of the transaction was already explicitly mentioned in his Legal Foundations of Capitalism (1924):

> A transaction [...] is the ultimate unit of economics, ethics and law. It is the ultimate but complex relationship.[106]

Already here he speaks explicitly of the plural "dimensions" that characterise a transaction:

> Thus every transaction has its physical dimensions of performance, avoidance, forbearance; its economic dimensions of opportunity, power, economy and expectation; its psychological dimensions of thinking, feeling, willing, persuading, coercing, commanding, obeying and expectation, its ethical and legal dimensions of rights, duties, liberties, and exposures, and its political or governmental dimensions of authority and authorization in the use of physical power, economic or moral power, according to common rules or working rules that set the limits and directions of conduct.[107]

Each transaction is thus indeed characterised by a *polydimensionality*, although in subsequent years Commons has, for pragmatic reasons, limited this diversity of dimensions to the three dimensions of law, economics, and ethics:

> [T]he problem of correlating law, economics and ethics [...] is the problem of discovering a unit of activity common to them.[108]

---

[103] Commons (1950/1956), p. 34.
[104] Jensen/Meckling (1976), p. 310.
[105] Commons (1934/2009), p. 53 (emphasis mine).
[106] Commons (1924/2012), p. 68.
[107] Commons (1924/2012), p. 83.
[108] Commons (1932/1996), p. 453.

In any case, "economic transactions" are no purely economic occurrences. The in itself only abstract world of the code of the economic system ("to pay or not to pay") exclusively shows only the economic dimension, and thus has a *mono*dimensional character. This abstract *mono*dimensionality is precisely not applicable for concrete transactions, however.[109] The concrete "transactions" are "events ", in which (at least) three *mono*dimensional dimensions, which are in themselves abstract, come together and become *concrete* ("actual") in every distinct transaction.

> In fact, transactions have become the meeting place of economics, physics, psychology, ethics, jurisprudence and politics. A single transaction is a unit of observation which involves explicitly all of them.[110]

In the real economy, therefore, nothing is just economic.[111]

6 Outro

The concrete world of business is a network ("threads", "societies", "going concerns") evolving out of countless transactions ("fibres", "occasions") with a polydimensional nature. But this.

> concrete world has slipped through the meshes of the scientific net.[112]

Attentive representatives of the economic sciences are well aware of this. For example, with regard to the "theories of the firm", representatives of the field themselves attest to a "present lack of realism ".[113] This deficiency is the result of economic formalisation efforts. Therefore, Whitehead is probably right in assigning metaphysical philosophy the task of criticising abstractions alien to reality:

> Philosophy is the criticism of abstractions which govern special modes of thought.[114]

Sure, it is the nature of scientific theories to come up with models which are abstractions or simplifications of the "messy" reality. This serves the purpose of being able to take a more precise look at *certain* aspects of chaotic reality. Therein lies the usefulness of both a city map and a scientific theory. Nevertheless, the map is not the landscape. So, Whitehead's "simple" message is:

> Seek simplicity and distrust it.[115]

---

[109] The "metaphysical complexity" of such a simple event like a payment is described by Searle (1995), p. 3 f.

[110] Commons (1924/2012), p. 5.

[111] "Wir argumentieren daher ontologisch [...]. Nicht alles in der Ökonomie ist ökonomisch." (Wieland, 1999, S. 63). Translated: "We therefore argue ontologically [...]. Not everything in the economy is economic".

[112] Whitehead (1936/1968), p. 18.

[113] Foss/Lando/Thomsen (2000), p. 646.

[114] Whitehead (1936/1968), p. 48 f.

[115] Whitehead (1920/1982), p. 163.

References

Bannenberg, B./Schaupensteiner, W. (2004/2007): Korruption in Deutschland. Portrait einer Wachstumsbranche, 3. Aufl., München: Beck.

Birch, Charles (2008): Why Aren't We Zombies? Neo-Darwinism and Process Thought, in Cobb, John B. (Ed.): Back to Darwin. A Richer Account of Evolution, Grand Rapids (Michigan):/Cambridge (U.K.): William B. Eerdmans Publishing Company, pp. 250–262.

Bohm, D., & Hiley, B. J. (1993). *The Undivided Universe.* Routledge.

Coase, R. H. (1937). The Nature of the Firm. *Economica, 4*, 386–405.

Coase, Ronald H. (1984): The New Institutional Economics, in: Zeitschrift für die gesamte Staatswissenschaft/Journal of Institutional and Theoretical Economics 140 (No. 1, March), pp. 229–231.

Commons, John R. (1924, 2012): Legal Foundations of Capitalism, Clark, New Jersey: The Lawbook Exchange.

Commons, John R. (1932/1996): The Problem of Correlating Law, Economics, and Ethics, in Selected Essays. Volume Two (ed. by Rutherford, Malcolm & Samuels, Warren J.), London Routledge, pp. 453–473. Original: Commons, John R. (1932): The Problem of Correlating Law, Economics, and Ethics, in: Wisconsin Law Review 8 (1932), pp. 3–26.

Commons, John R. (1934/2009): Institutional Economics. Its Place in Political Economy, Volume 1 & 2, 3rd Printing, New Brunswick/London: Transaction Publishers.

Commons, J. R. (1950). */ 1956): The Economics of Collective Action.* Macmillan.

Dennett, Daniel C. (1991): Consciousness Explained, New York/Boston/London: Little, Brown and Company.

Dyson, F. (1988). */ 2004): Infinite in all Directions (Gifford Lectures, given at Aberdeen.* HarperCollins.

Einstein, A. (1917). */ 2009): Über die spezielle und die allgemeine Relativitätstheorie* (24th ed.). Springer.

Ford, L. S. (1987). Creativity in a Future Key. In R. C. Neville (Ed.), *New Essays in Metaphysics* (pp. 179–197). State University of New York Press.

Foss, Nicolai J. & Lando, Henrik & Thomsen, Steen (2000): The Theory of the Firm, in: Bouckaert, Boudewijn & De Geest, Gerrit (Ed.): Encyclopedia of Law and Economics, Vol. III, Cheltenham U.K.: Edward Elgar Publishing, pp. 631–658.

Greene, Brian (2011). The Hidden Reality. Parallel Universes and the Deep Laws of the Cosmos, New York Vintage / Random House.

Greene, Brian (2020). Until the End of Time. Mind, Matter, and Our Search for Meaning in an Evolving Universe, New York: Alfred A. Knopf.

Harari, Yuval Noah (2015/2018): Homo Deus. A Brief History of Tomorrow, New York: HarperCollins (Harper Perennial).

Hartshorne, Charles (1936/1967): The Compound Individual, in Northrup, F.S.C. (1936/1967; Ed.): Philosophical Essays for Alfred North Whitehead, New York Russell & Russell, pp. 193–220. Also published in: Hartshorne, Charles (1972): Whitehead's Philosophy. Selected Essays 1935–1970, Lincoln University of Nebraska Press, pp. 41–46.

Jensen, M. C., & Meckling, W. H. (1976). Theory of the Firm Managerial Behaviour, Agency Costs and Ownership Structure. *Journal of Financial Economics, 3*, 305–360.

Krugman, Paul (2009): How Did Economists Get It So Wrong?, in The New York Times Magazine (Sept. 2, 2009). Download: https://www.nytimes.com/2009/09/06/magazine/06Economic-t.html

Lowe, Victor (1990): Alfred North Whitehead: The Man and His Work. Volume II: 1910–1947 (edited by J. B. Schneewind), Baltimore & London. John Hopkins University Press.

Meyer, Steven (2005): Introduction, in Meyer, Steven/Wilson, Elizabeth (Ed.): Whitehead Now, Configurations Volume 13, Number 1, Winter 2005 (Special Issue), pp. 1–33.

Nagel, Thomas (2012): Mind and Cosmos. Why the Materialist Neo-Darwinian Conception of Nature Is Almost Certainly False, Oxford: Oxford University Press.

Popper, K., & , Eccles, John C. (1977). */ 2003): The Self and Its Brain.* Routledge.

Popper, Karl R. (1963/1985): Conjectures and Refutations. The Growth of Scientific Knowledge, 4. Ed., London/Henley: Routledge and Kegan Paul.

Schramm, M. (2016). Wie funktioniert die Geschäftswelt wirklich? *Business Metaphysics Und Theorie Der Firma, in: Ethica, 24*(4/2016), 311–360.

Schramm, Michael (2017): How the (Business) World Really Works. Business Metaphysics & "Creating Shared Value", in: Wieland, Josef (Ed.): Creating Shared Value—Concepts, Experience, Criticism (Ethical Economy. Studies in Economic Ethics and Philosophy, Volume 52), Cham/Heidelberg/New York/Dordrecht/London: Springer, pp. 81–117.

Schramm, Michael (2019): Business Metaphysics und SustainAbility. Wie ein nachhaltiges Transaktionsmanagement generell funktioniert, in: Arnold, Christian & Keppler, Sonja & Knödler, Hermann & Reckenfelderbäumer, Martin (Hg.): Herausforderungen für das Nachhaltigkeitsmanagement. Globalisierung—Digitalisierung—Geschäftsmodelltransformation, Wiesbaden: Springer Gabler, S. 73–95.

Searle, J. R. (1995). *The Construction of Social Reality*. The Free Press.

Searle, J. R. (1998). */ 1999): Mind*. Basic Books.

Searle, J. R. (2010). */ 2011): Making the Social World*. Oxford University Press.

Thaler, Richard H. (2010): Conversations with History: Behavioral Economics (Richard H. Thaler interviewed by Harry Kreisler). Download: http://www.youtube.com/watch?v=4OdP3IADUVc

Thomasson, Amie L. (2015) Ontology Made Easy, Oxford New York Oxford University Press.

Urbich, Jan & Zimmer, Jörg (2020, Hg.): Handbuch Ontologie, Berlin: J. B. Metzler.

Wagner, C. (2019). *Managementethik und Arbeitsplätze*. Springer.

Weinberg, S. (1992). */ 1993): Dreams of a Final Theory*. Vintage Books.

Whitehead, A. N. (1919). */1925/2011): An Enquiry Concerning the Principles of Natural Knowledge, Paperback edition 2011 of the 2nd edition 1925*. Cambridge University Press.

Whitehead, A. N. (1920). */ 1982): The Concept of Nature (The Tarner Lectures Delivered in Trinity College November 1919)*. Cambridge University Press.

Whitehead, A. N. (1925). */ 1967): Science and the Modern World (Lowell Lectures 1925)*. The Free Press.

Whitehead, Alfred North (1926/2007): Religion in the Making. Lowell Lectures, 1926, 5th Printing, New York: Fordham University Press.

Whitehead, Alfred North (1929/1979): Process and Reality. An Essay in Cosmology. Gifford Lectures Delivered in the University of Edinburgh During the Session 1927–28 (Corrected Edition, ed. by D. R. Griffin/D. W. Sherburne), Paperback Edition, New York/London: Free Press.

Whitehead, A. N. (1933). */ 1967): Adventures of Ideas*. The Free Press.

Whitehead, A. N. (1936). */ 1968): Modes of Thought*. The Free Press.

Wieland, Josef (1999): Die Ethik der Governance (Institutionelle und Evolutorische Ökonomik, Bd. 9), Marburg Metropolis.

Wieland, J. (2001). Eine Theorie der Governanceethik. *Zeitschrift Für Wirtschafts- Und Unternehmensethik, 2*, 8–33.

Wieland, Josef (2005): Normativität und Governance. Gesellschaftstheoretische und philosophische Reflexionen der Governanceethik (Studien zur Governanceethik, Bd. 3), Marburg Metropolis.

Wieland, Josef (2014): Governance Ethics. Gobal Value Creation, Economic Organization and Normativity, Cham/Heidelberg/New York/Dordrecht/London: Springer.

Wieland, Josef (2018/2020): Relational Economics. A Political Economy (Relational Economics and Organization Governance), Cham: Springer Nature Switzerland.

Williamson, Oliver E. (1975): Markets and Hierarchies: Analysis and Antitrust Implications. A Study in the Economics of Internal Organization, New York/London: The Free Press/Collier Macmillan Publishers.

Williamson, Oliver E. (1981): The Modern Corporation: Origins, Evolution, Attributes, in: Journal of Economic Literature, Vol. XIX (December 1981), pp. 1537–1568.

Williamson, O. E. (1985). *The Economic Institutions of Capitalism*. The Free Press/Collier Macmillan Publishers.

Williamson, O. E. (1991). Comparative Economic Organization: The Analysis of Discrete Structural Alternatives. *Administrative Science Quarterly, 36*, 269–296.
Williamson, Oliver E. (1991b): Introduction, in: Williamson, Oliver E. & Winter, Sidney G. (Ed.): The Nature of the Firm. Origins, Evolution, and Development, New York/Oxford: Oxford University Press, pp. 3–17.
Williamson, Oliver E. (1991c): The Logic of Economic Organization, in: Williamson, Oliver E. & Winter, Sidney G. (Ed.): The Nature of the Firm. Origins, Evolution, and Development, New York/Oxford: Oxford University Press, pp. 90–116.
Williamson, O. E. (1991). Strategizing, Economizing, And Economic Organization. *Strategic Management Journal, 12*, 75–94.
Williamson, O. E. (1995). Chester Barnard and the Incipient Science of Organization. In O. E. Williamson (Ed.), *Organization Theory* (pp. 172–206). Oxford University Press.
Williamson, O. E. (1995). Transaction Cost Economics and Organization Theory. In O. E. Williamson (Ed.), *Organization Theory* (pp. 207–256). Oxford University Press.
Williamson, O. E. (1995). Hierarchies, Markets and Power in the Economy: An Economic Perspective, in: Institutional and Corporate. *Change, 4*(1), 21–49.
Williamson, Oliver E. (1995d): Transaction Cost Economics: How It Works; Where It is, in: De Economist Vol. 146, No. 1 (January 1995), pp. 23–58.
Williamson, O. E. (1996). *The Mechanisms of Governance*. Oxford University Press.
Williamson, O. E. (1996). Revisiting Legal Realism: The Law, Economics, and Organization Perspective, in: Institutional and Corporate. *Change, 5*(2), 383–420.
Williamson, O. E. (1999). Strategy Research: Governance and Competence Perspectives. *Strategic Management Journal, 20*, 1087–1108.
Williamson, Oliver E. (2000): The New Institutional Economics: Taking Stock, Looking Ahead, in: Journal of Economic Literature Vol. XXXVIII (September 2000), pp. 595–613.
Williamson, Oliver E. (2002a): The Lens of Contract: Private Ordering, in: American Economic Review, Vol. 92, No. 2 (Papers and Proceedings, May, 2002), pp. 438–443.
Williamson, Oliver E. (2002b): The Theory of the Firm as Governance Structure: From Choice to Contract, in: Journal of Economic Perspectives, Vol. 16, No. 3 (Summer 2002), pp. 171–195.
Williamson, Oliver E. (2005a): The Economics of Governance (Richard T. Ely Lecture), in: The American Economic Review, Vol. 95, No. 2 (Papers and Proceedings, May, 2005), pp. 1–18.
Williamson, O. E. (2005). Transaction cost economics and business administration. *Scandinavian Journal of Management, 21*(1), 19–40.
Williamson, O. E. (2005). Why Law, Economics, And Organization? *Annual Review of Law and Social Science, 1*, 369–396.
Williamson, Oliver E. (2009): Transaction Cost Economics: The Natural Progression, in: American Economic Review, Vol. 100 (June 2010), pp. 673–690.
Wittgenstein, Ludwig (1953/2009): Philosophical Investigations, 4th Edition (ed. by P. M. S. Hacker/Joachim Schulte), Malden/Oxford: Wiley-Blackwell.

Michael Schramm is professor of catholic theology and business ethics at the Faculty of Business, Economics, and Social Sciences at the University of Hohenheim since 2001. Before this, he held the chair of christian social sciences at the Faculty of Catholic Theology in Erfurt (1995–2001). He was a speaker of the Association for Social Ethics (2006–2009) and is a member of the German Economic Association and the German Whitehead Society. His main research topics include business metaphysics, transaction ethics, and process theology.

Relational Money—Working to Define the Conditions of Non-payment

Christian Fiedler

Abstract In the course of this analysis, my goal will be to show that the debt relation, as a relational form of contract, deals with polycontexturality and, in the process, introduces external reference, which, through self-reference, is subsequently returned to money in the form of interest. However, by doing so, the institution of money reveals its own instability as a measure of value, and can only serve as one if the shared value created by a given process exactly matches the discounting of the interest.

1 Introduction

As this paper will show, the task of overcoming the temporal distance involved in cooperation, the need to define processes at t1 but to only reap the benefits at t2, is achieved by the institution of money in its (according to Commons (1990, p. 510ff)) primary function of creating, negotiating and releasing debt, which lends money the form of a process, and which can itself be described using the temporal asymmetry of process and event.

Through the debt relation, a continuation of the relation that extends beyond the act of payment becomes possible. In this way, as will be shown through the distinction between incorporeal and intangible property, the debt form is also the form for specific invested parties, employees, suppliers and NGOs in a going concern. Moreover, the institution of money can only be conceived of in the coexistence of abstract property rights, and varies according to the economic organization of corporations, banks, and the credit and money markets. Its function as a medium of exchange is then derived from its debt-moderating function, thanks to the possibility of selling debt securities on the part of creditors, i.e., banks.

C. Fiedler (✉)
Zeppelin University, Friedrichshafen, Germany
e-mail: c.fiedler@zeppelin-university.net

L. Biggiero et al. (eds.), *The Relational View of Economics*, Relational Economics and Organization Governance, https://doi.org/10.1007/978-3-030-86526-9_14

2 John R. Commons' Transaction Theory of Money

The following section represents an attempt to contribute to the discussions regarding Commons' (1990, p. 390) transactional theory of money. For the most part, it will focus on the last chapter (IX. Futurity) in the first volume of his Institutional Economics. Remarkably, he begins this section of the book with a discussion of the negotiability of debt (390ff), which is based on MacLeod's credit theoretic perspective. Obviously, both debates have, at least in the realm of economic scholarship, been won by the currency side. Reviving Commons for the current discussion of modern monetary theory, in general, and for the transactional theoretical construction of money theory for Relational Economics in particular, is the ultimate goal of this section. I will not provide a detailed introduction to the transaction theory that forms the basis of Commons' monetary transaction, assuming the reader is familiar with it, and directly address his conception of the monetary transaction.

2.1 Futurity

Commons develops his theory of money in the chapter on futurity. Futurity, in his view, is one of the five principles of Institutional Economics, the others being scarcity, efficiency, custom, and sovereignty. All of these are dimensions of subjective and objective human will that gain an objective status through collective action. Commons uses them in various combinations to explain transactions.

The principle of futurity is inherently linked with the theoretical abstraction of Institutional Economics. Economics, as Commons argues is not a material science of things, but deals with the present disposition over future rights to things and services. What is of value in current bargaining transactions, in which economic value is determined, is the current expectation of future claims to property.

Notably, Commons begins his discussion of futurity with the legal institution of "negotiability of debts" and "saleability" of debt. He uses an analysis of claims to payment and performance, which have emerged from the evolving legal status of merchants and the structures of the feudal system (cf., Commons, 1990, p. 390ff), in order to develop the principle of economic behavior's future-orientedness (futurity) based on an abstraction of current rights to future access to the property, which represents a departure from Böhm-Bawerk's psychological approach (ibid.). To do so, he adopts a credit and claims a perspective to develop the subject of Institutional Economics on the basis of the chronological structure of property rights, distancing himself from commodity-theoretical approaches.

What is transferred, then, is a debt of a seller to deliver a good or service, the legal equivalent of which is a duty of performance, and, a debt of the buyer, equivalent to the legal duty of payment (cf., Commons, 1990, p. 395).

In this double coding, Commons underscores from a legal and economic perspective the "double transfer of ownership" (Commons, 1990, p. 394f) that takes place in a transaction. This perspective, which is socialized in the sense put forward by Simmel (1989), introduces the structure of the triad by differentiating the contractual rights and societal roles.

What shifts in the process is the temporality of when use-values (corporeal property) are manifested in negotiations between the transaction partners. Commons makes use-values the subject of past and therefore previously completed valuation processes, which nevertheless re-emerge in transactions as path dependencies or commodities of exchange. Commons makes, as previously mentioned, current negotiations between buyers and sellers concerning future access to the property into the subject of support, a context in which buyers and sellers become each other's debtors and creditors, provided there is a lapse of time between the negotiations and exercising of the payment and performance rights. In this case, the buyer owes the seller a debt of payment, while the seller owes the buyer a debt of performance. By being legally positioned in the future, these claims attain an objective status as incorporeal property.

In turn, Commons refines Macleod's definition by supplanting the debt-laden, incorporeal property with the intangible property produced by various property rights, liberties, and exposures, and which is accordingly not debt-laden. Hence:

> [...] intangible property is the entirely different expectations, such as good-will, patent rights, railroad valuations, the right to continue in business, the right of access to a labor market, whose present valuation depends on the expectations of quantities and prices to be derived from future transactions under control of collective action (Commons, 1990, p. 522).

> Intangible property is the present value of expected net income from *future sales*; whereas incorporeal property is the present value of expected *payment of debts*. (Commons, 1990, p. 452).

Based on this distinction concerning the underlying property rights, Commons presents incorporeal and intangible property rights as the separate forms of the "economic quantity" in Macleod, which he later equates to the "modern meaning of capital" (ibid., p. 441). Both types of rights are objectified forms reflecting the principle of futurity, as they represent current valuations regarding the future. More precisely, it can be said that the present value and the corresponding debt are what constitute capital for Commons, whereas the use-value, as a past "present" for the assessment of future debts and values, represents the current path dependency of the already completed value generation. Therefore, for Commons, it is the subject of Home and Engineering Economics, which focuses on commodities and not property rights. This aspect will be clarified in 2.4, together with the connection between debt discounting (process) and risk calculations concerning the profit (event), discussed below.

2.2 *Profit and Interest*

In his non-linear view of time, Commons clarifies the temporal component of current expectations for the future using the asymmetry between the process ("lapse of time") and discrete event ("instant") (Commons, 1990, p. 449). This process structure can be linked to the ongoing social relations between creditor and debtor, which, in their continuity, are always processes and, as described above, differ from discrete buyer–seller relations.

In this regard, it would seem essential that within the process of the creditor-and-debtor relation, the waiting on the part of the creditor (ibid.), who is remunerated via interest—or more precisely, via the promise of future interest—coincides with and depends on the risk calculations regarding an expected profit, which are themselves only objectifiable on the market after the fact. Both the waiting (and therefore the size of the current discount rate) and the risk-based discounting of the expected future profit depend on the subsequently achieved exchange value (ibid.). The identity of incorporeal and intangible capital consists in this "objectification," which stems from a purely subjective assessment of the transaction values' equivalence. In this regard, it should be mentioned that, consequently, investment is not a function of saving, but of debt.

More importantly, however, interest is a discounting of the process itself, i.e., it always applies to a single transaction. In contrast, the expected profit, which for assessment purposes represents a function of expected risk, is a parameter involving two discrete transactions. Interest is a process-based parameter, namely one based on the process of relations between creditor and debtor, while profit is an arbitrage involving discrete sales. This asymmetry is only dispelled when the sale takes place. At the same time, interest is an approximation of the expected increase in value, which is represented only by the current forecast, i.e., only imprecisely, in the "real economic" process running parallel to the debt process. Nevertheless interest, or more precisely the discount, not only assumes the role of remunerating the creditor, but also becomes the monetary measure of value creation itself, which the at times fluctuating risks of the day have to be judged by. From this monetary perspective, it is a rate and therefore an average over time.

But of course, interest is also, unlike profit, a legally enforceable claim.

> Interest is payment enforced by law and stipulated in contracts. The law guarantees that the debtor will pay, if he has the funds. Otherwise it declares him bankrupt. Interest is a legal relation between creditor and debtor. But profits are not guaranteed by law. They are a relation between buyer and seller, borrower and lender, employer and wage-earner, each of whom is at liberty to deal or not to deal, and each of whom is exposed to gain or loss on account of the liberty of the other to deal or not to deal. It is a liberty-exposure relation permitted and enforced by law. Profit is obtained by purchasing transactions at low prices, for materials, or low wages, or low interest rates, or rents, and by selling transactions at higher prices. If the procedure is reversed, the result is Loss. (Commons, 1990, pp. 528–529).

As such, whether or not one should enter into the status of debtor, and therefore into a legal obligation framed by degrees of liberty and exposure is of course a strategic question. In any case, this distinction also yields a differentiation between the concept of the going concern, which Commons finds particularly interesting from the standpoint of the debtor, and that of banks. The former deal in expected profits and, in Commons' model, secure the financing of banks, which in turn specialize in the function of waiting, which Commons views as a productive function.

> Hence, those who have legal control of corporations and business generally are seeking for profit and are fearful of loss. Their business, then, is twofold: Forecasting and Planning, while those who get pure interest are merely Saving and Waiting. Profit is the result of forecasting and planning, and this is the reason why, in a system of private property, those who can make a profit get legal control of industry, and if they cannot make a profit, they lose legal control through bankruptcy. So, in asking what is the share of profit, we are asking how much does the nation pay for Forecasting and Planning. But in asking how much is the margin for profit we are asking how much do individual business men and corporations have after paying their debts (Commons, 1990, p. 529).

Accordingly, when the financing of a going concern is conceived on the basis of bank debt, the result is a sequence of debts that accompany the process of capital formation. At a superordinate level, as mentioned, Commons remains unconvinced by the neoclassical claim that saving and investment are interchangeable.

2.3 The Institution of Money and the Monetary Transaction

The problem of money emanates from the principle of futurity; negotiations over future property rights take place in the present, when the corresponding value has not yet come into being. Accordingly, the problem of money is first and foremost a problem for the seller, or later, for the going concern, which, because it will only be remunerated after having providing the agreed-upon goods or services and after the buyer has paid their debt, must initially incur debt itself. As such, for Commons, money:

> [...] in its modern meaning, is the social institution of the creation, negotiability, and release of debts arising out of transactions. If the payment is made without a lapse of time worth measuring, we name it a purchase or sale, and it differs from short-time and long-time debts only in that the intervening stage of negotiability of debt is omitted. Thus money is secondarily a medium of exchange—it is primarily a social means of creating, transferring, and extinguishing debts (Commons, 1990, p. 513).

From the outset, then, Commons defines money as an abstract unit of account and in terms of its function of bridging the temporal distance between present and future. In this definition, money assumes the form of a claim, which conforms to the chronological structure of the debt form, namely overcoming the current unavailability of the means required to fulfill the obligations toward the buyer that the seller has entered into. For him, the relevant form is debt money.

Beyond the fact that the money the going concern borrows from the bank as credit for the process of value creation was only created by the banker for the purpose of this transaction, it is important to note that, until it has been repaid, the underlying bank debt is itself an ongoing creditor-and-debtor relation. In other words, money itself becomes a process that integrates the two relations introduced separately here: the financed transaction and financing transaction. Hence, when as a result:

> [...] each loan transaction creates its own money and the whole volume is created and extinguished every 30 days, then the definition of money should be converted from the static idea of a quantity to the dynamic idea of a process. The process is the billions of bargaining transactions, with the bankers as participants (Commons, 1990, p. 513).

The deadline created by debt, which attaches a fixed release date to the newly created bank debt, serves to define the beginning and end of the transaction and the accompanying sum of money, which is spontaneously created, only to later be extinguished. Consequently, money's function as a form of payment is a derived one, since the payments involved in the debt relation between firm and bank, when a chain of transactions is formed, can only be determined by the negotiability, creation and release of debt.

In Part 4.2, I will argue that this modification represents a further specification of the third variable used in the triadic basic structure introduced by Simmel (1989).

2.4 The Valuation Process

The previously discussed, largely artificial separation for analytical purposes of transactions that are actually assumed to be process-bounded must of course (in keeping with Commons' approach) be thought of in terms of processes, and in an integrative manner with regard to the valuation process as Commons develops it in his chapter on The Transactional System of Money and Value (Commons, 1990, p. 510ff). In my view, though brief, these deliberations constitute the positive part of his valuation theory, which resurfaces in Volume 2 of Institutional Economics in his socioeconomic reform.

Commons' thoughts on his valuation theory are somewhat cryptic, because he (most likely intentionally) does not introduce in detail all of the variables he has in mind (Whalen, 1993). I believe they lose a bit of clarity because they argue at both the measurement level and by employing various concepts of value and the not always explicitly mentioned dimension of human will, which he connects with the respective variables (ibid.). In the following, I will present those aspects that seem most sensible to me, and open them for discussion.

The general difficulty in describing a process is that the distinction between event and process is precisely due to the fact that, in the form of emergent processes, accurately "locating" values is essentially impossible; gauging them requires discreteness. Processes are fluid and therefore not entirely measurable, as can be seen in the distinction introduced above.

In this regard, for Commons, the bargaining transaction is:

> [...] none other than the process of pricing, valuing, and debiting, which create, transfer, extinguish, and recreate both economic quantities and the money which measures them as values. The price, the value, the debt, are each jointly determined, if not literally created, at

> the point in time when the agreement transfers the ownership of the economic quantity thus agreed upon, and all the variabilities, taken together in the sequence of time, are a process of pricing, valuing, and debiting by means of transactions (Commons, 1990, pp. 513–514).

In other words, it is a multiple causation system (cf., Commons, 1990, p. 456). This is further complicated by the fact that the process consists of the interaction between the "objective" influences of collective action and the subjective variables. In the course of introducing his variables, Commons identifies several ways of approaching a valuation theory.

> One is the transactional meaning of value as the multiple of price, quantity, and futurity discount, and therefore the equivalent of debt and "capital." Another is the purchasing-power meaning of value as an aggregate of prices. Third is the distributive meaning of value as real value, with money and prices as instruments for the distributions of wealth. Throughout these meanings are the several principles of scarcity measured by prices, quantity of use-values measured by physical units, and value as an aggregate of prices *times* quantities (Commons, 1990, p. 520).

The general intuition behind a transactional theory is a relation of the several meanings of value to be inferred from the process of transactions. Commons uses two different sets of specific manifestations of the variable (a varying description between Commons, 1990, pp. 514ff and 520) in his analysis and conclusion to the chapter.

Nevertheless, it becomes clear that the specific factors are derivatives of his five dimensions of human will, embodied in individual wants, desires, and habits, as well as institutions of collective action. These five dimensions, as mentioned earlier, are futurity, efficiency, scarcity, custom, and sovereignty (see also Whalen, 1993). Futurity expresses the present expectations for the future as portrayed in the above-mentioned concepts of waiting and risking, which, as Whalen points out, concern both the future state of the economy and the particular property rights transferred (Whalen, 1993, p. 1159). Efficiency is linked with the properties of commodities and thus consists of quantitative measures of goods. Custom is any institutional habit that accompanies the transaction. Sovereignty is essentially the state's third-party enforcement of individual rights and duties.

The following list of variables in the valuation process is provided by Commons (cf., 1990, p. 514ff):

- Scarcity of the Commodity or the Securities dealt in,
- Scarcity of Means of Payment,
- Scarcity of Waiting,
- Expected Lapse of Time,
- Risking (Profit),
- Quantity of the Commodity,
- Kind and Quality of the Commodity,
- Property Rights,
- Bargaining Ability, and

- Expectations of what Collective Action will do through Customs, Laws, Rights, and Liberties as Administered by Courts, Executives, Boards, and Commissions including Central Banks of issue.

Here it becomes clear that use-value, once banned from the focus of Institutional Economics, again becomes part of value assessment in the process of transactions, in the form of path dependency. It should be stressed once again that these manifestations view themselves as interactions between the dimensions of will, e.g., use-value is a relation between scarcity and efficiency and therefore, without the addition of futurity, a static concept. In contrast, risking is a futurity-scarcity relation, which integrates the aspect of future scarcity into the assessment. Although Commons does not explicitly say so, I believe the "expected lapse of time" is connected to the idea of turnover, and therefore thematizes the transactions' turnover rates.

3 The Nexus of Money, Going Concerns, and Banks

The previous part of this paper addressed the process form of the transaction, introducing it in a number of analytical steps. In the following, I will attempt to apply the process form of the transaction to the network form, which in this context consists in the nexus of the going concern, banks and a third party. To do so, I will, as previously stated, first clarify the connections to markets in the real economy and, in 3.2, the connections to money markets and debt markets. The analysis ends at the point where, as I will argue, money, through interest, becomes a self-contained monetary form of capital, which, due to interest, is marketable as a price (unlike a rate).

3.1 Forecast and Repetition System(s) Instead of Circulation

The goal of the following explanation is to combine the process perspective with the network perspective. At this point, the portrayal of the network remains limited to the relations between going concerns, banks, and money, and should be expanded elsewhere by addressing the networking of monetary and debt transactions (cf., Commons, 1990, p. 520ff). In this regard, the point of departure would be deliberations on interest, which will be discussed in the following section.

Here, the focus will be on describing the monetary transaction, in which we will discuss how money as credit money has established itself through the debt relations between transaction partners and their banks. In this regard, how Commons views this embeddedness of the transaction in the form of forecast and repetition systems (Commons, 1990, p. 510ff) would seem to be a decisive aspect. Here, he is namely arguing against the concept of monetary circulation that underlies the conventional quantity theory of money and is connected with the generally recognized money formula,[1] together with the speed of circulation (velocity). First of all, according to Commons such a formula can only be found in the transaction itself (cf., Commons, 1990, p. 513); secondly, by claiming the identity of investing debt and value, instead of the generally assumed identity of saving and investing, the formula is more complex than for consumption. This is because the process of value creation and debt does not arise from saving, or, put another way: if the money needed for investment is created anew by banks in the form of debt and based on an assessment of an entrepreneur's profit-making prospects and creditworthiness, then the notion of circulating money to create solvency is misleading.

Money, as the institution for the creation, negotiability, and release of debt, moderates this process in that, within the debt relation, it itself is a process, while also fulfilling the discrete function of a form of payment with the network. This should be considered together with the previously discussed aspects.

> [...] each loan transaction creates its own money. There is not a fund of money that "circulates," but there is a repetition of the creation, sale, and payment of short-time debts to the amount equivalent to the discounted values of the titles of ownership alienated. Two succeeding increases in value thus occur, based on forecasts of the prices of commodities: the increase in output of use-value of commodities to be added by the input of labor; and the increase in value of the discounted debt as it approaches maturity (Commons, 1990, p. 511).

However, this depiction of a process' outcome is only possible at the discrete point in the present at which a past process of capital formation with corresponding debt has been completed and, in so doing, is followed either by commercialization or further cooperation in the value creation chain, continuing the form of the process. In my view, this is precisely due to the temporalized view of future-oriented capital and the asymmetry of the process ("lapse of time") and discrete event ("instant"). The form of the process as moving through time, and the point-in-time-based perspective used in the network, demonstrate precisely this asymmetry of standpoints, because the uncertainty of success and validation of corporate forecasting are preserved in the process of creating value (and the corresponding debt). One could also say there is a degree of uncertainty as to the likelihood of a debt being successfully repaid, since the entrepreneur's intersubjective valuations only attain objectivity through the discrete act of payment. In this process, the value holds the status of a potentiality, which is maintained in every relation of value creation and debt, and is only actualized through payments, in point-in-time-based relationalizations of price within the network, which represent discrete transactions.[2]

---

[1] Money formula $PT = MV$, usually interpreted as the quantity (M) and velocity of money (V) preceding the price level (P) and volume of trade (V). This is a core assumption of the monetarist quantity theory of money in neoclassical economics, which is challenged by the Keynesians, who argue for reverse causation. Commons at least favors the second position, later adopted by Keynesian economics (cf., Commons, 1990, p. 513).

[2] The market can ultimately be understood as a network within which (nonetheless discrete) transactions are negotiated. The decision that arises with regard to value creation, namely, whether a transaction should be executed via the coordinating function of the market or via the cooperative coordination found in value creation chains, is then the subject of Relational Economics. In the context at hand, it is connected to the question of whether the capital formation process should be

In Commons, this asymmetry manifests in the multiple connections that a going concern has to the wholesale and retail markets, not to mention the money market and debt market.[3] When the process is successful, the results can be seen in discrete price increases on secondary markets:

> The first increase of value appears on the various commodity markets, as when the price of iron ore becomes the price of pig iron, then the price of rolled steel, of agricultural machinery, of knives and forks to be purchased by ultimate consumers. The second increase occurs on the money or debt markets, where each short-term debt increases in value by reduced lapse of time until it is paid (Commons, 1990, p. 511).

This quote is interesting because, in the context of value creation, due to the presumably process-bound quantities of capital, increases in value can only be recorded in a discrete, i.e., point-in-time-based manner. Elsewhere, however (namely with regard to employment markets), Commons addresses the transfer of debt within the network.

> When the laborer goes to work he is not paid in advance. [...] Each accrual of use-value accepted by the foreman for the employer is paralleled by an accrual of debt owed by the employer to the employee. The debt is liquidated on pay day, but the use-value is merged into a joint product which the employer expects will furnish him a credit against another debtor on a commodity-market or debt-market. The principle here is the same as when material men wait [...] for payments of their materials (Commons, 1990, pp. 506–507).

If we view the employment relation from a modern standpoint as a stakeholder relation that can, due to supply contracts with a temporal discrepancy between performance and payment, be portrayed as a debt relation, then cooperation, which is characterized by enforceable rights and obligations, also represents a transfer of the debt originally negotiated in the creditor-and-debtor relation between entrepreneur and banker. From a monetary standpoint, this is precisely the function of the entrepreneur, namely to initiate a process—based on his/her current profit-making prospects, which are determined by his/her discounting of risk and discounting of bank interest—that creates a debt for the cooperation partners in his/her network, which will be paid back ex-post, together with profits, upon commercialization. Within the network, the debt that was originally negotiated in the transaction between the banker and entrepreneur serves as a form of payment that sets the cooperative process in motion. Once the profit has been made on the market, all debtors are paid and, by repaying the debt accrued by the banker, the credit money they created by extending the balance sheet also disappears. The money does not circulate as credit; rather, it creates temporary networks that, depending on the type of transaction, can be measured in terms of their repeatability.

---

extended via the production channels, or whether (and at which points) it should be interrupted, so as to capitalize on the relative certainty of the market assessment. In my view, this is the operative question for potential connections to "secondary" supply markets and "primary" consumer markets alike. From a process perspective, precisely the opposite sequence would apply.

[3] The connection to subsequent deliberations on how the money market and debt market are linked is discussed in the next section.

Consequently, Commons replaces the notion of circulation with that of a forecast and repetition system, which can be assessed using the turnover rate of its transactions. The quantity of money cannot be empirically determined, as it varies constantly and can never be accurately predicted. As such:

> [i]nstead of a quantity of money we have a variable "turnover" of bank debts, the volume of which is negotiated, created, cancelled, and renewed every 30 days or so, varying in magnitude, however, with the expected prices and quantities of commodities, of services and of debts whose valuations largely determine the magnitude of further debts created by further transfers of ownership." (Commons, 1990, p. 512). "Hence the appropriate doctrine of cause and effect is found in billions of transactions, where the banker who creates the money participates as a guide to the transaction. (ibid., pp. 511–512).

> Multiply this over-simplified transaction of a supposed single bank by a repetition of billions and even trillions of similar transactions during a year, add all the banks […], and we have, not a circulation system of money, but a forecast and repetition system of money (Commons, 1990, p. 549).

What these two ideas have in common are quantities of money, dependent on the short-term supply of and demand for credit, which are limited by the cyclical negotiation and release of a debt on fixed dates, and which repeat depending on the type of transaction. Therefore, the idea of turnover is connected to the assumption of typical, transaction-specific completion times, which makes it possible to use the size of the bank debt to draw conclusions regarding the dynamics of capital formation. This fits with the process-boundedness of value creation and of the corresponding debt. However, Commons consistently uses the term "turnover" in quotation marks, reflecting his awareness of the artificial nature of applying such a dynamic statistical term with regard to the process of value creation.

Commons estimates that the resulting amount of credit money accounts for 80–90% of the total quantity of money, in contrast to 10–15% cash, which he refers to as "money in circulation" (here, too, in quotation marks). As such, he does not wholly disregard the concept of cash, but considers it to be irrelevant for going concerns. The amount of money debt now listed in M2 still accounts for the lion's share of the money produced by deposits from consumers, an aspect that we won't explore further here (cf., Commons, 1990, pp. 510ff). The reason why Commons gives a considerably higher estimate of this percentage can be attributed to a change in the capital intensity of value creation, which, at least in Western countries, has moved from capital-intensive physical goods to services and intangible goods. Nevertheless, the percentage of the total money that short-term debt constitutes remains considerable, especially in the financing of working capital, which wanders with high turnover through the accounts of banks and companies alike.

3.2 The Function of Interest as Price

We have now adequately discussed the short-term monetary connections made by firms, an aspect that forms the core of the following considerations, and will subsequently be discussed in terms of the prospects for Relational Economics. The discussion took place at the level of transactions, which, according to Commons, can be statistically described in terms of their "turnover."

In the following, I will argue that individual transactions are executed within relational contractual arrangements, provided the relation between entrepreneur and banker continues beyond individual transactions, which can safely be assumed. Here, the figures described in the transaction as the "banker" and "entrepreneur" must be assumed to be personifications and, in the framework of Relational Economics, be viewed as emergent organizations. Commons prefers—a sound choice in the context of the short-term capital described above—to characterize the respective functions of banks and firms as forecasting and waiting. Though firms take risks in the hopes of generating profit, while banks specialize in waiting, essentially both parties do both things, an aspect that will be clarified later in the paper. In any case, as far as banks are concerned, there can be no doubt that they also do their business in awarding credit on the basis of projected profits, i.e., that they also use the guiding difference earnings/costs.

Transaction-based debts are continued in long-term customer relations, which, with regard to the balance, are perpetuated as ongoing creditor-and-debtor relations. The argument that, in addition to temporal continuity, what we're seeing here are relational contracts, becomes evident when one considers the social relation between the banker and entrepreneur (Ingham, 2004). After all, the assessment of the latter's creditworthiness is based on the two persons' relationship to date. The credit assessment calculates the size of the debt on the basis of the past relation. In addition to certain objective values (etc.), the criteria used are person-dependent and transaction-specific; accordingly, they are influenced by, e.g., behavioral norms. At the same time, banks orient their choices on both "average banking behavior" and, in the broader societal context, on general ethical and religious norms (Ingham, 2004). Through the relation, all of these aspects inform the assessment of the transaction, which results in the application of a certain interest rate based on the debtor's rating.

As previously discussed, for assessments made in the present, interest is expressed as the discount rate. Interest rates decrease with increasing maturity, which implies a rise in value. Here it is important to note that the interest, which is expressed in the relation as a rate, is also the creditor's legally enforceable claim against the debtor (cf., Commons, 1990, p. 520). In the concrete form of this relation, the rights of the creditor and the responsibilities of the debtor are expressed as a rate. At the same time, as a price, interest allows bankers to sell debt as a generalized form of purchasing power, a context in which interest as the price of "good credit," as the price of the debt relation—which itself proceeds under the premises of future appreciation, of debt itself, and of the value creation process financed—represents a potential for earnings.[4] As such, there is a need to more closely scrutinize the banker's function as a merchant (Commons, 1990: 453), which, with regard to creating the money needed for the debt relation, has to date only been addressed in terms of the bank's assets, i.e., of customer demand.

Accordingly, the banker is a:

> […] merchant or middleman, buying and selling the "savings" of others in the form of their debts *not yet due* in exchange for his own debts *past due*. In such bargaining transactions it […] is the merchant's choice of opportunities, which we have previously analyzed as opportunity-cost, […] A manufacturer *without cost* is a merchant, […] a merchant, buying and selling the "savings" of the community (Commons, 1990, p. 454).

We have already discussed the first part of buying the debt "not yet due" in the context of the concrete relation between the entrepreneur as debtor and the bank as a creditor. From an accounting standpoint, credit creation can simultaneously be understood as a liability when the banker buys the current profit-making prospects and makes an entry on the asset side, corresponding to the entrepreneur's assessed value. In this regard, Commons claims, when it comes to this money created from scratch, the banker uses his "general 'good credit,' backed by his reputation, by his legal reserves, and by other legal requirements designed to strengthen his credit" (Commons, 1990, p. 454). The expression "debts past due" merely refers to the fact that the banker, by entering the debt in his or her ledger, creates his or her own debt, and extends the balance sheet. At this moment, money is created. In the process, and in Commons' notation this is represented by "savings" in quotation marks, the banker is not serving as a broker for those who want to deposit or borrow money; rather, they are dealing in the exchange values of debt, which they finance not only with debts of their own creation, but also with debts that have already been paid. As such, Commons is a proponent of an elastic supply curve for credit, one that depends not only on the intangible good of the banker's reputation, but also on legal rulings and decisions of the Central Banks, not to mention fluctuations in the willingness to take risks on the demand side.

The profit generated by these transactions and those succeeding them is the result of interest arbitrage, which capitalizes on the changing prices of debt, i.e., on interest as price. Accordingly, there are various long-term interest rates for longer-term debt transactions (bonds), which make the individual prices comparable to short-term bank debts and other securities. At the same time, this interest as the price of debt paves the way for a relationalization of the resulting debt market. After all, by being

[4] It is precisely here that we can see a crucial difference from post-Keynesian credit theories, which becomes apparent in Commons' (1990, p. 319ff) discussion of general vs. specific credit. For Commons, this is where the transition from incorporeal, i.e., debt-bound, and intangible, or non-debt-bound property, takes place. Accordingly, resold debt does not represent credit owed by or to anyone because, as intangible property, it does not involve any rights or obligations concerning performance or payment, which continue to reside in the concrete debt relation. This is where we can see, assuming the banker has certain opportunity costs – which are produced by the fact that he or she chooses not to pursue certain creditworthy transactions, despite his or her high confidence in the supply of and demand for credit–, the inherent instability cited by Commons (1990) and Minsky (1986, 2011).

issued, stocks and similar titles to intangible property can, through the discount of the profit-yield, be compared with the discount for debts as a form of interest (which, from a discrete standpoint, also becomes a price). This yields the market-perspective-based relation of profit-making prospects and interest prospects, which allows us to compare the "debt capital" and intangible capital, and to integrate the separate markets via discrete transactions.

In my view, on the one hand, the commercialization of debt occurs at the point at which money becomes its own norm[5]; on the other, this is also the point at which the relationalization of process and discrete event takes place, and money becomes capital, both in its own right and in relation to intangible property. After all, the process of debt continues to be evaluated using the approximation of an interest rate, which is dependent on discrete events on the debt market and money market. As such, the asymmetry of process (capital) and event (price) takes on this recursive form, both in the actual debt and in connection with intangible property.

According to Relational Economics, this point, namely that at which the commercialization of debt takes place, is from a monetary perspective also the point at which the relational contract concerning the specific debt relation gives way to classical and neoclassical contracts. As a next step, in order to further develop the governance perspective, the relation between the debt market and money market, which is structured by the Central Banks' hierarchy of the debt pyramid (cf., Commons, 1990, p. 395), would need to be precisely defined. I believe this hierarchy could be introduced as a variable of third-party enforcement in the context of flat relationalization, i.e., the intentionally hierarchically structured atopology of Relational Economics. However, I feel that the global financial movements of money themselves are more critical, and that the hierarchy of intervention on the part of Central Banks and governments is sufficiently reflected in an intermittent variable. A governance perspective, then, would concern itself with functional equivalents in the organizational and institutional control of dynamic debt networks and monetary networks.

For the firm itself, the strategic decision always involves a trade-off between accruing a debt subject to interest, while retaining ownership and controlling rights on the one hand; and relinquishing said rights, i.e., taking on other investors, but not having to accrue any debt on the other. This is the subject of strategic finance, the basis of which consists in accruing debt in order to finance operations, and in securing working capital through banks or (either strategically or as a means of last resort) by issuing long-term bonds. In contrast, issuing shares (market relations) and taking on investors (relational contracts) serve to support infrastructure investments.

[5] According to Commons: "Hence even incorporeal property becomes "intangible property" by the device of negotiability, because the debt has now market value, the "price" of debt, which rises or falls according to the changing relative scarcities of long-time, short-time, and demand debts. This market value of a debt is its scarcity-value, or price, and it is this market price that is "intangible property" on the debt market just as the expected prices of commodities, services, or labor are on other markets. Their intangibility is their scarcity and their futurity, whose expectation is property, whose measure is price, and whose "objectivity" is both the modern meaning of capital and the collective action which, independent of individual wills, creates the rights of property." (Commons, 1990, p. 522).

This aspect could be applied to the various cost categories employed in Relational Economics in order to reflect the financial side of forming strategic relations in connection with the strategic disposition of property rights.

4 Implications for Relational Economics

At this point, I would like to briefly review the insights gained so far, before connecting them to the logic of Relational Economics as delineated in Wieland (2018, 2020). These ideas emerged in the process of writing the paper and offer potential points of departure for further investigations of the ability to form relations. They are presented merely as perspectives in the form of hypotheses, and have yet to be assessed in terms of their plausibility or developed in more detail.

4.1 Discussion of the Implied Concept of Capital

The definition of money as an institution for the creation, negotiability, and transfer of debt, which can be derived from our discussion of Commons, highlights the execution, through the co-specialization of banks and entrepreneurs, of potentially profitable undertakings, in that the social, objective and temporal distance in the possession of claims to the future property is moderated by credit money. In the nexus of going concern and society, money acquires from this primary function the derived but equally important function as a medium of exchange, thanks to the possibility of trading in claims. In all of its functions, money is involved in the execution of transactions, making it real; after all, it structures the overcoming of distance by granting access to property rights. That being said, in this context money cannot be conceived separately from the organization of profit-making prospects at going concerns or from profit-oriented waiting at banks.

Using the form of the creditor-debtor relationship to systematically define money as a continuation of relations, in contrast to a one-time, pure seller-buyer relation, makes it possible to apply money, as both a relation and process form, to the schema of asymmetry between relational transactions and exchange transactions that can be found in Relational Economics. In this regard, Relational Economics represents a further evolution of Commons' theory, in that it develops the bargaining transaction, which I believe Commons intended as a market transaction, for the relationalization of societal and business networks. As such, it reintroduces the distinction between relational and exchange transactions in the seller-buyer difference, in order to describe the cooperative resources and property rights found among stakeholders, without the rigid assumptions imposed by hierarchies. Since, in these value creation processes, cooperation is the form of capital formation that produces an output of material and intangible values and simultaneously represents the relationalization of said values, I believe Commons' notion of capital, which is itself derived from

MacLeod's economic quantity, can be applied to cooperation. By applying the monetary perspective arising from the debt relation, existing relational contractual arrangements involving specifically investing stakeholders represent the incorporeal property. This refers to the entries in the balance sheet that are denoted with outstanding claims to and debts of performance, and which include the financial burden of debt. In contrast, those elements listed as equity are, in keeping with Commons, intangible property, and for the purposes of Relational Economics, they represent access to relational goods that can be privatized and are valuable for the organization of future collaborations.

Moreover, here the function of money as an institution for the creation, negotiability and release of debt has a co-determining influence on what I will cautiously refer to as the formation of relational capital, because in bargaining transactions, which take into account ex-ante the valuations of future collaborations for the purpose of shared value creation, the assessment of the corresponding money debt is included as a liability. The loan issued includes a deadline, and therefore a fixed end date for the financing of the debt and an interest rate. Thanks to this clear dividing line between negotiation and a fixed date for repaying the debt, the cooperation is separated into distinct processes and becomes quantifiable, even if doing so always represents an artificial intervention in the underlying societal processes. However, doing so also offers a means of approximating the dynamics of turnover in transactions, because the capital formation processes that can be typified using turnover can be classified according to their frequency, repetition interval, and duration. This is connected to a dynamic view of capital that matches the temporal structure of Relational Economics, which places the act of overcoming contingency in the present by forecasting future cooperative circumstances from a "real" and "monetary" standpoint, while also taking into account the path dependencies of past value creation processes, at the heart of the analysis.

4.2 Polycontexturality and Money

The creditor-and-debtor relation between bank and going concern, as this paper has sought to show by referring to Commons, is a transaction that effectively transforms polycontexturality into monolingualism. What makes it so unique is its level of organization through banks, which is unparalleled for the form of capitalism (Commons, 1990; Schumpeter, 2006). The focus on this transaction, in particular, is due to the fact that it represents the most commonly used form of financing for short-term debts and, given the high liquidity, in keeping with Commons, assumes the highest turnover of money forms (Bain & Company, 2019).

The distinction between interest as price and interest as rate serves to illustrate that the rate, in the course of the transaction and within the contractual relation, especially helps to temporally structure the social debt relation. I believe this represents a relational contractual form, especially if we assume that people's connections to banks go beyond transactions. However, this also means that polycontexturality continues to apply to debt relations. This becomes especially clear when we recall the valuation process; see above.

My logical interpretation of the transaction according to Commons, and drawing on Simmel, is that he employs the structure of the triad, namely the idea that every exchange involves a third party that adds a variable of collective action as an objectifying, socialized form to the transaction. In this interpretation, the introduction of potential buyers and sellers represents a division of the third value into several variables. If, in connection with bank debt, the bank is added, then we have a relation between buyer and seller in the monetary transaction, a relation that reflects the interactive effects of competition with potential buyers and sellers on the basis of their respective debt relations. His expansion of the triad with these values shows that he feels this interactionistic shift toward third-party enforcement should always be kept in mind, and that he is simultaneously open to using more variables of collective action. In my eyes, from a logical standpoint, the figure remains a triad.

In Simmel's work (1989) the triad, as the smallest social unit and, in this view, basic theorem of modern social network analysis, argues along the same lines. The third value can on the one hand be applied to personnel, e.g., in the figure of the mediator/broker, tertius gaudes (Bröckling, 2010). On the other, societal forms can also be used, e.g., with money as the mediator of exchange, norms, forms of property, and therefore the "objectivity" of emergent forms, allowing actors of collective action to return as relations within the relation. This is the common subject shared by Relational Economics, the network theory based on the works of Simmel, relational contract theory, and institutionalism as put forward by Commons.

In sociological system theory, the figure of the third was introduced using the distinction between codes and programs (Luhmann, 1994). With regard to money, the code is the distinction between payment/non-payment and determines the self-referential nature of money and the economy, namely, the fact that payments connect to other payments. Luhmann uses the secondary coding of property (possession/non-possession) to describe the overall economy as a dual cycle in which the exchange of goods in a transaction on one hand, and payment on the other, are analytically separate but interrelated (Luhmann, 1994). Both "cycles" can then be thematized in terms of their self-reference. Third values manifest in programs of profit or programs of law (Luhmann, 1994). I feel this offers a structurally equivalent solution to the problem, which is why the system theory can serve as a valuable foundation.

However, with regard to a theory of money and the argumentation of Relational Economics, my point (to more precisely define the content discussed in 1.1) is as follows: Relational Economics acknowledges the self-reference of societally differentiated functional systems, yet it is also and especially interested in external reference, in the relations between the programs that introduce external reference using various decision-making patterns, i.e., in polycontexturality and in successfully integrating external-referential logics in the context of polylingualism. In connection with relational deliberations on money, this also means (in my opinion): thematizing external reference. Any effort to do so has to address the polycontexturality of the programs that determine payment or non-payment and therefore the self-reference of money. I feel the previously discussed theories of money can, in various theoretical areas, be used to explore precisely this question. Ultimately, however, the goal is to understand the roles of the individual and objectivized economic, contractual, and normative forces that influence the transaction, against the backdrop of societal dynamics, in order to arrive at practice-relevant conclusions regarding the generalization of transactional patterns.

Here, I consider the current economic-sociological reflections on credit theories (Ingham, 2004; Sahr, 2017) to be of interest, as they argue that fixating on money's function as a means of payment in order to explain its self-reference means disregarding the dynamics of debt, which are even more relevant for analyses of the financial system that build on the ideas presented here.

4.3 Implications for the Logic of Cooperation

In this regard, the task is to connect a relationalization of the distinction between money, banks, and firms to the fact that value creation, as explained in Relational Economics, is the outcome of cooperative processes.

In this context, the concept of the underlying "economic quantity," i.e., of capital, is an important one, together with Commons' distinction between corporeal, incorporeal, and intangible property. Corporeal property is the present outcome of past valuations in the form of "realized" material and intangible use-values. Although they manifest as path dependencies in current transactions, principally speaking they are completed processes. As described above, intangible property and incorporeal property are, as the identity of value creation and corresponding debt, the current titles that are used to negotiate concerning future contingencies. This parallel coexistence of intangible and incorporeal property results in a dual connection to the market, which, as a potentiality, accompanies the process of cooperative capital formation: the connection to commodity or service markets on the product side, and to debt or money markets on the financial side.

On the financial side, a given firm now has the chance to make a financial-strategic choice regarding its debt or equity financing based on a trade-off of accruing debt subject to interest, while retaining ownership and control; or based on sharing its equity with a third party, which would mean not accruing any debt subject to interest, but having to relinquish ownership and control. This amounts to deciding, on the debt side, whether to enter into a bank relation or to accrue market-mediated debt by issuing bonds; or, on the equity side, to capitalize on its surrender of ownership and control by issuing stocks, pursuing collaborations in the form of joint ventures, or taking on partners. At the same time, banks shape the current valuations of future property rights in that, when providing credit money in connection with a debt assessment (which for Commons is equivalent to the negotiated value), they chiefly choose to be compensated in the form of mortgages and interest. Here we see their specific ability: waiting.

This relation to the "debt market" is, in my interpretation, reflected at the level of the "real economy" in the form of economic cooperation. Here, too, there are relational debt connections, in which the partners have, over time, made specific investments and in which the mutual exercising and fulfillment of their rights and obligations have continued, transcending discrete market transactions. At the same time, the process of societal value creation demands the constant adaptation and reevaluation of existing relations and making expenditures to cover relational costs, so as to enhance the ability to cooperate and chances for cooperation, and therefore, to have a say in controlling future collaborations deemed worthwhile, without attaining ownership of said collaborations.

The relation that, through the introduction of money at the level of the transaction, manifests in legally binding present claims to future property rights, represents a relationalization of capital and money against the backdrop of the relations between firms, banks, and money. At the abstract level of Institutional Economics, namely, the future disposition of property rights, Commons' notion concerning the difference between a "lapse of time" and an "instant" (Commons, 1990, p. 453) would seem to be the monetary connection for Relational Economics. What takes place in cooperative networks, in the continuity of contractual relational arrangements, i.e., in a "lapse of time" is, in relation to a discrete exchange on the market, i.e., to an "instant of time," the temporal difference resulting from the "production of capital" and the generation of profit-making opportunities that are only realized in the discrete event of commercialization. In this regard, firms are experts on the disposition of ownership and controlling rights, as well as securing access rights in the case of shared ownership. Capital, then, is the relation between value creation and corresponding debt, which Commons separates into incorporeal and intangible capital; and the output, which is the result of the realization process, is then commercialized to produce a rent (in the case of profit). In the simplest iteration of this relation, the firm structures its points of access to existing societal value creation processes, which are assessed on the basis of the corresponding debt made possible by banks through credit creation, and which are connected to the present by the institution of money in the form of bargaining transactions. Though this is the simple variant, and is now chiefly used in connection with firms' short-term working capital, it also represents the largest quantity of money (Bain & Company, 2019). If we assume that societal value creation, firms, banks, and money are co-specialized, this relation can also become far more complex—economically, legally, and ethically—especially considering the influence of collective action.

5 Summary and Outlook

This text represents an attempt to filter and distill certain ideas concerning a relational theory of money that would facilitate its endogenization in Relational Economics.

Its specific focus on Commons' transaction theory of money has, using the distinction between incorporeal and intangible property, shown that not all money is debt-mediated, although the percentage of bank-debt-mediated money continues to make up the lion's share of the total, especially in terms of financing the operations of firms, which are empirically speaking the object of analysis for Relational Economics. In this context, Commons' definition of money as the institution for the creation, negotiability, and release of debt was discussed by illustrating the process of the transaction and of the distribution within a given firm's network, which is what constitutes money's derived function as a means of payment. This was done in the framework of forecast and repetition systems, a concept that Commons uses for credit money, which is created and extinguished along with debt, representing his alternative to the idea of the circulation of money. I have subsequently argued that relational transactions in the debt relation are executed through relational contracts between banks and firms, and that consequently, polylingualism characterizes these relations.

This finding seems to be relevant in that, based on the polyvalence of the transaction, it makes the self-reference of money possible, while taking into account interest. After all, as the analysis revealed, it is only the translation of the polyvalence of the debt relation through interest as price, and taking into account the general societal and economic circumstances, that simultaneously allows debt to be discretely commercialized on the money market. In this regard, the interest is critical: through its dual role as a rate within the relation but also as the price of the titles resold by bankers, it allows money to be mediated on both debt markets and money markets.

Post Scriptum This article is an abridged version of Christian Fiedler's master's thesis. I had invited him to contribute to this book. However, this plan could not be realized, as he died on the 20 of November 2019. The core of his work and reflections, the reconstruction of the monetary theory of J. R. Commons as a possible contribution to Relational Economics, is published here. I am convinced that it may contribute significant thoughts and ideas to the discussion. Josef Wieland.

Literature

Bain & Company. (2019). Global private equity report 2019. Boston.

Bröckling, U. (2010). Gesellschaft beginnt mit Drei. Eine soziologische Triadologie. In Theorien des Dritten. Paderborn: Wilhelm Fink.

Commons, J. (1990). Institutional economics. London: Transaction Publishers. (Original work published 1934)

Ingham, G. (2004). *The nature of money*. Cambridge: Polity Press. Knapp, G. (2012). Staatliche Theorie des Geldes. Lindau: Unikum.

Luhmann, N. (1994). Die Wirtschaft der Gesellschaft. Frankfurt am Main, Suhrkamp. Macfarlane, L., & Minsky, H. P. (2011). Instabilität und Kapitalismus. Zürich, Diaphanes.

Minsky, H. P. (1986). *Stabilizing an unstable economy*. New Haven, Yale University Press.

Sahr, A. (2017). Das Versprechen des Geldes: Eine Praxistheorie des Kredits. Hamburg: Hamburger Edition HIS.

Schumpeter, J. (2006). *History of economic analysis*. London: Routledge

Siddiqi, M. (1983). *Banking without interest*. Markfield: Islamic Foundation.

Simmel, G. (1989). Philosophie des Geldes. Berlin: Suhrkamp
Whalen, C. J. (1993) Saving capitalism by making it good: the monetary economics of John R Commons. Journal of Economic Issues 27(4), 1155–1179.
Warde, I. (2000). Islamic finance in the global economy. Edinburgh: Edinburgh University Press.
Wieland, J. (2018). Relational Economics. Ökonomische Theorie der Governance wirtschaftlicher Transaktionen. Metropolis-Verlag.
Wieland, J. (2020): Relational Economics, Cham, Springer International Publishing.

Christian Fiedler studied Sociology, Politics & Economics as well as Corporate Management and Economics at Zeppelin University. He served as a student research assistant at the Leadership Excellence Institute Zeppelin.

Reasons Theoretical Underpinnings, and Core Features of a Novel Paradigm of Acting in Economics

Albrecht von Müller

Abstract Relational Economics reconceptualizes longstanding assumptions of the discipline. This paper tries to provide a philosophical framework and underpinning for this new form of describing and analyzing economic interactions. To this end, the paper focuses on a new paradigm of acting that becomes possible and eventually even necessary, once we start to appreciate reality as a process of ongoing self-unfolding.

Keywords Constellatory thinking · Autogenetic universe · Complexity · Homo instrumentalis · Mutual semantic unfolding · Rationality · Reason

1 Introduction

The purpose of this little note is to briefly sketch out: (a) the reasons why we need, (b) the conceptual underpinnings of, and (c) the core features of a novel paradigm of acting in economics.[1]

Relational economics is, I think, a very promising approach to reconceptualize some of the most fundamental assumptions of this discipline. A relational picture, I presume, is not meant to be in any way a static snapshot, but it provides us with a dynamic, constantly further unfolding representation of (economic) reality.

What I try to point out in the following can, thus, be understood as a trial to offer a small, philosophical underpinning and "flank protection" for Relational Economics, and I will focus specifically on the paradigm of acting, that—in my understanding—comes with this new way of appreciating business interactions.

[1] As the following argumentation refers to a number of novel conceptual approaches and concepts, which cannot be elaborated here in greater detail, I refer to my recently published book: von Müller, Albrecht (2020), Die Selbstentfaltung der Welt (The Autogenetic Universe), Siedler.

A. von Müller (✉)
Parmenides Foundation, Ludwig-Maximilians-Universität München, München, Germany
e-mail: albrecht.von.mueller@parmenides-foundation.org

L. Biggiero et al. (eds.), *The Relational View of Economics*, Relational Economics and Organization Governance, https://doi.org/10.1007/978-3-030-86526-9_15

2 The Three Reasons for Seeking a Novel Paradigm of Acting

In general, I see three reasons for being interested in a novel paradigm of acting. They are not independent, but it may be useful to distinguish them.

The first reason is the self-acceleration of evolutionary processes due to the very fact that the environment of all competitors is characterized by an increasing pace of adaptation. This self-acceleration of evolutionary selection processes has the side effect that: (a) the overall pace of change, (b) the relevance of speed as a selection criterion, and (c) the overall complexity increase continuously. One may even speculate that there is a second-order effect: The higher the overall pace already achieved, the more important becomes the speed of adaptation as a selection criterion.

Today, most strategic thinking and decision-making processes are increasingly overwhelmed by complexity and pace of change. This, I would argue, holds true for both domains, business as well as politics. The obvious danger of this development is the first reason to look for a further-developed paradigm of acting.

A second, at the first glance quite an independent reason, is that within the edifice of science, we see that at the most fundamental level, that is, in physics, the traditional notions of time and reality are no longer viable.

Given the still unresolved incompatibility between General Relativity Theory and Quantum Physics, there is not yet a clear, unified understanding of how we need to reconceptualize time and reality. However, one thing is clear: The old notions no longer suffice and need a foundational revision.

Interestingly, these problems at the very foundations of science have to a large extent not yet reached the higher echelons of the edifice of science. Biology and medicine, for example, still rely to a large extent on the notion of a fully deterministic, causally closed reality. This reality is at the very foundation of the scientific edifice, but is no longer available. In other words, the scientific edifice can no longer legitimately be derived from it. The same "bottomlessness" holds true for much of the social sciences, including economics.

It is quite possible that many of the unresolved open issues on these higher levels, for example, the quest for what constitutes life or consciousness, are due to these outdated conceptual foundations. The same may hold true for major deficits in economics: They are probably related to the fact that all markets are characterized by a high degree of self-referential unfolding, that is, by actors that appreciate their environment, interpret it and act based on these hypotheses. This inherent self-referentiality distinguishes social systems most fundamentally from highly complex, but purely physical, systems—like the weather. However, this basic discrepancy is hardly reflected in the models and the mathematics we apply.

The third reason for seeking a novel paradigm of acting is of a more philosophical nature. Asking where we stand in the overall evolution of mankind, especially the evolution of cognition, it probably is not unfair to say that the notion of a "homo sapiens" (or even "homo sapiens sapiens") may still be a bit premature.

We actually seem to be still much more of a "homo instrumentalis". Its state of cognitive development is characterized by very advanced skills to understand and manipulate what can be described in more or less linear-causal and deterministic relations, as is the case in the most traditional technology. The impressive abilities to handle this aspect of reality resulted in a self-accelerating increase in our instrumental powers. That said, all technical, respectively instrumental, interventions are embedded in larger human and societal contexts and frameworks.

Unfortunately, the skills required appreciate and shape those contexts in a responsible manner: the faculty of reason still drastically lags behind our instrumental powers. One can compare the "homo instrumentalis" quite well to the Sorcerer's Apprentice in Goethe's famous poem. He was able to unleash the most powerful forces, but he is unable to control or guide them in a meaningful way.

Unlike in Goethe's poem, however, there is no sorcerer in the offing that could bail us out. We have to master the transition to a real homo sapiens by ourselves—and for surviving the present spiral of escalating civilizational threats, we should rather start soon and be successful.

3 Some Remarks on the Conceptual Underpinnings

The following is by far the most tedious part of the entire argumentation, but I will try to summarize the main points in a few theses.

(1) Local spacetime is a very powerful mode of addressing reality, especially by allowing for descriptions that enable manipulating reality with a predictable outcome. This is the case for all forms of technology. But the local spacetime portrait is available only for the factual aspect of reality. In other words, it is incomplete as it cannot cover that and how facts come into being in the first place.

(2) The second aspect of reality is its actual taking place. Facts are the traces which this actual taking place leaves behind in local spacetime. Reality "in statu nascendi", that is, the actual taking place of reality still occurs outside local spacetime, in the time–space of the present. This present is neither a point-like now, nor a subjective confabulation. It is an aspect of (physical) time in its own right. The time–space of the present is the "primordial" form of time, out of which the sequential structure of time emerges. The present is a not-yet-local "platform" on which all of reality actually occurs. Only as something "*takes place*" there, it becomes part of local spacetime. Local spacetime emerges and becomes applicable only together with factization. Only then a prior starts to become separable from a latter in a clear-cut way.

(3) Our subjective experience of a present is not just a misleading, just subjective confabulation, as assumed in modern physics. In neurobiological terms, it is the most costly endeavor of our brain. As a result, it would hardly have survived evolutionary selection pressures if it did not reap huge benefits in interacting with reality. Seen from the novel account of time and reality introduced here, our experience of a present turns out to be quite to the point. It is hitherto the most advanced adaptation of cognitive evolution to the actual taking place of reality—as it occurs in the time–space of the present.

(4) The essential feature of the present is constellatory unfolding. All that is present constitutes a constellation in which it unfolds into what it subsequently is as a fact. Without this actual unfolding, the emergence of something genuinely novel cannot even be thought, because we are conceptually locked in a block universe picture—in which not even our quest for truth makes any sense. Within this picture, all that is present unfolds mutually, thus becoming what it factually is, thereafter. Reality in statu nascendi, that is, while unfolding, is not yet well defined enough that it could be tackled by the sharp means of Boolean logic or causality, the sequential order of time or a clear-cut separation of observer and observandum. Metaphorically, one can address this aspect of reality as the "concertus mundi". While the unfolding reality is both, (partially) pre-determined and thus foreseeable, due to already existing facts and what their perseverance implies for the future, *and* (partially) unpredictable due to genuine novelty. The actual taking place of reality is characterized by the interplay between fact-based predictability and genuine novelty. A good example of this interplay is improvisation, for example, the improvisation found in jazz. The different musicians authentically respond to each other, taking up what just emerged, expanding, and unfolding it further. If felicitous, an overarching, coherent piece of music emerges, which is a realization of both ultimate freedom *and* almost stringent necessity, that is, by being exactly right, "just as it is". The authentic experience of "Stimmigkeit" (approximately translatable as "elegance") is the only available criterion of "truth" in this second aspect of reality, namely its actual taking place in the time–space of the present.

(5) The novel account of time and reality, thus, comprises two complementary aspects of reality. Its two constituent layers are (Fig. 1).

(6) It should be mentioned that for reasons of philosophical completeness one can also formulate one more, namely a third fundamental aspect of reality, the so-called "apeiron aspect". This comes into play when we address all of reality under the aspect of its unity. Drawing on Heraclitus, one could characterize it as a "hen panta" appreciation of the reality that allows to consider how all is related to everything else in a most interesting superposition of unity and diversity. But, for the present context, it is sufficient and already demanding enough to just focus on the "factual" and the "statu nascendi" aspect of reality.

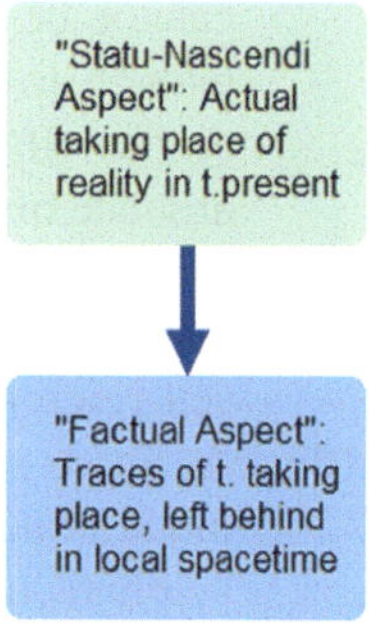

Fig. 1 The two aspects of the reality of the novel account of time and reality

(7) In order to understand and handle these two complementary aspects appropriately, we need to consider a hitherto unknown phenomenon for which the notion of an "underlying categorial apparatus" is introduced. Whenever we address reality, we draw on categories as the most fundamental structures by which we frame what we want to address. Immanuel Kant's great achievement was to make us aware of these primordial *preparations* that human cognition inevitably undertakes. What is new is that these categorial underpinnings do not come one by one but rather as an apparatus, that is, embedded into a set of interrelated and even fully interdependent components. Neither of these constituent components of an apparatus can be abandoned, or substantially modified, without unraveling the entire apparatus.

(8) The categorical apparatus that underlies and constitutes the factual portrait of reality is composed of four, as mentioned, fully interdependent components (Fig. 2).

(9) But this categorical framework, subsequently also referred to as "F framework" does not allow for a comprehensive picture of reality. It is especially incapable of handling two phenomena. The first is *strong self-referentiality*, which is defined as the phenomenon of something referring to itself in its entirety. (Gödel's ingenious proof of 1931 shows that strong self-referentiality

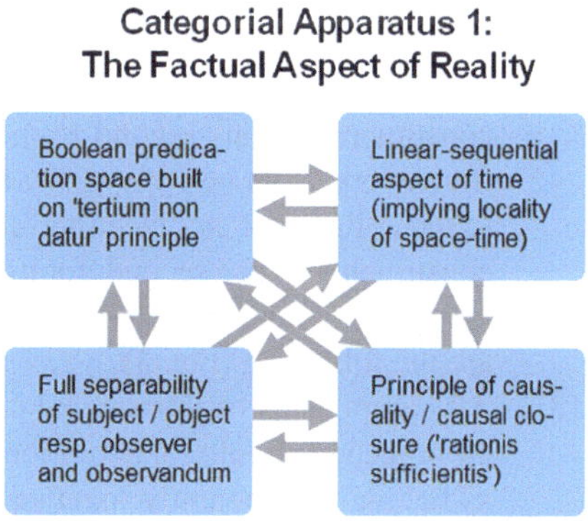

Fig. 2 The factual aspect of reality

cannot be avoided, even in the most basic formal systems, just strong enough to derive natural numbers.) The second phenomenon is *autogenesis* by which something unfolds in and out of itself—in other words, in the absence of external causation. A closer look at these two phenomena shows that they are closely intertwined: Strong self-referentiality is the structural portrait of autogenesis, while autogenesis is the procedural portrait of strong self-referentiality.

(10) As a side remark, it should be mentioned that most, if not all, the big "enigmatic issues" with which modern science continues to struggle to seem to be characterized by these twin phenomena. This applies to quantum physical reduction and the singularities of general relativity, the phylogenetic and ontogenetic self-constitution of life, and, based on the latter, the emergence of consciousness respectively mind. Seen from the novel account of time and reality, these three foundational enigmas, located at the roots of physics, biology, and cognitive science, can be interpreted as first-, second-and third-order self-referentiality. The strength of the F apparatus is that it allows for well-defined descriptions. But this is, incidentally, also its central weakness. It imputes that reality is infinitely well defined, which it is not as long as it is "still in the making", that is, as long as it is still unfolding itself in the time–space of the present. The F apparatus I is *structsurally* incapable of handling strong self-referentiality, and respectively autogenesis. Reducing reality to what can be appropriately addressed by means of the F apparatus I constitutes a "facticity imprisonment" that characterizes most of modern science.

(11) In order to be able to address these hitherto inaccessible phenomena, and the actual taking place of reality that is characterized by them, a second categorial framework is required. Building it requires to first gain an insight into the very existence of categorial apparatus (pl.), and second to understand their structure. A categorial apparatus has four constituents. It must comprise (a) the structure of a predication space, (b) a related aspect of time, respectively space, (c) a way how events can be interlinked, and, finally, (d) a basic epistemological setting.

(12) Based on understanding the basic structure of a categorial apparatus, one can develop a second categorial framework that allows to address "reality in the making", namely the actual self-unfolding of reality. Neither of the constituents of this second framework, subsequently also referred to as "E framework", can be put into the F framework. This would lead immediately to the collapse of any meaningful predication. But taken together, these four constituents form a second, for us today rather unusual, but inherently consistent, way of addressing reality. Its four components and their interrelations are the following (Fig. 3).

(13) All components of this second categorial apparatus have a long tradition in all branches of cultural evolution. Its components have just never been seen as belonging inherently together. "Constellatory logic" is a specific way to concatenate propositions. Like in a poem, the individual components unfold

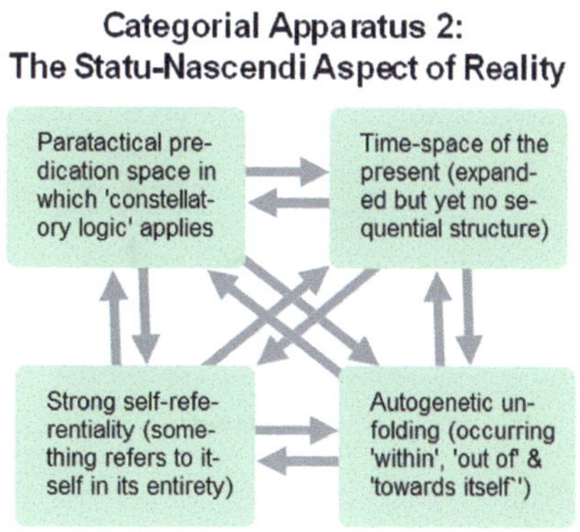

Fig. 3 The Statu-Nascendi aspect of reality

their meaning mutually, that is, only in the authentic *presence* of all components. This is the reason for the impossibility to formalize a poem and, thus, constellatory predications in general. Constellatory logic does not allow for any kind of formal conclusions. A good example of highly self-referential, constellatory unfolding is the already-mentioned improvisation in jazz. The different musicians authentically respond to each other, taking up what just emerged, expanding on it and unfolding it further. If felicitous, an overarching, coherent piece of music emerges, which is a realization of both ultimate freedom *and* almost alternativeless necessity, that is, being exactly right "just as it is". The authentic experience of "Stimmigkeit" (approximately translatable as "elegance") is the only available criterion of "truth" in the E framework.

(14) In addressing reality, we can now draw on both categorial apparatuses. The appropriate mix varies, depending on the degree of self-referentiality within the addressed object-space. But neither of the two can ever reach zero completely, that is, all predications about reality require both aspects irreducibly.

(15) Natural language is characterized by the use of concepts that are not completely well defined. Our concepts are moving targets that change their meaning while we use them. But this is not a bug. Instead, it is the crucial success factor of natural language. It combines the principle of semantic constancy and the possibility of semantic unfolding in a most sophisticated balance. This balance emerged during cognitive and cultural evolution. Only due to this most-sophisticated balance are we capable of addressing both: the factual aspect of reality *and* its ongoing, not anticipatable, unfolding. Via its semantic unfolding, natural language enables us to address and *re-present* the unfolding of reality—its actual taking place in the present (Fig. 4).

(16) The history of the categorial deprivation and its cost can be summarized as follows.

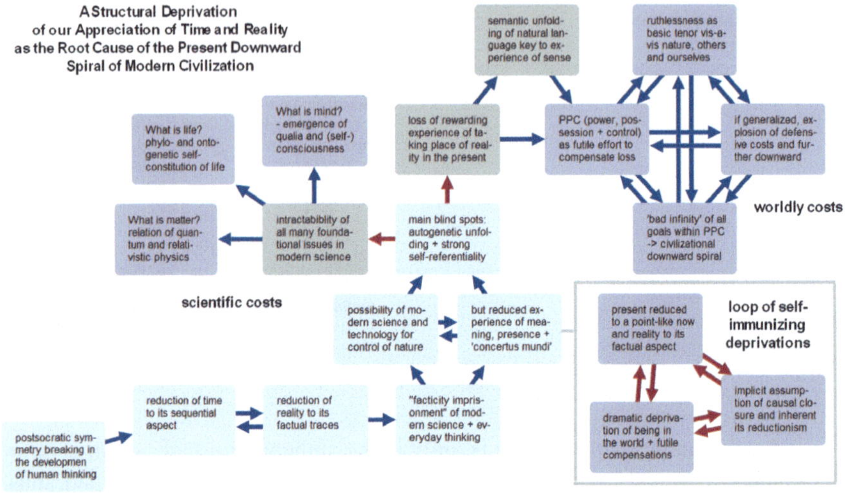

Fig. 4 A structural deprivation of our appreciation of time and reality as the root cause of the present downward spiral of modern civilization

(17) It is not the task of this paper to discuss the worldly costs of the post-Socratic symmetry breaking. For reasons of completeness, however, they should be mentioned briefly. At present, we observe a dangerous overfixation of modern civilization on power, possession, and control (PPC paradigm). This paradigm defines our basic tenor towards the world, others, and often even ourselves. Seen from the novel account of time and reality, it could be exactly this tenor, respectively the underlying categorial deprivation of our thinking that brings mankind to the brink of self-extinction. If the overall approach presented here is roughly correct, this ruthless PPC attitude is less an ethical than an epistemological problem: Focusing just on the sequential aspect of time makes time appear as the merciless "dent" (already Aristotle's metaphor) that constantly nibbles away everything there is. And the PPC paradigm—with its three versions clinging onto something—would just be a futile effort to stem against this misguided perception of time as an all-devouring maelstrom.

Concluding remark: The emergence of relations is the essential feature of the unfolding of reality. But we also cannot fully appreciate the first without being able to consistently think the latter. Therefore, the extremely interesting and promising approach of Relational Economics might profit from—and might even need—being complemented by a fundamental reconsideration and widening of the categorical foundations in which we frame time and reality.

4 Six Crucial Features of the Novel Paradigm of Acting

As the final topic of this little note, I would like to address the question of what this novel portrayal of time, in reality, means for our paradigm of acting. As long as we see reality as a more or less predetermined, causally closed process, we will resort to a rather mechanistic way of trying to intervene. If, instead, we appreciate reality as a process of ongoing self-unfolding, we, obviously, come to quite a different way of acting, that is, of trying to shape matters.

A key point in this regard is the difference between rationality and reason. Rationality can be defined as the "drill-down" mode of thinking. By this very important and powerful mode, we come to a more and more precise analytical understanding, and—depending on the epistemological framework—often also to causal accounts. This mode of thinking lies, as mentioned, at the root of the self-accelerating expansion of our instrumental power in modern industrial society. We can, however, iterate this mode of thinking as often as we want, it will never bring us back to a cognitive representation of the respective topic in its entirety. According to a convincing definition of the phenomenon of "reason" by the physicist and philosopher Carl Friedrich von Weizsäcker, it can be understood as "the ability to appreciate an issue in its entirety".

Based on two decades of interdisciplinary basic research on human thinking at the Parmenides Foundation, we possess today a much better understanding of how this equally important mode of thinking is actually implemented in the human brain. The core phenomenon is a process of mutual semantic unfolding between the constituents of a constellation. This occurs as a quite structured process that can be described as the so-called "logic of constellations". This may have evolved in response to the constellatory self-unfolding of reality. A one-sided, "facticity only" portrait of reality is closely related to the cognitive trap of ruthless, local optimization. In order to overcome this, we need not at all abandon rationality, but expand it and go beyond it towards reason and eventually even wisdom—the feature we prematurely made our signature characteristic in the notion "homo sapiens".

In the following section, I intend to introduce six crucial features of the novel, the reason-oriented paradigm of acting that in its epistemological roots goes back to the novel understanding of time and reality described above.

I start with our overall attitude towards reality, specifically the world we live in. The essential characteristic of unfolding is that on one side something genuinely novel comes into being while on the other side this is not a total "aliud", but it can—at least ex-post—be understood as a further developed form of a what has already been there. In this way, unfolding combines the feature of irreducible novelty or wonderfulness with the feature of partial explainability. The best basic tenor versus such a reality is, I would argue, an attitude that could be described as ***thankful attentiveness***. By this, I mean a fundamental openness and a caring approachability which at the same time is characterized by deep gratitude. Quite obviously, one would not come to this basic tenor if we would not appreciate reality as a process of continuous self-unfolding.

The second core feature is the new way of interacting with reality could be characterized as ***dialogic shaping.*** In a deterministic portrayal of reality, one would tend to intervene mechanistically, namely by having a fully defined idea of what one wishes to achieve, and then trying to find the most efficient causal interventions in order to make this come true. Dialogic shaping, instead, is much closer to how a potter or a gardener interacts with reality. They do something, and then they observe how reality reacts to it. They take up these interim results and make them part of both, a certain re-definition of what they want to achieve and a valuable input for further strategy and tactics. In this way, a kind of dialogue emerges between: (a) the intentions of the actor and the ways how she or he proceeds, and (b) the emerging responses by the respective object—which becomes almost a partner in this dialogue.

The third component is of a more technical nature. Whenever complex systems unfold, there are certain points at which the future orientation of the entire process is taking shape. These points I call ***Archimedean shaping points*** (ASPs). They are usually quite deeply embedded in the respective system and not easy to identify. But it is absolutely worthwhile to search for them, as utilizing them as the point of departure for one's own interventions boosts the efficiency and the effectiveness of these. Starting from the ASPs assures also a much more substantial and lasting impact than by just intervening at the surface as we usually do when trying to correct systems' behaviour, especially under time pressure. I would like to give two examples of ASP-based strategies—one from education and the other from health care. The most fundamental problem of today's healthcare systems is that we reward only "being occupied is treating diseases". We do not incentivize preventing disease in the first place or, at least, returning to a healthy status as quickly as possible. If, and only if, we redesign present healthcare systems from that ASP, we have a chance to really achieve better healthcare combined with more moderate cost increases. Regarding education, the quintessential factor of success is fascination—both, on the side of the teachers as well as on the side of the students. In today's practice, however, the factor of fascination is at least neglected, and often it is also almost systematically eradicated. Unless we change this and make fascination the pivotal point of our education systems, we will continue to waste enormous amounts of resources, while at the same time significantly harming the future prospects of students. Regarding all complex challenges, one can seek to identify these ASPs and this is by far the most promising way to have a substantial and lasting impact on the respective systems.

The fourth component of the novel paradigm affecting can be characterized as learning to see ***the problem as a partner***. What is the point here? Institutions are built to resolve upcoming problems. If a problem is severe and/or sticky, this problem, in a way, "makes something right". It manages to survive the "immune system" of the respective system or institution. Therefore, it makes sense to look at the problem like a little organism that has its own metabolism. Once we understand the key components of this metabolism, namely the main structures and processes by which the problem manages to survive, we can start to tackle the problem in a much more systematic and promising manner. Just like in antibiotics research, we can ask which are the crucial choke points at which one can stop this metabolism to work. In this way, the problem-as-a-partner heuristic can be seen as a very efficient way to search from where to tackle the problem. Often a crisp description of the metabolism can serve even as an ex-negativo blueprint for a highly successful strategy, in which we do not have to do much more than just "inverting" the key factors of the survival metabolism.

The fifth characteristic of the new paradigm of acting is again of a slightly more philosophical nature. In a just given universe, driven by a mixture of deterministic and random processes, the best I can do is trying to optimize my own interests through a certain form of local, eventually even ruthless, optimization. In a self-unfolding universe, instead, this way of proceeding easily turns out to be counterproductive—because it harms and deprives the further unfolding of the entire system. In order to ensure the best possible unfolding of the entirety, we have to become aware of the ***convergence of the ethically good with the most useful*** for the individual actors. Being aware of this convergence is crucially important for acting successfully in a self-unfolding universe—and respectively for our ability to tackle and successfully resolve the global challenges of modern civilization still in time.

Closely related to this fifth core feature of the novel paradigm of acting is also the sixth and last one. A very powerful and fundamentally novel heuristic for finding the best way to act in a given situation can be defined as ***joint option space unfolding***. This heuristic makes us try to imagine, respectively figure out what could expand the future option spaces of all the involved agents in the most efficient and lasting manner. Mathematically speaking, one can define this joint future option space as the product of an individual future option space. The goal of the heuristic is to find out how the future volume of this joint option space can be expanded as good as possible by one stone actions. In concluding this brief note, let me give an example also for this last feature of the novel paradigm of acting. Good education is what optimally unfolds the joint option space of children and parents. Education is meant here as combining good preparation for a chosen job with a familiarization of the core insights and values of humanism. Good education is, obviously, very important for the future of the children. As well-educated human beings, they will, however, also be able to interact with the parents on a substantially deeper level and in a richer way than without a good education. In this way, the future option space of the parents is also optimally unfolded by assuring the best possible education for their children. This, in turn, means that the mathematical product of the two option spaces is the biggest possible. (The reason for not just "adding" the volumes of the option spaces, but "multiplying" them is that only in this way one-sided increases are adequately "punished".) Whenever acting, the heuristic of joined option space unfolding can serve as another form of a "categorical imperative"—tuned to the specific features of a self-unfolding universe.

Instead of just summarizing some key points, the graphic on the following page, a so-called visual reasoning architecture, summarizes the essential steps of the whole argumentation (Fig. 5).

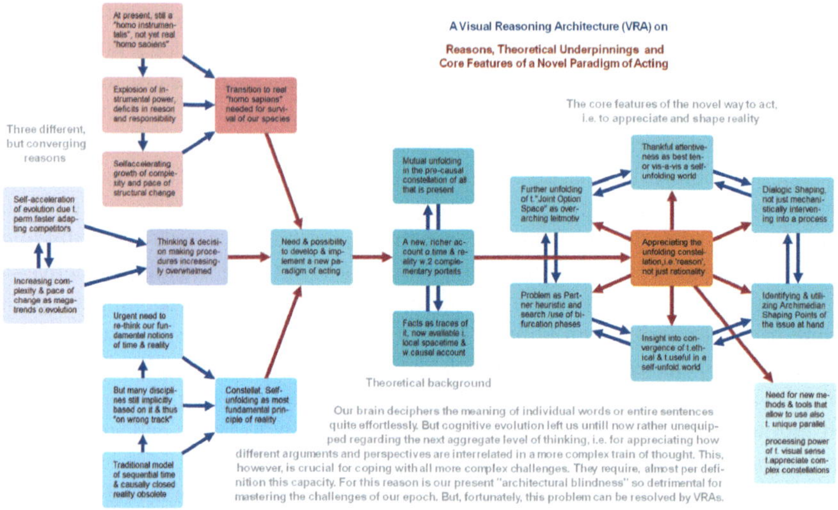

Fig. 5 Reasons, theoretical underpinnings, and core features of a novel paradigm of acting

Albrecht von Müller is professor at Ludwig-Maximilians-Universität, Munich. He is the founder and chairman of the Parmenides Foundation (www.parmenides-foundation.org). After his Ph.D., he worked at the Max Planck Institute for physics and became head of the "Stability-oriented Security Policy" research program. He was the founding director of the European Center for International Security and developed in 1983 the arms control paradigm of structural defense dominance, which later became a leitmotif of the CFE treaty. Müller developed the visual reasoning language Eidos. He publishes in the fields of philosophy, theoretical physics, complexity theory, cognitive science, and political studies.

Contracts as Cooperation: About an Implicit Ethics of Transactions

Jean Müßgens and Birger P. Priddat

Abstract The rational choice is based on the representation of a monoregular, balanced market environment. It ignores the fact that a minimal sociology is created through the transaction as the smallest unit of analysis. On this basis, allocative couplings are created which go beyond the assertion of efficient allocations. Away from the mutual advantage appropriation, under the premise of mutual mistrust contingency, it is also about exploring the potential for cooperation. In the bilateral relationship of the transaction, the actors are open to admitting something to the other beyond the maximization of their advantage. This insight is important if one considers that economic activity is constituted within social networks and relationships. These interrelationships become apparent in the dispositive of the gift-economy. It refers to the "implicit ethics" of bilateral service relationships, particularly effective at the digital economy's core.

Keywords Relational economy · Digital economy · Social networks · Gift-economy · Relational transaction · Markets and Non-markets · Ethics

Economic theory is based on a misleading assumption: rational actors who freely and independently optimize themselves do not yet bring about a transaction. Only when two transactants interact and when payments flow (Baecker, 2020), an economic operation is realized. Rational choice is, strictly speaking, only a unilateral contractual statement, neither an economically nor legally effective action, because it does not consider the formation process of decisions.

In this paper, the process of transaction formation is elaborated in three steps:

1. A bilateral bargaining process can develop an implicit ethic of mutualistic reciprocity.

J. Müßgens (✉)
Zeppelin University, Friedrichshafen, Germany
e-mail: Jean.Muessgens@zu.de

B. P. Priddat
University Witten/Herdecke, Zeppelin University, Friedrichshafen, Germany

L. Biggiero et al. (eds.), *The Relational View of Economics*, Relational Economics and Organization Governance, https://doi.org/10.1007/978-3-030-86526-9_16

2. The gift-economic dimension, which is evident in this, is fully developed in the digitalized markets.
3. It represents a complex entanglement of multiple transactions—a new facet of a relational digital economy.

1 Transactions as Bilateral Mutualities

The basic economic operator is the bilateral transaction. Its form is the contract. Only in the contractual consensus is the transaction economically confirmed. Economic contracting is always juridical—an old insight of J.R. Commons (1995). In the transaction, economic and juridical modes of action are brought into play uno actu.

The economic actor proves to be a multiple self, which follows two actor dimensions simultaneously—with the consequence of analyzing which actor modalities are actually in operation (Priddat, 2010). The transactions are institutionally embedded (Ostrom, 2005; Wieland, 2020, part. 1).

From a process perspective, transactions have

1. An individual search phase (search for potential contract partners) and
2. A collective agreement phase afterward.

In the final stages of this process, transactions, albeit temporary, are cooperations. In its transactional finale, the economy is based on a weak sociology because the core of contractual cooperation is communication and interaction. The transaction is a relational construct of law, economy, and ethics (Wieland, 2020, p. 20). Harald Münster (2020, p. 72 et seq) works out that the legal contract as a form of interpersonal interaction cannot be legally enforced but sets self-obligations as conditions.

Transactions are generally regarded as a coordination of mutual benefit (competitive coordination). It is assumed that actors only transact to maximize their respective benefits (see Priddat, 2016a). Such an approach is not efficient from the outset because it leaves cooperation potentials untapped. The contracts perspective as a competitive advantage does not fully sound out the negotiating potential, resulting in cooperation processes. Contracts can be interpreted across a broader range of contractual modalities. The usual economic interpretation of a contract, as a mutual advantage, is a construction of equilibrium theory, which is sufficient to prove that the exchange/transaction partners have chosen the best of the alternatives available to them (i.e., rational choice). However, in cooperative contract negotiations, further possibilities can open up. The object of a transaction can be expanded or changed. Furthermore, the subjects of the transaction can change as well. These aspects remain usually untapped (Gintis et al., 2005; Ostrom, 2005, p. 128).

Contracts do not form themselves, and they are not events for exchange coordination. Instead, they are generated or communicated consensus. The fact that most contracts in the market are treated in a standardized way is not an argument against the innovative potential of self-governance of collaborative cooperation. There are always reasons to offer, for example, discounts, leeway, time, and social conditions to others. When two people cooperate (which takes place in the broad dimension of bargaining), there is room for maneuver. Instead of price-taking, one goes into a state of price-making. In another context, one speaks about gifts.

Of course, you can leave bargaining at any time and ventilate other, new, third offers. Until then, the competition works (phase 1). Nevertheless, once you have entered into the contract process (phase 2), we have a transition phase: actors condition each other, gain trust, and gain new options in the collaborative process (which are no longer matched against third alternatives, unless you distrust each other—again). Trust (via a lock-in, a process of de-anonymization) defines the relative contract consensus. One varies, but within the partnership, one no longer competes against others (phase 2). The competition changes to cooperation when such a state is reached.

Successful contractual processes are mutual agreements with the emergent exclusion of competition. In phase 2, the market is excluded: one actor forms his own small new (bilateral) market, with potentially his own price and quality judgments.

One has to think about it in this way:

1. Markets are competitive events.
2. Markets are formed through contracts that have been executed.
3. Contracts are formed through contractual processes that can be cooperative in their finale (phase 2), i.e., exclude competition.
4. As a result, at times, non-competitive emergent structures can emerge in the core of the market.

If actors gain trust during the negotiation process, possibilities for action can be sounded out together, increasing the utility space—a dimension that is not perceived by the simple coordination utility maximization. It is a transition into an extended ontology or a space of possibility.

Instead of the neoclassical optimization of conditions, transactants can create new conditions in the contractual process that form their own local balances. They are, sui generis, potentially innovative instances, which are provided with a Hayekian (1969) analogy: they pursue their discovery process in the market, changing the conditions under which they entered by their joint design. It is, now, unlike Hayek, a form of collaborative discovery—an interplay that becomes possible in the transaction process, which can change into gift-economic gift-exchanges (Ferrary, 2003, p. 128 ff.).

But also independently of the shared feelings (Singer & Fehr, 2005, p. 340), the contract negotiations reach interference foci that are unique concerning the specific relationship (because other negotiations with other partners would have generated other interferences). According to this, every phase 2 process is solitary and only partially comparable—at least if one has engaged in real bargaining (and does not merely allow price-taking to take place).

A decision to omit phase 2, for example, would devalue the specific negotiation gains that have accumulated in the meantime. The alternative negotiations would first have to be conducted without knowing whether the same interference would be achieved. The social capital invested in the contract negotiation process would be devalued entirely (Herrmann-Pillath, 2000; Lin, 2001). It turns out that the emerging interference of phase 2 limits the economic advantage of drawing comparisons between alternative offers at any time. In their final process phase, contracts are subject to bounded compatibility, which could be described positively as Kompossibilität (Leibnitz's concept of Kompossibilität refers to a process of joint enabling).

Contracts do not optimize what the market wants but what they define. They define, in their local event space, what the market is. By doing so, all contracts form the market as the sum of collaborative local optimizations, not in general equilibrium, but as a market process of manifold variations of local results—a proximity to evolutionary economics is apparent (Herrmann-Pillath, 2010).

1.1 Networks and Markets

All actors are, in parallel, included in networks. This is not trivial: they move uno actu in other social dimensions than just markets. Networks are loose couplings of the actors (in various dimensions that are not coupled with each other), which form a social positioning matrix. Here, status questions are essentially clarified, as communicative couplings (Ferrary, 2003). In networks, the participants communicate social and economic meanings (e.g., relevance, focus, and attention). Networks are linguistic communities in which language games codify semantics (see White, 2008; White & Godart, 2007 a,b; Priddat, 2011, 2012, 2019).

We can safely assume that mutual agreement is more likely to be possible if both contracting parties belong to the same networks (e.g., possibly an industry, manager socialization, or an ethnic group) (Ferrary, 2003, p. 135). As a result, they have similar semantics and are positively encouraged in their network communication. If the networks differ, the chance of an emergent mutual agreement in the contract process decreases because we have unadapted semantics and neutral-to-negative "advice" in network communication (see Priddat 2011, 2012b).

Networks are functional bridges of the transition phase (from 1 to 2) in the contract process. The networks also influence the finding of transaction partners in the contract process (phase 1). We must abandon the idea that rational actors act independently of communication because they are frequently under influence. Even in undetectable acute communication, they act under the influence of the semantics of their network participation. Goods are goods + meaning (Priddat, 2006), which are produced by the media (e.g., advertising and social communication, practically in networks among friends, families, colleagues, communities, and peers). Consequently, the contracts are not concluded directly through the purchase but primarily through the preliminary communication of the relevance of the goods, i.e., economic and social validity. Network communication is part of the contract process.

However, in the contract process, the actors can free themselves from their bridge semantics, canceling their leading network influences. If they succeed in establishing a specific exclusion in the contract, both partners open new options for themselves. These changes are not based on individuals' hypothetical autonomy but on a successful (micro) discourse of the contractual partners in their respective contract processes. Thus, we have extended the bilateral transaction formation via network influences.

If we make this result more precise, we are no longer dealing with a bilateral transactional partnership—not only with a pair of interactions, but with a more complex network, in which each transactant is subject, for example, to influences, communications, norms, proposals for interpretation, and affect, which expand the number of participants and influences. We must understand the transaction as a process in which multiple actors intervene polylingual. When a transactant copies an ongoing communication in society, his decision is not only his, but hybrid: his and that of the communicative influence. Both transactants mutate into a duplex actor. Together they form a related quadruple so that the transaction can succeed. The fact that the actor person is considered to be the decisive one is related to the legal construction of holding someone liable in the contract.

However, these are not economic reasons which are simulated in the methodological individualism of economics in order to exculpate the juridical for the primacy of the economic, i.e., pure economics. Transactions represent a relational nexus, not a simple cause-and-effect principle.

For the analysis of transactions, networks are names for the dimensions of influence that cannot be categorized in rational decision routines. Economic, juridical, social, ethical, technical, emotional, political, and other dimensions play a role in transaction formation processes (Wieland, 2020). Let us focus on one of them.

1.2 Implicit Ethical and Gift-Economic Implications of the Transaction

Cooperation as a—latent, always possible—modus integralis of economic transactions is an ethical mode. But it is not norms or maxims, which function as restrictions (external to the economy), that come into play here but instead options for shaping one's relationships freely and confidentially. The ethical mode is generated bilaterally when trust prevails. It is a form of implicit ethics (see Vogd, 2018, ch. vii). What is decisive is the different attitude of the actants that appears in trust relationships: they are prepared to grant something to the other person instead of just benefiting themselves (see Ortmann, 2004, pp. 130 f., 137 f.). Systematically, we are dealing with an 'economy of the gift' in the core business of the market economy (see Elder-Vass, 2018; Ferrary, 2003).

This may seem strange at first. However, the gift-economy is not an exclusively pre-modern model of the economic (Hénaff, 2009; for fundamental analysis, see

Derrida, 1993; Enkelmann, 2010; Ricoeur, 1990, 2006, treatise III, ch. v), but rather co-present in the modern transactional worlds (Ferrary, 2003; Ortmann, 2004; Hillebrandt, 2009; Priddat, 2016b; Elder-Vass, 2018). If we reinterpret the above remarks in light of these concepts, phase 2 of the contract negotiations, when it is transformed into a trust-based mutual agreement, is neither a social space in which the maximization of individual benefit is seen as the goal nor—that on which the above analysis is based—the generation of cooperation rents. Beyond that, it is, possibly, a mutual giving based neither on value equivalence nor on unconditional reciprocity. For if you trust, you give to the other without knowing whether you will regain it. Ferrary (2003, p. 130) explains it as follows:

> In the Gift Exchange, the exchange is diachronous and rarely financial. The one who provides the gift anticipates that the other will one day provide the counter-gift in one form or another. The contract is implicit and uncertain because the provider takes the risk of not receiving a counter gift.

When we speak of an implicit ethics of transactions, it is not a question of contracts being normatively set ethically, but of the fact that they have always contained the reference to good relations among those who entered into them in terms of the logic of their negotiation. Of course, the milieu in which contracts are negotiated, i.e., the market milieu, is shaped by other mental models (of individual utility maximization). The ethical mode is always in danger of becoming marginalized in the optimization process. Therefore, we propose not to determine the actor in phase 2, but to let him find the contract's modalities: in this way, he can prove himself as homo cooperativus. This is a different type than Falk's (2003) homo reciprocans. He is not, quasi-anthropologically, subscribed to reciprocity, but to the free constitution of contracts. The transactant does not have to appear as homo oeconomicus and not as homo reciprocans, who enters a fair moment of retribution. One can also give a gift without expecting retribution (not necessarily in toto, but partially) in the contract. One could waive the first price, give a discount, reduce the rent, not optimize, or defer payment—all gifts that are not envisaged in the competitive market. Empirically, this may be rare (although we experience it frequently during the coronavirus crisis), but we simply have too little data about it to declare it irrelevant. In addition, we know that the logical structure of the contract allows this form of mutuality because the transaction contains a mutualistic dispositive that can be unfolded reciprocally.

On the one hand, to offer a gift in the transaction process, e.g., to give a discount, is a "generosity" (Hénaff, 2017) that can remain unrequited, which makes it risky. On the other hand, it is the initial prerequisite for giving in return on another occasion. This is not charged in monetary terms, but, in fact, indicates the closing of a reciprocal cycle that can be included in the transaction. The transaction takes place and, in parallel, in its structure, a reciprocal act, the priceless fulfillment of which takes place later (not immediately as in the monetary transaction). Via the gift-economic loop, the transaction is transformed into a mutualistic arrangement in which the two agents are in a different relationship with each other (i.e., interdependency) (Ricoeur, 2006, p. 289), than if the transaction had taken its usual market course, (i.e., reciprocity in the sense that "[t]he market is [...] reciprocity without interdependency") (ibid.).

The gift initiative is more of an investment in a shared social capital, with all the investment risks. However, it is only when one of the transactants initiates it that the chance of a counter-gift, a modification of the standard form of the transaction, arises. We can call it creating an atmosphere of gifting through the gift. What appears in the current transaction as a pure gift only becomes relevant for counter-giving later in other transactions. We are dealing with two modes of the transactional: a synchronous transaction and diachronic reciprocity. While the synchronous mode immediately completes the transaction as a transaction, the reciprocal moment appears to be asynchronous. This is because it is only answered in the diachronous mode. The gift, inserted into the transaction, connects the first with a later transaction so that we are dealing with a hypertransaction that modifies the form of the reciprocally coupled later/second transaction in a gift-memory way.

The economic model of hypertransaction is this: the gift from the first transaction has been reminded and reciprocated in the later/second transaction. We are dealing with a coupling of the transactants, over a personal bond that is tantamount to excluding competition, i.e., a kind of customer loyalty. This results from the obligatory character of the implicit reciprocal contract, the gift-economic moment of the transaction. The first transaction is indeed completed, but it contains a surplus that remains unfinished as an expectation of a response. The gift has a call character beyond the first transaction, which we, culturally disposed of, accept. This reveals the different scheme that is inherent in the gift-economy: give and take. The classical form of taking is the gratitude witnessed in accepting the gift, which is expressed in a later reproduction. In the joy of recognizing the gift, shame is mixed with the shame of not being worthy of it. Social norms and rituals are at work here. From a purely economic perspective, the gift does not have to be reciprocated; this form of acceptance is then a pure "take-away" (free benefit, generated from one-sided altruism). In this view, the social momentum of the gift-economy is absent.

The diachrony of the reciprocal hypertransaction has yet another meaning. Williamson (2002) treats it as transaction cost rationality: that actors enter into long-term relationships because these reduce the transaction costs of reviewing contracts. It is also possible due to another mode: that one does not want to reduce costs at all but wants to have good relationships (mutual agreements as social capital). These mutual agreements aim not to optimize the respective or common benefits but to achieve a commonality (joint utility) that binds the transactional relationality and familiar relationship to a nexus. One sees immediately that the respective benefit does not disappear. It is generated under new conditions: that one understands each other, i.e., that one does not enter into an anonymous relationship, but a humane one, in which one can exist before oneself and others in the good life (eupraxis). The good that is gained in this process is not an extension of the good, but rather its condition: that something can only be useful if it is received in a relationship context that is itself good.

Here we find an ethical dimension of the transaction: it forms relationships based on personalized interdependency (Ricoeur, 2006, treatise III, ch. v), not on anonymous reciprocity. This is a straight side of mutualistic commonality. Implicit contracts, in contrast, represent the other side of the same process. If the first transaction's gift is reproduced in a second, subsequent transaction, it becomes clear that a kind of debt relationship has arisen. This debt relationship tends to be unconscious in terms of the socialized pattern that gifts are reciprocated out of "gratitude".

2 Gift-Economic Aspects of the Digital Economy

So far, we have developed a gift-economic dimension in the core process of transactions, which refers to a mutualistic potential (gift-economy I). However, the field of gift economics is broader when we look at digital markets (gift-economy II). The simple reciprocity of the transactions' mutualistic potentials changes into a more complex nexus. We will unfold this reciprocity as a quaternary or multiply overlapping allocation. The gift-economic dimension finds a new expression in the digital economy.

We are entering a new type of transactional relationship in which a personal, bilateral actor relationship does not exclusively determine the transition phases within the contractual process. The essential operation within transactions, the bargaining within the contract process, is carried out via human-technology interfaces, which are not socially transparent because they follow independent cognitive processes. Here, bargaining is not the subject of a physical, personal heteronomous experience among people. In these transactions, human consciousness moves from the human to the non-trivial machine.

Assuming that there is no retrivialization by a human observer, the non-trivial machine forms a virtual cogito, which chooses its method in the representation of worldly modalities (Müßgens, 2021). The subject-relative given of the world is ordered on a pre-reflective level by guiding and aligning consciousness's subjective manifestation. For the actors, the world's scope shows itself in a wealth of newly appearing objects, whose intentional representation is not perceived. The intentional appearance of the world gains a new dimension. Data are set about the deliberate changing of the object world. One can speak here of a "data-setting power" (Popitz, 1992, p. 167), which performatively stages the transactional objects at the human-technology interface and thereby points beyond a classical subject-object (S1-O1) relation (see Priddat, 2014, p. 81). The virtual cogito generates an algorithmically generated transcendental subject (S2) from the actors' data points, which independently breaks down into the objects (O2). Within this process, the virtual cogito chooses an independent "method of phenomenological reduction" (Husserl, 1985, p. 201) by interpreting human existence's external conditions as informational data phenomena (Müßgens 2021). Thus, the virtual cogito asserts the "absolute, pure uniqueness" (see Husserl, 1985, p. 190) of its cognitive processes. We are dealing with the detachment of a transcendental idealism that simultaneously coincides with life itself. This becomes apparent when we consider the relationship at the human-technology interface. At first glance, this is a symmetrical communication relationship that deliberately stages a reciprocal relationship between an "I & You" (Buber,

2019) in order to create facts in the actors' life-world. This becomes visible in those cases in which the consumers are fed by algorithms with individually tailored offers from their statistically determined, past-based purchase biographies. The algorithmically generated transcendental subject (S2) can import offers that correspond to the actor's individual preferences (S1) and arouse his undreamt-of desire. It turns out that the offers, algorithmically formulated by (S2), exceed the processual capacity of the actor (S1) to identify the best possible alternatives (Priddat, 2014). The new algorithmically transcendental subject "(S2) offers a marked object (O2) that is identified as better" (ibid. p. 80), which is why the offers take on the character of a gift. Here the individual approach simulates a personal relation. We are dealing with a new transaction partner, the computer or big-data algorithms, which are able to input signals that pleasantly surprise us and invite us to cooperate, because they reflect a more efficient form of ourselves, so to speak: "Here someone thinks along with me, takes care of my personal well-being" (Priddat, 2014, p. 56). This form of machine-mediated interaction is imbued with an unexpected radicalism.

Against the background of the conception of a virtual cogito, a non-trivial machine's cognitive functions are attributed an independent quality. Based on this mental game, the virtual cogito can understand itself as the unshakable foundation of an act of being, it can maintain the "identity of the self - itself" (Lévinas, 2017, p. 304). The directly gained evidence of the virtual cogito becomes a "qualitas distinctiva" (ibid.). It gives the impression of being able to achieve something analogous in the transaction process. From here, one demands an intervention about what one communicates. Esposito (2018, p. 293) explains that

> One demands the processing and transformation of the original information into another. One requires the computer to act on meaning, although it is not a system that constitutes meaning.

The virtual cogito (S2) refers to the "beyond of being" (see Lévinas, 2011) of (S1), which promises to show the world as an extended, infinite experience space (ibid.), although a scientific "idea disguise envelops" it (Husserl, 1986, p. 258). In this thought lies an optimism of progress, which is directed towards opening up the "horizon of determinable indeterminacy" (Husserl, 1985, p. 173) as a restless boundary in the perceptual behavior of the actors (S1). In this context, it is overlooked that the one to represent comes from a context that cannot be represented. His person is the result of a difference.

Through the increasing integration of the actors in machine-mediated communication relationships, the digital markets' supply dynamics become the object of a formal, logical structural mapping. Through the genesis of "arithmetic ideals" (Husserl, 1986, p. 254) in the worlds of supply in the digital markets, the actors are relieved of their epistemic preparatory work. The algorithms of a virtual cogito announce themselves as meaning-generating forms. Taking an unmarked state into account, probabilistic probabilities of judgment are made about a bargaining process's successful course. Strictly speaking, it is a learning process that attempts to exploit the unmarked state's resources (Müßgens, 2021). This is achieved through the involvement of the other party in order to achieve the necessary convergence of the probabilities of judgment to the actors' life-world reality in a follow-up operation (ibid.). Although the intelligence of the virtual cogito points to something else here, this other does not meet one in the mode of one's personal insecurity, but in the mode of "individualized recognition" (Priddat, 2014, p. 56). Baecker (2019) describes this functional context as a movement that oscillates between its self- and foreign referentiality to "make the familiar visible in the unfamiliar" (p. 64). The result of this operation is an idealized, intentional representation (Lévinas, 2017, p. 157) of the transaction object. Within the contract process, the thinking of the actor is not unprepared. The communication that takes place in the contract process generates convergence.

This is successful if the latent risk of communication can be made observable from technology's perspective with the "category of risk" (Baecker, 2007, p. 247). It is essential to bear in mind that the bargaining process and the associated communication are always risky because the possibility of misconduct remains present (ibid.). For a virtual cogito's intelligence, this risk can be minimized by the informational evaluation of communication relationships with the other. The form of the information is explicit, "cumulative and additive" (Han, 2014, p. 56). Therefore, it is particularly suitable for technological operationalizations to establish a uniform formal communication relationship. In this context, language becomes the unit of a system, in which the "recursivity of functions and algorithms" (Bolz, 1995, p. 37) is in the foreground. Communication events become computable because "language is reduced to a casual function of information exchange" (Lévinas, 2017, p. 262). If the being coincides with the information, it is possible to send clear signals in identification offers through reasoned calculation (Müßgens, 2021). We are dealing with a conception of communication that is guided by the premise of a rational theory of communicative action. Locally, one considers "consensus to be more rational than dissent" (Luhmann, 2000, p. 53).

These processes are crucial for companies that operate in a big-data context and follow an informational processing imperative. They can place their offers much more precisely and control capacity by evaluating the purchase profiles. Coupled with the automated process control of production (Industry 4.0 and successor), market and production are combined in a self-controlling system, which is practically achieved through targeted mass customization of offers and their advertising. The advertising no longer appears like an anonymous advertisement, but as personal information on the mobile phone display, matched to the previous preference profile dynamics. Utilizing variations, the innovations become more personal. Addressed in this personal way, consumers react in thank-blame patterns. The "gift" cannot be turned down immediately. We are so socialized that we answer gifts with counter-gifts (Schmid, 2017). What can create disgruntlement in private life is not possible in business. For example, not responding to informational gifts with counter-gifts is damaging to business in Silicon Valley because this behavior is closely observed in social networks (Ferrary, 2003, p. 130 ff.). The young start-ups freely tell their company secrets because they are convinced that they can implement them in the market faster than the others, who have yet to design and organize an implementation. It is not a question of knowledge differentials but instead of the distribution of enforcement and implementation competence. However, for the information gift, it is expected that the others inform just as generously—give, take, and reproduce.

It inspires trust and, on a pre-reflective level, calls on the actors to compensate. It is not a contractually, i.e., formally necessary, defined response, but rather a guilty socialized informal regularity. Decision genesis in the contractual process is considerably accelerated because here one does not operate under transaction conditions that are merely judged to be reasonably just and fair, but rather demonstrates a unique form of generosity (Hénaff, 2017). From this perspective, it is understandable why users, in principle, give their data to companies for market exploitation. The gifts are thus not one-sided but reciprocal in their own way. Something is bought on the internet, and the resulting data (plus the data profiles and other information) are "returned" as precisely simulated offers for future purchases. If this is interpreted as a service, we are dealing with a reciprocal relationship with "no price", i.e., it is not based on the market, but on other scales: a non-market process in the middle of the market.

Michael Hutter (2012, p. 9 f.; see also Priddat, 2014, part. 2) has discovered a moral economy of indebtedness for the internet:

> The diversity and density of the networks that have emerged in recent decades are perhaps the most vital sign of the media change that digitization brings with it. In these networks, an exchange is rarely coordinated via payments. Mutual obligations connect the participants: Acknowledgements, source quotations, but above all, evaluative comments take on the role of promissory notes. Here, morality is created that is appropriate to the problem of the creation and exploitation of digital content. The goods markets' successes rather forgot social coordination through debt relationships in the last century.
>
> Under digitally mediated communication conditions, bonds such as gratitude and debt develop new possibilities for collectively organizing creative processes.

A gift-exchange economy is emerging on the internet (Ferrary, 2003; Elder-Vass, 2018, part. III, especially ch. x; Geyer, 2020), which has settled on a reciprocal commitment mode. Hutter's (2012) explanation makes the currency character clear: to respond to the bond is a debt settlement (Athané, 2004). In the modern economy, which is based primarily on voluntary transaction contracts that are often of use, this points to a new deontological dimension: if the users of network communication feel a mutual obligation to respond or comment, they form dynamic communities that repeatedly introduce new variants, focuses, and meanings into their communications. Social media organizes semantic and semiotic spaces (semi-spheres), which form meanings that become decisive for the transactions. It is a relational nexus between economy and society, or their communication of meaning and discourses of interpretation. The transfer economy of the welfare state is a gift-economy (transfer = unilateral payment), but more complex, integrated into a contractual system "between service providers (public authorities; social insurance funds) and service suppliers (social economy organizations), on which customers (or those entitled to benefits based on legal claims) have no influence" (Geyer, 2020, p. 39; Bellermann, 2015). Therefore, social "assistance is always based on incomplete contracts, which do not correspond to bilateral transactions' economic standard. [...] A bilateral assistance contract is concluded downstream between the beneficiary and the service provider, without an exchange value (price) being agreed if self-payers are excluded. These contracts nevertheless have a 'relational character'" (ibid.).

2.1 *The Gift-Economic Core Process of the Digital Economy*

The reciprocal character of the internet, with all the hopes that were placed in the early phases of transparent openness to communication, has now been absorbed into the cloud (Seele & Zapf, 2017; Avanessian, 2017, p. 37). Michael Hutter's gift-economic interpretation of the internet (see above; also Priddat, 2014, Chap. 2) refers to a free network community with its open-source ideology (Kabalak & Priddat, 2006), which is now being transformed by oligopolistic platform entrepreneurs (Zuboff, 2018).

> Given this transition, it is no exaggeration to proclaim an exodus from the internet to the cloud. The internet's dispersed architecture gives way to the cloud's central model of data storage and management, handled and owned by a handful of corporations. [...] In the cloud, such 'digital convergence' goes even further: data becomes more effectively and thoroughly harvested, analyzed, validated, monetized, looked into, and controlled through the internet; its centralization is not just one of protocol, but also location. (Metahaven, 2012, part 1, 2; see Staab, 2019)

All information used by, for example, Google, Amazon, Yahoo, and Facebook are gifts from users to the companies (Elder-Vass, 2018, pt. III). In the current version, we are dealing with asymmetric reciprocity: Google and others use the data gifts profitably, while the givers/users only receive their individually tailored offers, i.e., a service they have not ordered but 'gratefully' accept – as the comfort of life. This grateful acceptance implies that it is not noticeable that they have long since paid via an involuntary contract, which they "legitimize" post hoc, without knowing the prices. Within the markets, there is a transaction world far removed from the market, which has the appearance of a reciprocal moral economy (see Hillebrandt, 2009), although it is based on a (pronounced) asymmetry in value creation.

Parallel to this, however, there is another gift-economy. All uses of the internet are free, i.e., given. The argument of the corporations is: because all uses of the internet, but especially, e.g., Google's search engines, are free, the corporations can, of course, freely use the data generated by these uses. This is another quasi-contract: a reciprocal arrangement that knows no prices, cannot charge anything, and remains asymmetrical and undefined in its quantity dimensions.

We are dealing with three interlocking reciprocal arrangements or cycles of gifts (**K** = corporations, **G** = gift, **u** = user):

1. Free web and search offers: Gifts (1) from Big Data corporations to users. K → u <G1>;
2. Corporate utilization rights of user data, as they were a gift (2) of the users to the corporations for (1): u → K <G2>; and
3. Gifts (3) as specific offers (services) – based on the use of network data – by the groups: K → u <G3>.

G1 to G3 form the reciprocal or gift-economic core process of the digital economy. Based on K → u <G1>, a reciprocal cycle of return is formed (u → K <G2>), which leads into a second return (K → u <G3>). All three gift relations form a hypercycle, which is the core of digital markets. Hypercycle means superimposing several individual reciprocal cycles. The gift-economic hypercycle is a non-market nexus around which the digital markets first form, based on the gift-economic infrastructure.

We do not want to give the data away because it is private (G2). If one declares it as an involuntary gift, the offer of precisely fitting purchase options is also a counter-gift that one does not necessarily want to "receive" (G3). We are then dealing with "negative reciprocity", which raises the question of the extent to which users have rights of disposal over the handling of their data, i.e., how they can stop or cancel the process and "return to sovereignty over the data" (see Hofmann & Schölkopf, 2015; Koenig, 2019). The lawyer Marietta Auer (quoted in Krischke, 2020, p. N4) adds:

> On the one hand, the individual's consent to using his data does not justify use in statistical collectives such as those on which the scoring systems are based. On the other hand, the individual's defense rights against data misuse offer no protection against discrimination against the groups thus formed.

Confronted with the "collective ontology" of algorithmic profiling, such protective instruments aimed at the individual were useless. Collective data protection rights would be necessary to protect disadvantaged groups' interests and fill the individual rights gap (ibid., p. N4). The point is that the autonomous person's legal figure, which presupposes indivisibility, is at risk. Auer (quoted in Krischke, 2020, p. N4), regarding Gilles Deleuze, explains it as follows:

> However, this very indivisibility is lost through digitization, for example, through algorithmic customer profiling. The individual becomes a combination of statistically determined characteristics and patterns of behavior. Indivisible, equal, and free persons become divisible and calculable. The 'individual' tends to become an 'dividuum'.

2.2 Quaternary Allocation: On the Interlocking of Markets and Non-Markets

Many uses of the internet are free of charge, i.e., they have no price (see G1): "Google's search engine does not operate in a conventional market. Users are not customers, because they do not pay for their search queries" (Staab, 2019, p. 30). Google's free "search engine" offer is a gift to the users. Philipp Staab's (2019) differentiation between customers and users points to the difference between the market and non-market economy: customers pay in transactions, whereas users accept gifts. Nevertheless, this gift-economic dimension is embedded in a (quasi-classical) economy: Google (like the other Big Data companies) acquires payment for the use of its search engine through advertising. Around the non-market 'search engine' exists a market.

However, the context is complex. Google sells access to advertising companies (market 1) to the non-market of search engine users, where they can place advertising. This advertising market (Market 1) presupposes what we described above as gift 2 (G2): the use of users' information to optimize advertising offers. Market 1 and search engine non-market together form an infrastructure for a second market that serves the real transactions (market 2), i.e., what you buy after the search or based on the search's advertising. We are dealing with a triangular double market-non-market hybrid. Google continuously increases the variance of its offer, i.e., Google increases its attractiveness to its users, binds them, and attracts them by offering new services and applications (e.g., Maps and the entire Google Play Store). With this increased impact, more advertising can be sold to companies. Investing in the gift-economic dimension increases turnover and profit from the advertising market (market 1). Google can accordingly increase advertising price because it has increased the number of users via its non-market (see Staab, 2019, p. 31 f.).

So far, we have talked about reciprocal, i.e., ultimately bilateral, structures. Now we see an entanglement of gift and market economies in the sense of a triangular allocation – between providers and users (non-market), between providers and firms as advertising customers (market 1), and between firms and customers (market 2); with a user/customer transformation taking place in this process). If the companies, that place advertising on Google and Amazon, are also customers on the platform (on Google in the Google Play Store; on Amazon directly), we are dealing with a third market (market 3). The platform is the market, and it has the peculiarity of belonging to a private company. Philipp Staab (2019) speaks of a proprietary digital capitalism (p. 27).

From this quaternary structure, we can easily see that the gift-economic dimension accounts for only a quarter and that we are dealing with a complex form of market entanglement. The free offers on the internet form the core of the digital and platform economies. This is where the data/information is created, which the Big Data companies see as compensation for their free offers. The Big Data groups use the information to make specific offers that appear to be reciprocal (G1 **R** G2). However, one has to look at it carefully. From the perspective of the transactants, the information that every transaction generates digitally is given away because the data is useless to the consumer himself. All information is not valuable as outgoing information. However, all information is valuable as incoming information in the stochastic aggregations of the algorithms. Only within the algorithmic network individual information becomes meaningful. It is the price for the algorithm being able to work.

Tim Cook, the CEO of Apple, differentiates Apple from social networks like Facebook: "If an online service is free, you are not the customer, but the product" (Cook, quoted in Iid, 2018). The user is the product that Facebook sells on address and profile markets. What Facebook is accused of as misconduct in the Cambridge Analytica case is just its regular business model (as is the case with Google), hence the evasive answers of Zuckerberg in the US Senate. The gift of free and unrestricted communication in social media is the production prerequisite for personal data sale, which was previously provided voluntarily or involuntarily.

When the Big Data groups use the data from the market 2 customers' transcriptions, they exploit it by showing or offering more precise advertising relations to market 1 (with corresponding price variations). The circle closes when more customers buy from the advertising companies because of successful advertising (market 2) so that the rising advertising costs compensate the companies. If the companies then place themselves on the provider's platforms, the platform companies (or these company markets) earn commissions (market 3). The argument that the companies give something back to the customers cannot be dismissed. But these are all services that come from the three, in effect classic, markets. New is that these markets only become useful through the information/data generated from the customers' purchasing behavior and the users' search behavior. It is the interlocking of the three markets with the gift-economic-dimensioned non-markets. It should not be overlooked that the 'gift' of data to the Big Data companies is a counter-gift, as many services and features on the internet can be used free of charge, including search engines, apps, and maps. For the structuring and listing of offers by Amazon (as well as the convenient comparisons that this makes possible), see G1.

The free offers on the internet create the free economic structure, which puts users in a (sudden) state of debt, but which is actuated by the payment of free use through data. It is a kind of implicit reciprocity contract that users deliberately do not enter into but allow them to apply. It is their counter-gift that frees them from the (gratitude) debt. Jaron Lanier (2014) points out that here the capitalist system is suspended: Google et al. would have to pay the users—if it were economically viable—for every use and exploitation of the information, i.e., buy the respective rights of use from them. Only then we would be back in a (classic) market. Raghuram Rajan (2020) also advocates customer ownership: "every user and consumer should be the owner of his or her data" (p. 497). However, Rajan points out that "most people will not be able to manage their data, but where a need arises, a market emerges", i.e., "information providers" and "chargeable bargaining bots" (ibid., p. 498).

If property rights for data were enforced, other markets would also emerge because if you owned your own data, it would become transactional, and you could give it to companies in return for payment. But then you are guaranteed to be excluded from your data afterward. If we go back to the quadruple complex, we have to deal with other markets (market 4 for external data management; market 5 for data ownership). The digital-economic nexus can grow into a sixfold entangled structure of five markets and a—core-forming—non-market. Above all, the possibility of data ownership, which has so far only been discussed, transforms the gift-economic dimension: the production of positive externalities of data through digital search and purchase actions into a market (market 5). The data would no longer be "given away" but traded. In the sixfold intertwined digital-economic nexus, the reciprocal non-market would disappear, and we would no longer be dealing with a market-non-market hybrid but with an intertwined multiple market field.

When it comes to the question of data ownership, we are dealing with two possibilities, both of those end in market solutions. Usually, the Big Data companies declare themselves as the owner of the data.

> Most of this data has never been deliberately transferred by users to Internet companies, it is a collective good, but it is not available as common property. The companies decide how and whether the community benefits from the use of this data. They insist on their ownership of 'their' data. Therefore, with foresight, the Internet companies try to persuade their users to register and stay logged in explicitly. In this way, the data from unclear ownership relationships are subject to the terms of use of the corporations. (Hofmann & Schölkopf, 2015, p. 14; see Koenig, 2019)

This strategy amounts to the fact that the corporations let users and customers assign access rights to them, i.e., having these rights given to them as a gift. In other words, what was previously illegitimate appropriation of data, only functionally a gift, is now transformed into an intended gift, given a second time (for legal protection). In this way, the illegitimate appropriation is made legal. It also remains free of charge.

The second possibility, i.e., the appropriation of the users '/customers' data, is costly if the users/customers then make it available to the companies or sell the right of use. The "donating" registration in option one becomes here a costly purchase of the right of use. In this second option, a new market is opened (market 5), while in the first option, the Big Data companies' market scope is legalized.

But there is a completely different argumentation, which was already hinted at earlier: the disclosure of private data and information is the payment to use the internet. In this sense, the internet is not free at all. However, this argumentation remains trapped in a bilateral transaction model. In contrast, we have shown that we are dealing with an unfolded quaternary nexus of three markets and a non-market which can unfold into a sixfold intertwined digital-economic nexus. If one reflects on this economically, the internet's free use has long since been financed by other business models. On the provider side, we are not dealing with pure gifts, but with free offers (for the users, i.e., the non-market), which others pay for (market 1 and market 3). Only with the external effects that users generate, which are used as data/information by the corporations (to use the data, information system infrastructures, and above all investments are needed). There is no direct market relation between users and providers, but there are indirect relations: if the users' data lead to the fact that they become customers of the companies that pay the providers, they indirectly finance the free offers. The system of quaternary allocation is based on a transformation of users into customers. It can be tested in reverse: if users would only use the gift-economical free use but react aversively to advertising and the transactions linked to it, the system would collapse.

Free usage on the internet, the gift-economic dimension, is a teaser that ultimately leads back to markets (markets 1 and 3). The magic of an alternative economy, which according to Mauss (1990) was repeatedly attested to the gift-economy, has been transformed in the digital economy into a functional, albeit necessary, process.

3 Coda

We can hardly call the reciprocal action in the digital economy a gift because nobody believes in giving, but everybody feels entitled to take with a certain self-evidence (the data companies as well as the internet users, who take everything for free). Taking, it seems, dominates giving (giving < taking). On the one hand, the digital economy's core appears to be a big takeaway—a new level of consumerist freedom. Giving, on the other hand, has no economy. The gift-economic dimension we are discussing here proves to be a reduced or semi-gift-economy, at least in the digital world.

However, we do not only pay in transactions, but we also give—especially information. In other words, we give unintentionally. It can be said that the data groups owe us something, but these are loosely knit obligations. They take the data to give us something: more, better products, better access, and more personalized allocation, everything that Staab (2019, p. 31) identifies as behavior that is unlikely to harm consumers, but at the same time, they promise higher transaction rates and sales to those who pay for this attribution advertising. What they give us in terms of information and personalized advertising, they give in parallel to the advertising companies and take the revenue from the advertising sales. We find ourselves in a hybrid economy where gift-/non-markets and markets interact and are entangled several times:

1. Data groups take the information from our buying processes;
2. They sell this data to advertising companies. (It would be euphemistic to say that they "give" it to them. They do, but for money. Thus, the semantics of giving is not correct.);
3. They give us specified and personalized advertisements. These are, in fact, return gifts. But we have not given anything intentionally, nor do we necessarily want to have the offers of return;
4. However, we accept them by gratefully transforming them into purchases, i.e., to pay our debt, out of gratitude for the personal specificity (see p. 3). They take place in a socialized atmosphere of the donation conventions. Precarious is the "gratitude" as the motive of reciprocity. The personalization of information is not a gift, but a strategic advertising intention, which makes it seem as if one is individually awarded. The deep grammar activated here wants reciprocity, but out of naïve loyalty (give-take-return) and not the gracious characteristic of gratitude. Here no grace is granted for which one should be grateful.
5. Are we not dealing with a give-and-take guilt cycle? It is not economic, but rather has a sociological basis: from socialized forms of gratitude for gifts.

In the hybrid matrix, purchases are: (a) real transactions and at the same time (b) reciprocally returns. The economic line is: take, sell, give and take (i.e., give back). The cycle would be complete when new data emerge from the purchases, which the data groups then take. The gift-economy is a fact, but it exists within the market networks in the digital domain. It opens the economy by providing priceless arenas in which new markets can establish themselves. The gifts and gift-economic relations create transactional potentials that only come into play based on digital media.

In standard economic theory, we deal with two unrelated agents that behave juxtapositionally in a transaction (Priddat, 2016a). It seems to be the economic transaction's quality to anonymously encounter each other—and not the other, but only his offered commodity for the offered money. The relationships that are established in this form of the transaction are relationless (interactionless interaction), anonymized reciprocity. But the transaction—which we try to trace in this essay—contains a mutualistic dispositive to refer to each other: in consideration of the other as other (without the juxtapositional ruthlessness that remains foreign or anonymous in the transactional act), in personalizable reciprocity and potentially in obligation/responsibility.

The fact that this mutualistic dispositive of the transaction also contains a gift-economic dimension was our third step, which can be traced especially in the digital economy. The transaction is not only a possibility to relate to each other, i.e., a social imputation. In its mutualistic process, new perceptions and interpretations can be generated through listening and responding, which can transform the crude subject-object conception of rational choice into a mutual process of becoming aware of what the transaction is based on.

However, it becomes apparent that the bilaterally intertwined actors are part of networks of relationships and influences that "have their say". The methodological individual of economics proves to be illusory since it is instead multiply interpreted in a polylinguistic nexus. The transaction turns out to be a complicated process, revealing a relational structure that unveils its intrinsic entanglements in the digital market. Every transaction is in a crossover network of diverse transactions and markets.

The gift-economy is a significant core process that indicates a nexus of markets and non-markets—a different economic spectrum. Like the juridical, it is a necessary institutional condition of the economy—an infrastructure in a complex digital market network. The gifts in the digital market possibly serve to create incentive milieus for new transaction possibilities. They are a medium of new opportunities, not an alternative economy.

References

Athané, F. (2004). *Schulden zwischen Gaben und Pflicht*. Das Gefrorene Meer. Retrieved May 15, 2021, from: http://www.germe.de/no5/donetdevoir_de.html.

Avanessian, A. (2017). *Miamification*. Berlin: Merve.

Baecker, D. (2007). *Form und Formen der Kommunikation*. Frankfurt am Main: Suhrkamp.

Baecker, D. (2019). *Intelligenz, künstlich und komplex*. Leipzig: Merve.

Baecker, D. (2020). Die Form der Zahlung. In D. Baecker (Ed.), *Wozu Wirtschaft?* (pp. 141–154). Marburg: Metropolis.

Bellermann, M. (2015). Sozialstaatliche Rahmenbedingungen in Deutschland. In B. Wüthrich (Ed.), *Soziale Versorgung zukunftsfähig gestalten* (pp. 53–62). Wiesbaden: Springer Fachmedien.

Bolz, N. (1995). *Am Ende der Gutenberg-Galaxis*. München: Wilhelm Fink Verlag.
Buber, M. (2019). *Das Dialogische Prinzip*. München: Gütersloher Verlagshaus.
Commons, J. R. (1995). *Legal Foundations of Capitalism*. New York: Macmillan Publishers.
Derrida, J. (1993). *Falschgeld. Zeit geben I*. München: Wilhelm Fink Verlag.
Elder-Vass, D. (2018). *Profit und Gabe in der digitalen Ökonomie*. Hamburg: Hamburger Edition HIS.
Enkelmann, W.-D. (2010). *Beginnen wir mit dem Unmöglichen. Jacques Derrida, Ressourcen und Ursprung der Ökonomie*. Marburg: Metropolis.
Esposito, E. (2018). *Soziales Vergessen – Formen und Medien des Gedächtnisses der Gesellschaft*. Frankfurt am Main: Suhrkamp.
Falk, A. (2003). Homo Oeconomicus versus Homo Reciprocans: Ansätze für ein neues Wirtschaftspolitisches Leitbild? *Perspektiven Der Wirtschaftspolitik, 4*(1), 141–172.
Ferrary, M. (2003). The gift exchange in the social networks of silicon valley. *California Management Review, 45*(4), 120–138.
Geyer, C. (2020). Hilfe als Ware auf digitalen Marktplätzen? Überlegungen zu einer realistischen Utopie zwischen Coopetition und Commons. *Zeitschrift Für Wirtschafts- Und Unternehmensethik, 21*(1), 34–61.
Gintis, H., Bowles, S., Boyd, R., & Fehr, E. (2005). *Moral Sentiments and Material Interests. The Foundation of Cooperation in Economic Life*. Cambridge/Massachusetts & London: MIT Press.
Han, B. (2014). *Im Schwarm. Ansichten des Digitalen*. Berlin: Matthes Seitz.
Hayek, Friedrich August v. (1969). Der Wettbewerb als Entdeckungsverfahren. In F. A. Hayek (Ed.), *Freiburger Studien* (pp. 249–265). Tübingen: Mohr.
Hénaff, M. (2009). *Der Preis der Wahrheit: Gabe, Geld und Philosophie*. Frankfurt am Main: Suhrkamp.
Hénaff, M. (2017). Die Schuld der Zeit. Gabe und Anerkennung in den Beziehungen der Generationen. *Lettre International*, 17–22.
Herrmann-Pillath, C. (2000). *Social Capital and Networks: A Proposal for Conceptual Integration*. Retrieved May 15, 2021 from: https://papers.ssrn.com/sol3/papers.cfm?abstract_id=949088.
Herrmann-Pillath, C. (2010). *The economics of identity and creativity. A cultural science approach*. St Lucia: University of Queensland Press.
Hillebrandt, F. (2009). *Praktiken des Tauschens. Zur Soziologie symbolischer Formen der Reziprozität*. Wiesbaden: VS Springer.
Hofmann, T., & Schölkopf, B. (2015, January 29). Vom Monopol auf Daten ist abzuraten. *Frankfurter Allgemeine Zeitung*, 14.
Husserl, E. (1985). *Die Phänomenologische Methode - Ausgewählte Texte I*. Stuttgart: Reclam.
Husserl, E. (1986). *Phänomenologie der Lebenswelt - Ausgewählte Texte II*. Stuttgart: Reclam.
Hutter, M. (2012). Vom Haben zum Greifen. Auf dem Weg in eine digitale Abrufgesellschaft. *WZB Mitteilungen, 136*, 7–10.
Iid. (2018, April 3). Schlagabtausch zwischen Cook und Zuckerberg. *Frankfurter Allgemeine Zeitung*, 24.
Kabalak, A., & Priddat, B. (2006). Open Source als Produktion von Transformationsgütern. In R. A. Lutterbeck, B. Bärwolf, M. Gehring (Eds.), *Open Source Jahrbuch* (pp. 109–122). Berlin: Lehmanns Media.
Koenig, G. (2019). *La fin de l'individu: Voyage d'un philosophe au pays de l'intelligence artificielle*. L'Observatoire.
Krischke, W. (2020, April 29). Der Algorithmus kennt keine Moral. *Frankfurter Allgemeine Zeitung*, N4.
Lanier, J. (2014). *Wem gehört die Zukunft? "Du bist nicht der Kunde der Internetkonzerne. Du bist ihr Produkt"*. Hamburg: Hoffman & Campe.
Lévinas, E. (2011). *Jenseits des Seins oder anders als Sein geschieht*. München: Karl Alber Verlag.
Lévinas, E. (2017). *Die Spur des Anderen*. München: Karl Alber Verlag.
Lin, N. (2001). *Social Capital. A theory of social structure and action*. New York: Cambridge University Press.

Luhmann, N. (2000). Was ist Kommunikation? In P. Gente, H. Paris, M. Weinmann (Eds.), *Niklas Luhmann-Short Cuts.* (pp. 41–63). Frankfurt am Main: Zweitausendeins.
Mauss, M. (1990). *Die Gabe. Form und Funktion des Austauschs in archaischen Gesellschaften.* Frankfurt am Main: Suhrkamp Verlag.
Metahaven. (2012). Captives of the Cloud. Part I, II. *E-Flux Journal, #37,38.* Retrieved May 15 2021 from: https://www.e-flux.com/journal/37/61232/captives-of-the-cloud-part-i/.
Münster, H. (2020). *Jenseits von Markt und Staat. Differenztheoretische Grundlegung einer Philosophie des Sozialen.* Würzburg: Königshausen & Neumann.
Müßgens, J. (2021). Zur Komplexität der neuen Kommunikationsverhältnisse in der ökonomischen Theoriebildung und ihre ethischen Implikationen. In J. Müßgens (Ed.), *Eine dynamische Kartografie der Ökonomie.* Marburg: Metropolis (in planning).
Ortmann, G. (2004). *Als Ob. Fiktionen und Organisation.* Wiesbaden: Springer VS.
Ostrom, E. (2005). *Understanding Institutional Diversity.* Princeton, NJ: Princeton University Press.
Popitz, H. (1992). *Phänomene der Macht.* Tübingen: Mohr Siebeck.
Priddat, B. P. (2006). Moral als Kontext von Gütern. In P. Koslowski & B. P. Priddat (Eds.), *Ethik des Konsums* (pp. 9–22). München: Wilhelm Fink Verlag.
Priddat, B. P. (2010). Das Dritte in der Ökonomie. Transaktion als multipler triadischer kommunikativer Prozeß. In E. Esslinger, T. Schlechtriemen, D. Schweitzer, A. Zons (Eds.), *Die Figur des Dritten* (pp. 110–124). Frankfurt am Main: Suhrkamp.
Priddat, B. P. (2011). Kollaborative Vertragsprozesse und Netzwerke. Williamson and beyond. In St. Grüninger, M. Fürtst, S. Pforr, M. Schmiedeknecht (Eds.), *Verantwortung in der globalen Ökonomie gestalten. Governanceethik und Wertemanagement* (pp. 111–146). Marburg: Metropolis.
Priddat, B. P. (2012). *Akteure, Verträge, Netzwerke. Der kooperative Modus der Ökonomie.* Marburg: Metropolis.
Priddat, B. P. (2014). *Homo dyctos.* Marburg: Metropolis.
Priddat, B. P. (2016a). Die Transaktion als Juxtaposition und als Kooperation. Differente Interpretation des Marktes. In H.-C. Schmidt am Busch (Ed.), *Die Philosophie des Marktes* (pp. 207–226). Hamburg: Felix Meiner Verlag.
Priddat, B. P. (2016b). Mehr als Effizienz? Über Allokation und die gabenökonomische Infrastruktur der modernen Ökonomie. In W.-D. Enkelmann, B. P. Priddat (Eds.), *Was ist?: Wirtschaftsphilosophische Erkundungen. Definitionen, Ansätze, Methoden, Erkenntnisse, Wirkungen, Bd. III / von III* (pp. 111–148). Marburg: Metropolis.
Priddat, B. P. (2019). Märkte als transaktionale Netze. In D. J. Petersen, D. Willes, E. M. Schmitt, R. Birnbaum, & J. H. E. Meyerhoff (Eds.), *Perspektiven einer pluralen Ökonomik* (pp. 137–155). Wiesbaden: Springer.
Raghuram, R. (2020). *Die dritte Säule.* FinanzBuch Verlag.
Ricoeur, P. (1990). *Liebe und Gerechtigkeit.* Tübingen: Mohr Siebeck.
Ricoeur, P. (2006). *Wege der Anerkennung.* Frankfurt am Main: Suhrkamp.
Schmid, W. (2017). *Vom Schenken und beschenkt werden.* Berlin: Insel Verlag.
Seele, P., & Zapf, C. L. (2017). *Die Rückseite der Cloud.* Berlin/Heidelberg: Springer.
Singer, T., & Fehr, E. (2005). The Neuroeconomics of Mind Reading and Empathy. *American Economic Review, 95*(2), 340–345.
Staab, P. (2019). *Digitaler Kapitalismus.* Berlin: Suhrkamp.
Vogd, W. (2018). *Selbst- und Weltverhältnisse. Leiblichkeit, Polykontexturalität und implizite Ethik.* Weilerswist: Velbrück Wissenschaft.
White, H. C. & Godart, F. C. (2007a). Märkte als soziale Formationen. In J. Beckert, R. Diaz-Bone, H. Ganßmann (Eds.), *Märkte als soziale Strukturen* (pp. 197–215). Frankfurt am Main: Campus Verlag.
White, H. C. & Godart, F. C. (2007b). Stories from identity and Control. *Sociologica.* Retrieved 15 May 2021 from: https://www.rivisteweb.it/doi/10.2383/25960.
White, H. C. (2008). *Meaning Emerges in relational Dynamics, Manuskript für den workshop 'Relational Sociology – Transatlantic Impulses'*, Berlin 25.9.2008 (unpublished).

Wieland, J. (2020). *Relational Economics. A Political Economy*. Cham, CH: Springer.
Williamson, O. E. (2002). The theory of the firm as governance structure: From choice to contract. *Journal of Economic Perspectives, 16*(3), 171–195.
Zuboff, S. (2018). *Das Zeitalter des Überwachungskapitalismus*. Frankfurt am Main/New York: Campus-Verlag.

Jean Müßgens is a research assistant at the Chair of Institutional Economics of Prof. Dr. Wieland at Zeppelin University. He studied Business Economics (BA) and Ethics & Organization (MA) at the University of Witten/Herdecke. The focus of his research is on Relational Economics. Against the background of the Digital Economy, he studies questions in economic theorizing. In addition, he tackles issues of strategy and governance in innovation research.

Birger P. Priddat is senior professor of economics and philosophy at the University of Witten/Herdecke and Zeppelin University in Friedrichshafen. Previously he held the chair of economics and philosophy at Witten/Herdecke (since 1991) and Zeppelin University. His primary research interests are philosophy of economics, institutional economics, history of economic thought, and digital modernization.

The manufacturer's authorised representative in the EU is Springer Nature Customer Service Centre GmbH, Europaplatz 3, 69115 Heidelberg, Germany. If you have any concerns regarding our products, please contact ProductSafety@springernature.com

Printed and bound by CPI Group (UK) Ltd, Croydon, CR0 4YY
30/09/2026
02225699-0010